BRAND MANAGEMENT STRATEGIES

BRAND MANAGEMENT STRATEGIES
Luxury and Mass Markets

William D'Arienzo

Fairchild Books
An imprint of Bloomsbury Publishing Inc

B L O O M S B U R Y
NEW YORK · LONDON · OXFORD · NEW DELHI · SYDNEY

preface

As global economies grow and the cost of doing business increases, the brand is the preeminent business asset needed for success in global business development and offers the most sustainable way to avoid pricing wars and margin erosion. It can also be, if properly planned and executed, a fast track for entering and reaching the emerging middle classes in foreign markets and for penetrating and optimizing latent potential in mature home markets.

The active roster of books on brand management tends to be focused either on fashion for non-luxury brands or on luxury brands exclusively. Currently, there is no book available that integrates both perspectives, thus presenting a holistic view of the brand management marketplace. This book fills that void.

Brand Management Strategies: Luxury and Mass Markets presents the luxury and mass brand experience on a market continuum. This includes brands that are characterized as mass, mass fast fashion, fashion, premium, and luxury across diverse products and services from Burberry to BMW, from Coca-Cola to Chanel, from Starbucks to Starwood's and beyond and seeks to connect them while exploring their essential differences. This book's value lies in its unique viewpoint, a result of the author's experience as a corporate marketing professional, a consultant, and a university professor. The content is underpinned by a strong theoretical framework built on five premises:

1. Luxury is a distinct culture that mass brands often attempt to emulate. Yet, each has influenced the other. Brand management strategies can, and often do, successfully migrate across business boundaries. This book explores what mass and luxury markets owe to each other and how they differ in their brand management strategies.

2. Brand managers are not in the business of selling things to consumers, they are in the business of solving problems and serving practical needs and aspirational wants for consumers.

3. For luxury, the axis of engagement goes beyond needs and wants to desires and points to one of the fundamental differences between luxury brands and others.

4. The most successful brand companies are those that are market oriented and consumer-centric and thus recognize what business they are really in.

5. Great product is a necessary precondition for market entry, but without a brand strategy and brand management, it is not sufficient for market success.

This book details the proven steps necessary to develop, build, and sustain a brand, a brand strategy, and a business and alerts students and budding brand managers to the avoidable pitfalls inherent in doing business in a competitive market landscape.

Because of the range of brands introduced in the text, brand managers can learn and apply best practices from successful companies outside their competitive space and business sector and thereby derive fresh insights. To that end, this book offers examples of strategies used in a wide range of industries from fast food to fashion and seeks to identify the strategies that work irrespective of the sector.

In a rapidly changing business climate, the book goes one step farther to explore how the web and digital communications have altered the way mass and luxury companies communicate the brand to the global and domestic consumer and discusses the metrics that measure the return on investment (ROI) of their digital and web-based brand strategies.

APPROACH

Many books on brand management are filled with citations of research rather than with prescriptions for action. This book is both informed and experiential. It is written in a manner to be useful for both business and academia—a manual for brand managers and a primer for business schools. It is conversational in tone but analytical in content. Students will find it friendly, managers can reference it, and start-ups can use it as a guide. We don't provide solutions for every contingency that might occur, but we do teach a way of thinking, a framework, which transcends historical circumstance.

1. The concept of **marketing myopia** is, in this book, a core idea that calls for a primary focus on the consumer and not the product, which leads to the key question that we ask in relevant chapters, *"What Business Are You Really In?"* Failing to raise the question and obtain a clear and actionable answer can explain Coca-Cola's monumental "taste test" debacle in 1986, point out costly errors in repositioning that Starbucks experienced in 2006, and account for the sudden downward spiral in sales and market share of U.S. teen retailers in 2014.

2. Continuing with our focus on the consumer, we develop and apply the concept of **archetypes** to better understand the need for brand DNA and personas and how to align them with consumer segmentation models and brand promises. Our consulting experience with various brands underscores how brand managers apply this.

3. **Brand equity** driven by consumer markets and **brand valuation** driven by financial markets are, in this book, the concepts used to describe the two sources of brand value. They are interdependent in how they influence each other

but need to be understood as two separate concepts.

COVERAGE

The book is sectioned into four parts: Part 1, "The Evolution of Brands"; Part 2, "Building the Brand"; Part 3, "Maintaining the Brand"; and Part 4, "Brand Perspectives in the Global and Digital Worlds." Part 1, "The Evolution of Brands" (Chapters 1 through 3) introduces the concept of the brand and a brief survey of its historical evolution. Chapter 1 contains a brief history, Chapter 2 focuses on the unique aspects of luxury brands, and Chapter 3 focuses on the similarities and differences between luxury and mass brands.

Part 2, "Building the Brand" (Chapters 4 through 8), introduces the usage of segmentation models (Chapter 4) followed by strategies for maximizing brand loyalty and how these models fit in (Chapter 5). We then discuss managing the brand promise to engender and maintain brand loyalty (Chapter 6), measuring and managing brand value to quantify the contribution the brand provides to both consumers and companies (Chapter 7), and finally (Chapter 8) a method for generating brand names followed by a review of over a dozen court cases which provide the essential strategies for registering and protecting intellectual property (IP)/brand assets.

Part 3, "Maintaining the Brand" (Chapters 9 through 11), builds upon the foundation in Part 2 by providing insights into how retailers stay "on-brand" for business success (Chapter 9), reviewing the strategies and tactics available to brand managers for optimizing the brand's life cycle (Chapter 10), and analyzing consumer engagement strategies for maximizing brand health (Chapter 11)

Part 4, "Brand Perspectives in the Global and Digital World" (Chapters 12 through 15), begins by exploring the unique challenges in terms of measurement and communications that the digital space introduced into brand management (Chapter 12). This is followed (Chapter 13) by a similar analysis from the perspective of luxury brands per se and how they have navigated the challenges without tarnishing their image and rarity. Continuing the expanded universe within which brand management must deploy resources and strategies, Chapter 14 discusses the unique challenges of global marketing and communications and how experiential and emotional symbols connect global brand consumers to markets. Merging the new horizons discussed in the prior chapters of Part 4, Chapter 15 concludes by exploring the ultimate horizon, the human mind, and what neuropsychology has taught us about how we as a species process, determine, and act upon brand messages from both the digital and global worlds and what brand managers must know to be successful brand guardians.

FEATURES

The book is replete with "example-rich" *Case Studies* including discussions of strategies of global corporations and local businesses, drawn both from my own consulting practice and from the world at large; here lessons learned are from both failures and successes. A *"what could have been done"* practicum characterizes the resulting principle derived from the experience. It is then reframed into a big-picture understanding by our concepts and theoretical frameworks.

Cases of successes and failures in brand strategies are headlined, *"Brandstorming"* and are found in every chapter. This feature provides instructors, seminar leaders, and brand managers with actual business cases and the brand strategies that worked, those that didn't, and why; for the latter, the nature of the "failed" strategy is complemented by a thorough explanation of an alternative strategy. The missed opportunity is discussed in terms of the brand's identity and the book's thesis on principles of successful brand management. These can be used as pedagogic tools for teams to dissect and assess or for individual learning.

Similar learning components are at the end of each chapter headlined "*Chapter Conversations*" and *Chapter Challenges*." The "Conversations" are brief ticklers whose function is to provide food for thought and/or a way for instructors to engage students in intellectual exchanges during lectures. The "Challenges" are more

demanding and are formulated as problems which can be solved with a variety of strategies. These could be used as take-home or in-class exam questions or as a way for brand managers to review their takeaways from their readings.

INSTRUCTOR AND STUDENT RESOURCES

Brand Management Strategies STUDIO:

This book features an online multimedia resource—*Brand Management Strategies STUDIO*. The online *STUDIO* is specially developed to complement this book with rich media ancillaries that students can adapt to their visual learning styles to better master concepts and improve grades. Within the *STUDIO*, students will be able to:

- Study smarter with self-quizzes featuring scored results and personalized study tips
- Review concepts with flashcards of essential vocabulary

STUDIO access cards are offered free with new book purchases and also sold separately through Bloomsbury Fashion Central (*www.BloomsburyFashionCentral.com*).

Instructor Resources

- Instructor's Guide provides suggestions for planning the course and using the text in the classroom, supplemental assignments, and lecture notes
- Test Bank includes sample test questions for each chapter
- PowerPoint® presentations include images from the book and provide a framework for lecture and discussion

Instructor's Resources may be accessed through Bloomsbury Fashion Central (*www.BloomsburyFashionCentral.com*).

acknowledgments

A book takes a person from being a writer to being an author, a humbling and monumental transformation. It is the result of the intercession of things seen and unseen. To those that can be seen, my profound gratitude; to my teachers, to my associate, Cathy Healy whose insights and love for the manuscript often kept it afloat and always on even keel, for Sara Sparano and Andrei Popov interns from the Rider University, who selflessly gave their best and yeoman's work towards its publication, to my students at The Fashion Institute of Technology, NYC whose passion for Brand Management motivates me to continue to believe in the brand as our most important business asset and to my children Marc and Dana, for whom I hope this book will prove to be my legacy to them. And to my parents, unseen, but never forgotten . . . and to my Muse, whose creative spirit truly deserves whatever accolades this book may earn.

I'd also like to personally thank the editorial team involved in the publication of this book for their expert guidance, and infinite patience: Corey Kahn, Development Editor; Amanda Breccia, Senior Acquisitions Editor; Kiley Kudrna, Senior Editorial Assistant; Edie Weinberg, Art Development Editor; Gail Henry, Photo Researcher; Eleanor Rose, In-House Designer; Claire Henry, Production Manager and Christopher Black, Project Manager. Bravo!

The Publisher and the author wishes to gratefully acknowledge and thank the academic reviewers who contributed their time and feedback on the project: Melissa Abner, University of Central Missouri, US; Bridgett Clinton, University of Maryland, Eastern Shore, US; John Conte, Wade College, US; Mark DeFanti, Providence College, US; Phyllis Fein, Westchester Community College, US; Julie Haworth, University of Texas, US; Christopher Hopper, University of Southampton, UK; Ruth Jindal, De Montfort University, UK; Jaehee Jung, University of Delaware, US; Nicole Kirpalani, LIM College, US; Gulnur Tumbat, San Francisco State University, US; Catherine Weiss, Lasell College, US.

June 25, 2016
Princeton, NJ

The Emergence of Brands

CHAPTER 1

AFTER COMPLETING THIS CHAPTER, YOU WILL BE ABLE TO:

- Describe the origins of brands and brand management and their evolution into business strategies.

- Contrast product-centric and consumer-centric business models and explain how market dynamics affected the transitions of the former into the latter.

- Assess brands as business drivers and their role in avoiding "Marketing Myopia."

WHAT IS A BRAND?

Brands are complex entities which defy simple definitions. As there is no authority that determines these
types of meanings, there is no agreed-upon definition.

Often we think of them as logos or registered
trademark names such as Coca-Cola®. This doesn't
tell us much. For example, if registered trademarks
were enough to understand brands, why does Coca-
Cola have a variety of related names associated with it
(Diet Coke, Coke Zero, etc.) and why (per the title of
this book) do they need to be managed? To learn more,
we may decide to explore where they appear in daily
life. When we do, we find that brand names, logos,
or other associations pop up in people's conversations
and appear to be a type of shorthand for expressing
the images they hold in their minds of a brand's message or its features and benefits. As we dig deeper, we
also discover that people often have emotional relationships with brands, discussing them as if they were
real (literally often "loving" them or "disliking" them,
as the case may be). This kind of emotional intensity
can be seen generated by the Apple logo, bite and all.
It is often associated with various degrees of customer
affection as are many brands, which we will examine
in the chapters ahead. This preliminary exploration
gives you some idea of the richness and complexity of
the search for understanding what a brand is.

Brands versus Branding

Continuing our exploration about what a brand is,
many people fall into the trap of confusing brands
with branding. Brands are nouns, things; branding is
a verb, an action which creates the symbols and elements which we mentioned in our introduction and
through which the brand's message is communicated.

figure 1.1
An icon: A classic example of a branding element,
the Nike swoosh.

As an example, the Nike swoosh is a branding element
(an icon) and what an ad agency might create along
with a logo, tagline, or ad copy to convey a brand's
message (Figure 1.1).

These elements exist only to enhance and market
the brand and should be expressions of, and consistent
with, the brand's business management strategy.

Branding, therefore, should be understood as the
process of creating and communicating a brand strategy and these elements should provide the consumer
with information regarding the nature of the business. Without a strategy to integrate the elements and
unify the message, the branding message will confuse
the consumer and fail in its purpose.

Brand Concepts

Consequently, throughout this book, we are going
to make a distinction between brands and branding.
When we speak of the "brand" in a business context,
our language will reflect classic business concepts:
brand development, the process of developing
a name or label into a brand through first creating
brand elements (various intellectual property assets
such as brand names, logos, and associated identities);
brand building, the steps such as awareness to create
brand strength or equity; **brand loyalty**, the most
dependable consumer purchasers of the brand and its
products; **brand strategy**, how the brand elements

can support business objectives, and **brand manage-ment**, a business approach to differentiate, build, and measure the value of a brand or the process of managing all of the above. All of these terms present the brand as a primary business driver.

Public Brands versus Private Label

To continue to clarify the concept of a brand, we are going to draw another distinction and that is between **public brands**, whose products are widely distributed and often nationally advertised such as Polo Ralph Lauren, and **private label**, those products with names and symbols on tags and packaging that are exclusively owned by a retailer and only available at that retailer. An example would be "Worthington®," a women's sportswear and dress label found at JC Penney. Here is where it becomes important to distinguish the product from a label and the product from the brand.

Private label names and symbols placed on products and packaging are not brands, no matter how creative their names or artistic their logos. Private labels such as the generic names that retailers create for their exclusive use (i.e., Charter Club® at Macy's, and Walmart's Metro 7®) are simply names or marks of identification until the consumer begins to perceive them as brands. Brands are purveyors of consistent values, promises, and emotional relationships with their consumers, who cocreate the brand by their perception of its importance in their lifestyles. Their emotional attachment to the message and their commitment to continuing to purchase the product results in and reflects brand loyalty. This is especially the case in fashion and luxury products where the emotional quotient is high, and less so with consumer package goods (CPG) such as groceries, drugs, and home supplies where the emotional quotient is low but the necessity quotient is high.

The following attributes distinguish private labels that are not perceived as national brands from national brands:

- Private labels have no sustainable consumer awareness; they are not **top-of-mind**—that is, consumers do not readily recall them.

- Private labels cannot command a consistent price vis-à-vis competitors.
- Private labels are seldom on consumers' pre-shopping list.
- Private labels do not readily engender consumer forgiveness for mistakes.
- Private labels do not maintain consumer loyalty over time. Private labels have shorter life spans and generate lower margins than brands.
- Private labels are seldom what one recommends to family and friends.

The Origins of Brands and Brand Management

Anthropologically, brands have their origins in the universal tendency of human beings to use symbolic communications. Historically, brands emerge from the dynamics of modern economies.

In their comprehensive research on the emergence of the brand (a historical survey spanning 4,000 years), Karl Moore and Susan Reid charted the development and purpose of symbols and branding (as precursors of brands), concluding, "*Two key roles are witnessed during each (historical) period of interest: first, as a conveyor of information (origin and quality) regarding goods and/or services and second, as a conveyor of image or meaning (power, value and/or personality).*"[1]

Symbols and Brands

But clearly, symbols are not brands. Symbols such as crests or images of animals or nature are an artisan's attempt to convey an identity and/or to confirm a degree of quality represented by the symbol. Brands, therefore, began as literal works of ownership and authority. A potter's imprint on the base of clay pots, domestic cattle hinds branded by branding irons, and imperial wax seals on proclamations are found in every culture, ancient and modern.[2]

For example, in China, "stone chops" (flat, small, tablet-like rocks) were used for centuries by the Imperial Court for imprinting official documents conveying status and authority. These continue to find a place today in many traditional Chinese weddings, both in China and in the United States, as symbols of vows exchanged by bride and groom as they "brand" their experience and seal their promise.

In medieval Italy, watermarks as brands first appeared on paper, conveying the source of the product and its artisan. In the Middle Ages, coats of arms, communicating one's social rank and political fealty, were and continue to be forms of symbolic messaging.

A parallel found in many other cultures are totem poles (Figure 1.2). Here, images of clan affiliation and status suggest the global range and universal tendency of humans to use symbolic language for establishing ownership, authorship, and authority. In all instances, a unique identity and emotional connection with observers was sought and often realized.

figure 1.2
Symbolic communications: An example of a totem pole.

Symbols and Luxury Brands

In the world of luxury products, we find the very same tendency and development. The name of the original artisan or location often was "branded" into saddles or other works. For example, Hermès, founded in 1837 in Paris, embossed "Hermès, Paris" under the saddles (Figure 1.3). The intent was not to create a brand because the concept as we know it didn't exist then, but to inform those who might request the location of the artisan and where he might be found. Thus began the meaning of "brand" as a communication effort in so far as the "branding" of the saddle with a distinctive and consistent imprint, together with the name and the location of the artisan, suggest some of the very early and basic origins for today's brand strategies.

As an example, Brooks Brothers® continues to use the logo of the sheep being weighed in a certain stance. This weigh-in procedure would, in times past, suggest honesty in that the weight of the animal, and therefore its value in the market, was not being compromised or influenced by outside factors. Merchants in Europe would often hang this sign outside their shops and ships, signaling that the merchant dealt in wool. An added plus was that the symbol had been the crest of a highly selective order of chivalric knights and the symbol was seen as a sign of honor and integrity (Figure 1.4).

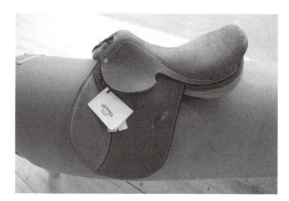

figure 1.3
An Hermès saddle with Paris location imprinted: An early example of luxury branding.

figure 1.4
The "Standing Ram" as Wool Shoppe logo:
Forerunner of Brooks Brothers' current logo still found on apparel.

Brands and Market Dynamics

Brands, beginning as communication symbols, served a wide variety of purposes in a broad swath of cultures, societies, and historical periods. Continuing with this historical development, let's take a look at how brands and brand management and their prerequisite, **consumer-oriented economies** (those focused on the needs of the end user for building business strategies), emerged over time in Western society.

The rise of consumer-oriented economies was preceded by several hundred years of a dramatic shift in market dynamics. It begins with the evolution from an agrarian society to a manufacturing society. The shift required a revolution in thinking and the creation of new modes of weaving, forging, and manufacturing.

For thousands of years people lived on, and tended to, the land around them for social life and economic subsistence. In Europe, with the fall of the Roman Empire around 500 CE, knights and warlords often built castles and fortifications around which peasants and craftsmen gathered for protection and lived. For example, the lord of the manor upon whose land the serf (or farmer) would live and farm was "paid" with crops in exchange for protecting the serf from pirates, marauders, and thieves.[3] This political arrangement was known as **feudalism,** a system for structuring society around relationships derived from the holding of land in exchange for service or labor. Because there were no nation-states overseeing money and commercial transactions, currency (unless it was gold) was of questionable value. A system arose called **bartering**, the exchange of goods and services in lieu of currency that was to be the medium of commercial exchange in place of money. This was a natural outgrowth of the feudal system in which such modes of barter were commonplace and presaged the development of outdoor markets where goods and services could be found, exchanged, and purchased and where an early form of branding communication took place as sellers often would seek out the same location in the market so buyers could recall where they could be found.

Over time, there emerged a new way of thinking about the creation and distribution of goods and services. What was traditionally made in the farmhouse for use within the family and on the farm and for barter was seen as a commercial opportunity. New modes of inventions, such as weaving for creating handicrafts, gradually generated more products than a family or farm needed or could use. The idea of taking surplus goods to market and generating hard currency (rather than the traditional bartering of goods and services) began to emerge as a commercial opportunity.

With this new economic reality, a system of small industries emerged. These were called **cottage industries**, wherein business manufacturing activities were carried on within a person's home or cottage often using an individual's own tools and equipment (e.g., spinning wheels).[4] The name derived from the farm cottages and countryside, which characterized the early manufacturing locations.

By the mid-18th century, feudalism was ending, creating the possibility of new economic mobility. Nation-states such as France, Spain, England, and Holland emerged, creating currencies of dependable value. Having currency or money also made it possible not to be bound to the land and to the barter system with its limited view of value. With this came a surge in inventions such as the steam engine. As more and more inventions came to be, the complexity and cost of buying and using them led to the emergence of the factory system and the displacement of the cottage industries, followed by vast migrations of many of those former farmers into cities in search of higher wages and a more predictable lifestyle. This became known as the **Industrial Revolution**, the transition to new manufacturing processes beginning in the 1760s in Great Britain.

The Industrial Revolution and Product-centric Business Models

The Industrial Revolution and its aftermath have been described by authors Robin Lewis and Michael Dart as characterized by the Four Waves. These waves are described as running from 1850 to the present day and are meant to portray general but significant shifts in production, distribution, and marketing of goods and services rather than specific historical periods per se.[5]

Wave I is seen as starting in 1850 and continuing until 1945. An extraordinary number of inventions and technologies emerged, such as the harnessing of electricity and steam power, which made possible the emergence of the assembly line. With the assembly line came the ability to mass produce products. We will characterize this as the "product-centric" century during which **producer power** prevailed,[6] wherein the demand for goods and services was much greater than the supply, resulting in the producer having more power over the product's pricing and distribution, and brands, with some exceptions, were hardly a factor and played a peripheral role in business strategies. This is because, in this period, consumer choice was dictated by the manufacturer and limited as demand far exceeded supply. This is reflected in that widely quoted phrase of Henry Ford in 1928 regarding his Model T automobile (Figure 1.5): "*Any customer can have a car painted any color he wants so long as it is black.*"[7]

Embedded in this phrase we can see a hint about the emergence of not only brands (the reference to the "Model T," for example) but also what then follows, the brand management system. George Low and Ronald Fullerton, complementing Lewis and Dart's analysis, have framed this into "four distinct but overlapping eras" from 1870 to the 1990s: "*During the first era, from about 1870, to the early 1900's, determined firm owners-entrepreneurs and high level managers created the first large wave of successful, nationally branded products.*"[8]

This was followed by the second era (1915–1929), during which functional product managers who were

figure 1.5
A black Ford Model T: An example of the first mass-produced automobile.

experts in efficiencies and mass production (such as those who managed the Ford Model T product into becoming a national icon) created a new management model focused on the product and reducing manufacturing costs per vehicle.

This product-oriented management perspective was soon to be challenged by Procter & Gamble (P&G), the consumer package goods company which today is the largest in the United States. Following what was a revolutionary idea at the time (1930), P&G undertook to reconstruct how the company's portfolio of products was managed. Now consumer brands would be the focal point to be managed, and product categories such as toothpaste or soap became business categories guided by brand strategies and the modern brand manager was born (1930 to 1949).

It took several decades for this management model to become the corporate norm, and this adoption constitutes the last era, 1949 to 1995, which roughly corresponds to Wave II discussed below.[9]

Wave II emerges post–World War II and runs from 1945 to 1980. In this environment, radio, print, and then television advertising was controlled by a few large networks. Late in the period, televisions may have been in some homes, but with only three stations and national broadcast rights, the content was limited to what the networks and their sponsors wished to sell. Here the mega-brand dominated the consciousness of the consumer. The role of the brand was to describe the product and its practical and dependable benefits rather than to differentiate it from its competitors. Manufacturers and brand owners operated product-centric business models with an *"if we build it they will come"* (they will buy it!) business mentality. So long as the needs of the consumer outweighed the production capacity of the factory system, this business model was sustainable. When this was no longer the case, a new model was needed. This set the stage for the advent of **mass marketing**, or targeting large segments of the population to sell, and **mass brands**, those packaged and distributed to reach the largest number of consumers, at the lowest cost to the manufacturer.

The efficiency of the factory system had redressed the post–World War II imbalance between supply and demand. When the demand for consumer goods had exceeded the supply, the product-centered system could continue. When the supply began to exceed the demand, a more aggressive marketing model was required to sustain the production levels of the factory system, which continued to produce for markets that were gradually becoming saturated. Over time, as the availability of products begins to meet and exceed demand, the need for products for everyday living is gradually supplanted by the want for products and the emotional pleasure they bring to the consumer. With this comes the emergence of **lifestyle fashion brands**, such as Polo Ralph Lauren, which begin to promote the brand as a source of stories on how the brand can complement and add satisfaction with its products to various aspects of the consumer's daily life. For example, fashion apparel becomes an aspiration to be enjoyed emotionally, something that you want rather than need or purchase out of necessity. As wants become distinguished from needs, the importance of **desire** (an overwhelming passion that drives human consumption and remains even after needs and wants are met) as a driver of consumption, in contrast to needs and wants, becomes more apparent and presages the advent of luxury products and brands.[10] With this, consumer behavior takes on an added dimension. Desire is recognized as an aspect of our passions, more intense and permanent and part of our makeup as human beings. In the words of one scholar, *"Needs are anticipated, controlled, denied, postponed . . . gratified through logical instrumental processes. Desires, on the other hand, are overpowering."*[11] As we will see beginning in Chapter 2, luxury brands align more with desire than with needs or wants, which helps in part to explain their success.

Wave III, from 1980 to 2000, begins the ascendency of the consumer. The advent of the internet and cable television opens up literal and figurative channels of information never before available to the everyday consumer.

Luxury products begin their ascendency in this period as well, offering images and lifestyles that extend the brand story to **heritage narratives**—that is, those brands that have deep roots and continuity with the past and build their brand narratives around this.

This ascendency was made possible by the advent of the luxury brand portfolio system first initiated by Bernard Arnault, CEO, and his creation of LVMH, which began from the merger of Louis Vuitton luggage and Moet-Hennessey spirits in 1987.[12]

The rise of corporate brand portfolios is the beginning of **luxury brand management**, a business tool to help differentiate and protect the value of the luxury brands, and the importance of both innovation and heritage as their unique brand elements to drive business development. At this stage, the lifestyles of the rich and famous are seen by many consumers who do not have the immediate means to purchase luxury products nonetheless as brands to own and lifestyles to emulate.

The Post-Industrial Revolution and Consumer-centric Business Models

David Aaker was one of the first to recognize this shift and the power of brands to drive business performance.[13] Aaker wrote, *"Sometime in the late 1980's, an explosive idea emerged, the idea that brands are assets, have equity, and drive business strategy and performance . . . and unless the business strategy resonated with the customers, the strategy was all but doomed."*[14] Enter the era of the brand and consumer power!

The final wave, Wave IV from 2000 to today, is the era of the brand, brand management, and consumer power. Brands proliferate! In 1947, there were some twenty automobile brands in the United States; today, there are about eighty-five. In 1980, there were six major blue jean brands; today, there are over 800. In the same period, there were around fifty major apparel brands; today, the estimate is over 4,000![15]

Brand managers begin to search out ways to engage their customer base and interact with them as solution and service providers rather than just product providers. Different types of solutions and services emerge.

For example, this might include solutions to the expense associated with furnishing a home or apartment, such as Ikea offered through affordable and simple-to-assemble furniture, or the unique pick up at home service offered by Enterprise Car Rental for drivers whose vehicles may be in the shop or for one-car families temporarily in need of two but with no means of transportation to get to the car rental office. The objective becomes not only to be different from their competitors but, more importantly, to be more relevant to the aspirational lifestyles of their consumers. Now the question becomes, "What do they want us to build so they will come?"

The practice of **experiential brand marketing** emerges. This entails a refocus away from the product, the price, and the availability as the center of the business strategy (Waves I, II, and III) to the feelings that consumers experience when they interact with the brand at every **touch point**—that is, the experience consumers take away from their interaction with a brand's operations and its personnel. The brand's **mission** (its marketplace purpose) and **vision** (its future aspirations) are the basis of values that engage and animate the brand's employees. They, in turn, bring those values and their emotional effect to the brand's consumers. Technology and mobile communications give even greater leverage to the consumer over market dynamics.

A central focus becomes the need to avoid strategic blunders such as a failure to transition to experiential marketing and to incorporate these changes into the company's business plans. Therefore, companies more and more transition from being product-centric to consumer-centric. Table 1.1 shows a summary of the two business models.

BRANDS AS BUSINESS DRIVERS

The emergence of the brand and its evolution into a primary facilitator of business strategies (rather than just a mode of communication) is the result of a gradual change in consumer mind-sets.

Table 1.1 Product-centric versus Consumer-centric Models: A Snapshot of How Consumer-centric Strategies and Brands Emerge Together

Business Categories	Product-centric	Consumer-centric
Strategic Focus	Create the best product	Create the best solution for the customer
People/Culture	New Product Culture: Looking for new products to develop	Customer Culture: Looking for new needs to fill / The Brand Ideal
Operational Focus	New Product Development; Research and Development	New Brand Solution Development, Customer Experience Management
Rewards/Metrics	Rewards new product development launches	Rewards people with consumer insights about customers
Organizational Structure	Product Divisions with Profit and Loss	Customer Brand Segments with Profit and Loss

As mass production provided a seemingly endless assortment of products and brands, and the web created an open forum for evaluating both, consumers began to share information as a means of validating their preferences. This led to higher levels of consumer expectations and has resulted in ongoing consumer dialogues with brands and their managers as consumers press the managers for higher levels of service and satisfaction. This change in consumer perspective is permanent and includes a necessary shift in business strategies from a **product-centric** business model which is focused on what can be produced and sold ("if we build it they will come") to a **consumer-centric** business model which is focused on what the consumer wants and is willing to buy ("what shall we build so they will come"); this aligns with this new consumer influence and more demanding consumer expectations. It also sets the stage for business practices (which we will explore in subsequent chapters) which no longer place profitability at the center of the business enterprise but see business in terms of a social undertaking whose responsibilities are not only to stockholders but also to the environment, social causes, and consumer well-being.

As a consequence, brand management becomes more **strategic** and looks toward long-term objectives rather than just tactical and only concerned with how we communicate and implement and operate the strategy. Managing the brand from a consumer-centric perspective is now essential for business success.

Avoiding Marketing Myopia

As products and services are branded as a means of communication and differentiation, and as products and services depend more and more on the brand in a fiercely competitive marketplace, brand managers need to be aware of the dangers of marketing myopia.

Marketing myopia[16] is a form of business "near-sightedness" where images of distant objects (the big picture) become out of focus because we bring them too close to us to see them clearly. Brand managers often suffer from this by being too close to their products, which limits their ability to adapt to changing market conditions. This inability of brand managers to see clearly can result in drastic business outcomes. These might include thinking tactically or short term rather than strategically or long term, a failure to innovate, and a tendency to be overly risk averse and not take necessary chances. However, there is a way to avoid the marketing myopia trap. Brands should be defined as solutions, not products.

This "solutions mentality" openly challenges some traditional business wisdom. One of these is the concept of **unique value propositions**, the benefits and solutions offered by a company and communicated through its brand that differentiate it from its competitors.

The classic unique value proposition by which a company in the product-centric age defined its **core competency** (its fundamental capabilities or what it does best), and its brand, was built from a product perspective and often a single product at that. This often limited change and growth. Now, the ability to meet business challenges requires a brand platform that supports flexible product innovation as a response to changing market conditions and commensurate changes in consumer demand.

A responsibility of brand management is to anticipate change, which should include the creation of a brand platform upon which to organize a potential group of related but distinct products (a product portfolio) as solutions to consumer demand. This new brand portfolio of products has to be developed so the products complement rather than compete with one another and, overall, the brands are **positioned**, or presented as providing solutions that differ from those of their competitors, as the company's core competency. Then, this is communicated in the company's **brand identity**, or what it does best, and **brand promise**, or what it conveys in its messaging to consumers regarding its identity. All of this has to remain consistent with what the company does best or has the capability to do with the proper changes and visionary leadership. These are steps in avoiding marketing myopia. What follows is how it can be managed from a company's beginning.

Adapting to Market Dynamics

Companies should launch with the broadest consumer-centric market view possible. This is consistent with empirical research data which confirms "*that a customer focus is the central element of a **market orientation**. . . . a philosophy of business management based upon a company-wide acceptance of the need for customer orientation.*"[17]

The following case provides us with an example of how marketing myopia can be avoided and how brand elements can capture a company's customer-centric solutions and market orientation and help it to readily pivot when market conditions change.

A company can adapt to **market dynamics**, or the competitive factors and the social, political, and economic environment, more readily when its mission and vision reflect a market orientation. There is also empirical evidence that companies that are market-oriented tend to post better performance metrics than those that are not.[18] In later chapters, we'll explore this connection between customer-centricity and performance and take it to another level by adding the concept of consumer engagement to the process and how it increases performance outcomes.

To demonstrate the process by which marketing myopia can be avoided, we've created a fictitious manufacturing company that makes shovels—the American Shovel Company (ASC). Let's take a look at it in *Brandstorming: American Shovel Company*.

Failure to Adapt to Market Dynamics

Railroads in America have held a fabled position in our society as reflected in movies, TV series, and pop music. The railroads are portrayed by these sources of entertainment as bastions of dependability and adventure that opened the West to settlement, offered mobility to those who wished to begin a new life, and connected far-off places in America, helping to make it into one country. This gave the railroads an iconic status in our society confirmed by the folklore of our culture, but it also reinforced a false perception by railroad management of competitive invincibility, rendering strategic flexibility unnecessary.

But by the 1960s, the railroads were on the brink of nationwide bankruptcy. They had been outmaneuvered by more agile and innovative carriers of people and freight such as ships, airlines, and the trucking industry, the latter catapulted forward by the completion of the U.S. interstate highway system in the late 1950s.

American Shovel Company (ASC) is a company name and a brand identity tied to a product and a category. But what if market dynamics (competitors' innovations, change in consumer lifestyles) make shovels marginal or obsolete? What if the internal culture of the company is so tied to a product that there is little or no consumer perspective and little if any motivation to innovate new product solutions? In addition, if ASC has been advertising as the premier "shovel" company, it may be difficult to convince consumers that the company is as competent to deliver other high-performance, more sophisticated product solutions.

So what business is the company really in? If it were just starting out, the company may have had the vision and leadership to think beyond its product and create a brand strategy that prepared it for adapting to changing market conditions, such as envisioning its business as providing consumer-centric solutions to environmental challenges. How might the company rethink its identity to position itself for such change and growth?

The purpose of a shovel is found in the problem it solves. If you were putting up a fence and needed to put some fence posts in the ground first, the purpose of a shovel is not to dig a hole per se, but to remove the soil which is an obstacle to putting up the fence. The shovel enables you to better manage your environment. The same applies with snow. One removes snow not to remove snow but to get it out of one's driveway. Notice the word "shovel" snow was not used in the preceding sentence and it should be avoided in any future ad copy, opening a window for developing other products to better manage and help solve the environmental problem that snow presents.

Now, consider what business this company is really in. It is in the business of removing natural obstacles, such as soil and snow that impede constructive changes or lifestyle needs. If ASC began with a problem-solving orientation, it may have called itself "The Environment Management Company" or a name to that effect. It could have devised the following brand assets such as a logo ($E = MC^2$), condensing its corporate name into a brand asset and leveraging a very famous symbol of cosmic energy. Building upon this branding, it could have added the tagline "managing mother nature"([SM]), and conveyed this brand promise in its mission statement and brand story, website, and advertising. It also indicates the company serves and solves beyond the ordinary—that is, to the second power (MC^2)! It can still make shovels, but now the company has positioned and branded itself in the consumer's mind to be a credible maker, for example, of steam shovels, backhoes, and snow blowers. The product mix, at the appropriate time, can be extended, consistent with the competitive market challenges and the perception the public now has of the company's core competency. This also sends an internal message to research and development. It can liberate the research and development teams within the company who now imagine their roles are to create innovative solutions to nature's obstacles beyond shovels. The company is poised to pivot, meet change, and be a part of the solution by more readily adapting to market dynamics (Table 1.2).

(continued on next page)

Table 1.2 Two Branding Models for the American Shovel Company: Contrasting Product-centric with Consumer-centric Thinking and Seeing How Marketing Myopia Emerges from the Former

Classic	Contemporary
• Successful Brands convey images that differentiate them from competitors	• Successful Brands conjure up feelings that connect with consumers' deepest emotions
• Brands are created by companies in light of their mission	• Brands are created by the interactions of consumers and companies
• Brands never vary in their image	• Brands grow, evolve, and change (like people)
• Successful Brands occupy previously unoccupied space in consumers' mind-sets	• Successful Brands are traveling companions, joining consumers on life's journey
• The Objective of Branding is to position oneself first or better than competitors in a competitive arena	• The Objective of Branding is to build trust in the Brand

As an example from the real world, in 2006, the Apple Computer Corporation changed its name to Apple Inc. Over the last ten years, this change sent a message heard internally and externally that Apple was no longer simply a company that made computers. Both consumers and the company's research and development team got the message. The change in its corporate brand identity enabled Apple to begin to reposition itself from a computer manufacturer to the premier innovator of electronic lifestyle communications (the business it was really in!) that devised and unleashed a creative avalanche in product and service solutions (Figure 1.6).

figure 1.6
Apple Watches: Apple is not in the computer business; it's in the lifestyle business!

The railroads, so focused on the product they offered, suffered from marketing myopia. The railroads were unable to see themselves in the business of transportation solutions, which is the logistics business. They knew logistics or how to move people and things from point to point swiftly and safely. Unfortunately, they saw themselves as being in the railroad business. What they didn't know was "the business they were really in." In Theodore Levitt's seminal piece "Marketing Myopia" in the *Harvard Business Review*,[19] he mused about what the U.S. railroads might have become had they not been figuratively and literally tied to the railroad tracks—that is, that they could see the business they were really in. Not only the corporate brand names (e.g., the AT&L Railroad, the Union Pacific Railroad, the Baltimore & Ohio Railroad) but, as discussed above, the folklore surrounding the sector in songs and stories so reinforced and romanticized the railroad experience that it assumed a certain mythic hero status in American culture. American railroads provide a snapshot of how a failure to adapt to market conditions can happen and how archetypes can help or hinder this adaptation. **Archetypes** (not to be confused with stereotypes) are universally held social roles rooted in our biological mental makeup which frame our social values and expectations regarding types of human behavior.[20] The examples that follow will give some idea of how important they are.

The railroads can be understood as the archetype of the hero who courageously traversed plains and mountains to open up the American West. As an example of how this theme resonates in brand marketing in the U.S., think for a moment of the Marlboro Man ad campaign, an iconic depiction of the American cowboy as a Hero archetype, representing freedom, individualism, and a willingness to go it alone for a good cause.

The Marlboro Man, always on horseback, can be seen as a complementary brand persona to the legendary "Iron Horse," or the railroad trains (a common metaphor used in the late 19th and early 20th centuries to describe railroads)—courageous, independent, and forging westward (Figure 1.7).

figure 1.7
The Marlboro Man: A symbolic image of how American culture views Western heroes.

However, because every archetype has within it its opposite tendency, the railroads over time became arrogant (the corresponding opposite to the "courage" of the hero) and when under competitive pressure developed an "us versus them" mentality (another corresponding weakness of the hero archetype). The result was their inability to see themselves as part of a broader market in which to reinvent themselves. Therefore, the possibility of transitioning into logistics companies through mergers and acquisitions with non-railroad competitors was obscured by their failure to fashion a fresh archetype by which to characterize their brands and their businesses.

The Brand Ideal

The evolution of brands from platforms that differentiate your product from the competition finds its next consumer-centric stage in the **brand ideal**.[21] The brand ideal holds that the customer's hopes and aspirations should serve as the basis for the brand's business strategy. Brand managers are now charged with discerning emotional drivers within their consumers' psyches by discovering their passions and their values and emerging with innovative solutions regarding how the brand serves those values. Here is where the consumer and the brand intersect to create the brand experience. This forms a further iteration of the limits of product-centric models and the need to avoid marketing myopia.

The Customer Is Boss

The classic expression of this can be found at Procter and Gamble (P&G) and its pivotal commitment to consumer engagement. The company's CEO, A. G. Lafley, sounded the trumpets when he announced in 2001 that "*the consumer is boss.*"[22] It heralded a shift resulting in unprecedented growth in market share and profits. In place of a business model focused on beating the competition and creating products in response to the market and the company's agenda, the shift was to the agenda of the consumers and their fundamental human values. Here are the words of Jim Stengel, CMO at P&G, who was called upon to drive this initiative: "*If you want great business results, you and your brand have to stand for something compelling . . . truly sustainable business models are linked to fundamental human values—an ideal of improving people's lives.*"[23]

What Business Are They Really In?

Examples of the brand ideal and how it links with "knowing the business you are really in" can be found in various types of businesses. What follows are examples of very successful companies that follow this strategy.

We've condensed these examples into short stories that explore how companies have avoided marketing myopia by staying focused on the brand, remaining consumer-centric, and understanding the business they are really in!

VF Corporation (VFC)

VF Corporation is the world's largest apparel and footwear company.[24] As of 2014, its brand portfolio was comprised of over thirty high-profile, consumer-focused brands (Wrangler, Vans, North Face, Nautica, Timberland) and generated over $11 billion in annual revenues. The corporation's success comes from a well-operated brand portfolio management model and a focus on consumer-centric brand strategies. The business it has been in is identifying brands that can align with the *passions* of its targeted consumer. Here is the view from Eric Wiseman, president and CEO, about the company's consumer-centric approach to brand building when it decided to become a major player in a competitive space relatively new to VFC:

> *The outdoor and action sports industry became a place that we really wanted to be. Apparel and footwear, in that sector, are worn by people when they're pursuing their passions . . . what they wear matters to them because it has a function . . ., in some cases, a life-saving function; people develop real emotional connections with that stuff. Those brands (in the sector) are sustainable if you can keep the emotional connection strong.*[25]

The business that VFC is in is discerning and tapping into these consumers lifestyles and dispositions and creating brands that matter to them. The companies which are able to transcend being product-centric tend, therefore, to be more open to innovation. They define the essence of who they are and therefore the **DNA**, or the essence of their brand identity, in more imaginative ways, which enables them, all other things being equal, to be more competitive.

This, as we have seen, has become a more prevailing requirement for success, as consumers intensify their demands for influence over the product offer and the brand experience.

Under Armour

As another example, let's take a look at Under Armour. On first reflection, many would identify the brand with functional athletic apparel and footwear for the avid sports activist. This might be one way of describing the business the company is in. However, it also could be in the technology business (its market entry signature athletic shirt that wicked away perspiration was, in part, a technology breakthrough). Listen to Under Armour's founder and CEO, Kevin Plank, on wearable tech:

It's going to move at lightning speed . . . all of a sudden it's as simple as swiping something to change the color of my shirt . . . It's just a matter of when and who's going to do it. I'll be damned if I'm going to cede anything to Silicon Valley, because I believe we are a technology company.[26]

And his further expression of this vision:

And if the phone is going to get integrated into the shirt, should that be a technology company making apparel or the apparel company starting to make technology? I choose the latter and that's exactly where I'm pushing my company.[27]

Here we have the classic expression of consumer engagement as the brand evolves with and meets the lifestyle needs of its core consumers. We also have a classic example of the CEO as brand manager (Figure 1.8).

The Marriot Corporation

Ostensibly, the Marriot Corporation at its inception was in the business of selling hotel rooms. J. W. Marriott, in *The Spirit to Serve: Marriot's Way*[28] explained the company's approach and why it was successful:

Expertise in managing the processes that make those sales possible by nailing the basics into place, systems allow employees to provide more customized

**figure 1.8
Under Armour retail display in a Chicago store:** The brand now sees itself as in the business of "wearable technology."

customer service, SOP's and Great Systems nip common problems in the bud so staff can focus on uncommon ones and act energetically (free from normal operational concerns) to solve the problem quickly . . . In a service industry, this and "A Bias for Action" is the key to success.[29]

Notice the emphasis on solving problems for consumers, again the high-water mark of successful consumer-centric business models, and transcending the product and service trap in defining the company's business model. Once this key to success was discovered, other business opportunities emerged for Marriott. It went from building hotels and owning them to running them.

Marriott's in-house manual, *Sixty-Six-Steps-to-Clean-a-Room*, is symbolic of the expertise which leads "to consumer satisfaction," then to franchising. Once a consistent brand has been developed, business development extensions flow naturally from the core DNA, as reflected in the niche properties of Marriott.

However, even Marriott can experience missteps in the strategies, especially when it deviates from the consumer-centric model. Here's an example. In 1977, the company entered the cruise ship market. Fifteen years later it exited the business. Let's look at its assumptions and why it failed.

Marriott came to owning and operating cruise ships from a strategic business perspective of viewing them as "floating hotels." Cruise ships appeared to be a natural, organic extension of the business the company was in. The Marriott Corporation was proficient in:

- Food Service Preparation and Delivery
- Housekeeping
- Family-Oriented Environments

All of these were core requirements for managing a successful cruise ship business. However, these were necessary but by no means sufficient competencies. What Marriott discovered was that it knew little about how to develop "family entertainment" and to engender an atmosphere of "Creative Adventure" on board. These are two key ingredients for success in the cruise

ship business. As for the "floating hotel" metaphor, occupancy was more erratic than in brick-and-mortar hotels. If a reservation was cancelled, it was difficult to fill the rooms at the last moment. Add to this that maintenance requirements on board an oceangoing vessel are much more stringent than simply *Sixty-Six-Steps-to-a-Clean-Room*! Given that the company was so good at making a hotel or restaurant work, Marriott tended to downplay the fact that consumers aboard cruise ships had different expectations than at a hotel. Because of this, the cruise ship venture was not successful, and Marriott exited the industry.

What became clear by the late 1980s was that any extension where customized customer service could be effectively managed or outsourced was Marriott's true business. Once the company discovered this, it successfully developed, built, and sold or franchised (and then managed) hotels, time-shares, and, recently, senior assisted living facilities. All sit comfortably on the brand platform and all flow naturally from the business that Marriott is really in, the business of managing customized customer service. The purchase and successful managing of the Ritz-Carlton luxury hotel group where customized service reaches its pinnacle (see our discussion of Ritz-Carlton in Chapter 4) points to the power of consumer-centricity and knowing "What Business They Are Really In!"

Polo Ralph Lauren

Knowing "the business you are really in" also applies to an aspirational luxury business model. Here, the clearer the understanding of the values and dreams of the targeted consumer, the wider the field of the business opportunity. The key caveat is that the product, service, or experience be perceived as authentic.

So when Ralph Lauren says, "*I'm not in the business of fashion, I'm in the business of dreams,*"[30] he is stating a marketing message about consumer aspirations to enter his world. But to do so effortlessly, one has to feel its genuineness. As with a good movie or play, consumers are willing to suspend reality and embrace the illusion if it feels that it mirrors who they are within themselves.

Polo Ralph Lauren as a corporate culture understands this. In each brand extension (Purple Label, Black Label, R.L. Sport) there is a consistent theme that conveys the DNA of the brand that Polo core consumers embrace.

What are these "dreams"? What business is Polo Ralph Lauren really in? It's not the apparel, fragrance, or fashion business. What one experiences is a brand that trumpets the lifestyle of America's old money elite, a world of equestrian farms, Cape Cod compounds, and, of course, polo and its lifestyle extensions. It is the closest America has to an aristocracy, and Ralph Lauren has tapped into a deeply felt need and an aspiration to be part of it. This is the business Ralph Lauren is really in!

Starbucks

Howard Schultz (founder and CEO) began the process of launching his business by committing to finding and building a company "with soul."[31] How does one experience this at Starbucks?

- Couches to sit on and read
- A place to meet friends and linger; table turnover is not a Starbucks business metric
- Free wireless internet service was added early, before most stores envisioned this as an added value
- Small gifts and then the big add-on—the commitment to being a center where music was as much a part of the culture as coffee
- Special CDs for sale
- A "Hear Music" media bar with free downloads
- Sponsoring concerts and making donations to music-related causes

The business that Starbucks is really in is providing a comfortable community gathering place for the literati, the young sophisticate, and the music lover. Starbucks is in the business of creating (on every street corner) a community living room with soul. This especially resonates in urban life where, given transitory lifestyles and an absence of community, alienation often prevails.

Such a transformation would not have been possible if Howard Schultz had thought of Starbucks as simply being in the coffee business. But early on, he had a vision "*of creating a culture of warmth and belonging where everyone is welcome, a neighborhood gathering place . . . a 'third place' between home and work.*"[32] This is the business Starbucks is really in!

American Girl

In business since 1988 with retail stores, an online business, a mail-order catalog, and a magazine, American Girl has sold and serviced over 21 million dolls plus accessories and created lifestyle events, generating over $650 million in revenues in 2013.[33]

Owned by Mattel, the company's challenge from the very beginning was how to sell dolls and accessories to tweens and pre-tweens in light of the dominance of Barbie and the ascendancy of modern notions of feminism. The solution, the business that it is really in, is not to sell dolls!

A visit to an American Girl store provides immediate confirmation of this. In four floors, the history of America is represented by perfectly costumed period dolls for each defining event (the Revolutionary War, the Civil War, etc.). The full spectrum of ethnicity (Native American, African American, etc.) is represented in history through stories of the dolls as heroines in each historical event. This makes them role models for the girls. A theater with live performances of the different periods, plus the magazine (with over 1 million subscribers), reinforces the feel-good, uplifting tales that the story lines convey. A website with millions of hits per month broadcasts these values (Figure 1.9).

At retail, dolls can buy new outfits, get their hair done, be admitted to the "hospital" for repair for any "injuries," and then join their owner and her family for lunch or dinner, while seated in their own separate chair. In the Café, service is on china by waiters and waitresses serving real food and no sodas! Every meal, irrespective of what you order, begins with a cinnamon bun, warmed, sweet nostalgia, which symbolizes the traditional values of home and family. This brand

figure 1.9
American Girl dolls:
In spite of these images, the company is not in the doll business; it is in the business of honoring young girls!

experience has been so successful that advance reservations are required.

This brand experience reinforces the bonding between grandmothers and granddaughters, mothers and daughters, and aunts and nieces and begins to tell us what business the company is really in. American Girl is in the business of building self-esteem in young girls by embracing traditional values. By providing a wholesome counterpoint to the racy images and self-indulgent values of current pop music and movie stars with strong role models through soft dolls, reliving their stories of sacrifice, hard work, overcoming adversity, and community service, this is the business American Girl is really in!

Build-A-Bear

In the Build-A-Bear store signage is the word "Workshop." The Build-A-Bear Workshop is in the business of selling teddy bears. The Build-A-Bear sign suggests that this isn't the real business the company is in. The brand byline "Where Best Friends Are Made" opens the portal a bit more so we can begin to get at the DNA of the brand.[34]

A Build-A-Bear fact sheet on the company's website states that the company was founded in 1997 as

"an interactive entertainment retail experience based on the enduring love and friendship that connects us all to stuffed animals, and especially to our teddy bears."[35]

In the final section of its website on trade mark and editorial usage, the corporate communications department asks the following of those who write about the company: "*Only use capital letters when referring to our products and services,*" and "*Build-A-Bear should not be used as a verb!*" (such as in "Building-A-Bear").

Perhaps the most telling in our search for the soul of this brand and what business it is really in is the "request" from the company website that "*in reference to the process of making stuffed animals, you use the word 'make' not 'build.'*"

What should we, if you'll excuse the play on words, "make" of all this? Let's take a closer look at what's being "made" in the "workshop."

Build-A-Bear, founded in 1997, is another experiential retail phenomenon. This publicly traded company has become a $500 million business operating over 400 stores in the U.S. and Canada and overseas.

The concept and operational business model is to offer "guests" (as customers are referred to) a platform, "a workbench" for creating their own experience through making a teddy bear. Children can choose from various voices or songs on computer chips, and satin hearts with "Love & Wishes" on them, and place them within the bear; add a bar-code chip for its "Find-A-Bear" tracking program; and sew the final stitch to complete their very personalized Teddy. Should a bear be lost, it can be tracked and returned to its owner; thousands have, in fact, been returned.

The bear can be "groomed," dressed in separately purchased outfits, and named (birth certificates are issued in Spanish or English). A "Cub Condo" carry-case and a "Buy Stuff Club®" card, with discounts toward future purchases, complete the transaction. Throughout the process, staff advisors such as "Pawsonal Shoppers®" or "Pawlette Coufur®" fashion advisors guide purchasers along the way. Co-branding with such brands as Sketchers® for "footwear" or the NBA® and WNBA® for apparel adds excitement to each child's experience.

The brand experience has its own music as well as birthday party facilities, stores, and Build-A-Bear Workshop Cafés. A recently launched "Friends 2 B Made®" adds another experiential dimension to the brand's promise. Girls can come to the same workshop setting and make a very cool doll dress in the latest fashions, fuss and shop for their "friends," and have a birthday party to boot.

What's clear is that the company is not in the business of selling Teddy Bears. Then what business is it really in and how does the brand enable the core business to morph and reinvent itself?

First and foremost, Build-A-Bear is about "Doing," not "Buying." The "Doing" clearly rides the wave of consumer-centric customization. For Build-A-Bear, self-expression is the key. A business that can deliver this experience has touched the soul of its customers.

Such expressions of intimacy authenticate the Build-A-Bear brand and legitimize the extension of its brand to cause-related marketing events, such as creating NYPD/FDNY bears in supportive sympathy for the victims of September 11 as well as joining with UNICEF.

Build-A-Bear is in the business of engendering self-expression and providing a "workshop" (not a retail space!), which means that there is an opportunity for a brand extension that migrates past kids and tweens to teens and adults. Here's another business opportunity, which emerges once one truly understands the business it is really in!

SUMMARY

There is no agreed-upon definition for what a brand is. Consequently, the approach taken here is to look at consumer communications and behavior as a path to begin to understand a brand's richness and complexity. Brands began as symbols of authority and ownership. A distinction between branding and brands reflects the role of the former as a means of communication and the latter as an object of ownership and business development.

Brands evolved over several centuries to become business drivers as modern economic systems emerged. At the beginning of the Industrial Revolution as demand exceeded supply, the product-centric business model made brands less important in business. Business management emerged which sought to minimize production costs and maximize production output in factories. In the post–Industrial Revolution era, as supply exceeded demand, the consumer-centric model emerged and brands became part of business strategies for communication and consumer engagement. Here, a new management model emerged which focused on brands to organize and manage the business rather than on product categories. Brands became a means of reflecting and capturing consumers' needs and wants. Luxury brands went further and aligned with desires, a deeper and more intense behavioral driver. A distinction was made between private label and public brands as the latter engaged the consumer on an emotional basis which the former does not and the consumer responds in kind. A further shift occurred in consumer-centricity, as managers saw the brand ideal as a company purpose which looked beyond profit to serving customers' needs and wants as the basis for business strategies.

Brands provide a basis for these strategies which enable businesses to prepare for growth and to meet

14. Ibid., p. 7.

15. Lewis and Dart, "The New Rules of Retail," p. 32.

16. Theodore Levitt, "Marketing Myopia," *Harvard Business Review* 38 (1960).

17. Ajay K. Kohli and Bernard J. Jaworski, "Market Orientation: The Construct, Research Propositions and Managerial Implications," *Journal of Marketing* 54, no. 2 (April 1990): pp. 1–18, p. 2.

18. For an early empirical confirmation of this correlation, see John C. Narver and Stanley F. Slater, "The Effect of a Market Orientation on Business Profitability," *Journal of Marketing* (October 1990): pp. 20–35, and Bernard J. Jaworski and Ajay K. Kohli, "Market Orientation: Antecedents and Consequences," *Journal of Marketing* 57 (July 1993), pp. 53–70.

 A later replication of the 1990 study by Narver and Slater confirmed their earlier findings and broadened the relevancy by confirming those findings for additional markets. See "The Positive Effect of a Market Orientation on Business Profitability," *Journal of Business Research* 48 (2000): pp. 69–73.

19. Levitt, "Marketing Myopia."

20. The brand as an archetype is based on Jung's *Psychology of the Collective Unconsciousness*. For applications see: Margaret Mark and Carol Pearson, *The Hero and the Outlaw* (New Jersey: McGraw Hill, 2001).

21. Jim Stengel, "The Case for the Brand Ideal," *Strategy Business* (May 12, 2012).

22. Ibid.

23. Ibid.

24. "2013 Annual Report," VF, January 1, 2013, http://reporting.vfc.com/2013/.

25. Eric Wiseman, Interviewed by Robin Lewis, Personal Interview, January 10, 2012.

26. Kyle Stock, "Under Armour's Kevin Plank on Retail's Future," *Bloomberg BusinessWeek* (November 6, 2014), http://www.businessweek.com/.

27. Ibid.

28. Kathi Ann Brown, *The Spirit to Serve: Marriott's Way*. (N.p.: HarperCollins, 1997).

29. Ibid.

30. "Introduction," in *Tabletop Book—Polo Ralph Lauren 2008 Runway Collection*.

31. Mathew Dollinge, "Starbucks, 'The Third Place,' and Creating the Ultimate Customer Experience," *Fast Company*, last modified June 11, 2008, http://www.fastcompany.com/887990/starbucks-third-place-and-creating-ultimate-customer-experience.

32. Ibid.

33. Annual Report, Mattel Inc., 2013.

34. Build-A-Bear website, www.buildabear.com, home page.

35. For the founder's view of the DNA of the business and brand, see: Maxine Clark, *The Bear Necessities of Business: Building a Business with a Heart* (N.p.: John Wiley & Sons, 2006); www.buildabear.com.

The Nature of Luxury Brands

CHAPTER 2

AFTER COMPLETING THIS CHAPTER
YOU WILL BE ABLE TO:

- Establish craftsmanship and authenticity as the roots of luxury brands.

- Explain luxury as a culture driven by desires and values beyond price.

- Assess exclusivity and availability as luxury brand strategies.

"When I see two Porsche on the same street, I begin to worry."

—Porsche® CEO

THE ROOTS OF LUXURY BRANDS

The reality of corporate brand portfolio management, publicly traded luxury brands, and the efficiencies of modern global production all have impacted today's luxury business model. There is less and less space for handmade and the artisan, yet the business model still seeks to maintain an aura of **craftsmanship**, or the role of the artisan, in both its product designs and its brand narrative.

> *Every luxury object should have some part, even small but spectacular, that is hand made. This is the dimension that makes it stand out from the series, from the world without surprises of the factory.*[1]

This is not to imply that craftsmanship is not present in product creation or that artisans no longer play a part, but simply that they have become less prominent and, therefore, less of a purchase driver in the twenty-first century as luxury companies more and more mass produce in global factories. This is a reaction to the pressures of global demand and quarterly **corporate earnings calls**, those Q&A conference calls by stock market analysts, which are exerting pressure on luxury brands to develop growth strategies that could further limit the role of the artisan in favor of mass production. As one writer has commented, "*Society, (globally) has become dependent on industrial over-production for a market that over-consumes.*"[2]

As there is no agreed-upon definition of luxury, these assertions regarding the role of the artisan and craftsmanship in the creation of luxury products still need to be stated in a measured manner. In our next chapter, we will attempt to delineate the various iterations of luxury, premium, fashion, and mass brands and examine how they border on each other or mix to create hybrid brand models. We also will look at the role of craftsmanship, if any, in each category.

In this chapter, rather than attempt any definitions, we've opted for a narrative approach to their identities and differences. We will present how they behave strategically and tactically in the market using the leaders in each class (e.g., Louis Vuitton and Hermès for luxury, Ralph Lauren for fashion/premium, Zara for mass fast fashion, etc.) and by showing examples of how they contrast and intersect in the real world.

We will see that some of the luxury brands presented in this chapter are more heritage- and history-focused than others and, therefore, emphasize craftsmanship with greater frequency (Hermès). Other brands have begun to underplay the past and are constructing a more contemporary history (Burberry). What they share in common is an anchorage in a fabled history which they honor with differing degrees of ritual, plus an unyielding commitment to excellence and creative innovation. In our next chapter, we will broaden our discussion of luxury by analyzing various iterations of luxury that are brand marketing concepts as opposed to the implicit brand management definition of luxury that we are presenting here.

There are values from the original artisans, and their workshops and workbenches, that remain the bedrock of all things luxury. This is reflected in a brand management strategy exercised by every major luxury house. Some examples of this strategy are: Gucci curating and presenting its historic collection of handbags in a South Korean museum; Mulberry showcasing an artisan handcrafting a handbag at an English craftsmanship show and offering visitors an opportunity to be a temporary apprentice and craft their own "Mulberry" leather bracelet; Hermès providing videos of the artisans creating handbags from the Hermès workbenches; Fendi showing its "craftsman @ work" video in 2013 at Harrods in London for public view as part of the company's "The Handbag Narratives" promotion. These products are often subtitled and presented as expressions of "wearable art," further evidence of the omnipresence of the artisan in the creation and dissemination of **luxury brand narratives**, in which the pedigree of the brand in terms of its ancestral or genealogical line, reaching back many generations, is woven into the present tapestry of marketing communications.

This commitment to heritage is not limited to accessories brands. Witness, for example, the Swiss luxury watch brand Patek Phillipe, whose horological museum houses four centuries of artifacts and stories of all things related to watchmaking as an art, as well as the history of Patek Phillipe itself, which began in 1839. The company continues to support handcrafted production by training artisans. In its quest for a universal standard of excellence, Patek Phillipe launched an institute in 1886 that trains artisan watchmakers and awards a certification, **The Geneva Seal**. This certification has become the industry standard for creating and measuring the highest skills of watchmaking craftsmanship.

The Mystique of Handmade

Consequently, irrespective of their business strategy, luxury brands are united in their commitment to, and conversations regarding, the lure of handmade and the corresponding concept of craftsmanship. Why does this continue to resonate with consumers so long after the necessity of handmade has been virtually displaced by the reality of mass production?

The Craftsman Archetype

We submit that "The Craftsman" in this regard is an archetype as discussed in Chapter 1, a psychological imprint as to social roles that is anchored in the deepest recesses of our souls and minds.[3] The **Craftsman Archetype** is based on timelessness as its primary dimension.[4] Craftsmen who labored, and who labor with their hands, represent a tradition of passing down from generation to generation the skills and the spirit of what creativity means to human fulfillment. Over countless generations, Masters taught Journeymen,

Journeymen taught Apprentices in an unbroken tradition over time (Hermès still operates an apprentice training program in France). This process is a multigenerational transfer of skills and craftsmanship, a *"desire to do a job well for its own sake."*[5] There is a romantic element, a soulfulness to this that is captivating. Here is an expression of it: *"the craftsman . . . does his tasks with the perfect balance of beauty and function; he works with his hands . . . he wants to be connected to his project."*[6]

It is timeless in the sense that each handmade product is seen as a monument to imperishable beauty. The craftsman seeks immortality by leaving behind an impression of his soul.[7] It represents a form of immortality that we long for as finite beings, to transcend the temporal and be connected to the eternal. This again returns us to an earlier reference in this chapter, wherein one writer on luxury argues that every luxury object should have some part of it that is handmade, as with the grille of a Rolls-Royce (Figure 2.1) or the twisted silk thread that adorns the neck of a Nina Ricci perfume bottle (such a thread is also found on the Chanel bottle)![8]

> *When something is handcrafted* by an artisan . . . it has a legacy of stories, history, traditions, passed down through generations . . . a soulful feel.[9]

Needs, Wants, and Desires

The introduction of the concept of soulfulness opens a portal to another unique dimension of luxury brands, the power of desire in animating consumer behavior. As we discussed in Chapter 1, the shift from product-centered to consumer-centered brand strategies brought to the forefront the focus on being market oriented. Brand managers now have to understand what motivates different types of consumers to purchase which products. In the analysis, **needs** became identified with must-have commodities, things necessary for daily living, and **wants**, products or services that weren't necessary but were perhaps aspirational choices. So one needs footwear to safely navigate the streets of New York (need),

figure 2.1
Rolls-Royce grille being hand-assembled. An artisan's touch should prevail, even in assembling luxury automobiles.

but doesn't necessarily need Converse sneakers with which to do so (want). In the luxury space one might, in making this comparison, replace Converse with Christian Louboutin, which leads to our discussion of luxury and desire.

In introducing desire, we first draw a distinction between how we make need decisions versus want decisions. (We explore this in even greater detail in subsequent chapters.) The former are made in a rather nonreflective manner, while the latter involve a more reflective process. Desire raises the bar by adding the role of the passions and of the soul. "*Consumer desire is a passion born between consumption fantasies and social situational contexts.*"[10] Such "social situations" could include the influence of social stratification and our quest for social recognition that stratification both engenders and obstructs.[11] Such "fantasies" could be the quest for social recognition that some consumers seek through displays of luxury ownership in light of luxury's commitment to rarity and inaccessibility; many desire it but few can afford to enjoy it as this is part of the luxury strategy for maintaining a highly ordered system of value. "*The exclusive element of luxury is that it should always be beyond the reach of many*

people."[12] The greater the inaccessibility, the greater the desire.[13] Consequently, although consumers may express desire for things found in other categories such as mass, fashion, and premium products, luxury brands tap into deep desires—dreams, for example: "*The basic product corresponds to a need ... The luxury product corresponds to a dream.*"[14]

The degree to which this dynamic relationship between "desire" dreams and luxury has real business and brand management implications can be seen in the debate that broke out in early 2016 around runway shows in all major cities during fashion weeks. These shows are where the next season's collections debut before the fashion press, high-profile **fashionistas** (consumers who follow fashion and want to be the first to wear the latest trends), and style setters from movies and music. Burberry, in its strategy of being ultra consumer-centric, was the first to announce that it would sell directly from the runway shows, a timing challenge that was unheard of in the luxury business.[15] Usually the collections are not available at retail until four to six months later. In the interim, the desire for what was glimpsed in streaming video and in glossy fashion magazines escalates.

The reaction to Burberry's announcement was immediate—that this would undermine luxury's approach to business; in the words of Carlo Capasa, the president of Italy's luxury trade organization, Italian fashion is driven by "*a spirit to create desire*" (boldface added) while fast fashion, "*to satisfy a need*" (boldface added).[16] Henri Pinault, the chairman of the Kering luxury brands group mentioned in Chapter 1, added that Burberry's approach "*negates the dream*" (boldface added).[17]

In this context, products are more than just the fulfillment of needs or wants; what we purchase becomes "social markers" by which we claim membership in select social groups by dint of our purchase and ownership as well as how we define ourselves.[18] As Belk and others argue, consumers solidify this dynamic by being open to ads and following fashion media, cocreating with marketing managers their dependency by "*being complicit in their own seduction*."[19] Add to this that especially in the fashion market, "*the dynamism of the market does not depend on fulfilling desires but rather on their perpetual re-creation*."[20]

Here is where luxury parts company with fashion as a brand experience. Fashion is based on creating **obsolescence**! This season's merchandise is meant to offer a temporary satisfaction which makes way for next season's merchandise successor. Consequently, the very satisfaction of the desire regenerates the desire. Fulfillment is wanting. There is inherent in the process a degree of manipulation.

However, luxury brands are not in the business of engendering obsolescence. Luxury is based on timeless innovation and this provides the foundation for differentiating their relationship with consumers and their desires. In this, luxury brands face a different challenge. Because the desire for luxury is tethered to deeper issues of personal identity and social status, its liberation is more challenging and the opportunity for fulfillment more remote. Luxury would be doomed if it followed fashion's commitment to obsolescence.

This has led to a different business model for luxury. Luxury seeks to transmit the soulfulness of its creative process to the souls of its core consumers; it seeks to generate an experience beyond manipulation, an experience based on **authenticity**, or the genuineness of the creative process and the timeless innovation of its craftsmanship. Here is where desire may find its fulfillment.

For consumers, luxury brands offer the opportunity to be connected to this dream experience through the purchase and through the participation in the brand narrative. For some, the participation is only by reflecting on the experiential elements of which the runway shows and the waiting are a part. This creates a sense in the luxury consumer of authenticity in both the brand and the product in that it requires time to create a commercial expression of the runway collections. Maintaining this expectation adds to and confirms that the various narratives on craftsmanship are authentic, which results in a seamless brand experience.

How is this complement maintained? The answer requires that we explore the twin principles of today's luxury, exclusivity and availability.

Exclusivity and Availability

Returning to the roots of craftsmanship, we find latent within it the concept of **exclusivity**. Early artisans, limited by time and animated by timelessness, created unique and often singular expressions of their artistry. This was especially the case if the artisan was commissioned by royalty or the town's affluent to create a particular piece. The result was an exclusive piece of work since the opportunity for ownership did not "include" those who could neither afford nor perhaps conceive of such an indulgence.

Availability

This exclusivity made the owner feel special. It was exclusively his, and in a very real sense, he became exclusive. Add that the work was not readily accessible, if at all, to the mass of society and we have the second principle of a luxury strategy, **availability**, or the limitation of access to a select few. The latter concept is originally a function of one-offs, or the absence of, or limitations in, inventory that characterizes an enterprise of handmade objects.

Today, these have morphed into strategies for maintaining brand value. These strategies manifest themselves as part of brand management with unique product identity or innovative design, commensurate with the image and persona of the brand (exclusivity), and coupled with controlled retail distribution and/or limited inventory (availability). It is these two elements together that imply rarity and create the perception of value. (We'll revisit these strategies in more detail later in this chapter.)

Rarity

In luxury, **rarity,** or controlled scarcity (a function of the intersection of exclusivity and availability), can be understood on several levels.[21] One aspect is found in the product, which may be made of rare and exotic elements such as a special-issue timepiece from Piaget; the other is the number available. Rarity also aligns with the rarity of its consumers' financial standing, which is generally much greater (and therefore "rarer") than others in the social system.

This is confirmed by the final element, price. High premium pricing solidifies the exclusivity and availability dynamic. Alone, it cannot establish luxury as a class of objects, but together with exclusivity and the availability quotient, it can. It also confirms the perception of consumers who often use price alone as a **heuristic** (i.e., a mental shorthand confirmation by which to arrive at a decision) for quality.

How Luxury Differs from Fashion and Mass Brands

We've already introduced into our discussion the idea of timelessness and how it relates to luxury. We should add that a test of luxury is that objects appear fresh far past their launch date. Objects seem timeless and often appreciate in monetary value as well as in intrinsic beauty. Perhaps most importantly, they do so because they do not age precipitously as in the accelerated life cycle of fashion, where trends come and go at warp speed. They are not beholden to the market but claim each market as their own.

Obsolescence

In this way luxury and mass brands differ markedly. Fashion brands such as J. Crew and Club Monaco are driven by fashion trends and build obsolescence into both their product offerings and their brand narratives. They are at the mercy of their own strategies. They must guess right in the present moment. Luxury is driven by heritage, craftsmanship, and a vision linking past and future to constitute the present. As such, it is not enslaved to the trends but can lead the trends.

Leaders and Followers

So mass **Fast Fashion** brands, such as Zara and H&M, have turned the latest trends and speed-to-market into an operational mantra. Their strategy is to bypass both the past and the future for an intense deep dive into the present. Fast Fashion icons such as Zara and H&M turn their inventory every two to three weeks. Luxury brands think in seasons. For their iconic **signature pieces**, those styles with which the brand is uniquely associated and timelessly identified and which are part of the product line assortment each season (such as a Hermès Birkin handbag), they think in decades. This is an element of the cultural values that constitute a luxury brand.

THE LUXURY BRAND AS A CULTURE

What is "culture"? Here we mean culture not in the sense of the arts, such as music or painting or ballet, but in the sociological sense. **Culture** is shared patterns of behavior and values by which one group or society identifies itself and delineates itself from another.[22] Luxury is a culture in a social system. And at the foundation of every social system is social stratification.

Social Stratification, Cultural Values, and the Psychology of Luxury Consumption

Every society displays some form of **social stratification**. It can best be described as a tiered system of ascending and descending degrees of privileges and power that differentiates members of the same social system from each other by rank. For this purpose, rank can be a function of wealth, prestige, knowledge, status, talent, and the like. In terms of behavior and the purchase of luxury products, it manifested itself in late-nineteenth-century industrial societies in what Thorsten Veblen described as *"conspicuous consumption."*[23]

Describing their behavior as **conspicuous consumption**, Veblen posited that the new moneyed classes that arose from the Industrial Revolution accumulated wealth often to display it as a sign of their accomplishments rather than to consume their acquisitions as a function of their practical needs. This often led to garish displays of opulence such as was dramatized in F. Scott Fitzgerald's 1925 iconic novel **The Great Gatsby**, which presented a fictionalized account of such indulgences and the personal downfalls that ensue from their excess.

Four Types of Luxury Consumption

This "Culture of Conspicuous Consumption" marks a very early stage in the evolution of the luxury consumer in industrial society. Here the need to separate oneself from one's original class, or to make a pronounced statement that you are different from the mass of society, is paramount and is what animates this psychological dynamic.

It has also been described as Stage I in a four-stage model by Greg Furman, CEO of The Luxury Council.[24] These "stages" are not necessarily experienced by every luxury consumer. Perhaps we should think of them not as a necessary progression but as a set of **typologies**—that is, generalizations about types of personalities and how they psychologically process luxury brands (Table 2.1).

Stage I: Acquisitive. The consumer is concerned with "bragging rights," or the notion that whoever finishes with the most obviously ostentatious possessions wins! This has been referred to as an "Outer Directed" personality type.[25]

Stage II: Inquisitive. The consumer realizes that luxury is something intrinsically valuable but looks to authorities (fashion magazines, luxury trendsetters, etc.) to educate herself on how to discern this and choose accordingly.

Table 2.1 Typology of Luxury Consumers: How Different Personality Types Are Motivated to Buy Luxury Products	
Stage I: Acquisitive	**Stage II: Inquisitive**
Customers make their decision because: They are concerned with "bragging rights."	*Customers make their decision because:* Luxury goods are valuable, but they look to authority (e.g., fashion magazines) to educate themselves.
Stage III: Authoritative	**Stage IV: Meditative**
Customers make their decision because: Of the exclusivity experience and a sense of brand community.	*Customers make their decision because:* Luxury experiences have been integrated into their lives and inner beings, which leads to a sense of fulfillment.

Stage III: Authoritative. The search continues for the unique and the exclusive luxury experience. Brand narratives become important sources as guideposts.

Stage IV: Meditative. This is where we find the "Inner Directed" personality type. Luxury experiences have become integrated into their lives and inner beings. There is a sense of naturalism and fulfillment in this without affectation. There is a return to soulfulness in the luxury experience, such as a desire for things handmade.

Participating in the Brand's Culture

In Stage III, and especially in Stage IV, it is not so much what to buy but why to buy it that drives the behavior.[26] This is where the "Culture of Excellence" returns the consumer's focus to the appreciation of Craftsmanship. There then occurs an emotional bonding with the brand through this craftsman or artisan idea, which now symbolizes that excellence.

Luxury brands such as Rolex display and nurture this sense of timeless excellence and make it part of their culture. The brand narrative sets the stage for transcending the product. On the Rolex website we find the following brand promise to the consumer in the form of a tagline: "*The Rolex Way, our craft is timeless.*" The symbols of luxury, the brand logo, its

figure 2.2
A Rolex watch being "presented" to a customer.
Even the presentation is part of the luxury brand experience.

promise, and its associated dreams of timelessness become paramount elements in the brand narrative. The narrative continues as Rolex then proclaims in its website section entitled "Our Philosophy," "*Look in all the dictionaries, there is no word for what we do . . .*" These narrative elements create a new symbolic definition of value as the brand asks you to transcend the product and join it in an agreed-upon suspension of reality. You are now entering the dream world of mega-luxury (Figure 2.2).

This is something that is not replicated in mass brands such as Timex, which is widely distributed, defines quality as functionality, and is sold at a low price. Or **fashion brands** such as Swatch which seek to capture fashion trends and translate them into watch designs. This is part of the luxury culture and can be thought of as the emergence of **symbolic consumption**.

SYMBOLIC CONSUMPTION

Symbolic consumption, as with other forms of luxury consumption, is a function of social stratification. Here more advanced luxury consumers seek to further differentiate themselves from their peers through "consuming," through emotional bonding with the symbolic components of the luxury brand.[27] These include participation in brand experiences and experiential events such as celebrity chef dinners or invitations to charitable events closed to the public. These exclusive experiences place the consumer in still another and higher tier of difference from those in the social system. This desire is driven by the very essence of what motivates luxury consumers; quoting J. N. Kapferer, in *The Luxury Strategy*: "*The essence of luxury is the symbolic desire to belong to a superior class . . .*"[28]

Through brand management and the active participation of the luxury consumer, the brand becomes one with the product or the creation. There is no distinction; the brand drives the business rather than the business driving the brand. The brand is no longer a separate value add, it no longer simply "represents" the product or service, but it is identified fully with the objects that it "presents" to the world.[29] The ultimate rarity becomes the brand itself "*and the values it respects.*"[30]

One of those constant values is the unyielding commitment of luxury brands to, and the participation of the luxury consumer in, the brand narrative.

The Brand Narrative

When we speak of the brand narrative, we are speaking of storytelling. This may be based on a long company history and/or the creation of a contemporary conversation. We introduce the notion of "conversation" to emphasize that one-way narratives no longer resonate in the consumer-centric marketplace. The web and social media, with their consumer-centric dimensions, have changed the nature of brand management and, thus, the nature of brand narratives. Brand managers have gone from "storytellers" to "story-listeners."[31] We have transitioned from monologues to dialogues.

This change has affected both luxury and mass brands. But there is a difference in how they manage this change. Luxury brands bring the consumer into the brand rather than having the consumer become the definer of the brand. The strategy requires that the DNA of the brand be ensured and be the guiding light in inviting participation.

Burberry, for example, set up "*The Art of the Trench*" on its website. This feature asked consumers to post personal narratives, experiences, and photos of themselves with their Burberry signature product. Displayed by consumers, a dialogue ensues, participation prevails, and the brand, through its trench coat heritage and its history, continues to speak while it writes into its brand narrative current vignettes adding story lines from and for a new generation.

Mercedes-Benz had a similar online conversation with its customers. Mercedes owners were asked to post "selfies" in a Mercedes-branded chat room. Included with the photos were personal stories and experiences of the owners.

Brand Communities as Cults and Culture Clubs: Luxury versus Mass

A further expression of this is in the development and embracing of **brand communities**, which are ownership clubs whose members exchange insights and experiences focused on brand products, or brand **culture clubs**, whose members have voluntarily joined, bonded together by their emotional tie to a brand identity and its values (although not limited to, these clubs are most often associated with vehicle owners, Harley-Davidson being a notable example).

One of the early proponents of the importance of brand communities in understanding the consumer's social behavior in regard to brands can be found in Albert Muniz and Thomas C. O'Guinn's seminal work on the sociology of forming and joining such communities and their pivotal role in maintaining brand loyalty.[32] "*A brand community is a specialized, non-geographically bound community, based on a structured set of social relationships among admirers of the brand.*"[33] What is central to the concept, and most important to brand managers, is O'Guinn's conclusion about how such communities play "*a vital role in the brand's ultimate legacy.*"[34]

These communities are managed in very different ways by luxury and by mass brands, but what they have in common is how the brand values guide the relationship with the community and that they need to be approached as part of a brand management strategy and not merely a **brand marketing play**, or a strategy with which to sell products. It should be viewed as an opportunity to serve the ultimate guardians of the brand, the ultra-loyalists.[35]

A classic contrast of luxury versus mass is Ferrari and Harley-Davidson. These two brands both have extremely deep relationships with various consumer loyalists and brand communities. What they share in common is that each community borders on a **cult culture**, whose members share an intense sense of being an insider, with those who are not in the community viewed as outsiders.

A classic example of the cult culture is the Apple brand and what one commentator has called "The

Harley-Davidson has over 1 million club members throughout the world and has created subsets based upon demographics. There are, for example, a Hispanic riders group, a Women riders group, an African American riders group, and several others. They are bound together by what is called "the HOG culture"—that is, the Harley Owners Group community and the love of the open road. All share in the history of the brand and its identification with a certain **Outlaw Archetype** which corresponds with movies and music that honor the rebel in American culture. The annual "Sturgis Rally" each August in Sturgis, South Dakota, brings together a wide swath of diverse ownership types for riding, racing, and reviewing the latest in customized Harleys. (In 2015, a contingent of HOG owners, a first ever, came from India to participate!) The rally is open to all and draws a considerable number of attendees as well as press coverage for its more than occasional excesses (Figure 2.3).

figure 2.3
A Harley Owners Group (HOG) license plate.
Brand community members feel so connected that even "HOG" is OK!

Ferrari clubs are equally global, though fewer in numbers and members, as one might expect. If the watchword for Harley is "Freedom," then the watchword for Ferrari is "Passion": a passion to "Live the Dream," its brand tagline and the mission as formulated by founder Enzo Ferrari—"*You cannot describe the passion, you can only live it.*" "Living it" includes following the Formula One racing circuit (which Ferrari often dominates), driving a Ferrari, having a unique brand experience, and expressing a passion for excellence and innovation regarding the design and the feel of the ultimate racing car. Here is where luxury meets desire through authenticity.

One element is the audile experience. A common thread between the two brands is the sound of the engines. "*Soft, yet confident rumble*" as one owner describes the Harley, and an "*aural animal . . . like no other*" as a Ferrari owner describes the sound of the engine. Each brand tunes its engines to retain the sound, which is clearly identifiable and differentiates the brand from would be imitators. The precise calibration is kept secret! While there are similarities between the two brand experiences, there also are differences.

Anyone can go to Sturgis; one must be invited to go to Maranello, Italy, the location of Ferrari's headquarters and factory. Customized cars that one has purchased in other locales are personalized at Maranello. Test drives can be experienced only on a certified Ferrari track (the brand managers are concerned that the brand experience will be compromised on a less-tested track whose provenance is uncertain).

(continued)

The innovative 950 hp La Ferrari Hypercar was made public in December 2014. It could only be purchased at Maranello and by invitation only! Some 499 Ferrari connoisseurs were invited to do so at a cost of €1million. Taken together, we are witnessing an expression of the **Ruler Archetype** who commands through natural authority the allegiance of his subjects. When Ferrari stays true to this brand persona, it combines the artisan with the innovator, which results in a true measure of the luxury brand. As with Rolex, Ferrari is another expression of the meta-brand and symbolic consumption.[38]

After a Swiss collector drove the Hypercar and made a purchase, he was quoted as saying: *"This is not a car; it is everything you can imagine . . . it is a piece of Italian culture."*[39] What business do you believe Ferrari is really in?

Cult of Macintosh."[36] Here the sense of being part of a new social order counter to the corporate establishment (Apple versus IBM and Microsoft), a messianic leader (Steve Jobs), and product creation not for the money but for creating "neat stuff" all animates the cult's followers.[37] This generates perhaps the very highest degree of brand loyalty, reinforced by rituals and practices which confirm the brand's unique identity and, through this, the members' sense of privileged participation

EXCLUSIVITY AND AVAILABILITY IN THE MANAGEMENT OF BRAND VALUE

It should now be apparent that luxury brands thrive on social distinctions and social hierarchies. Mass brands thrive on social similarities and social equalities.

Luxury brands require that they be widely known and appreciated by everyone, but available to and owned by only a few.[40] For luxury brands to be perceived as luxury, they must remain somewhat out of reach. This paradox must be managed. Welcome to the implicit and continuing tension between Exclusivity and Availability! The platform upon which this takes place is brand portfolio management.

Portfolio Management

Brand portfolio management, as discussed in Chapter 1, is generally thought to have originated with Procter and Gamble (P&G) in the 1930s when the company CEO restructured responsibilities and created separate business managers for each product brand owned by P&G. Prior to this, the businesses were managed by categories (e.g., soaps, home supplies, etc.). This shift from category to brand management was needed in order to avoid having several brands in the same category **cannibalize** one another by competing for the same internal resources and external markets.

Returning again to David Aaker, brand portfolio management should be understood as a business strategy; *"The brand portfolio strategy specifies the structure (sometimes referred to as the 'architecture') of the brand portfolio . . . and the scope, roles and interrelationships of the portfolio brands."*[41] They should be a reflection of the corporation's business objectives as well as align with and be readily understood by each brand's target consumer segment.[42] In this regard, several brands can be found within the same product category: *"Different brands can co-exist in the same sector because they address the value curve of different segments."*[43] So, for example, in the laundry detergent sector, P&G markets Dreft, Cheer, and Tide, each positioned and priced for a different consumer segment within the aforementioned sector.

This model continues today and can also be found in the mass fashion and luxury fashion apparel space, such as exists in the structure of VF Corporation and, to some degree, in the structure of the luxury space in LVMH and others. However, mass, and luxury brands have different strategies of portfolio management.

Mass brands such as Tide and those mentioned above in the P&G corporate brand portfolio, or Old Navy and Athleta in the Gap Inc corporate brand portfolio, are focused on market trends and responding to the presence of consumer-centric demands. Although focusing on what one author has called **need states**, "*the intersection between what consumers want and how they want it . . . ,*"[44] to more effectively manage the explosion of brands across mass market landscapes and help generate more focus in meeting real needs, the brands become secondary to the product launches which are frequent tactics in the company's growth strategy and needed to meet both consumer and market demand.

In contrast, luxury brands manage the business through each brand's DNA and how the various brands complement each other within the corporate portfolio. Here the philosophy is that the product is only one manifestation of the brand (others would include the advertising, the website, the models, runway shows, etc.) and that "*Brand identity resides beyond the product which the product cannot betray.*"[45]

From this vision of luxury, brand strategies must drive product portfolio development and not vice versa. This impacts brand and product extensions, sub-brands and licensing strategies, and, of course, global expansion and the quest for new customers, all of which are an integral and consistent part of the mass and fashion brands' growth strategies.

Another key difference between mass and luxury strategies is in the global distribution arena. Here, the locations of flagship stores on **High Street** (high-rent/high-visibility locations with grand architectural imagery) are key elements in both the expectations that world travelers who are luxury consumers have of the brand (they expect to be able to find a brand's store in major cities around the world) and the brand's rarity and exclusivity quotient (consumers expect that visiting the flagship will be an extraordinary experience). This latter expectation is a function of the location of the flagship, its subtle but world-class service, and its stature as an architectural wonder.

For luxury, the product strategy is more selectively planned and more judiciously managed. A good example is with licensing as luxury brands tend to limit themselves to fine fragrances, cosmetics, and eyewear. The exceptions are Hermès and Louis Vuitton, each of which has its own perfumery facilities. It is important to note that in spite of both distributing their range of products only in their boutiques, fine fragrances (perfumes) are distributed in upscale department stores as well. This is a nod to the realities of the need for growth.

The Growth Challenge

"*Growth challenges the exclusivity that is part of every luxury brand's aura.*"[46]

The prevailing issue for luxury brands continues to be how to manage that growth without suffering the dilution of exclusivity. So, what is a strategy that works?

For luxury to sustain itself and be poised for growth, it must first reach what has been called **The Post-Artisan Stage**. This is an integrated strategy for brand extensions, production, distribution, and the transformation of the artisan into designer.[47] It is more likely at this juncture to be able to incorporate several strategies that can help navigate what Kevin Lane Keller has labeled "*The Growth Tradeoff.*"[48] These tradeoffs include exclusivity versus accessibility, classic versus contemporary imaging, and new customer acquisition versus core customer retention.[49] The first strategic recommendation is to be ever cognizant of the degree of brand equity by being "*extremely close to both existing and prospective customers*"[50] and second is to be cautious with the brand architecture so as not to dilute brand equity by engaging in brand strategies which have short-term growth possibilities but long-term deleterious effects on brand image. For example, deciding which brands to delete from one's portfolio or to retire from competition requires as much strategic thought as a new brand launch;[51] will customers be upset and migrate to a competitor,[52] and what impact does this have within the other brands within the portfolio?[53]

In this regard, line extensions, brand extensions, and launching sub-brands need to be undertaken with the managerial caution referenced above.

Growth Strategies

One prominent approach is **brand extensions,** which we use here as a strategic category wherein the brand name appears in various iterations and the product sector remains the same (automobiles, apparel, etc.). This differs somewhat from the traditional concept as used in a widely referenced article by Aaker and Keller[54] but is more adaptable to premium and luxury products, which we discuss in this section.

What both luxury and mass research tends to confirm is the critical importance of **fit**, or the consumer's perception that the brand's associative features fit naturally into the new product category.[55] However, for luxury brands, the notion of fit is defined more by nonfunctional associative attributes than is the case with non-luxury brands.

"This result provides empirical support of the notion that luxury brands, in comparison to non-luxury brands, more heavily rely on aspects beyond functional value as determinants of extension success."[56] The so-called **hedonic value,** or calculus, is such an aspect, whereby the luxury brand carries a high prestige value, giving it more emotional pull with the consumer's assessment of fit.

For non-luxury products, the similarities between the mother brand category and the extension category especially, *"when both brand associations and* brand affect, *the degree to which the communication cues resonate with the recipient consumer are held constant and may be the most valid basis for evaluating an extension . . ."*[57]

Brand extensions are products designed within a brand that are priced, designed, and imaged to align with and appeal to different consumer segments. Brand extensions take the form of three tactics that are widely used by both mass and luxury portfolios:

- Line extensions, often as entry-level products (opening price)
- Limited edition offerings (often called capsule collections)
- Sub-brands, which reference a mother brand in their name/logo

Line extensions such as BMW's 700, 500, and 300 series are launched *"to better meet the demands of segmented markets."*[58] They are tiered by price points (high to mid to lower) and by different levels of innovation and luxury accommodations. However, they all carry the BMW brand name and logo. And although each iteration of the series is different in size (the 700s being longer and more luxurious than the 300s), they are all similar in body type design (e.g., the four-door sedan). There is a common genealogy in their styling that ensures that each model appears as an offspring of the brand. Additional customization such as larger motors or special driving features (i.e., racing suspensions) adds to the possibility of more growth by appealing to subsets in the company's customer base.

Each BMW is marketed with the same brand promise through its advertising voice-overs and copy. The thirty-year "having-stood-the-test-of-time" tagline, *"The Ultimate Driving Machine,"* unifies the product extensions and attempts to validate the standing of any new entrant into the merchandise mix.

In managing the brand portfolio in this manner, brand messaging and brand value are consistent. This helps ensure that these original extensions do not compromise the brand's integrity. This tiered system is perceived as a form of **laddering** similar to identifying different product attributes which lead to an eventual trading up where customers can "dream" of ascending to the next tier. For BMW, this led to the creation of the 1 Series.

The motivation for the 1 Series, a recent addition to the merchandise mix, was to introduce the brand to the next generation of future loyalists by providing a compact profile and lower opening price, thus bringing the brand within reach, perhaps for the first time, to the younger luxury car buyer. This included families that were just starting out.

However, the styling, pricing, and positioning of the 1 Series seemed less aligned with the "ultimate driving machine" position of the parent brand. Also the styling tended to be boxy and more pedestrian. These types of downstream extensions are always risky.[59]

A sign of disparity is the "remove the logo test." When this is done, is the brand identifiable? For the BMW 1 series, such identification was difficult.

The 1 Series, launched in 2004, was discontinued in 2014. Yet, the performance reviews for the car were extremely good. Was the issue one of poor brand management?

Line extensions are risky for the true luxury brand because they can blur the distinction and core identity of the parent or mother brand. Let's recall that the luxury philosophy is that the portfolio is managed from the perspective of protecting the brand, not simply launching the product. In addition, although the brand manager may survey the core consumer of the mother brand, the objective is not, as is usually the case with non-luxury brands, to determine what the trends are but to obtain insights into a potential line extension launch that is currently being considered; thus, luxury brands in a portfolio setting are consumer-centric without being consumer-reactive.

One such occurrence points in this direction and shows the effectiveness of brand portfolio management in the luxury sector. The case in point is the strategic approach undertaken by Richard Purdey & Sons (RPS), handcraftsman of firearms and part of the Richemont luxury group.

Producing a limited number of firearms each year, RPS felt that the customer base that could afford to buy its guns (at $75,000–$100,000 per firearm) had already purchased most of what they might wish to own. Concerned that a lower-price collection would alienate this group of firm and committed loyalists, the company asked them if such a launch would diminish the equity and value in the brand and their current product ownership. The current owners were overwhelmingly supportive of the idea. As a result, the Purdey manager needed to take the next step— take the idea for assessment to the corporate portfolio managers: "*At Richemont, new product ideas go to a brand committee . . . if they don't like your idea, they throw it out. . . . you can protest, but you better have a good argument.*"[60]

A strategy that continued the exclusiveness and availability promise that the RPS brand had always stood by was adopted. And the new line extension was successful without diminishing the mother brand's identity.

Another growth strategy can be undertaken through launching limited editions of product categories. **Limited editions** are generally a launch based on maintaining the rarity quotient and therefore exclusivity. The rarity could be the special materials that constitute the limited edition and/or a limited window and unit availability.

Ferrari creates 7,000 cars a year. That is all. And this fact is known to both those who can afford a Testarossa® (the firm's "signature" motorcar) and those who can't but are aware of its iconic standing. The two feed the exclusivity objective by underscoring the stratification difference we referenced earlier in the chapter.

All Ferraris are subject to the same brand management approach that we discussed earlier. Authenticity is confirmed by the rarity of the product and how the brand nurtures those products and creates the Ferrari experience. The result is a waiting list and the ability when needed to raise prices, which increases the perception of value and increases demand at the same time; this is opposite the effect of price increases on premium, fashion, and mass fashion brands and is a characteristic of true luxury brands.

Sub-brands are an added growth strategy. Fashion brands such as Armani and Polo Ralph Lauren have mastered the art and science of differentiating their various sub-brands and aligning them with very specific consumer segments, prices, and distribution channels. This three-part strategy partly accounts for their success. The remainder is driven by the brand.

For Armani, his portfolio is as diverse as Armani Exchange, Armani Jeans, Emporio Armani, Collezione, Giorgio Armani, and Armani Privé (his haute couture collection). His strategy is to make sure that they are not found in the same retail environments as each other. They are all united by one photographic style, the Armani brand name coupled with the master's presence and persona, and Italian sophisticated understated design.

Ralph Lauren pursues a strategy similar to that of Armani. Purple Label (women and men) and Black Label (for men) are his "made in Italy" luxury component to his portfolio to Lauren Ralph Lauren, his more moderately priced rendition of Ralph Lauren Sportswear for women. Each sub-brand taps into the persona of the designer and the cachet that resides in the brand's intellectual property assets, the Polo "horseman" and the brand name or extensions of it (Polo Ralph Lauren, RL Golf, Blue Label, etc.). There is a distinct brand persona that unites the portfolio—the look of Americana and the lifestyle of America's old moneyed lifestyle, our non-hereditary aristocracy!

As part of the portfolio management strategy, Ralph Lauren has eschewed licensing and has taken back licenses, sometimes at significant expense (e.g., the Japan license ten years ago at a cost of over $40 million, and Lauren Ralph Lauren from Jones New York after a protracted legal battle over the licensing agreement). The objective, much like the luxury brands, is concern over maintaining the brand image and the desire to control major business opportunities. **Licensing,** which entails the "renting" by another company of a brand and its IP assets to be used in manufacturing and distributing a product not made by the brand owner, leaves the management of the business to the licensing partner in the geographic market. This often means the **value chain** as well, which includes the process and strategy of brand marketing, product creation, and distribution.

Licensing has become less of a "go to" strategy for both luxury and fashion brands. The traditional upside—faster market penetration with less monetary and organizational investment—is now often seen as potentially exposing the brand to value issues because the entire process and strategy of product creation and distribution is outside the direct control of the brand portfolio manager.

Distribution Management

Luxury brands manage the value chain by managing exclusivity and availability as they are complements to each other.

Managing availability goes to the heart of authenticity and the perception of the brand's value. The expectation of the luxury customer, and those who wish to be, is that the brand will be found (and not found) in certain locations. Also, there is an expectation that the product may be limited in number, colors, and/or sizes, as well as limited in availability due to the need for craftsmanship, which requires time and may limit production. So for luxury, the brand has three major aspects. The first aspect is retail availability, the second is product availability, and the third is **country of origin,** or the place where the product is made and the impact of that location on the perception of the brand. "*All studies reviewed indicate that country of origin does indeed influence buyer perception . . . the issue of how much . . . is not yet decided.*"[61] The following section explores this consumer dynamic in more detail.

Sourcing Strategies

"*Country of origin . . . is an increasingly important driver of relevance and differentiation.*"[62]

Where a product is made (known as sourcing and country of origin or **provenance**) has become part of the brand narrative. The associations that consumers hold between countries and brands are acute, especially in the luxury and fashion worlds. Germany tends to be associated with engineering and luxury cars, Italy with cutting-edge fashion design, France with fine fragrances and couture, Switzerland with watches, Japan with advances in denim fabrics for high-fashion jeans, England with Saville Row tailoring, and the U.S. with casual lifestyle sportswear, to name just a few.

These associations with locales go to the heart of consumer perceptions regarding authenticity. The psychological association with locations serves as a form of shorthand (again, a heuristic) to establish a particular credibility regarding design expertise, quality, uniqueness, and heritage.

We saw this in our previous discussion of Ferrari and its location in Italy. Building the cars in any other location would challenge the perception that they are authentic. Recall as well that it is not only the country (Italy) that lends credence to the brand here but also Maranello, the town identified with the brand's fabled heritage.

We see similar association in such brands as L'Oréal, Paris. In this instance, L'Oréal is calling on the city's reputation as a locale for a certain type of luxury.

Mass brands may attempt similar associations. Witness a Chrysler campaign, "Imported from Detroit," cleverly reversing the accepted relationship between excellence, foreign automobiles, and the locations from which they originated and in which they are made. The campaign's 2015 extension takes the idea a step farther: "America's Import"! This continues the association with the brand's origins.

The success of this type of campaign will also be related to how well the city itself fares because there is a relationship between the perception of the locale and that of the brand.[63]

This is known as the **halo effect** whereby a related element can benefit from being associated with the positive perception of its surrounding elements. This applies to both mass and luxury. Luxury sees this as part of the culture and the heritage of the brand. For mass, there is often a need to be reminded. In speaking of the perception of the Mini (an automobile designed in and originating from the UK), Peter Schwarspenbauer, CEO, BMW/Mini/Rolls-Royce, observed: *"We need to be more sensitive to 'Britishness', to do more to show Britishness to the outside world . . . Look at Fashion. If you mention a label people immediately know it comes from Paris or Milan and its better perceived because of that."*[64]

However, the question remains, when does **outsourcing**—that is, manufacturing a product outside the country with which the brand is traditionally identified—negatively impact the perception of exclusivity? For luxury, this *"cuts the connection . . . with cultural specificity."*[65]

One can argue that mass products which tend to speak about price and functionality, and mass production, can more readily make this transition to outsourcing without the negativity that luxury brands might have to endure.

But how will outsourcing, if at all, limit the growth potential of luxury brands? Will consumers accept the product as luxury if it departs from its associated creative origins? Something of the original connection should be maintained, but much of its success will depend on the product category and deepen the association with the location. As we will see in the next section, this is a challenging issue.

To maintain some connection with the country of origin, brand managers have engaged in some remarkable creativity. Here are some phrases that show up on packaging, in ads, and on garment hangtags and labels, especially in the fashion industry: *made in, created in, invented in, woven in, yarns spun in* (found in a Macy's private brand sweater label), *built in* (followed by the city or country), and, of course, *designed in*, just to name a few. Apple uses as a differentiator *"Designed in California"* rather than acknowledge too overtly that the products are *"Built in China"*![66] We'll return to this discussion in Chapter 5, when we explore the consumer's psychological underpinnings for brand loyalty and how country-of-origin brand strategies apply and inform the brand loyalty objective.

Accessibility and Availability at Retail

"I want my stores to be our statement."[67] This is followed by Moncler's (the luxury skiwear and outdoor apparel brand's) affirmation on its website that its aim is to "pursue development *of the luxury goods brand, worldwide, with a direct strategy."*

When so many retail brick-and-mortar channels are wavering under the blistering attack of the web and B2C (business to consumer) sales transactions, luxury continues to believe in the flagship store and the traditional retail platform as essential to the luxury brand experience. This is not meant to imply that luxury brands are not building a web presence for they are, and very often one that offers B2C commerce. In fact, Moncler has operated an online boutique since 2011. But the firm continues to build and rent on the most prestigious streets and high-visibility global locations available in retail.

Luxury operates in part by controlling demand while simultaneously stimulating that demand. Mass has no such latitude, or does it? We return to Zara and examine its product development and merchandise distribution strategies (Figure 2.4).

We know that Zara is the standard for fast turnaround and fast fashions. Through the most sophisticated of global operations, the company is able to get freshly designed fashion merchandise to its thousands of stores every two to three weeks. However, the key to Zara's success is not only that it must be **trend-right** and identify, in the heat of the fashion season, what its customers are likely to buy (and most often is right) but also that it has trained its customers to buy almost upon sight the new merchandise. Waiting for a sale for a better price is not a sound option because there are few if any sales at Zara.

One major reason is that the amount of merchandise is limited. Each style may have twelve pieces in two colors in a size range of small, medium, and large, and some may have only eight units (two small, four medium, two large). Because Zara has a reputation of being on trend, its customer, whose dressing style is young contemporary, wants the newest first. This gives Zara a great advantage because the company now can manage through managing availability. Zara creates demand by limiting supply.

This approach is similar to luxury brands' rarity strategy. For this fashionista with a contemporary taste level, being the first to obtain the incredible dress is an indication of her savvy as a style leader among her peers and her exclusiveness as a shopper. Again, social stratification is at the heart of the ability of the Zara brand managers to successfully maintain this global strategy.

However, Zara is unique as luxury is unique, but in a different way. The luxury experience may require a wait for the product and a limited access to it because it is offered in a limited range or number. For the Zara customer, there is democratization of the brand because the price and the multitude of locations make the brand readily available and accessible, something that the luxury brand seeks to avoid. Democratization and its implications will be examined in more detail in our next chapter.

figure 2.4
Zara storefront. Zara does no formal advertising but lets its store windows be its advertising platforms.

Accessibility and Availability on the Web

Partaking of the web and social media is a must for luxury brands as it has emerged as the future forum for stimulating demand. But luxury succeeds on rarity, mystery, and limited availability—all of which add up to the exclusivity quotient. The web is a milieu which thrives on the opposite end of the value spectrum: many, transparency, open inventory, and the democracy quotient. Several strategies have emerged, all of which will be discussed in greater detail in a separate chapter. For now, the accessibility value is maintained through several approaches. Some luxury brands will not sell on the web, others only by invitation, and still others (such as Burberry) offer a limited range of samples that they stream on their site after a major fashion show and catwalk presentation of next season's collection. The result is that limited availability is maintained and with it exclusivity, as the styles cannot be widely distributed as inventory comes from the show samples. Rarity is preserved while interest in the brand is stimulated and heightened. Demand is stimulated and controlled.

SUMMARY

Luxury brands honor craftsmanship as the brands' heritage. This imbues luxury brands with timeless character and exclusivity, features which differ from mass brands which are tied to fashion trends, broad availability, and obsolescence. Authenticity is an objective which naturally emerges out of the artisan's creative sensibility and becomes part of the brand experience shared with core consumers.

Another unique dimension of luxury brands is the power of desire in animating consumer behavior. We need to draw a distinction between needs, which are more biologically driven and rather nonreflective in how we reach our decisions, and wants, which involve more reflective choice. But desire raises the bar by adding the role of the passions and of the soul to decision making. Consumers' fantasies and social situations combine to make the desire for luxury a deep passion. Such "social situations" would include the influence of social stratification and our quest for social recognition that its presence both engenders and obstructs.

Luxury brand consumers are part of a culture of rarity and excellence and its value goes beyond price. It thrives on differences in rank as reflected in forms of social stratification. Consumers participate in this culture in various ways, including symbolic consumption of brand narratives, purchasing experiences, and brand communities. They are also drawn to luxury by various motives, including conspicuous consumption, pride of ownership, and a sense of being part of timeless artistry.

Luxury brands must grow but brand value must be preserved. Limited availability and selective accessibility help preserve the brand's rarity and its exclusivity. The strategies to do so include careful portfolio management, limited product offerings, and high-visibility/high-touch retailing, combined with a limited and highly managed web presence.

KEY TERMS

High Street
Authenticity
Availability
Brand Affect
Brand Communities
Brand Extensions
Brand Marketing Play
Cannibalize
Conspicuous Consumption
Corporate Earnings Calls
Country of Origin
Craftsman Archetype
Craftsmanship
Cult Culture
Culture
Culture Clubs

Exclusivity
Fashion Brands
Fashionistas
Fast Fashion
Fit
Halo Effect
Hedonic Value
Heuristic
Laddering
Licensing
Limited Editions
Luxury Brand Narratives
Need States
Needs
Obsolescence
Outlaw Archetype

Outsourcing
Provenance
Rarity
Ruler Archetype
Signature Pieces
Social Stratification
Sub-brands
Symbolic Consumption
The Geneva Seal
The Great Gatsby
The Post-Artisan Stage
Trend-Right
Typologies
Value Chain
Wants

CHAPTER CONVERSATIONS

- How would you describe the differences between luxury and mass regarding fashion trends?

- In what ways are luxury brands a culture?
- Why is managing growth more a challenge for luxury than for mass brands?

CHAPTER CHALLENGES

- The artisans of your luxury brand are slowly disappearing as they retire and with this goes the mystique of handmade. Should you as brand manager maintain the mystique? If so, what are the strategies you would use?
- Luxury brand communities are growing, but their membership threatens the brand's exclusivity. How can you increase communities without diluting the perception of luxury as exclusivity?

- You are the brand manager for a luxury handbag and accessories brand. Your CFO wants to increase margins by manufacturing in China. Would you consider this? If not, why not? How would you suggest margins be increased?

ENDNOTES

1. J. N. Kapferer and V. Bastien, *The Luxury Strategy: Break the Rules of Marketing to Build Luxury Brands* (London: Kogen Page, 2012), pp. 98—99.
2. Bruce Montgomery, "The Value of Contemporary Craft," in *The British Crafts Council* 4, (2011).
3. For the seminal work on archetypes and brands, see Margaret Mark and Carol Pearson, *The Hero and the Outlaw* (N.p.: McGraw-Hill, 2001).
4. Karen Kiester, "The Craftsman Archetype." *Path of the Sacred Masculine* (blog), October 24, 2013, http://www.pathofthesacredmasculine.com/2013/10/craftsman-archetype/.
5. Richard Sennet, *The Craftsman* (New Haven: Yale University Press, 2008).
6. Kiester, "The Craftsman Archetype".
7. Manfredi Ricca and Rebecca Robins, *Mets Luxury: Brands and the Culture of Excellence* (N.p.: Palgrave Macmillan, 2012).
8. Jean-Noel Kapferer and Vincent Bastien, *The Luxury Strategy* (N.p.: Kogan Page Ltd., 2012).
9. Amanda North, *The Neuroscience of Beauty: The Soul of Design* (blog), June 24, 2014, www.Artisanconnect.com/blog.
10. Russell Belk, Güliz Ger, and Søren Askegaard, "The Fire of Desire: A Multi-Sited Inquiry Into Consumer Passion," *Journal of Consumer Research* 30, no. 3 (December 2003), p. 327.
11. Ibid., p. 330.
12. Joanne Roberts and John Armitage, "Luxury and Creativity: Exploration, Exploitation or Preservation?", *Technology Innovation Management Review* (July 2015), p. 1.
13. Kapferer and Bastien, *"The Luxury Strategy,"* p. 71.
14. Ibid., p. 198.
15. See "Burberry to Sell Styles Straight from Catwalk in Fashion Shakeup," *The Guardian*, February 5, 2016.
16. "Italy's Fashion Chamber Rejects Immediacy," *Business of Fashion*, February 27, 2016, www.businessoffashion.com/articles.news.
17. "Fashion Calendar Shake-up 'Negates the Dream' of Luxury Says Pinault," *Business of Fashion*, February 27, 2016, www.businessoffashion.com/article/news.
18. Kapferer and Bastien, *"The Luxury Strategy,"* p. 18; for added insight into the notion that we are what we possess, also see Russell Belk, "Possessions and the Extended Self," *Journal of Consumer Research* 15, issue 2 (September 1988).
19. Belk et al., "'The Fire of Desire,'" p. 328.
20. Belk Russell, Güliz Ger, and Søren Askegaard, "Metaphors of Consumer Desire," *Advances in Consumer Research* 23 (1996): 369.
21. Kapferer and Bastien, *"The Luxury Strategy,"* p. 99.
22. Talcott Parsons, *Essays in Sociological Theory*, rev. ed. (New York: The Free Press, 1954).
23. Thorsten Veblen, *The Theory of the Leisure Class* (N.p.: Macmillan, 1915).
24. Greg Furman, "CEO Talk: Greg Furman, Founder and Chairman, Luxury Marketing Council," *The Business of Fashion*, June 10, 2009, http://www.businessoffashion.com/2009/06/ceo-talk-greg-furman-founder-and-chairman-luxury-marketing-council.html.
25. David Riesman, *The Lonely Crowd* (Reprint; New Haven, CN: Yale University Press, 2001).

26. Klaus Heine, "The Luxury Brand Personality Traits," http://www.brand-management.usi.ch/Abstracts /Monday/BrandpersonalityIII/Monday_BrandpersonalityIII_Heine.pdf.

27. Michel Chevalier and Gerald Mazzalovo, *Luxury Brand Management: World of Privilege* (N.p.: John Wiley & Sons, 2008).

28. Kapferer and Bastien, *The Luxury Strategy*, p. 18.

29. Ibid., pp. 143–142.

30. Ibid., p. 99.

31. Lauren Johnson, interview of Kimberly Kadlec, vice president of global marketing for Johnson & Johnson, May 18.

32. Albert M. Muniz Jr. and Thomas C. O'Guinn, *Journal of Consumer Research* 27, no. 4 (March 2001): 412–432.

33. Ibid., 412.

34. Ibid.

35. Susan Fournier and Lara Lee, "The Seven Deadly Sins of Brand Community Management," Boston University School of Management, June 2008, http://smgapps.bu.edu/smgnet/Personal/Faculty /Publication/pubUploadsNew/wp2008-6.pdf?did=756&Filename=wp2008-6.pdf.

36. See Russell W. Belk and Gulner Tumbat, "The Cost of Macintosh," *Consumption, Markets and Culture* 8, no. 3 (September 2005): 205–217.

37. Muniz and O'Guinn,

38. For an exploration of the concept of the "meta-brand" and meta-luxury, see Manfredi Ricca and Rebecca Robins, *Meta-Luxury, Brands and the Culture of Excellence* (London: Palgrave Macmillan, 2012).

39. Andreas Tsaousis, "Swiss Ferrari Collector Picks Up His La Ferrari from Maranello," carscoops, December 22, 2014, http://www.newscodex.com.

40. Brand Unique, "Marketing a Luxury Brand," brandUNIQ, 2013, http://branduniq.com/2013 /marketing-a-luxury-brand-part-1/.

41. David A. Aker, *Brand Portfolio Strategy* (New York: The Free Press, 2004), p. 13.

42. Ibid.

43. J. N. Kapferer, *The New Strategic Brand Management*, 5th ed. (London: Kogan Page, 2012), p. 60.

44. Stephen Carlottie Jr., Mary Ellen Coe, and Joesko Perrey, "Making Brand Portfolios Work," *McKinsey Quarterly* (November 2004), p. 1.

45. Chevalier and Mazzalovo, *Luxury Brand Management*, p. 60.

46. KPMG, "Managing Luxury Brand Growth" (2006), http://www.kpmg.com/CN/en/IssuesAndInsights /ArticlesPublications/Documents/luxury-brand-growth-0610.pdf.

47. Jean-Noel Kapferer, *The New Strategic Brand Management: Advanced Insights and Strategic Thinking* (N.p.: Kogan Page, 2012).

48. Kevin Lane Keller, "Managing the Growth Tradeoff: Challenges and Opportunities in Luxury Branding," *Journal of Brand Management* 16, no. 5/6: 290–301.

49. Ibid., 293.

50. Ibid., p. 294.

51. See R. Varadarajan, M. P. DeFanti, and P. S. Busch, "Brand Portfolio, Corporate Image and Reputation: Managing Brand Deletions," *Journal of the Academy of Marketing Science* 34, issue 2: 195–205.

52. Nirmalya Kumar, "Kill a Brand, Keep a Customer," *Harvard Business Review* (December 2003): 4.

53. Henrik Uggla, "The Sins of Brand Portfolio Management," *IUP Journal of Brand Management* 10, no. 4 (2013): 13.

54. For a further exploration of this distinction, see David A. Aker and Kevin Lane Keller, "Consumer Evaluations of Brand Extensions," *Journal of Marketing* 54 (January 1990): 27–41.

55. Carmen-Maria Albrecht and David Moritz Woisetschlager, "Drivers of Brand Extension Success: What Really Matters for Luxury Brands," *Psychology and Marketing* 30, no. 8 (August 2013): 647-659, 657; see also Aaker and Keller's landmark study, "Consumer Evaluations of Brand Extensions," p. 29.

56. Albrecht and Woisetschlager, "Drivers of Brand Extension Success."

57. Susan M. Broniarczyk and Joseph W. Alba, "The Importance of the Brand in Brand Extension," *Journal of Marketing* (May 1994): 215.

58. Kapferer, *The New Strategic Brand Management*.

59. For an in-depth analysis of the issue, see Michelle L. Childs, "Effective Fashion Brand Extensions: The Impact of Limited Edition and Perceived Fit on Consumers' Urgency to Buy and Brand Dilution" (PhD diss., University of North Carolina, 2014).

60. KPMG, "Managing Luxury Brand Growth."

61. Warren J. Bilkey and Erik Nes, "Country of Origin Effects on Product Evaluations," *Journal of International Business Studies* 13, no. 1 (1982): 94; see also Papadoupolous and Heslop's 1993 book on country of origin and its impact on brand management.

62. "Made In: The Value of Country of Origin for Future Brands," *FutureBrand*, 2014, http://www.futurebrand.com/images/uploads/studies/cbi/MADE_IN_Final_HR.pdf.

63. Mark McNeilly, "Where Do You Come From: Tips for Creating a Powerful Provenance for Your Brand." *Fast Company*, May 21, 2013, http://www.fastcompany.com/3009750 /where-do-you-come-from-tips-for-creating-a-powerful-provenance-for-your-brand.

64. Ibid.

65. Ibid.

66. For a comprehensive quantitative analysis of the COO literature, see Robert A. Peterson and Alain J. P. Jolibert, "A Meta-Analysis of Country of Origin Effects," *Journal of International Business Studies* (April 1995).

67. "Moncler Strategy Page," Moncler website, 2014, http://www.moncler.com.

From Luxury
to Mass

AFTER COMPLETING THIS CHAPTER
YOU WILL BE ABLE TO:

- Describe the differences and commonalities in luxury and other brands.

- Compare luxury with non-luxury brand marketing strategies.

- Assess the strategies of luxury brand portfolio management.

CHAPTER 3

"Some people think Luxury is the opposite of Poverty. It is not; it is the opposite of Vulgarity."

—Coco Chanel

DELINEATING LUXURY BRANDS FROM OTHER BRANDS

How do we define **luxury**? Is luxury *"something that everyone wants and nobody needs"*[1] or is luxury a matter of consumer perception? Here is the view from that perspective: *"Luxury brands are regarded as images in the minds of consumers that comprise associations regarding a high level of price, aesthetics, rarity and specialness."*[2]

These definitions are a long way from the original meaning of luxury, which in Latin means a form of *"excess."* This was based on the idea that opulence cast an ethical shadow over those who displayed it because it suggested that the person was excessively self-indulgent and therefore of questionable character.

The opening quote by Coco Chanel expresses a more modern view that luxury is not about money or price but about the opposite of **vulgarity**, or overstated or excessive attempts at displays of style. However, in contrast to the classical idea of excessive indulgence, and short of making a character judgment, she is suggesting that the opposite of luxury is "trying too hard" to be elegant. Later in this chapter, we will return to this view as a way of benchmarking luxury and contrasting it with its opposite (Figure 3.1).

In a certain sense, the view of luxury as indulgence continues to be the case today. What has changed is that the social stigma, in some quarters, has been removed, making indulgence an acceptable behavior. An exception to this view is those who see luxury as an expression of a timeless way of life. It can serve as the basis for a more refined understanding of what luxury means and be the foundation for a different brand management strategy from those that embrace indulgence as luxury. This idea of luxury as transcending time and trends will be revisited later in the chapter.

figure 3.1
The legendary Coco Chanel: Founder of the luxury brand Chanel and definer of luxury.

The differences in what luxury means can be seen in the ways that brands market themselves in attempts to associate the luxury category in the mass consumer's mind. This brand marketing of "mass luxury" messages and images are what we will refer to as "quasi-luxury" or **premium brands** (brands that touch on luxury in some aspect of their business strategy) and we will suggest how they differ from true luxury brands.

Quasi-Luxury Brands and Business Models

Because there is not a single source of authority that determines the parameters and definitions of market positions and brands, premium brand managers often take liberties with the descriptors for their brands. So we find the adjectives such as "affordable," "accessible," and "modern" preceding the word *luxury* and thereby generating what appears to be a hybrid brand. The purpose seems clear. By attaching these words to brands, it seemingly gives them both unique **positioning** (differentiating them from their competitors) and an association in consumers' minds with luxury.

Yet questions remain. Are these marketing communication tactics rather than real differences or delineators of the brand? Will these change with a change in strategy? How strong and successful are these brands likely to be by following such a strategy? Will a change in the descriptors lead to consumer confusion and disengagement from the brand?

Affordable, Accessible, and Modern Luxury

Let's explore these questions by looking at Coach. Coach was founded in 1941 as a traditional and somewhat conservative (but upscale) leather attaché case, handbag, and wallet brand. Craftsmanship and product handmade in New York were part of its brand promise.

Lew Frankfort took over as CEO in 1979 and began to **reposition** (to retool or redirect a brand to make it more relevant to another market or consumer) the brand by changing its target audience and market position to a younger and more trend-driven consumer. Classic Coach styling in accessories such as brass trims and finishings and fine leathers were given updated touches. Fabric handbags made with trendy fabrics were added to the merchandise offering at a lower opening price to make the brand more attractive to a younger customer. Frankfort called this "accessible luxury," a phrase that had no previous meaning. Speaking about the Coach brand, here is how Frankfort gave it some meaning and relevancy: "*I dreamed it might be the egalitarian Louis Vuitton; where they were exclusive, we would be accessible; where they were pricey, we would be affordable; where they were snotty, we would be friendly.*"[3]

Lew Frankfort used "accessible" and "affordable" together, probably for the first time, to describe a premium brand. Now these words are used interchangeably to describe upscale brands that were once called **bridge lines**. Bridge lines are a category in retail departments where products are priced between better and designer/luxury merchandise and the styling tends to be more contemporary. This is where the crop of "accessible" brands like Michael Kors, Tory Burch, and Kate Spade (all direct competitors with Coach in the accessories category) are positioned.

Over the next two decades, Coach experienced solid growth and profits and, apart from a misstep into sportswear, seemed to be on a sound footing. Fast forwarding to 2014, Coach found itself under severe competitive pressure from its entry into the accessories space of Michael Kors, Tory Burch, and Kate Spade, in addition to some less prominent brands. These brands appealed to a younger, more fashion-forward consumer who was less likely to embrace the overall classic image associated with the Coach brand. Store closings followed and a rethinking of the brand's positioning strategy was undertaken again (Figure 3.2).

The new direction was described as "*modern luxury.*" Here are the words of Coach's president of North America Retail: "*The overarching objective is to change brand perception from accessible luxury to modern luxury.*"[4]

What do these phrases "accessible luxury" and "modern luxury" mean? What does this tell us about the brand management strategies of this and similar brands, such as Michael Kors, positioned as "*affordable luxury*"?[5]

Coach in its implementation of modern luxury began with the product and creative direction. They hired Stuart Vevers as creative director in 2013. Vevers had extensive leather accessories experience with the

figure 3.2
The Coach logo on a Coach black handbag. Logos were kept on some Coach styles while more modern styles made them less apparent.

Mulberry and Loewe luxury houses as well as stints with Calvin Klein and Marc Jacobs. This signaled to the market a change to a hipper, more contemporary merchandise direction.[6] The change included younger styling (for example, leather miniskirts), new locations for the photo shoots, quirky models, and a modernizing of the company's retail stores. With this new positioning came a commitment to transform Coach into a lifestyle brand. This would include extending sportswear and footwear for women into the firm's seasonal merchandise offerings and increasing the range of products in the menswear line.

This movement toward "modern" included investing in flagship stores in twelve major international fashion markets to showcase the collections to make them globally *accessible* and *exclusive*, which was only partially served by increasing the prices of upper-price-level products and adding more opening-price styles.

This strategy stops short of luxury's approach to diminished sales. For example, Gucci's response in 2014 to the slowing of sales from double digits to mid-single digits was to follow classic luxury tactics. The objective was to increase the Gucci brand's exclusivity and reduce accessibility by:

- Reducing the number of entry-level-priced products.
- Increasing the prices of upper-level products.
- Strengthening the finer and more exotic leather bag offerings.
- Halting new store openings.

In 2014, to buttress this strategy of "modern luxury," Coach purchased Stuart Weitzman (the contemporary designer footwear brand) for over $500 million. At that time, Coach's footwear business was about 15 percent of revenues. The question remains whether this is a separate business venture within a corporate portfolio that management sees as a category growth opportunity, or one that will be integrated into the current Coach brand. The high brand recognition, and the contemporary style positioning of the brand, again sends a signal of "modern" to the

market. What remains to be seen is how the brand portfolio is managed in terms of the style direction undertaken by the creative director. Will all other Coach product categories begin to take on a more contemporary look? Using the Weitzman brand as a signal and a complement to the Coach brand will require a change not only in the style direction of the latter but in the brand management of the overall business. Will the brand be in its own free-standing stores or will it be merchandised with other products at the Coach boutiques? How will the Weitzman brand be imaged? What heritage story can be told that is consistent with Coach's heritage and history? What strategy would you recommend?

Taken together, "modern" at this stage means catching up to its competitors rather than adopting a unique brand management strategy. So, for example, opening-price handbags, which constitute up to 50 percent of the revenues in the accessories category, did not increase in price in any appreciable manner, thus keeping the brand "affordable." The opening of high-profile, High Street shops in targeted luxury retail locations in major international cities helps ensure that the brand continues to be "accessible." This is especially important for the affluent international traveler who expects to find high-profile global brands present in high-visibility urban locations.

The above suggests that these descriptors—"modern," "affordable," and "accessible"—are marketing terms, and this is how they should be understood. The strategies which characterize these descriptions have no fixed parameters. They will vary in meaning and tactics depending on brand management's objectives and the creative director's vision. So in looking at Michael Kors, his brand is described by the trade media as both "accessible" and "affordable" luxury—again the terms are used interchangeably.

A close look at the brand positioning clearly shows that what Coach now terms as modern is part of what Coach's competitors have been doing for some time. For example, Michael Kors is a fully lifestyle brand, with a men's and women's sportswear collection. Kors has opened stores near luxury brands such as Louis

figure 3.3
Michael Kors store opened next to luxury brands such as Rolex. Part of the premium brand's strategy for being thought of as luxury.

Vuitton and Gucci in all major international fashion markets. Kors draws on the stature of these competitors and benefits by the associative proximity of its retail stores to those of these marquee brands.[7] Kors, taking affordability a step farther, designs many of its handbags to mimic design details of Gucci, Louis Vuitton, Chanel, and others.[8] These design details are a code that leads young, fashion savvy shoppers to the Kors brand as a way of partaking in the luxury they can't afford (Figure 3.3).

Therefore, Coach's repositioning is both a public announcement regarding a change in direction and a guideline for redirecting the internal company mission so everyone is on the same page. It is directed toward the staff, the fashion press, and Wall Street. How the firm's new direction will appeal to a fresh customer base while retaining the loyalty of current Coach loyalists remains to be seen.

The need to mimic luxury finds its expression not only in premium brands but in what has come to be called **masstige brands** (brands created by incorporating upscale packaging and presentation into what was traditionally a basic product category). These reflect the rise of not only a more numerous and affluent global consumer class that can afford more and higher-priced brands but also one that has been exposed to some of the intangible values that luxury trumpets but whose products may be out of such consumers' financial reach. The brand strategies and business objectives, and what these categories of brands have borrowed from luxury, will be explored in the section that follows.

How Do Premium, Masstige, and Luxury Brands Differ?

Masstige brands and premium brands would not exist without luxury brands. However, luxury brands can exist without masstige and premium brands. Masstige and premium brands are attempts to partake of luxury and qualify as luxury in terms of consumer perception; thus, they must be defined and understood in terms of luxury. A consequence is that these brand categories, although on a **brand concept continuum** (a graphic representation of the degrees of difference between mass and luxury brands), cannot successfully migrate across the landscape of trading up to or down from luxury. For example, there are limitations as to how

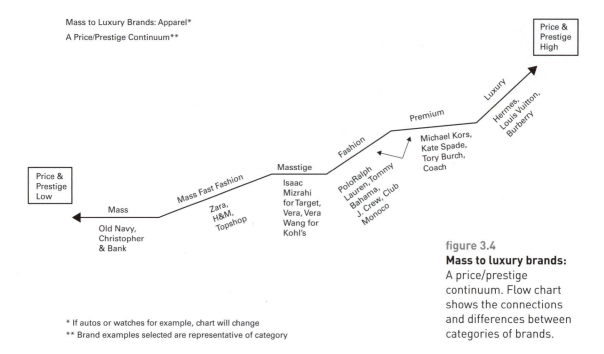

Mass to Luxury Brands: Apparel*
A Price/Prestige Continuum**

Price & Prestige High

Luxury
Hermes, Louis Vuitton, Burberry

Premium
Michael Kors, Kate Spade, Tory Burch, Coach

Fashion
PoloRalph Lauren, Tommy Bahama, Club J. Crew, Club Monoco

Masstige
Isaac Mizrahi for Target, Vera, Vera Wang for Kohl's

Mass Fast Fashion
Zara, H&M, Topshop

Price & Prestige Low

Mass
Old Navy, Christopher & Bank

* If autos or watches for example, chart will change
** Brand examples selected are representative of category

figure 3.4
Mass to luxury brands: A price/prestige continuum. Flow chart shows the connections and differences between categories of brands.

far down the slope of our model (Figure 3.4) a luxury brand can go in new merchandise/lower-priced products without slipping into a premium image and damaging the overall brand identity. By the same token, for premium brands to enter the luxury sphere would require a change in both the business model (e.g., a release from dependency on trends) and a shift in consumer perceptions, two very difficult undertakings to achieve. The merchandise model in Figure 3.4 offers a graphic representation of the connections and distinctions between and among these brand categories and offers some perspective on this question.

In introducing these brand categories together on a continuum, we are recognizing that some people view them as based on pricing and prestige. Others suggest that these distinctions are based on personal perspectives. As one pundit has remarked, "*The classification of brands in to luxury and premium is, above all, a personal assessment.*"[9]

We don't agree. As we have already suggested, there are clear differences in how to manage brands

to maintain a distinction between, say, premium and luxury. The final outcome will be the combined effect of consumer perception and brand management, the latter in part a function of how effective the brand managers were in achieving their objectives for the brand. We'll examine how these objectives are understood in the luxury market and brand management world. The result will show that these are not mere concepts in search of meaning but distinctive ways of managing different types of brands, in different types of markets, with unique identities appealing to different but often overlapping consumer segments. Just as the distinction between luxury brands and premium brands is the manner in which they present themselves to the market in which they do business, the same principle pertains between luxury and masstige brands. As a further example of the distinction between luxury and premium, let's look at the launch of the Lexus in the U.S. market.

For its entry into the U.S. market, the Lexus ES 350 was positioned against the Mercedes C300 series.

This model is Mercedes' next to opening price point and its best-selling sedan. The Lexus brand message was characterized by references to both its lower price and its superior functional utilities (such as trunk space). This already separates it from the luxury category because price and function are not definers of luxury.[10] Neither is positioning against competitors. (We will return to the positioning issue later in this chapter.) The C300 continues to outsell the Lexus ES 350 against which it is positioned. The question that arises is whether the Lexus brand strategy was appropriate vis-à-vis a luxury brand that doesn't emphasize price, utility, or positioning per se.

The launch in 2014 of the Mercedes CLA listed at $29,750 is another example of a strategy that might be questioned for its positioning and potential negative impact on the brand. It raises questions about the standing of the Mercedes brand as a luxury brand, as this under-$30,000 sticker pricing comes perilously close to "affordable" luxury!

The Maybach, the ultra-luxury Mercedes, was relaunched very soon after the CLA and targeted for the "Ultra-Rich" ($200,000 price tag). It has a luxury heritage going back to the 1920s, which was widely known to the Mercedes community. At this price point, no significant sales were expected, and one wonders if this was more a marketing message to counterbalance any negative perception regarding the CLA by assuring the ultra-loyalists that Mercedes is still in the luxury business.

The consumer will tell us if the CLA is perceived as a premium entrant into the luxury circle. If the latter, we'll know if there has been a decline or an increase in purchases of the upper-numbered Mercedes models (the 300, 400, and 500 series) because the CLA is extremely affordable and therefore easily accessible as a middle-class price-point. The risk is that the CLA could put the Mercedes brand in the premium mix and perhaps below, with some of the upper-priced models following the CLA and being perceived as less than a Mercedes. This would continue to make it too expensive for the CLA consumer and too "non-luxury" for those who purchase the 300 series and above. Given

its price, the CLA is approaching the point where it might be thought of as competing with the likes of Buick's Lacrosse or even Toyota's Avalon model!

The upbeat affirmation that the CLA Mercedes entry-price-point model will not dilute the equity in the overall Mercedes brand is fraught with certain difficulties. Here is a response of the CEO of Mercedes when he was asked about the CLA and brand dilution: *"The huge excitement which goes around the CLA is beneficial for the brand altogether . . . It brings more . . . coolness to the brand."*[11]

The question that arises is whether luxury brands wish to be "cool." This clearly goes contrary to the idea of maintaining a certain distance, a degree of aloofness, which adds to the mystique and source of value. The Maybach, for example, is counter coolness! In addition, the coolness factor can be promoted without possible damage to the brand when it is marketed in a way which honors the brand, but not necessarily by trumpeting price in an effort to sell the product. This is one of the unique dimensions that separates luxury from masstige and premium brands. *"Marketing a luxury brand requires attracting brand enthusiasts that will never afford it, but are very passionate about it, . . . the brand has to be known and appreciated by everybody and owned only by few."*[12]

The emergence of masstige brand strategies has found great success in the cosmetics and personal care products industries. Bath & Body Works, for example, is able to command pricing 30 percent higher than a comparable Vaseline brand product but less than a prestige and considerably more expensive brand such as Kiehl's, both of which offer body and skin moisturizing products of comparable quality but of incomparable packaging and presentation. Here, packaging and visual promotion create the perception of prestige for consumers and, therefore, of added value.[13] It offers an opportunity to trade up without having to pay a luxury price that is seen as prohibitive. This masstige strategy enables pricing and margins to be higher than those of mass brands or private label, providing funding for the added marketing costs while offering middle-class consumers a small taste of luxury.

The migration of consumers to premium fashion brands, such as Ralph Lauren and Calvin Klein, has been successful when the companies position signature products as masstige (e.g., Ralph Lauren's men's Polo and Calvin's fragrance such as Obsession or Eternity) and adhere to certain brand management strategies.

In a landmark research study of masstige consumers by Troung and Kitchen, consumers were found to be most receptive to masstige strategies when two variables in the marketing mix were honored:[14]

- The brand was imaged and positioned to convey high perceived levels of prestige (status + conspicuousness) closer to classic luxury brands like Louis Vuitton and Prada.
- The price levels, although somewhat higher than those of comparable products from mass fashion brands (H&M or department store private labels), were perceived as affordable.

Overall, the conclusion drawn was that these brands have successfully differentiated themselves from middle-range mass brands below them in terms of perceived prestige and, with reasonable price premiums, have devised a winning strategy. What we also have here is the influence of luxury on mass brand management. Storytelling, imaging, and other brand communication intangibles are critical to success as price (so long as it is reasonable) becomes less of a determinant in its outcome.

Can Luxury Brands Be Lifestyle Brands?

As luxury brands seek to grow, brand expansion strategies become paramount considerations. In the previous chapter we saw various strategies including sub-brands, product extensions, and licensing. These strategies all have different degrees of challenges for both luxury and other types of brands, but what they have in common is the focus on lifestyle. *"Lifestyle is about enriching consumers' lives in a credible way."*[15] This quotation provides a good beginning for it takes a

consumer-centric perspective as well as introduces **credibility**. The latter honors the brand and its relationship to the consumer by insisting that the product or service which is added to the brand's portfolio must be authentic to the core identity of the brand. Failure to do so can also lead to a dilution of the brand image and of its prestige. This recalls the risk inherent in the CLA/Mercedes strategy discussed earlier in the chapter.

An additional challenge is that adding lifestyle to the brand's offerings blurs the distinction between luxury brands and premium fashion brands. As discussed in the preceding chapter, fashion brands, and therefore premium brands, which are all fashion driven, must embrace a high degree of disposability or obsolescence in design direction. Luxury brands, on the other hand, favor timeless innovation. Premium brands are trend-driven; luxury brands are trend-drivers.

Lifestyle is a response to market trends and consumer direction. As one luxury observer has commented, *"Luxury brands sell style,"*[16] the implication being that luxury transcends trends. Style is either the expression of the brand owner's creative genius such as Armani and Armani Casa (his brand extension for hotels and luxury apartments where his aesthetic decorates the interiors), or it is a clear brand identity that the creative director uses to frame the product or service extensions and determines which are authentic to the brand.

Having a founder is not always a precondition for luxury product management and successful extensions. Montblanc, the luxury writing instrument and accessories brand, provides an example of how the brand does not need a founder to be able to maintain its identity while extending its style through extending its product offerings. Rather than just reacting to lifestyle changes in the market, the strategy is to embrace both the process of **organic extension**, meaning that the product additions fit together with the core offerings creating a cohesive and integrated brand story, and **gradualism**, or a reasonable pace in introducing each additional extension. Together, both processes honor the brand and honor its loyalists.

The key is to determine the brand's intrinsic identity and *the feelings* that having, for example, the iconic Meisterstück pen (or writing instrument!) engender. What narratives are known? What does fountain pen writing mean? How is it an art form? Why is the color black so prominent in its image displays and presentations? Here we can begin to align Montblanc "style" with credible products, infusing them with the brand's identity and confirming that the extensions correspond naturally to how the consumer would be using the writing instrument in her life. What naturally "gravitates" around the pen? Luxury stationery and appropriate holders; leather briefcases cannot be far behind. These provide the legitimacy for any subsequent extensions which should take place gradually, giving the initial extensions time to adhere to the brand's history and be confirmed as legitimate by the consumer's purchases and satisfaction. Perhaps additional leather products can now be added. Items we hold in our hands or place in our clothing (as we do the pen)—wallets, cell phone holders, iPod or tablet cases are appropriate. As these take hold as part of the brand's collective offerings, there is an implied permission granted to move somewhat beyond the brand's origins—cufflinks or watches, still "instruments" of a sort, continue to express the brand and both increase revenues and extend the consumer base. Here again, the brand honors the consumer by honoring itself first. This is the luxury meaning of "lifestyle."

We should recall that luxury brands must manage accessibility. Therefore, the more extensive the brand offerings are, the greater the risk that this principle of luxury brand management will be violated.

At a certain point, after overextensions and/or inappropriate extensions, brands can suffer. Pierre Cardin can no longer be considered a luxury brand as its name has been licensed to every imaginable product category (including wigs, key chains, and men's underwear). As a revenue generator it has been successful, although it is legitimate to ask if the strategy could be replicated today as opposed to the 1960s when Cardin was one of the few high-profile designer names and luxury brand portfolio management hardly existed.

By the same token, it is possible that some brands, under financial pressures, seek to license to almost any category with dire consequences. Such was the case with Harley-Davidson, which in the 1980s licensed its brand for both fragrances and men's neckties (among other anomalies), neither of which were successful and which further exasperated the firm's financial woes by almost permanently tarnishing the brand's image and forever alienating its loyalists. How the company avoided falling over this precipice and going bankrupt is dealt with in Chapter 4.

KEY STRATEGIC MARKETING DRIVERS OF LUXURY BRANDS

A fundamental distinction between luxury brands and other types of brands is in the understanding of "positioning." Positioning finds it classic expression in Jack Trout and Al Ries's *The 22 Immutable Laws of Marketing*. Here the thesis is developed that all branded businesses need to differentiate themselves from their competitors by finding a unique value proposition (one that is not presently marketed or is marketed poorly), and communicate their brand and this proposition to a set of targeted consumers. The key is to occupy, to the exclusion of the competitors, the cherished space in the consumer's mind which consumers can readily access when they are in the process of a purchase. The role of the brand manager is to create the strategy and marketing communications that clearly and compellingly convey the brand's attributes and why it is superior to those of the competitors. Trout and Ries offer no distinction in strategy between luxury, premium, fashion, or mass brands.

The process of developing a positioning strategy first begins with a look at the competitive landscape relative to your product, price, promotions, and place (or points of distribution). Constructing a competitor's map, sometimes referred to as a **perception map** because much of the information that goes into it derives from how consumers perceive the competitive landscape, is a good way to visualize where opportunities may or may not exist. Where data are not available, the insights and perceptions of seasoned managers and executives are often a source for mapping. Figure 3.5 shows an example of how such a map might look for premium handbags in the American market.

Assume that all the information is correct and comprehensive. The map suggests that unless you can compete at a very low price, the two lower boxes are well covered and the upper-right box is a little better because there is some white space showing. Remember that even if you see an opening, your brand and company must have the core competency at least in products and marketing to compete. There are no brands in the upper-left box perhaps because it is difficult to be highly innovative at a low price.

The next step would be to take a consumer-centric approach to the concept of **relevancy** (sometimes referred to as "saliency"), or the extent to which a brand is important to a consumer segment because it fits their lifestyle. What is it that you do and for whom do you do it? Is your brand and its product or service highly or uniquely relevant for the core consumer? We join brand and product because all really strong positioning strategies position the brand together with its product. The reasoning is that the connection with the consumer is strongest when the connection is emotional. The brand can deliver on that objective through intangibles better than the product which is more tangible. In addition, unless the product is innovative, or patented so it cannot be immediately copied, there is a major risk that the claim to uniqueness will be compromised by a competitor that can **knock off**, or copy, the product's unique features and attributes

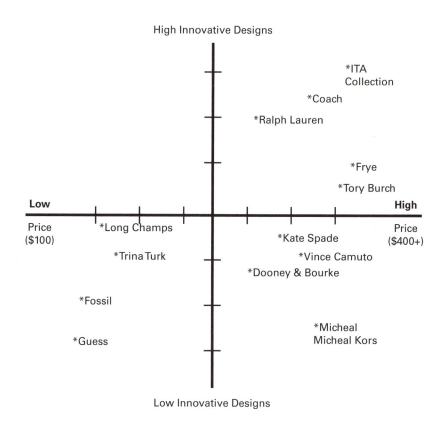

figure 3.5
Competitive perception map of U.S. Premium handbag market: A visual focus on who your competitors are and where there is opportunity.

and with it a brand's claim to relevancy. Here is where consumer research and consumer input can play a pivotal role in formulating strategies, something which we'll explore in greater detail in Chapters 9 and 10.

Following relevancy, the second dimension of positioning is **competitive differentiation**. This requires a clear awareness of who your competitors are and not who you wish them to be, and how you intend to be different. Researching the industry by speaking with retailers, industry pundits, and trade and media reporters, and reviewing relevant discussions on blogs and other social media sites, can help you accurately define the competition. If possible, survey your current customer base (or your targeted one) and ask the basic question, "If you couldn't purchase my brand for the product you want, from whom would you buy it?"

If the brand is in its **pre-launch** (preparations prior to being introduced into the market) or is being repositioned, it is of great importance that relevancy be established prior to competitive differentiation. This is to avoid falling back to a product-centric business model. If the brand promise and its offerings are relevant, the differentiation will follow because the consumer already is alerting you to the differences that the brand manager needs to focus on. Relevancy should drive differentiation because it brings us back to our mission, which is to solve consumer problems and/or service consumer needs.

Positioning and Differentiation as Counter Luxury

"Forget about positioning, luxury is not comparative."[17] With that bold assertion, Kapferer and Bastien begin their argument of how and why luxury brand management and its marketing drivers are, and must be, different from those of other brand types.

Luxury brands have distinct identities, and their uniqueness rests on this. They know who they are. Positioning strategies are variable; brand identity is not. Luxury brands know "the business they are really in"!

The Role of Heritage and Craftsmanship as Differentiators

As we saw in our last chapter, heritage and craftsmanship are maintained by luxury brands because they are anchored in timeless artisanship and history. Chanel is Chanel because of Coco Chanel and her groundbreaking vision of women and fashion. Louis Vuitton is Louis Vuitton because of the founder's commitment to craftsmanship and his appreciation of the elegant lifestyle of his customers, whom his exquisitely crafted steamer trunks served. Neither brand looked to the other for positioning. Even as they both introduce products such as timepieces or fragrances, they do so in terms of their brand and their identity and not in response to competitive differentiation.

The Role of Symbolic Experience as a Differentiator

Continuing from our prior chapter, the ultimate sign of success for luxury brands is that they have transformed tangible benefits of usage into the intangible but often deeply more satisfying symbolic experiences for their loyal customers. Symbolic experience transcends positioning slogans.[18] It touches the soul of its followers and therefore is not in competition to occupy the mental space to which Trout and Ries refer.

Core Customers and the Next Generation

The quest for the next source of brand loyalists begins with the entry into the market of the next generation of consumers. The lifeline of a business and a brand is based on successfully appealing to this next generation. This echoes the management guru Peter Drucker and his definition of a business: *"the purpose of a business is to find and retain a customer."*[19]

The challenge is that these two objectives, to *find* and *retain* a customer, can be in tension with each other. In fact, this is the case and the challenge of luxury brand management, which has been confronted with the democratization of luxury and the erosion of scarcity and its complement, exclusivity.

The Democratization of Luxury

The democratization of luxury is the accessibility of aspects and symbols of luxury products and services to a very broad swath of consumers. It emerged as a social and economic dynamic with the turn of the twenty-first century and the globalization of luxury brands.[20] It manifests itself in the following ways:

- The World Wide Web has "flattened" the world and made luxury brands easier to view and to desire, reducing their mystique.[21]
- The globalization of luxury brand retailing and the availability of luxury products in major cities and throughout the world.
- The increase in the emergence of middle and upper middle classes in major markets around the world and their desire to own and experience luxury brands.
- The strategy of some luxury brands that, to appeal to a younger generation, offer models well below traditional luxury price points (e.g., Mercedes and the CLA model).
- The rise of hybrid brands ("affordable luxury"), discussed earlier, that mimic some of the activities of luxury brands, creating the perception that they are luxury brands.
- The mixing of mass products with luxury products (sneakers and tights worn with Gucci bags) as a counter-snobbery trend in fashion.
- Capsule collections and co-branding between luxury designers and mass fashion brands (such as Karl Lagerfeld and H&M).
- Luxury fashion designers who stage fashion shows replete with messages regarding the compatibility of democratic fashion with luxury creations.[22]

The underlying question is the impact of the above on each brand's traditional base of loyal customers.

Will they begin to shop other brands, feeling not only that their judgment regarding their purchase and the brand's superiority has been put in question but also that a deeper emotional violation has occurred—that democratization is a breach of an unwritten code of loyalty which perhaps has been forever compromised? How can luxury brands embrace some aspects of democratization, appeal to the next generation, and continue to retain the commitment of their loyalists? Here are some reflections on risks and rewards.

Collaboration of Luxury and Mass Brands

What began as Target's unique value proposition **The Democratization of Design** (a collaboration between a department store and a well-respected designer, bringing a designer's aesthetic to a mass market) has become part of a global brand management strategy. Target was the first major retailer to co-brand and develop unique and exclusive products from the likes of designers such as Missoni and Isaac Mizrahi in fashion to Michael Graves in Home. All major department stores and many specialty chains have followed, including Kohl's co-branding of a sportswear collection with Narciso Rodriguez, Derek Lam, and others, and culminating in fall 2015 with Elie Tahari. But none brought more attention to the market and consumers alike than the collaboration of the legendary Karl Lagerfeld, creative director of Chanel, and H&M. The collection, concise and available for only a short time, was a huge success, with most of the pieces selling out the first day. How can this be managed so the brand is not tarnished in the process?

From a brand management perspective, collaborating with H&M provided a window to the next generation of young fashion followers. H&M is known as a leading fast fashion, mass market trendsetter. For H&M, this temporary alliance with Karl Lagerfeld confirms its positioning as a trendsetter. For Lagerfeld, it introduces the luxury world to its next potential generation (Figure 3.6).

figure 3.6
Promotional building poster for Lagerfeld's collection at H&M: Collaboration breaks the luxury norm of inaccessibility.

The key to maintaining the luxury mystique was clearly in evidence in Lagerfeld's strategy. First, it was not the Chanel brand that was offered but his own Karl Lagerfeld brand. However, given the fashion sensibilities of the H&M customers and the media coverage of the event, there is little doubt that the association with Chanel was evident. Second, the collection was a "one-off"—that is, never to be repeated and with no chance of reorders (limited availability, both a luxury and fast-fashion strategy). Third, it was limited to only selected markets, notably high-visibility locations (again, the luxury limited accessibility factor is at play here).

Finally, the very stature of Lagerfeld himself and his aura, which rises above issues of commercialization, offsets the fear that democratization will compromise future creativity or the brand's iconic status. His stature is part of the brand and its continued promise of exclusivity. This aura is also an essential element in successful luxury brand portfolio management. This is another critical part of how luxury brands stay both relevant and exclusive with their unique approach to brand portfolio management.

MANAGING THE LUXURY BRAND PORTFOLIO

Implicit in the preceding section are the principles that are needed for successful management of luxury brand portfolios. We should first restate the distinction between luxury and other types of brands and then place this understanding in a portfolio management context. Drawing a distinction between luxury portfolios and Consumer Package Goods (CPG) portfolios (sometimes referred to as **FMCG**, or "fast-moving consumer goods" or basic commodities, describing how frequently they are purchased—for example, items found in Procter and Gamble's portfolio of household brands) is, given their contrast of the types of brands, a good point of departure. Then an example of a strategy different from that of a premium brand rounds out our analysis.

Managing the Business through the Brand

The power of CPG brands rests on tangibles such as book value or salability, or how they fend off competitors and produce market share and profits. They are often sold or downsized and closed if not performing. In 2015, J. F. Lafley, then chairman of P&G, finalized the sale or closing of close to 50 percent (or over

CASE STUDY
The Mercedes CLA and BMW Mini

In the April 2014 issue of *Entrepreneur* magazine, Kia, a division of Hyundai known best in the United States for SUVs and entry-level pricing, announced the launch of the K900, its self-proclaimed entry into the luxury automotive space, with a trademarked tagline in the two-page-spread ad that read: "*Challenge the luxury you know.*"[TM] Mercedes appeared in the issue several pages prior to Kia's ad with its own two-page ad spread. The Mercedes ad was not of roadsters or elegant sedans but of vans/SUVs, and contrary to classic Mercedes brand management, with starting prices prominently displayed! Ironically, this was the magazine's issue on brand strategies widely read by young entrepreneurs, the very consumer target that Mercedes had in mind when it launched its CLA model in the prior year.

At a price point of $29,750, far below the pricing for the 300 Series, the CLA was to supplant, by its "affordable" luxury sticker price, the 300 Series as the usual first consumer purchase of the brand. The question arises as to how this launch could have been better strategized from the perspective of brand portfolio management.

The thought that an under-$30,000 price point for a Mercedes would jump-start new, younger customers to gradually trade up to higher-priced models as they prosper failed to factor in what one automotive pundit has called "*our brand-diluted world.*"[27] The strategy is seen by this analyst as a further dilution of the Mercedes brand and therefore the undermining of the very asset, the brand's aura, which helps ensure lifetime customers. It fails to consider that the road to a Mercedes, if it remains a path to luxury, is driven by a rarity/exclusivity index and the ability of a new customer to successfully enter that rarified atmosphere called "luxury automobiles." The launch of the CLA seriously compromised this index.

By comparison, BMW's acquisition of Mini is a good example of a successful luxury brand portfolio management strategy targeting a younger demographic. When BMW wanted to enter the market and appeal to the next generation, it first launched the BMW 100 Series. With a price in the mid-$30,000 range, it seemed a perfect entry-level model. However, even with the high performance ratings by automotive magazines, it never reached its sales goals and in 2014 was discontinued. The Mini Cooper brand, which BMW had owned and had for a decade housed in showrooms attached and adjacent to BMW showrooms, became the vehicle for this younger target. The association with the BMW brand but without any sub-brand reference lent great credibility to the Mini brand without tarnishing the BMW nameplate. In addition, the brand's consumer perception was that the brand was fun and a bit quirky, which aligned well with the target consumer's mind-set. Once the brand had established itself, the Mini was housed in showrooms and locations separated from BMW, which made the Mini presentation stand on its own. The new ads were clearly youthful and quirky in their content and copy. Record sales and repeat customers have followed, and the BMW halo has had a positive effect on the Mini without tarnishing the aura of the BMW brand. Knowing that it is manufactured and marketed by BMW maintains the emotional connection with BMW, and this remains as a potential purchase driver for the current Mini owners as they trade up.

sixty brands) within the company's portfolio which were assessed as underperforming.[23] This would be unheard of in luxury portfolio management.

Luxury brands, as we have seen, have deep, intangible, symbolic value. This is in part why the role of the creative director is so essential to the health of the brand and its business. These brands have been created over decades of nurturing and tend to generate **market valuations**, such as stock market prices, which are much higher in proportion to their revenues than are those of CPG brands.[24] Thus, when business is tough, they are not readily disposed of, which can be attributed to the value of the brands and the emotional attachment that both consumers and brand managers have for them. This is, in part, what gives them the title of "luxury."

As a variation on managing and integrating brands in a portfolio, one premium brand, J. Crew, aligning with market trends, has embarked on a strategy which recognizes that head-to-toe dressing in a single brand is no longer the norm. J. Crew identified Converse in footwear and Levi's in jeans as brands complementary with the J. Crew brand. Until this undertaking, J. Crew was the only brand offered in its retail platforms. J. Crew saw an opportunity for mixing its brand with these high-profile, iconic brands with deep American roots (much like itself) and as management identified these brands as leading lifestyle choices of J. Crew's core consumers. Rather than incur the costs to manufacture these categories, J. Crew purchased product from these complementary brands under a special arrangement. There is no ownership of these brands, or the categories, and each benefits from the halo effect of the other. This also reduces J. Crew's downside risk because if sales do not materialize, the firm can discontinue offering the outside brands without damaging the image of the J. Crew brand. At the same time, each brand brings both its own and overlapping loyal customers to the J. Crew retail platforms—consumers that each brand may not have access to and may not have successfully engaged without such a concentrated multi-brand effect.

This is clearly a strategy that luxury brands, concerned with avoiding dilution of the mother brand image, would not undertake. However, this does not preclude from luxury portfolio management a strategy of finding synergies within a corporate portfolio of owned brands. Thus PPR, the French luxury conglomerate and owner of the Gucci brand among others, changed its corporate name to "Kering," which it hopes sends an internal message to the brand managers about the direction of the overall portfolio of brands. The CEO explained that this change is a call for synergies and cross-pollination of fashion ideas (we'll return to this in more detail in Chapter 4).

A high-fashion house such as Kering, which contains brands such as Gucci and Saint Laurent, would be challenged to include in its portfolio an athletic brand. So a question that has been raised is whether the Puma athletic brand fits into Kering's portfolio.[25] Can the other creative and brand elements which characterize the other brands infuse Puma with a common sensibility, making its role in the portfolio assortment more complementary with the other brands?

In the luxury realm, the business is managed through the brand, not the brand through the business.[26] Failing to manage this correctly can have dire consequences for both entities.

The Creative Director as Luxury Brand Manager

Bernard Arnault, CEO of LVMH, in speaking of brand identity and managing luxury brands, cautioned, "*the last thing you should do is assign advertising (of a brand) to a marketing department . . . (you must) have proximity between designers and the message to the marketplace.*"[28]

Over the last two decades, the role of creative director has dramatically changed. Once responsible for ads, models, and media, the creative director and the design director have been merged in luxury brands (and often in premium brands) into one overarching role of brand guardian. This is a measure of how central the brand and brand management have become to business development and how the creative, innovative dimension has been recognized as paramount in sustaining luxury businesses. Witness the role played by Christopher Bailey in a resurgent Burberry and, likewise, Lagerfeld for Chanel and John Galliano for Dior. Their influence in developing company strategies is part of the confirmation that these brands have matured from artisan beginnings into global businesses; *"the creative director is more than just designing a product; it's about an overall vision . . . marketing, retail . . . presentations."*[29]

Premium brands have adhered to this change as well. Here is what Jenna Lyons, president and design director of J. Crew, said regarding her call for a single vision: it is imperative that *"to create a coherent brand and drive the business forward every piece of the creative organization has to be unified."*[30] Thus the merging of the president and design director positions at J. Crew.

CEO/Creative Director Collaborations

We conclude with what some have argued was the strongest CEO/creative director relationship in luxury—that is, of Domenico De Sole and Tom Ford together at Gucci. When they first arrived the brand was a shadow of its original self. De Sole devised the business plan and oversaw its implementation, while Ford infused the brand with an elegant sensuality. Within a decade they turned the business around to where the Gucci brand and the business were once again both glamorous and profitable. Asked about their collaboration and the basis for their success, De Sole observed: *"We've known each other for a long time. We're very different but we have the same vision about what a brand ought to be and what the vision of the brand should be."*[31]

SUMMARY

Luxury brands are based on exclusivity, which combines the management of retail accessibility and product availability; rarity, innovation, and craftsmanship must be their norm. Premium brands are known by how they market themselves. Often the price may be near or at some of the opening prices of luxury products, but the message is not about heritage and craftsmanship (which characterizes luxury) but about functionality and price/value of the features offered in the product. Premium brands often tap into the halo of luxury by creating hybrid names for their business sector, such as "affordable" luxury. These should be seen as marketing strategies rather than as characteristic of the brand, as the words themselves ("affordable," "accessible," "modern") are often changed by premium brand managers when there is a change in their business strategy. Masstige brands embrace some of the prestige elements of luxury (such as packaging and imaging) but with prices that are closer to those of mass brands. Finally, there are mass fashion brands, especially those associated with "fast fashion" retailers, who are trendsetters, which makes them close to the next young generation which shops their brand. This also makes them attractive collaborative partners with luxury brands.

The concept of positioning is very different for luxury brands when compared with the others mentioned above. Positioning is carving out an identity for the brand which is both relevant to the target consumer and different from the market competitors. So its origins are outside the brand; for luxury, this external dependency for its identity is unacceptable. Luxury brands know who they are. Growth challenges are met by being true to the brand and its loyal consumer base rather than by being reactive to market trends. This organic extension from flagship products and a gradualism in introducing new product extensions are what characterize successful luxury brand management. The ultimate objective of luxury brands is to achieve a loyal following by symbolic consumption; other brands seek concrete consumption. This is why so many of the latter's communications are about utility measures: price, comfort, and the number of colors in which the product is available. Luxury customers do not "consume" products, they experience brands. The democratization of design and accessibility challenges luxury, especially when the temptation arises to co-brand with Fast Fashion brands for a "next generation" strategy. Caution and a strong creative director/designer plus "one-off" limited collections help ensure that the luxury brand does not fall prey to commercialism.

The brand drives the business of luxury, and strategies including portfolio management are managed through the lens of the brand. Creative directors are the new brand managers responsible for innovative designs, brand marketing, and brand integrity. This requires a strong CEO who legitimates this new brand manager role and partners with the creative director, merging innovation, creativity, and business objectives into a single strategy orchestrated by the brand's identity.

KEY TERMS

Brand Concept Continuum
Bridge Lines
Competitive Differentiation
Credibility
FMCG
Gradualism

Knock Off
Luxury
Market Valuations
Masstige Brands
Organic Extension
Perception Map

Positioning
Pre-launch
Premium Brands
Relevancy
Reposition
The Democratization of Design
Vulgarity

CHAPTER CONVERSATIONS

- How would you go about explaining what a luxury brand is?
- In what ways do luxury brands tap into consumer emotions that non-luxury brands do not?

- What brought about the change in the role of design director to creative director?

CHAPTER CHALLENGES

- You are the brand manager for a line of luxury automobiles; the CFO, wanting better margins, higher revenues, and a larger market share for scalability, has asked you to launch an opening-price-point family car with the luxury brand name plate. How would you respond?

- The marketing director has been approached by a mass fashion retailer to collaborate, co-brand, and feature the company's line of luxury hand-bag. What questions should be asked and by whom, and what answers would confirm that this is a sound collaboration?

- The CEO of a premium brand has decided to promote the design director to the position of president; she would retain her position as design director. The board of directors feels that this is a conflict in roles and will undermine her effectiveness as a designer. How would you respond to the board?

ENDNOTES

1. KPMG International, "Managing Luxury Brand Growth," KPMG, October 2006, http://www.kpmg.com/cn/en/issuesandinsights/articlespublications/pages/luxury-brand-growth-200610.aspx.

2. Klaus Heine, *The Concept of the Luxury Brand* (N.p.: n.p., 2012).

3. Nancy Hass, "Couch on the Edge." *The Business Journals*, March 17, 2008, http://upstart.bizjournals.com/culture; Miriam Gottfried, "The Accidental Fashionista." *Barron's*, May 19, 2012, http://online.barrons.com/articles/SB50001424053111904571704577404383078606746.

4. Vicki Young and Lauren McCarthy, "Coach Plans to Close 70 North American Stores." *Women's Wear Daily*, June 20, 2014, http://www.wwd.com/accessories-news/leather-goods/coach-plans-to-close-70-north-american-stores-7746906.

5. Astrid Wendlandt and Brenda Goh, "Accessible Luxury Snaps at the Heels of Mega Brands," *Reuters*, March 5, 2014, http://www.reuters.com/article/2014/03/05/us-luxury-affordable-analysis-idUSBREA241HO20140305.

6. "Stuart Vevers's Live Mosaic," *Business of Fashion*, February 20, 2016, www.businessoffashion.com/community/people/stuart-vevers.

7. Wendlandt and Goh, "Accessible Luxury Snaps at the Heels of Mega Brands."

8. "Luxury vs. Premium Brands," *Modern Wearing*, http://www.modernwearing.com/trends-news/luxury-vs-premium-brands/.

9. Jean-Noel Kapferer and Vincent Bastien, *The Luxury Strategy: Break the Rules of Marketing to Build Luxury Brands* (N.p.: Kogan Page, 2012).

10. Mira Oberman, "As Luxury Reaches Masses, Will Auto Brands Lose Prestige?" *GMA News Online*, January 15, 2014, http://www.gmanetwork.com/news/story/343901/economy/companies/as-luxury -reaches-masses-will-auto-brands-lose-prestige.

11. Michael, "Marketing a Luxury Brand: Part 1," *BrandUNIQ*, http://branduniq.com/2013/marketing-a -luxury-brand-part-1/.

12. Y. Truong, "New Luxury Positioning and the Emergence of Masstige Brands," *Journal of Brand Management* 16 (2009): 375–82.

13. For one of the first articles on Masstige, see Michael J. Silverstein and Neil Fiske, "Luxury for the Masses," *Harvard Business Review*, April 2003.

14. Thomas. Tochtermann and Linda Dauriz, "Luxury Lifestyle: Business beyond Buzzwords," *McKinsey & Co.* November 2012, http://www.mckinsey.com.

15. Ibid.

16. Jack Trout and Al Ries, *The 22 Immutable Laws of Marketing* (N.p.: Harper Business, 1994).

17. Kapferer and Bastien, *The Luxury Strategy*.

18. Klaus Heine, "The Relationships between Luxury Characteristics and Brand Identity," April 1, 2012, http://www.conceptofluxurybrands.com.

19. Peter Drucker, *The Practice of Management* (N.p.: Harper Business, 2006).

20. Liselot Hudders, "The Meaning of Luxury Brands in a Democratized Luxury World," *International Journal of Market Research* 55, no. 3 (2013): 391–412.

21. Thomas Friedman, *The World Is Flat: A Brief History of the 21st Century* (N.p.: Farrar, Straus and Giroux, 2005).

22. Marie Driscoll, "Globalization and Democratization Impact Fashion, Too," *The Robin Report*, April 30, 2014, http://therobinreport.com/globalization-and-democratization-impact-fashion-too/.

23. Phalguni Soni, "Procter and Gamble Divestitures: Is the 43 Brand Coty Deal the Last?," www.marketrealist.com/2015/07.

24. Driscoll, "Globalization and Democratization Impact Fashion, Too." .

25. Bloomberg, "At Kering, Turmoil and Soft Profits Are in Fashion," *The Business of Fashion*, December 17, 2014, http://www.businessoffashion.com/2014/12/kering-turmoil-soft-profits-fashion.html.

26. Ibid.

27. Peter De Lorenzo, "The Democratization of Luxury: Coming to a Mercedes-Benz Dealer Near You," *Auto Extremist*, November 12, 2013, http://www.autoextremist.com/current/2013/11/12 /the-democratization-of-luxury-coming-to-a-mercedes-benz-deal.html.

28. Suzy Wetlaufer: *Harvard Business Review*, October 2001.: "The Perfect Paradox of Star Brands: An Interview with Bernard Arnault of LVMH"

29. Kim Winser, "Why Do Luxury Brands Need High Profile Creative Directors?," *Forbes*, July 9, 2013, http://www.forbes.com/sites/kimwinser/2013/07/09/why-do-luxury-brands-need-high-profile -creative-directors/.

30. Ibid.

31. Christian Barker, "Interview Domenico De Sole", April 29, 2014. www.billionaire.com

CHAPTER 4

Segmentation Models

AFTER COMPLETING THIS CHAPTER,
YOU WILL BE ABLE TO:

- Discuss how segmentation models serve business objectives.

- Explain why different consumer cohorts require different types of models.

- Apply personas, archetypes, cultural codes, and segmentation models for brand management.

THE PURPOSE OF SEGMENTATION MODELS

In the preceding chapter, we explored various positioning strategies on the mass/luxury continuum and discussed how brand portfolio management differs with different types of brands; we also explored how it plays a role in organizing and implementing a variety of successful business strategies. A natural outgrowth of this management dynamic is the development of consumer insights, as consumer-centric brand equity building recognizes that the customer or consumer affects, through his or her perception, the brand's image and therefore can serve as a business builder or a business inhibitor.[1]

With this chapter, we begin Part 2, "Building the Brand." Brand managers as brand builders have many resources available to them. These include broad-based scientific theories, which generate useful insights, and more hands-on everyday tools, which generate useful outcomes. Both seek to forge a better understanding of human decision making and how the brand impacts consumer behavior. From the former, we'll explore in Chapters 14 and 15 some of the current research and its applicability from **neuropsychology** (which studies the dynamics of biology on human behavior), **behavioral economics** (which studies the impact of economic stimuli on human behavior), and **cultural anthropology** (which studies how cultural values or codes differ within and among nations and their influence on human behavior); because they take a big-picture view, these are sometimes referred to as the **macro-determinants of human behavior** (Figure 4.1).

From the latter (**micro-determinants**, used to designate segmentation models that seek to discover granular, detailed drivers of consumer behavior), we proceed to look in this chapter at tools and techniques that are more hands-on and used in everyday planning and operations. One of these is segmentation modeling.

Segmentation modeling is a technique used to structure and create a deeper and more granular understanding of the micro-determinants, or the most detailed explanation possible regarding your customers' behavior so that you can better align with their wants and needs and dreams. It is based on the premise that there is no such thing as the "average" customer, but varieties of similar customers with different reasons and motivations for their shopping habits. Both mass and luxury brands develop segmentation models; luxury is often motivated by the objective of creating greater intimacy and aligning with consumer desires and dreams without being intrusive—a delicate balance; mass brands tend to be more focused on wants and needs and differentiating consumers by their purchasing proclivities and the degrees of difference between different cohorts. What they share in

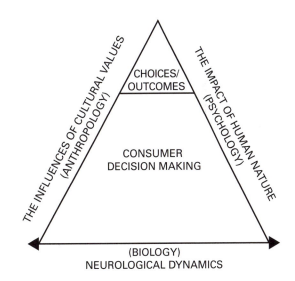

figure 4.1

Macro-determinants in consumer decision making: How the three systems of thought converge to influence behavior.

Table 4.1 The Three-Step STP Process: Graphically Portrays the Linkage Between the Three Major Variables in Marketing		
1. Market Segmentation	**2. Target Marketing**	**3. Product Positioning**
Determine to whom you wish to sell	Identify the best potential or best actual cohort	Craft relevant product, message, offer for best cohorts

common is a similar approach when they are operating on a more macro level, referenced earlier.

Market segmentation models are part of a more widely applied method of discerning business opportunities and serving consumers called the **STP process**, the business planning and executions sequence comprising the three steps of segmentation, targeting, and positioning of a brand and its offering to the market. This process has been described as *"the essence of strategic marketing."*[2] Thinking about our discussion in the preceding chapter on *positioning* enables us to integrate the concepts of *segmentation* and *positioning*, with *targeting* being the bridge that links the two. Table 4.1 visually captures this process and sequence.

Looking back at our positioning map in Chapter 3, we could align consumer types with the various brands in one of the four occupied quadrants on the map to strategize where the best opportunity is, given our core competencies and market conditions. It's important to remember that STP and position mapping are as much art as science and constitute just some of the available ways to think about how to proceed in creating a strategy. Experience and good business instincts (don't discount "gut" insights!) should be part of any decision-making process.

Segmentation modeling starts out by dividing existing customers or targets into two or more discrete groups that share similar characteristics–for instance, brand shoppers. Members of this group may all be department store shoppers or even prefer to shop consistently at one retailer. They may also prefer one brand over another. Within these similarities there are often distinctions. One group may shop the store infrequently and only when the brand is on sale; another may be **loyalists**, people who shop often

and are committed to buying the latest fashions and are not concerned with what is on sale. These **target groups**, or selected **cohorts** (as they are often referred to in the literature) are or can be prime customers and are organized within segmentation models by a variety of information categories, which differ depending on your various business objectives (Figure 4.2).

Figures 4.3 and 4.4 show two pyramids which display a shopper spending model and a shopper frequency model, both of which can be used to chart degrees of brand loyalty to a store or a product brand. This focus on targeting enables us to identify the best opportunities and then construct relevant messages and offers which are consistent with customers' lifestyles and shopping habits. This focused marketing communication increases the likelihood that it will resonate with the consumer and positively affect the purchase decision.

figure 4.2
Gradations of differences among consumer cohorts: The differing tiers provide an idea of how segmentation seeks differences among similar consumers.

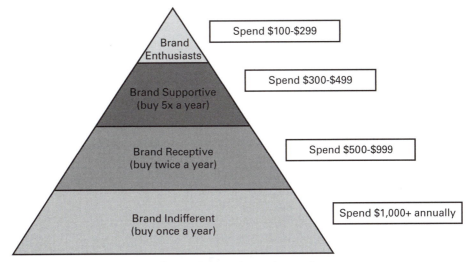

*Numbers used for example only (depend on product, price, etc.)

figure 4.3
Annual consumer spending segmentation model:
One way in which consumers can be segmented depending on your business objectives.

- Categories represent consumer types
- Types are defined by the impact of the activity of their emotions and needs
- Activity is present in different degrees
- Each may require different marketing messages, media, and methods to reach them

figure 4.4
Annual shopping frequency model:
Another segmentation model based on a different set of business objectives.

Types of Segmentation Models

The simplest way to segment customers is by using **demographic** data (such as age, gender, education, race, occupation, or income, which is readily available from U.S. census tracts). **Geo-demographic** segmentation (organizing data by region, city or metro size, population density, or climate) is another common type of segmentation that also uses census tract data. This data source is free and readily accessible online by searching http://www.census.gov/. These are two useful points of departure for new businesses as well as other businesses whose objective is to first target and then determine by sales responses which consumer segment will want their business offerings. One has to begin somewhere and demographics together with geo-demographics, both readily accessible and offering a broad view of the market, provide a good starting point.

A commonly used hybrid model is the following framework which focuses on age ranges (or generations) of Americans and the cultural times in which they came of age and then develops a general description of who they are and what their values are. For example, the baby boomers (born between 1946 and 1964) have been influenced by World War II, postwar prosperity, certain social values such as a high regard for formal education, and an exodus to the suburbs for a distinctive lifestyle. Following is an outline of this overall segmentation model:

- Traditionalists: Born prior to 1946
- Baby boomers: Born 1946 to 1964
- Generation X: Born 1965 to 1980
- Generation Y (or Millennials): Born 1981 to 1995
- Generation Z: Born 1996 to 2010

This model is often used to chart population growth and life stages (certain social actions such as when a driver's license becomes available) to determine if the trend lines favor or challenge certain brands given their core customer identity, or **brand persona**, a generalized and somewhat fictitious description of what is seen by the brand manager as the typical core consumer of the brand. This model has been used by Harley-Davidson, for example, to ascertain how population trends by generations may impact the brand's available pool of potential customers in the U.S.[3]

Socio-graphic segmentation modeling, sometimes called **lifestyle segmentation**, looks at social patterns of how people live their lives as a way of seeing their priorities. This segmentation model emerged from the realization that this type of data was superior to demographic and geo-demographic data for predicting consumer behavior. As mentioned earlier, the latter models are static and deal not with activities but with an identity or social category (e.g., income level or age).

A segmentation model similar to lifestyle is **life stage segmentation**, an approach to segmenting markets which recognizes important life events as delineators for marketing strategies. In every society and in its subcultures, there are **rites of passage** (patterns of behavior structured by predefined events in one's life such as getting married, starting your first job, or buying your first home) that result in certain types of purchases. Because these are "must-buy" life stages, they are more predictable as patterns of consumer behavior. Data here are often gathered through consumer surveys which provide the opportunity to project how large a potential market there may be.

The realization that lifestyle and life stage are better predictors of behavior than demographics has also led to the gathering of data from point-of-sale transactions (cash registers) and credit cards. Shopping patterns at stores or online generate data that are transformed into **behavioral segmentation**, such as frequency of store visits, patterns of in-store shopping, departments or brands shopped, and the use of credit cards, cash, or checks. All of these behaviors provide the brand manager with information and distinctions that lead to the profiling of consumers through their shopping and purchasing patterns and result in more effective business decisions.

The ultimate model is called **psychographic segmentation**. If the other models deal with who the consumer is and how he or she lives or behaves, the psychographic models determine the "why" of behavior or the attitudes that motivate the behavior. Knowing the "why" enables brand managers to forge a much more intimate relationship with customers and a much deeper emotional experience between the consumer and the brand.

Aligning Models with Business Objectives

The choice of how you design the model depends on what business objectives you want to achieve. For example, the extensive use of shopper behavior segmentation models stems from the need to identify different consumer purchasing motives and patterns. Here, the objectives may be to **optimize merchandise assortments**, or to have the right merchandise in stock, or to intensify the focus of marketing messages and offers to a highly sought after segment of consumers. In this instance, delineating your database by customers' shopping habits as to frequency and purchase patterns would be useful. Another database delineation objective might be to inform short-term and long-term **cost per customer** (a calculation of the cost to find and/or retain a customer relative to the return on investment) decisions which tell us our best and worst customers (such as those who buy at full price versus those who buy only when there is a deep discount and what we spend to retain them) to determine how budgets should be distributed that maximize the best return on generating and retaining new customers. A model that examined the database and mined information on customers' history and the dollar amount and potential amount of spending in a department or retail store would be useful.

Customer segmentation also allows guiding and prioritizing of research and product development initiatives. Knowing the different types of consumers who frequent and embrace the brand enables brand managers to provide targeted **product-message-offers**, or mass marketing communications customized to each customer segment's wants or needs. Depending on their profile, these may include different categories of **types of purchasers** such as frequent shoppers, ultra-loyalists, bargain hunters, or new shoppers buying the brand for the first time. In this situation, reaching out and surveying those who offer the greatest return on investment could lead to a product development assortment tailored directly to their needs. This sets the stage for brand managers to embark on **co-creation** programs with key consumer cohorts—that is, customized and/or personalized products for them and theme development for advertising from them. These initiatives are key strategic dynamics that confirm the brand managers' promise to optimize the principle of consumer-centricity. We will discuss co-creation in more detail in Chapters 11 and 12 and throughout the text and explore the role of brand communities cocreating **brand images** (what the market reflects back to the brand managers as to its perception of the brand) from within.

Segmentation research can also help uncover both the common thread that unites a potential brand community and the distinctive way each segment aligns its purchasing motives with the brand. Discovering this unifying principle means the brand can devise strategies to encourage the creation of brand communities, such as those we discussed in our last chapter (and which we'll explore later in this chapter with an in-depth look at the seven types of Harley-Davidson consumers), which are powerful generators of brand loyalty.[4] In the Harley-Davidson example, brand managers became privy to very granular data from these seven types of consumers and were in a better position to respond to different customer types while honoring the brand's overarching DNA, thereby maintaining its brand identity (the personality and values of the brand).

This achieves two important business objectives. First, it meets the desire of today's consumers to receive offers of products or services that are of special interest to them, also known as **targeted marketing**, which can lead to **mass customization**, or the creating of products which reflect the brand's identity but also give consumers the opportunity to infuse a product with their own individuality. This can take many forms, from embroidering a simple set of initials on a shirt that is already offered to the general public to customizing a pair of Nike sneakers through a "Designed by You, Made by Nike" online program.[5] Second, it optimizes the impact of these marketing messages to increase sales, profits, and **market share** (a percentage of a company's sales reported in units or dollars in the category and market in which the brand competes) because less time, money, and personnel are needed as a better focus leads to better business outcomes.

This offers an example of how a brand manager might integrate these key concepts and brand elements for robust and sustainable business development. What strategies might you add to this?

Resources for Building Databases and Segmentation Models

Developing segmentation models requires consumer data. The data can be from secondary sources such as the census bureau mentioned earlier or from **primary research**, a source of research data such as focus groups or sample surveys that directly query and interface with core consumers of the brand with customized designs to ensure that the results align with specific business objectives.

Online, many companies have created primary research panels of targeted consumers who have agreed to participate in ongoing research. P&G's "Tremor" panel is one that is well established and provides the firm with data on demand. For the more robust socio-graphic and psychographic types of models, two of the most widely used and actionable research platforms are VALS and PRIZM.

VALS is an acronym for *Values, Attitudes, and Lifestyles*. It segments consumers into eight psychological types based on their personality dynamics and describes how these are markers of behavior patterns.

Marketers and brand managers, once they discover the types that align with the brand's identity and image, can tailor messaging to the **cluster** (individual consumers with common behavior organized into groups for research and marketing purposes).

PRIZM, or *Potential Rating Index for Zip Marketers* is a similar model but works more on the socio-graphic level than VALS. It segments by households, shopping patterns, preferences, and geography the entire U.S. population, which it has clustered into sixty-six distinctive types of consumer cohorts. Given that there are approximately 120 million U.S. households, this creates on average 2 million households per cohort. In order for brand managers to locate targets, these cohorts are then organized into **Zip code clusters** of cohorts with similar lifestyles. The 42,000 U.S. Zip codes are broken down, reorganized, and clustered around several of the sixty-six consumer cohort groups, providing a critical mass of on average approximately 700 targeted Zip codes per cohort or type of consumer group. Lifestyle overlaps (consumers in more than one of the sixty-six clusters), open up an even more significant number of households to this Zip code cluster marketing.

What makes this model useful is the tendency of people with the same lifestyles to live in the same neighborhoods or Zip codes. For example, the Zip codes for Westchester, New York (a suburb of New York City), Buckhead, Georgia (a suburb of Atlanta), and Walnut Creek, California (a suburb of San Francisco) show, in spite of their geographic distances, closely aligned types of consumers by lifestyle. *"Consumers of a feather flock together!"* Because of this access to data, brand management and marketing communication strategies can now take on a broader geographic reach and a larger market segment and remain consistent in the message, further enhancing the brand profile, awareness, and business potential. Strategies can be more effectively focused and implemented and outcomes more readily measured and managed. An example of a PRIZM cluster and the socio-graphic information it offers can be seen in Figure 4.5.

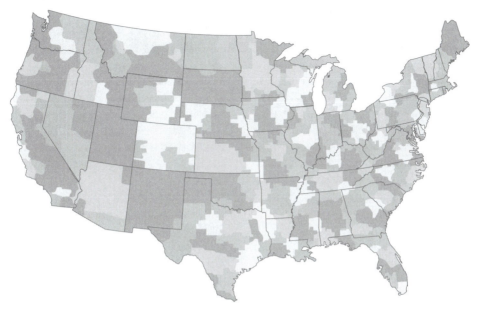

figure 4.5
PRIZM clusters: Map of the United States with colors showing degrees of different concentrations by Zip codes of a particular consumer cluster.

The following is an actual case of a client and a retailer where the absence of a segmentation model obscured business opportunities and the use of a PRIZM analysis provided new insights and fresh opportunities.

The Role of Segmentation Models in Engaging Consumers

As we have seen, there are a variety of segmentation models to assist in brand management. The choices are driven by a combination of the availability of data, budgets, time, and business objectives. The models we will examine all seek to **engage** the customer— that is, to meaningfully connect and ultimately form a relationship which leads to brand loyalty. This again is a manifestation of consumer-centricity in the successful management of the brand. It is also important to remember that these models are thumbnail clips of reality and are generalizations. They should not be confused with the reality of the entire class from which one may extract a sector in order to focus on targeted consumers and to devise a business strategy to reach them.

Luxury

Let's begin with a psychographic model because it provides the most granular and in-depth detailed framework. The models generally revolve around two independent variables such as the degree of wealth and the need for status. In the following model, this results in four consumer segments, each psychologically driven by less desire or more desire for overt signs or codes of luxury status.

A pivotal hypothesis in the model is that there is an inverse relationship between low wealth and high status. The lower the wealth of luxury seekers

Jhane Barnes was an award-winning designer of premium priced menswear. She was known for her unique sweater and sport shirt patterns which she designed using advanced geometric formulas resulting in eye-catching patterns and prints. She had a successful business and advertised in *GQ* and occasionally *Esquire*, the premier trendsetting magazines for men's fashion.

One of her clients was Neiman Marcus where, over a decade, she had built up a small but steady clientele with her menswear collection. The business for the past year had been stagnating and questions arose regarding the reasons and the profile of the Jhane Barnes customer. Who was he, what was his lifestyle which led to his purchase of the brand, and what (if anything) had changed? The company hired my consultancy firm, WDA Brand Marketing Solutions, to find out the answers to these questions.

We were able to draw a random sample of the Zip codes which were the predominant and reoccurring sources of the brand's most loyal consumers. From here, we applied a PRIZM cluster analysis. Several key facts emerged from the drill down into the customer base.

First, there wasn't one Jhane Barnes cohort but three. Each tended to buy different parts of the collection (knit tops, woven tops, etc.) at different times of year. Second, there were two distinct age sets: a younger and smaller consumer base who often shopped online and a much older and larger one that preferred the likes of Neiman's; the latter tended to be golfers and belonged to country clubs while the former tended to be tennis players and belonged to health clubs. And a third cohort, a smaller segment, bridged the patterns of the first two.

The product line has always been trend right and reflected Jhane's young attitude and her ability to design into trends without losing the brand's identity. As style trends became younger, she followed suit. For example, the fit patterns of knits and sweaters were made to mirror the trending fashion toward trim *metrosexuals*, those young, professional urbanities who stayed in shape. However, the bigger and core customer base was the older and somewhat less active cohort. Not only did we discover that the new fit patterns made some of the garments too tight for comfort for this segment, we also learned that the current ad campaign did not align with the magazines that this customer tended to read. We found that the golfers were subscribing to *Forbes*, *Fortune*, and *Golf Digest* and not to *GQ*, *Esquire*, and *Sports Illustrated*. This was one of several distinct socio-graphic lifestyle variables that the PRIZM clusters confirmed which contrasted with where the brand was advertising. We were getting to the bottom of why the business had slowed and what could be done to get it moving again.

We were now able to recommend, with confidence, that a two-tiered business existed. This two-tiered business required the creation of a sub-brand for the younger cohort and a

(continued on next page)

stronger presence online. We recommended the name *JB by Jhane Barnes*. We felt that *Jhane by Jhane Barnes* might be too feminine. But referencing Jhane Barnes seemed sound given that there was a following and brand recognition. To revitalize the core business, we recommended a review of the fit patterns and, if budgets warranted, a shift in some ad dollars to the magazines that the core customer read.

This provided the brand with a marketing and merchandising strategy more aligned toward its core customer and, by creating a sub-brand, opened up the opportunity to market the brand in a more targeted way to a younger demographic. The latter strategy provided the potential not only for creating additional revenue but also for developing the next generation of potential brand loyalists.

and the greater the need for status, the more likely they will define luxury by products or services that display frequent and overt signs of brands, logos, and a social style with which they wish to be identified such as being seen in upscale luxury social settings. Conversely, the study identifies a psychographic segment (item 2 in the following list) that has precisely the opposite psychological and sociological dynamic.

1. High wealth/high status
2. High wealth/low status
3. Low wealth/high status
4. Low wealth/low status[6]

The study, from *The Journal of Marketing*, provides a profile by which to identify the segment that each customer occupies. This would enable the retail associate to approach each customer as part of a psychographic subset, each in a different yet appropriate manner. Associates would be trained, as they are now in luxury retail, to discern a customer's preference or distaste for certain forms of status symbols. Discrete inquiries by the associate, or an intimate knowledge of the taste and proclivities of existing clientele, completes the experience expected by luxury consumers.

There are also implications for advertising messages and for special event planning and targeted invitations. The customer base, refined by the segmentation model, provides the data for forging strategic decisions regarding the appropriate brand narratives, the content of conversations with clientele, and the invitees who should be kept from a VIP list so as to avoid a serious faux pas.

In conclusion, the preceding policies seem a reasonable deduction given that the key research finding regarding logos and other luxury brand signs or codes is "*different consumers prefer quiet versus loud branding because they want to associate themselves with and/or disassociate themselves from different groups of consumers.*"[7]

The segments or cohorts in this model are described as follows. Patricians, Partisans, Pretenders, and Patrons are both concepts and names for the consumer types and capture the differences in values and perspective that each carries and conveys. So, for example, *Patrician* is a term for an aristocratic ruling class in ancient Rome, while *Patron* is someone who supports a cause with a degree of indifference to any public honor that may be bestowed upon him or her (Table 4.2).

It is worthy to note that the researchers used PRIZM in the same manner that we did in the Jhane Barnes study. They were able to locate by Zip code and validate the income ranking and lifestyle values by clusters (these include the three wealthiest segments in America, all of which had a high awareness of luxury brands) and find the very consumers they wished to interview.

Table 4.2 The Four P Types:
A Luxury Consumer Segmentation Model Based on Degrees of "Signaling"

Patricians	Partisans
High Wealth/Low Need for Status: A desire for subtle or "quiet" signals They signal to each other, which can only be discerned by the like-minded.	*High Wealth/High Need for Status:* Want to disassociate from have-nots They prefer "loud" signals and are partisans for luxury symbols.
Pretenders	**Patrons**
Low Wealth/High Need for Status: Want to associate with the "haves," especially the "Partisans"; mimic need for "loud" signals They are pretenders about their ability to afford luxury goods (most likely to buy counterfeits).	*Low Wealth/Low Need for Status:* Don't need status consumption, or wish to associate with wealthier cohorts; Not concerned with signaling by using Luxury goods. They are somewhat patronizing about the status needs of others.

The brand management implications suggest that differing tones of messaging as well as differing design elements in the products have different appeals to different segments of shoppers of the same brand. The challenge becomes to offer this distinctiveness that the segments call for without compromising the integrity of the brand's identity. Here is where luxury brands and their brand managers have stood the test of time. The tendency of non-luxury brands is to compromise the brand's integrity and let the dominant brand image determine the brand identity (as defined by the heritage and craftsmanship of the brand). This is never the temptation for luxury brands as it is for premium or mass fashion brands.

Unity Marketing, a specialist in the luxury research sector, has developed a behavioral segmentation model which complements the study in *The Journal of Marketing* referenced earlier. Here are the consumer profiles based on the Unity Marketing Segmentation Model.[8]

- *X-Fluents:* Extremely affluent. Spend the most on luxury and are most highly invested in luxury living.
- *Butterflies:* The most highly evolved luxury consumers who have emerged from their luxury cocoons with a passion to reconnect with the outside world. Powered by a search for meaning and new experiences, the butterflies have the least materialistic orientation among the segments, yet they have strong spending potential for the right brand experience.
- *Luxury Cocooners:* Those who are focused on hearth and home. They spend most of their luxury budgets on home-related purchases.
- *Aspirers:* Those luxury consumers who have not yet achieved the level of luxury to which they aspire. They are highly attuned to brands and believe luxury is best expressed in what they buy and what they own.
- *Temperate Pragmatists:* A newly emerged luxury consumer who is not all that involved in the luxury lifestyle. As their name implies, they are careful spenders and not given to luxury indulgence.

To activate this model requires lifestyle secondary data such as PRIZM to provide socio-graphic profiles that correspond to the types outlined above as well as geographic locators so they can be reached.

Finally, Kapferer and others suggest another segmentation model based on wealth and non-wealth and conservative lifestyle versus a "modern" or advanced lifestyle.[9] This model again results in four major segments and is used to explain how those without significant wealth can be included as ongoing and potential luxury purchasers.

The lifestyle and the life stage concepts are at the foundation of this model. Consumers, made aware of luxury brands through the internet and through global marketing, have in addition to rising incomes, rising expectations of how they wish to live. This includes both partaking of luxury brands as experiences and as life stage gifts, often to themselves as personal rewards for life achievements. This helps to explain how luxury brands seemingly affordable to only the very wealthy—also called the **Super Rich**, or **Ultra High Net Worth (UHNW)**, constituting just 1 percent of the U.S. population—have experienced, over the past two decades, phenomenal growth.

But this growing segment, apart from the Super Rich, can also be segmented by their attitudes toward luxury as a system of social values. In this model, purchasing decisions are largely based on personal values. Brand managers would do well to track these segments not only because of their size and growing purchasing power but also because the Super Rich are harder to locate and less amenable to interviews and survey research.[10] Table 4.3 shows the Value-Based Segmentation model that describes them and which provides brand managers with a more granular idea of how to approach them.[11]

Again, the brand manager should be framing the customer base in terms of the above types or categories. This is helpful in informing store personnel and for creating general brand marketing communications.

The challenge in applying this model is twofold: first, it requires in-depth sensitivity training of store personnel so they can discern, from in-store conversations with clients, verbal cues as to which value system the client might embrace. Then they would make the appropriate presentation and recommend the appropriate product that aligns with the client's unique perspective. Second, there is a conceptual flaw in the model: "Individual Psychology" is not a value, it is a concept (remember, this is a "value-driven" model—for example, "premium pricing," "uniqueness," "conspicuousness" are drivers). Therefore, we don't know the types to which "psychology" refers, or their "values," and how this integrates, if at all, with the other value segmentations. How would it work into the training session, and if it doesn't fit into the model, does this invalidate the usefulness of the model as a whole?

The objective in building and applying these models is **brand engagement**, or fostering emotional relationships with targeted segments.[12] The process is to seek, communicate, connect with, and create brand loyalists. In each brand management strategy, there is a unique and compelling brand experience where the product is secondary to the engagement between the brand and the consumer.

Table 4.3 A Personal Values–Based Luxury Segmentation Model: Based on How Luxury Complements Their Personal Values	
Financial	**Functional**
The premium price is the fundamental benchmark of luxury and the value driver	The perceived uniqueness of the product and its quality is the value driver
Pretenders	**Patrons**
The individual purchasers' personality in terms of their view or perception of luxury	The need for conspicuousness or group affiliation achieved through the luxury purchase

Mass and Premium

The three major types of brand engagement are "Involving" customers, "Romancing" customers, and "Delighting" customers. P&G was an earlier adopter of engaging consumers online as a way of ensuring a consumer-centric alignment with product development. It also saw the dual benefit of market research as a tool for data collection and a means of consumer engagement.

As we introduced in a previous section of the chapter, P&G early on recognized the shift in power to consumers that the web had created and the ability of web-based activists to impact the general public's perception of the brand through social media. Co-opting the blogs and other platforms, P&G created online communities of consumers who agreed to join opinion panels and to participate in brand marketing surveys regarding product development and launches. Each of these permanent survey panels were segmented in different ways in various cohorts of age and lifestyle. One survey panel, "Tremor," has over 500,000 "Moms" who agree to test products, packaging, and the like before these items go to market. This strategy was one way A. G. Lafley, CEO, ensured that P&G implemented his mantra, *"The Customer is the Boss."*

The strategy also recognizes the shift to consumer-centric market planning and the new role of customers as active participants in the brand's evolution. This is a forerunner of what we will introduce later in the chapter—the shift from storytelling by brand managers to story listening from those told by consumer loyalists, and how the integration of these two narratives generates brand engagement.

A second form of brand engagement is "Romancing" customers. The J. Peterman catalog accomplishes this by creating beautiful pen-and-ink watercolor product sketches for each classic upscale item that is offered for sale. But what is really being offered is a brand and emotional engagement.

The catalog assortment is curated to reflect the lifestyles of defining moments in the periods, places, and events of Western history and culture. The insouciant lifestyle story lines that accompany each sketch transport the reader into another time and place as reflected in the catalog's brand positioning statement, *"Clearly, people want things that make their lives the way they wish they were."*

The catalog cover, which is numbered (and purposely smaller than most catalogs), describes its contents as an "Owner's Manual," suggesting that it is to be kept as a source of "solutions" for those who *"want things that are hard to find. Things that have a romance, but a factual romance about them."*[13] The story lines are clearly targeted to a generation (many of whom are baby boomers) that finds the content relevant to their own education and/or life experience.

A third type of engagement can be found in "Delighting" customers. KLM Airlines® (Figure 4.6) used a "surprise campaign" to delight its customers, many or most of whom were Generation Xers. Tapping into the power of mobile devices to reach and align with customers' specific lifestyles, KLM devised a rewards program second to none for its immediacy, differentiation, and personalized customer relevance. Tracking their flights via their customers' use of mobile device check-ins and reviewing their frequent flyer customer profiles (which they could readily access), the airline employees would locate, prior to each flight, each person inside the terminal's waiting area. They then handed each a small gift that was unique to that passenger's lifestyle and trip destination—for example, a New York City guidebook with sports bars highlighted for a soccer fan passenger bound for New York, or a headband for a customer going on a ski trip in the Alps! This targeting recognized how this cohort communicates and its lifestyle dynamic.

Brand Communities

Building brand communities is not a marketing function per se; it is a business strategy that should be aligned with corporate-wide goals. Engagement helps engender these communities, which define target customers, loyalists, and advocates.

We can confirm that it is a business strategy because "Engagement" is a quantifiable metric that moves the

figure 4.6
The KLM brand experience goes well beyond the aircraft.

purchase and profit needle. The most successful outcomes are in those companies that have monetized this metric and can correlate it with measurable loyalty outcomes. One engagement scale from FedEx has been created which, in the words of Michael Glenn, its executive vice president (quoted in "The Positive Economics of Customer Engagement"), confirms that *"Every one percent increase in customer loyalty represents approximately $100,000,000 in revenue. We spend a lot of time looking at how to build customer loyalty."*

A classic example of an approach to engagement and community can be found in the challenge faced in 1984 by the iconic Harley-Davidson® (HD) brand. In 1984, the company teetered on the brink of bankruptcy and possible liquidation. Management responded by reformulating the competitive strategy and its business model around the philosophy of a brand community. It restructured every aspect of the company, ranging from its culture to the operating procedures, to align with this revitalization.

The foundation for this revitalization was the "brotherhood of riders" community idea. The company began to sponsor community-outreach events, enlisting employees rather than temporary hires to participate in the events. This motivated many employees to become riders as well as riders to join

the company, both of whom often became vocal brand advocates.

More and more, decisions at all levels were grounded in the community perspective as the company acknowledged the community as the rightful "owner" of the brand. What preceded this was the shift to a consumer-centric mind-set and the development of a highly detailed customer segmentation model. Here is how it unfolded.

The crises faced by HD stemmed from its brand strategy which assumed that the brand's appeal was, in part, from its selective distribution and limited availability. Dealers, however, were clamoring for more units as sales hovered around 60,000 bikes a year and consumer demand suggested that perhaps as many as two or three times that number of units could be sold. It was clear distribution wasn't an issue; the dealers had budgeted to buy more than what had been manufactured. The key question to be answered was, "Can we ramp up production without compromising the cachet of the brand?"

The executive team feared that the increased production would alienate the core loyalist, but they had only impressionistic and anecdotal evidence of this customer. More granular and deeper insights of the riders' attitudes toward the brand were needed.

A customer sample survey was designed, and 16,000 questionnaires were sent out. Expecting a typical response rate of 2 to 5 percent max, the returns numbered over 4,000—a 25 percent return! This suggested an intensely interested and perhaps very loyal customer base. The resulting data confirmed the best of both possible worlds.[14]

There were seven distinct demographic/lifestyle customer segments, each of which experienced the brand in lifestyle settings that were different and aligned with their various socioeconomic backgrounds (Table 4.4). The next insights were the most dynamic in terms of leading to a fresh brand strategy:

1. A broad swath of brand loyalists existed who, in spite of their social and economic differences, were united around a singular perception of the brand experience as reflected in the brand

Table 4.4 Harley-Davidson Cohorts within Their Segmentation Model: Portrays the Differences and the Unifying Commonalities of the Brand			
Name	**Demographics/Values**	**Attitudes/Psychology**	**Model Owned**
Sensitive Pragmatics (29%)	Tend to be blue-collar workers Easygoing and practical	They like the "high" of riding	Touring Model owners
Laid-Back Campers (24%)	Quiet and softspoken These bikers are patriotic, labeled as "Made in America"	They like to use the bikes to cruise around, not to speed or race	Sportster owners
Cool-Headed Loners (17%)	Higher income "white-collar" individuals	Consider a Harley the perfect getaway Call the Harley a "fingerprint"	Softail owners
Adventure-Loving Traditionalists (10%)	Love risks and seek thrills	Ride a Harley for independence, freedom, and adventure	They purchase all models
Classy Capitalists (8%)	Described as "Rich Urban Bikers," or RUBS Represent the traditional American success story 45–50 years old	They love the attention they get when riding a Harley	Softail owners
Misfits (7%)	Enjoy having the reputation of being a "bad guy" or "wild man"	The sound and speed of a Harley are most important to this group Love to get a chance to "open up" on the road	Dyna owners
Stylish Status Seekers (5%)	Young, stylish, and elite	"Riding a Harley separates you and makes you stand out"	CVO models Custom Harleys

persona of the Rebel archetype. The "*open road*," the "*freedom*," the expressive unique sound of the Harley-Davidson engine, the pride of ownership, and other attitudinal dynamics were mentioned as brand attributes by almost all the respondents. Here was the basis for the brand community and for sustainable growth.

2. Building on both the unity and the differences, Harley-Davidson was now able to plan unique product-message-offers to different segments in different marketing venues. The company now knew by segment which media to use, which message would most likely resonate, and which model was preferred as well as its lifestyle end-use. Yet there was still a community bonded together by the brand archetype.[15]

In a decade unit sales increased from 60,000 to over 130,000 a year. This was all the more impressive because it was accomplished in a competitive sector that also experienced the more aggressive marketing of Japanese brands (Kawasaki, etc.) and, to a lesser degree, German, British, and Italian challengers as well!

The use of segmentation models and targeting to create a community can also be tied to a strategy of building engagement through first creating a community on social media. This could include aligning a brand with a segment that is not your traditional consumer.

Returning for a moment to the CLA example, this is what the Mercedes brand managers did when they began the process of launching the CLA model. Although we will examine in greater depth the social media strategy in later chapters, here is a brief capsule of how Mercedes brand managers proceeded.

In 2010, the average age of the Mercedes-Benz consumer was 57. The challenge of the brand manager was to appeal to a younger and more spirited demographic without alienating the core consumer whose purchases sustained the business. This required three shifts in strategy.

First, two demographics were targeted—Millennials and Generation Xers, focusing on an age range of 25 to 39. The second strategy shift required a change in the attitude and the corresponding message. Classic Mercedes brand ads focused on the engineering attributes of the brand persona. Innovation and efficiency were the personality attributes of the brand. These new targeted cohorts were edgier in their lifestyles and somewhat more adventurous in their dispositions than the engineering/performance values which were the content of the classic ads. The third and final shift focused on moves toward social media. The medium by which the targeted segments tended to receive their information was not magazines, where many of the classic ads appeared, but social media wherein the targeted consumers were heavily influenced by key **opinion leaders**, trend makers, and influentials from within their cohorts.[16]

THE BRAND PERSONA AND SUCCESSFUL ENGAGEMENT

Successful brand engagement requires the alignment and balancing of brand identity with brand image. Brand identity is what the brand manager, in the form of the brand's DNA (where the brand's archetype and its cultural code resides) brings to the market; brand image is what the market reflects back to the brand managers as to its perception of the brand. The mix results in the brand persona. When the description is the result of listening to the narratives of key customers and blending with this narrative the brand's DNA, we arrive at a concept that anchors both marketing and merchandising, keeping them from drifting off course. This also sets the stage for the brand's segmentation model, which we explore further on in this chapter. The chart in Figure 4.7 outlines the engagement dynamic and the key roles and contributors to the outcome.

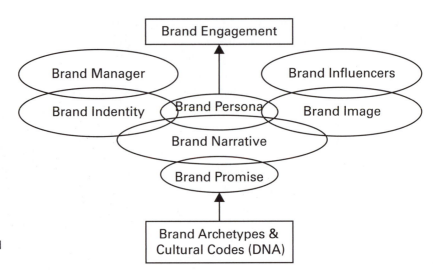

figure 4.7
Engagement:
The Components Needed
to Achieve Success

Brand Personas in Mass and Premium Brands

This use of the brand persona is widely used for apparel and for fashion brands. Here's how it works. Advertising and marketing campaigns need to be focused on a typical consumer who represents the brand. The look of the photography, the imaging and setting, the model chosen, all must be guided by the brand. The content may vary, but the tone and image should be consistent. The persona serves as the silent director of an ad campaign, ensuring that it consistently captures and communicates the personality of the brand and its values. Referring back to the "persona's" attributes and personality is a good way to maintain a consistent brand message.

The same guideposts are used for determining the appropriate merchandising decisions for the target customers.

Mass

Here's an example of how personas serve as guardrails for a large U.S. specialty chain located in the Midwest which markets moderately priced women's apparel. The company is Christopher and Banks with over 400 stores and $500 million in sales. The brand

persona is named "Mary," who is 40-something years old, wears a size 10, and has two children, as determined by focus group research. Here's how she is described by the brand manager: "*Mary could work as a teacher, nurse or bank teller. She drives a minivan. Her husband drives a Jeep. She prefers sit-down restaurants such as TGI Friday's to McDonalds. She reads* People *and* Good Housekeeping *but shuns* Vogue. *She is someone you would want to sit down and have lunch with.*"[17]

Company managers take field trips to check out typical "Marys" in their everyday activities at grocery stores or at movie theaters and record what she is wearing. Pictures of "Mary" which are in various places at headquarters are updated. These serve as merchandising guideposts for the design teams so everyone is clear as to the target consumer for whom the product is being designed and for whom the brand is being positioned. This is a definitive model of a mass apparel brand and its strategy for ensuring that a moderately priced, mainstream fashion, classic women's sportswear product comes out of its design and merchandising departments. This helps to ensure that the creative vision of the brand—and not the design team's personal choices—informs the design effort. Consistently executing this set of deliverables to the targeted consumer is the essence of the brand promise (Figure 4.8).

figure 4.8
Mary, the brand persona: Picture of the prototypical Christopher and Banks customer for merchandising & and marketing guidance.

Several tactics in this strategy should be noted. Although most personas begin with an idea of what the targeted customer is about, it must at some point be confirmed or adjusted by actual consumer input. The danger in failing to do so is that the brand can become irrelevant to the consumer lifestyles even though the product may continue to be differentiated from the competitors'.

Both the focus groups and the field trips provide a stream of market data which, while totally useful for formulating generalizations, cannot be used for projecting propensity to purchase in any specific way. Confirmation of their accuracy remains best confirmed by sales.

Premium

Another model of brand personas is found in the Kate Spade brand. Here we have a more contemporary consumer than with Christopher and Banks. In fact, the Kate Spade consumer places the brand within the so-called accessible luxury space.

The first step was defining the DNA of the brand and its target customer.[18] Here is how the executive management team describes the process of developing the brand persona, starting with Craig Leavitt, CEO: "*We had to get the DNA of the brand first, then the rest would follow.*" And Mary Beech, the chief marketing officer: "*the Kate Spade woman lives in a ten-floor walk up but has champagne glasses. She does not take hours doing all her holiday cards perfectly; she has a glitter party with her friends.*"[19] The consumer is not defined by her demographics (although she is described as age 25 to 44, over $100,000 in annual income, married, and college educated) but by her lifestyle and her personality "*an ageless mindset.*"[20] Again, Mary Beech: "*She sings off-key, but with great spirit, and she has wallpapered the rental apartment.*"[21]

In a similar vein, here is how Deborah Lloyd, president and chief creative officer of Kate Spade, describes Kate, her lifestyle, and the brand promise: "*Our brand promise is to help our girl lead an interesting life, to live her life in colour in every sense of the word . . . it's about encouraging our girl to live this colorful life*"[22] (Figure 4.9).

This concept of color and colorful is not simply a metaphor for an "interesting life" but serves as a merchandising guide by embedding color as a constant in product development and as an aesthetic for the colorful interiors of the Kate Spade boutiques. The brand persona guides business development.

These and other persona attributes are used within the company to ensure a common understanding and internalized focus on the part of the management team on who "Kate" is and what her lifestyle looks like. But we still need consumer input to authenticate the descriptions and a strategy to manage it.

The key to authenticating the descriptors that Mary Beech and the others use was to tell the brand

figure 4.9
The Kate Spade customer reflects her love for color and the "colorful life" brand persona.

ARCHETYPES, CULTURAL CODES, AND SEGMENTATION MODELS

The brand persona is the centerpiece for developing customized segmentation models which when properly designed can drill down into segments such as the Single Mom and discover cohorts that have been hidden from view. The business opportunity increases with the degree of granularity generated by the model. The following is an example.

Aligning Archetypes with Consumer Cohorts

There are currently over 10 million single mothers in the United States with children at home under age 18.[25] At one time this segment may have been seen as a monolithic consumer segment, and a homogenized product-message-offer would have missed serving these consumers' differing needs. However, a study done at Women at NBCU generated the following segmentation model. Again, this is one example of what could be various ways to segment this market. The cohort names (such as "Girl Interrupted") were devised by the researchers and are meant as descriptions, not judgments, and serve to suggest the differences among the cohorts within the segment. This technique is based on the fact that these consumers have an overriding cultural code which they share (maternity/motherhood), yet each is unique in her subcultural influences (e.g., social standing) which drive attitudes and values.

> *"Girl Interrupted"*: This cohort most often describes young girls who became mothers in their teen years. These women are more likely to be Caucasian, young, and lower-income. They also tend to live with extended family, but without receiving much support. Yet, they are the most technologically connected of all.
>
> *"Dream Girls"*: More likely to be from a minority group and receive a lot of family and friend

story digitally, online, in social media. An essential part of the strategy was to be in ongoing communication with her. This was to be both storytelling and story listening, or a dialogue between brand managers and core consumers, which has become an essential part of fashion brand strategies. Again, Mary Beech observes, "*A brand's voice begins with your brand promise; it begins with . . . your real customer.*"[23]

The research, confirmation, and evolution of the brand persona is ongoing. This transcends fashion brands and applies to any brand that is truly consumer-centric. Witness this similar expression from the vice president of global marketing for Johnson & Johnson, the pharmaceutical and consumer products goods company, in her comments on consumer-centricity and the dynamic role of the consumer in the evolution of the brand persona: "*One of the most important factors in building a relationship is listening . . . we need to spend more time listening because in storytelling that still keeps us in charge of the beginning, middle and end, and that's really not how it works anymore.*"[24]

A similar expression of the power of the brand persona occurred during a client presentation by our company to the management team of the Tommy Bahama brand. This is an upscale premium brand of cruise and vacation sportswear largely for men. It is currently distributed in Nordstrom and Bloomingdale's and in its own free-standing stores. There is a strong Caribbean Island context in which the brand and its product are presented (Figure 4.10).

We were asked to provide our client with a presentation to Tommy Bahama management for the license for men's aftershave fragrance. We put together storyboards and mocked up bottles, labels, and boxed gift sets to show how the product would be displayed at retail and how our merchandising captured and conveyed the essence of the Tommy Bahama brand and the Tommy Bahama lifestyle.

As we completed our presentation, the management team began to analyze the various elements of the merchandise packaging. The questions that they asked were: Would Tommy like this color label? Is this the kind of scent that Tommy is likely to wear? Is this the shape of the bottle that is "Tommy"? Clearly they all shared in an approach to evaluating whether product and packaging were *on-brand* (adhering to the brand values as a set of guidelines for merchandise, marketing, and brand management); that is, did it capture and convey the brand persona?

This was confirmed by the "answers" that were generated from their almost rhetorical questions. As a discussion ensued among them, it was as if "Tommy" was in the room and existed as a real person when in fact the very brand name was a construction; there was no actual Tommy Bahama. The result of this internalization by management of the brand personality, attitudes, and values was the emergence of a consensus from the group on each aspect of the presentation that impacted on the brand. The brand's authenticity in the internal organization gave it a consistent personality, and this clarity helped to ensure its consumer engagement in the external marketplace.

figure 4.10
"What would Tommy want": The brand as a "person"; humanizing the brand persona.

support, Dream Girls have a more positive outlook on life and are excited about being moms.

"*Survivor Mom*": She is older, struggling financially, and more likely to be divorced or widowed. She is confident in her parenting choices and buying decisions and is the most brand loyal.

"*Second-Life Moms*": Also older and more likely to be divorced, these moms tend to be more educated, work full time, and be financially secure.

How might a company that designed and marketed baby carriages approach this segmentation model as a business opportunity? In what ways could a company better serve these consumers in each of their differing circumstances? First, the decision as to what business they were really in might generate the archetype of the Caregiver. Providing safe and comfortable caregiver solutions in the form of baby carriages would serve this cohort well. Next, the personas could be developed for each which would create a subset of Caregiver-Mother archetypes as anchors for the four personas. The Caregiver would be the constant, but their differing life stages and life circumstances would alter the "product-message-offer" to ensure its relevancy for each segment. These could include special content and communications which offer advice tailored to the particular segment's life stage.

The above provides an example of how a brand manager might integrate these key concepts and brand elements for robust and sustainable business development. What strategies might you add to this?

Connecting Consumers to Experiential Marketing

The addition to brand messaging of special content and communications referenced above has become the basis for **experiential marketing**, or interfacing with brand touch points beyond the product itself resulting in an emotional connection with the consumer.[26] This contrasts with the **features and benefits approach**, a product-centric approach to marketing that stresses product functionalities and practical benefits. There, product features and benefits (such as "*tastes better*," "*30 percent MORE*," "*same size/lower price*") were the essence of what was communicated to the consumer as the reason to purchase. Today, most consumers, and not only luxury consumers, are demanding that companies do more than just provide quality services or products from their brands. Now, devising a brand personality as part of the brand persona wherein the brand displays through its marketing mix "human characteristics" sets the stage for considering a brand/consumer relationship as something more than just a concept or a metaphor.[27] Emotional fulfillment and a seamless brand experience from first "hello" to post-purchase thank-you notes to consumers have become protocol and factors in creating and maintaining consumer loyalty. As we shall see in the next several chapters, the brand experience and the emotional dynamic it creates and sustains have become priority brand management objectives. Add to this that in addition to the brand experience, this emotional dynamic now requires that "*brands can and do serve as viable relationship partners*"[28] and their brand personalities are now seen as a major factor in driving brand loyalty.[29]

SUMMARY

Segmentation modeling enables brand managers to obtain a deeper understanding of their core consumer. Models are designed to capture drivers of smaller, targeted groups (micro-determinants of behavior) and broader, culturally distinct, targeted national types (macro-determinants of behavior). This in turn provides the platform for customizing messages and offers. The need for different segmentation models is based on the idea that there is no average customer but clusters of similar ones who need to be organized by what they have in common as well as how they differ within that commonality. This enables the brand manager to maintain consistencies in the brand identity while varying the product-message-offers for more personalized communications. The Young Motherhood clusters as well as the Harley-Davidson model are examples of this. Although demographic data provide a starting point, lifestyle, life stage, and psychographic data are more useful. The process called STP provides an integrated model of how brand managers proceed in their planning and execution of brand marketing strategies. Segmentation targeting followed by positioning provides an operational model for decision making.

Collecting data can be done through primary and/or secondary research sources. Several strong secondary sources such as PRIZM and VALS and others are available from which to draw excellent consumer profiles and locate concentrations of targeted consumers.

Luxury models and mass and premium models all tend to build their profiles in a similar fashion except that the luxury businesses have identified more complex variations of luxury buyers including various levels and modes of engagement.

Building brand communities is an excellent way to build consumer loyalty. Brand personas, archetypes, and models all aid in engaging consumers and preparing brand strategies which lead to experiential marketing.

KEY TERMS

Behavioral Economics
Behavioral Segmentation
Brand Engagement
Brand Image
Brand Persona
Cluster
Co-creation
Cohorts
Cost Per Customer
Cultural Anthropology
Demographic
Engage
Experiential Marketing
Features and Benefits Approach
Geo-demographic

Life Stage Segmentation
Lifestyle Segmentation
Loyalists
Macro-determinants of human behavior
Market Share
Mass Customization
Metrosexuals
Micro-determinants of human behavior
Neuropsychology
On-Brand
Opinion Leaders
Optimize Merchandise Assortments

Primary Research
PRIZM
Product-Message-Offers
Psychographic Segmentation
Rites of Passage
Segmentation Modeling
Socio-graphic Segmentation
STP Process
Super Rich
Targeted Marketing
Targets
Types of Purchasers
Ultra High Net Worth (UHNW)
VALS
Zip Code Clusters

CHAPTER CONVERSATIONS

- Why are segmentation models important for brand management?
- What research techniques are useful in developing segmentation models?

- How are brand personas and archetypes related?

CHAPTER CHALLENGES

- A research firm has contacted you suggesting the creation of a segmentation model for your flagship brand. They are specialists in demographic modeling. What questions would you ask and what might be your concerns?

- Your marketing director wants to create a brand community by sending emails to brand owners. What might your advice be?

- Brand personas are thought by some to be outdated because of segmentation models. Do you agree or disagree? Why?

ENDNOTES

1. For the linkage alluded to here, see Kevin Lane Keller, Brian Stern Thal and Alice Tybout, "Three Questions You Need to Ask about Your Brand," *Harvard Business Review* 80, no. 9 (2002).

2. Phillip Kotler and Kevin Lane Keller, *Marketing Management*, 14 ed. (Upper Saddle River, NJ: Prentice Hall, 2011), p. 34.

3. Charles Sizemore, "Blame Harley-Davidson's Downfall on Baby Boomer Demographics," *Forbes*, November 13, 2013, http://www.forbes.com/sites/moneybuilder/2013/11/13 /harley-davidsons-downfall-baby-boomer-demographics/.

4. Albert M. Muniz Jr. and Thomas C. O'Guinn, "Brand Community," *Journal of Consumer Research* 27, no. 4 (March 2001), pp. 412–432.

5. See NikeiD Products on www.nike.com.

6. For a scholarly exposition of this model, see Y. J. Han, "Signaling Status with Luxury Goods: The Role of Brand Prominence," *Journal of Marketing* 74 (July 2010): 15–30.

7. Ibid.

8. Ibid., p. 16.

9. Pam Danziger, "Luxury Report 2014: The Ultimate Six-Year Guide to U.S. Affluence." Unity Marketing. http://www.unitymarketingonline.com.

10. Jean-Noel Kapferer and Vincent Bastien, *The Luxury Strategy: Break the Rules of Marketing to Build Luxury Brands* (N.p.: Kogan Page, 2012).

11. Doug Gollan, "Building a Profile for Today's High Value Luxury Customer" *Media Post*, September 10, 2014, http://www.mediapost.com/publications/article/233936/building -a-profile-for-todays-high-value-luxury-c.html; for a value-based research study of luxury segmentation, also see K. P. Widemann, "Value-Based Segmentation of Luxury Consumption Behavior," *Psychology and Marketing* 26, no. 7 (July 2009): 625–51.

12. For a more detailed exploration of relationship theory in brand/consumer interactions, see the seminal work by Susan Fourier, especially her groundbreaking "Consumers and Their Brands: Developing Relationship Theory in Consumer Research," *Journal of Consumer Research* 24 (March 1998), pp. 343–368.

13. Ibid.

14. "Harley-Davidson, CEO," Blog Spot, http://www.blogspot.com/2009/11/interview.

15. Kyle LaMalfa, "The Positive Economics of Customer Engagement," *Allegiance*, 2008, http://www.allegiance.com/documents/AllegianceEconomicsofCustomerEngagement.pdf.

16. Harley-Davidson, "Harley-Davidson 2009 Annual Report," *Harley-Davidson*, 2009, http://www.harley-davidson.com/en_US/Media/downloads/Annual_Reports/2009/HD_Annual2009.pdf.

17. Stephen Zoeller, "How Mercedes-Benz Uses Marketing Segmentation," *Stephen Zoeller's Marketing Blog*, November 25, 2014, http://www.stephenzoeller.com/how-mercedes-benz-and-german-luxury-car-brands-use-marketing-segmentation/.

18. Amy Merrick, "Christopher and Banks Shuns Trends in Fashion, Targets Mothers in 40s," *Wall Street Journal*, May 9, 2003, http://www.wsj.com/articles/SB105242830433329600.

19. Robin Mellery-Pratt, "Can Kate Spade Become a $4 Billion Business?" *The Business of Fashion*, November 26, 2013, http://www.businessoffashion.com/2013/11/can-kate-spade-become-a-4-billion-business.html.

20. Ibid.

21. Julia Neel, "Kate Spade's Mary Beech Talks Brand Storytelling," *Women's Wear Daily*, July 21, 2014, http://www.wwd.com/media-news/marketing/mary-beech-kate-spade-new-york-7806158.

22. Ibid.

23. Ibid.

24. Ibid.

25. Lauren Johnson, "Johnson and Johnson Exec: Mobile Is More Strategic Than Promotional," *Mobile Marketer*, May 18, 2012, http://www.mobilemarketer.com/cms/news/content/12849.html.

26. Stephanie Azzarone, "Marketing and the Single Mom," *Media Post*, October 26, 2011, http://www.mediapost.com/publications/article/161086/marketing-and-the-single-mom.html; Bernd H. Schmitt, *Experiential Marketing: How to Get Customers to Sense, Feel, Think, Act, Relate* (N.p.: Free Press, 2009); for a complement to this approach, see Marc Gobe, *Emotional Branding: The New Paradigm for Connecting Brands to People* (N.p.: Allworth Press, 2010).

27. Jennifer L. Aaker, "Dimensions of Brand Personality," *Journal of Marketing Research* 34 no. 3 (August 1997), p. 347; Fournier, "Consumers and Their Brands."

28. Fournier, "Consumers and Their Brands," p. 344.

29. Aaker, "Dimensions of Brand Personality."

CHAPTER 5

Brand Loyalty

AFTER COMPLETING THIS CHAPTER, YOU WILL BE ABLE TO:

- Explain how co-creation and brand touch points drive brand loyalty.

- Develop strategies and methods for managing touch points.

- Evaluate methods of measuring and managing brand loyalty.

"The purpose of a business is to create a customer."

—Peter Drucker

BRAND LOYALTY AND BRAND TOUCH POINTS

In the last chapter, the implications of consumer-centric brand management were seen to extend into the creation of consumer segmentation models and into consumer profiles with which to discern socio-graphic and psychographic consumer values and attitudes. This led to the idea of the brand experience and the realization that every interaction between brand elements and brand symbols or **brand touch points** as discussed in Chapter 1 (logos, brand representatives, sales associates, and everyday business contacts) with consumers, have a cumulative effect on the ultimate objective of brand management, which is to establish brand loyalty. *"The brand experience, the essence of a relationship, is created by brand touchpoints."*[1]

Brand loyalty, as we saw in Chapter 1, is the faith and commitment that a consumer has toward a brand. That is, it is both attitudinal and behavioral. It results in more robust, more frequent, and repeated purchases, a willingness to pay premium prices and to forgive mistakes, a resistance to marketing pressures from competing brands to switch allegiance, and a natural desire to recommend the brand to friends and family.[2]

On the market side, the positive effects include reduced costs for marketing, leverage in the trade which helps ensure appropriate distribution and retail presentation, attracting new customers through heightened brand awareness, and time to respond to shifts in competitors' strategies.[3]

As we'll explore in more detail in Chapter 11, degrees of loyalty are also a function of sociological experiences and historical eras in which cohorts find themselves. For example, the purchasing motives of Millennials (Generation Y) and Generation Z (the last two generations of consumers referenced in a preceding chapter) are also impacting this change toward experiential consumption. Globally, shoppers who fit into the Generation Y (born between 1980 and 1995) cohort tend to define themselves not by what they own but by what they do. This naturally aligns with the type of experiential brand management strategies we will be discussing and leads to further extensions of these experiential offerings by the brand managers. Those that fit into Generation Z (born between 1996 and 2005) provide a contrasting dynamic. Experiential offers will change in their relevancy and may be considered but perhaps with a more discerning eye, as this generation tends to be less responsive to marketing messages and less likely to be brand loyal.[4]

Brand Touch Points and Co-creation

Brand managers, therefore, need to be aware of the touch points where the brand interfaces with consumers, creating the brand experience. These touch points range from the simplest contacts such as answering the phone to more complex contacts such as handling the return of merchandise. Think for a moment of the various touch points you experience when checking into a vacation hotel. From the moment you drive up and hand your keys to the parking attendant to the moment the bellhop brings your luggage to the room, you are experiencing the brand identity and formulating your perception of its image. This perception is an emotional experience that when replicated with a recurring positive impact over time generates an **affective commitment**, *"a customer's emotional attachment to a particular brand . . . based on their identification with that . . . brand."*[5] This attachment has been shown in empirical studies to be strongly correlated with brand loyalty.[6] The concept of **brand essence**, which has been described as quality expectations, perceived evidence of its existence, and an absorption of the brand's identity described as **contagion**[7] (a psychological phenomenon wherein people believe that products become imbued with the values associated with a famous owner, maker, or location), helps explain the power of country of origin as a brand preference driver, which we discussed in Chapter 2 and which now reappears here as a brand loyalty driver. As a loyalty driver, it helps to explain the personalized attachment to brands that loyalists feel. A recent empirical study of this contagion phenomenon confirmed that it appears in both luxury and mass brands.[8] In the test study, factories in different countries were said to be the production home for the same products. Those locations that appeared more "authentic" to consumers were thought to convey greater value onto the products they produced—"*that is, consumers believe that products from the 'original' factory have absorbed the 'essence' of the brand which in turn drives authenticity and, thus, value.*"[9] This underscores the co-creation which, as we shall see below, is a key dynamic in experiential marketing.

Experiential Branding

In Chapter 4, we introduced the notion of consumer engagement and how brands create different experiences to achieve it. Here we explore the experiential dimension in more detail. As we will see in this chapter, this experiential dynamic is very different from the traditional "features and benefits" model of traditional brand marketing communications. This latter model assumes that consumers are driven in their decisions by a rational weighing of product or service offers. In this model, the offers are called **utilities**, or the rational value of a product or service derived from its features and benefits. It is assumed that we weigh competitive features and benefits and then, by adding and subtracting positives and negatives, we purchase or praise the highest measured outcome.

Whether this excessively rational model was ever the case is questionable; what we do know is that the utility model of consumer behavior no longer works.[10] Consumers have told us, and research confirms, that the emotional and neurological drivers of decision making are a better explanation as to why and how we behave.[11] An early expression of experiential

marketing that takes the brand experience beyond the product and the purchase can be found at Mitchell's and in the Mitchell's retail company culture.

Mitchell's is a legendary luxury menswear and women's wear retailer with four locations and a flagship store of over 10,000 square feet in Greenwich, Connecticut. The firm's customer base and segmentation model has very detailed data for each customer regarding birthdays, family events, and gift preferences, as well as the personal style and brand choices in apparel, footwear, and accessories. Data are available at the point-of-sale cash registers, which also serve as database computers. Any sales associate can access data and serve the customer in a highly focused service manner. Here **Customer Relationship Management (CRM),** which seeks to optimize customer loyalty and long-term customer engagement and which in mass brands are most often managed through impersonal telephone call centers or internet chat boxes, takes on a very personal level of involvement with each customer and delivers the type of service that wins his or her allegiance.

One example is a story told by Mitchell's equally legendary former CEO, Jack Mitchell, in his book *Hug Your Customer.*[12] The Greenwich store received a call from a customer who was in New York City and said he was summoned by his employer's headquarters in London to leave immediately for an emergency meeting. He had no time to get back home and pack. Store personnel checked the database for the customer's profile and created an appropriate wardrobe for the trip including suits, shoes, and even an umbrella. They then met the client at the airport just prior to departure with a bag packed and ready to go!

This extraordinary service component is well known to luxury brands. The expectation held by luxury consumers when they enter a luxury brand boutique is that they will become part of what is termed the **high-touch** brand experience. This includes extraordinary service, subtle indulgences, and understated aesthetics in the store's environment. These may include champagne and fresh flowers and an elegant space that is not consumed by excessive merchandise. Properly dressed, charming, and unobtrusive sales associates are a given. There is never an attempt to effect a sale. This is part of the expectations of value beyond the product or the brand elements per se and a touch point for luxury brands, which, in this context, "*requires skillful and well trained staff who can successfully engage in an appropriate dialogue with ultra-high and high net worth individuals.*"[13] The atmosphere and service are part of the purchase experience and are a form of symbolic brand consumption, as referenced in prior chapters.

This experience is present in some luxury automotive brands as well. Mercedes-Benz, mimicking Apple's "product geniuses," has created the **product concierge**. The "product concierge," although in the showroom, does not sell the product but helps customers understand the product and how it works.[14]

The Brand Experience

The experiential model is given an even more "direct touch" in the brand notion of **participatory entertainment**, or the co-creation of the brand experience, by how the consumer interacts with the brand and its participatory business model. Build-A-Bear and American Girl, as discussed in Chapter 3, are two very successful examples.[15] Here, if you recall, the opportunity is offered to every customer to experience the brand in terms of her or his own values and personal wants and needs. From creating the bear to dressing the doll, the experiential brand offers personalized outcomes that transcend the product and forge an emotional bond between the consumer and the brand. Brand loyalty begins with this type of personalized, emotional experience allowing customers to "feel" the brand. It fulfills the growing need for brand experiences that are meaningful.[16]

This experiential dimension is blurring the distinction between luxury and non-luxury brands as both sets of brand managers embrace experiential business strategies. What follows are some examples of these strategies.

The rise of experiential marketing has culminated in the fostering of brand sponsorships (i.e., events, offers of exotic and educational travel, or celebrity one-on-ones) that are connected to the brand's values and directly reflect the core consumer's values and lifestyle.[17] An example of this can be seen in American Express's marketing efforts. The company sponsored the U.S. Open Tennis Championship (aligning itself with its customers' lifestyles) as well as sending out a call to its cardholders that it would serve as the conduit for donations in response to the Haitian earthquake disaster in 2011 (aligning itself with its customers' values).

For luxury brands, the experiential offer may include visiting a workshop or meeting a designer. For instance, Gucci has begun to invite good customers, who are not at the top of the spend list, to tour its workshops in Florence, Italy. Here is the view of Patrizio di Marco, Gucci's former CEO: "*Getting our clients to understand how much history, tradition, quality and passion there is behind our work means winning their loyalty.*"[18]

Gucci and others are also selectively inviting customers to store openings, an event usually reserved only for celebrities and the fashion media. Occasionally, the invite may include an exclusive look at a very limited new design that only a handful are invited to preview and, if they wish, purchase (Figure 5.1). As an example, Lanvin recently made five black python handbags priced at $4,000 with a very short list of invitees.[19] Here are the words of Dante D'Angelo, brand director at Valentino, on this experiential phenomenon: "*Everything has become more experiential . . . It's a new way of providing exclusivity, making customers feel important, unique.*"[20]

Co-creation in luxury, as we see from the above examples, requires a similar but a more far-reaching outreach as the influences which animate brand value and sustain brand loyalty in luxury emanate from a broader universe. These include a network of "*official and unofficial brand communities,*[21] experts including the curator of a national museum . . . designers across

figure 5.1
A Gucci store opening event in China: The process of store openings is a consistent luxury brand event.

a range of fields . . . symbols of popular culture . . . as well as editors and journalists."[22]

This dynamic is being driven by several permanent changes in the macro-economic picture—fundamental and sweeping economic patterns—that have occurred in the luxury space, such as "*In an era of overconsumption, people are realizing there is more than just buying products . . . Buying experiences provides more pleasure and satisfaction.*"[23]

The strategy of co-creation goes beyond a sales or service interaction and crosses both mass and luxury brands. P&G's CEO A. G. Lafley set the tone when in 2000 he issued a challenge and an innovation objective: 50 percent of all new product innovations were to come from outside the company—a goal reached in early 2015. Microsoft engages its consumer base by asking for ad formats that engage rather than enrage its readers and its loyalists. Burberry, leading the way in the digital luxury space, not only pretests marketing ad content but seeks suggestions for new trench coat designs. In addition, the firm allows its loyalists to purchase styles from its runway fashion shows shown in streaming videos, in effect cocreating the

final merchandise assortment by factoring in, when the final collection is mass produced, the preferences of these engaged consumers.

For IKEA, the mass home furnishings retail brand, co-creation takes the form of being solutions oriented and developing a culture and programs which pursue consumer-needed home solutions. The touch point that helps sustain this is the company's Home Report, which is a form of anthropological research whereby the marketing and product development teams visit with customers and perform a Home Tour, listening to needs and proposing solutions.[24]

Community and Brand Connectivity

The creation of brand experiences is also sustained and expanded through the creation of brand communities. These can be encouraged by the initial strategy of the brand's management or, as we will explore in Chapter 11, engendered by the co-creation by brand loyalists themselves in terms of how they interact with one another and connect with the brand.

Luxury Brands

As one example of encouraging community, Mercedes-Benz has designed a restaurant-showroom community center for artists and young professionals in Germany to be a digital center for this next generation. It offers what the social media world expects from a brand, a seamless execution between offline and online brand communications and the opportunity to connect and create a community.

This center is now a major touch point as it is a place for community and meets the need for **connectivity** between those various technology platforms and venues that engage members of the same brand community; this characterizes how younger consumers interact with brands, and each other, in a digital world. The main purpose for the creation of "Mercedes Me," the twenty-second century gathering space (aka showroom) in Hamburg, is not for the participants to buy cars but rather to become immersed into the Mercedes brand experience through showroom motifs and a nonintrusive environment.[25]

A similar facility called BMW "Welt" (The BMW "World" in English) has been developed by BMW in Munich, Germany, near the firm's corporate headquarters. As with the "Mercedes Me" concept, the BMW facility is a gathering space for people who want to participate in the brand experience, especially those who are technologically savvy. Futuristic displays, interactive visuals, and audio presentations create a world where the brand appears as a natural part of the future (Figure 5.2).

Mass Brand Centers

Connecting through community also has become part of the non-luxury expression of experiential brand management. One example is the Red Bull brand. Red Bull is an extremely popular high-energy drink targeted for the Millennials. It was one of the first brands to sponsor action sports and competitive events when these sports were considered excessive expressions of inner-city youths. Red Bull continues to support these events (which have become mainstream) as well as sponsor young athletes. This involvement gives Red Bull enormous credibility with its target consumer (Figure 5.3).

The company's centers around the world provide a similar opportunity to embrace the brand by connecting with the lifestyle in technology, music, equipment,

figure 5.2
BMW Welt in Munich, Germany: These venues are not to sell products but to present the brand's narrative.

figure 5.3
A Red Bull–sponsored race car: Red Bull has identified sports that its core consumers are committed to and sponsors those events to co-create the brand community.

and related activities (for example, the company has a special physical training and nutrition center for athletes in Santa Monica, California) that the brand persona conveys.

MANAGING THE BRAND EXPERIENCE

As we review the prior examples it becomes apparent that given its complexities and importance, the brand as an experience needs to be managed. Essential questions must be asked and answered. What are the expectations and deepest desires of the core customers? What are the attribute **drivers**, those values and aspirations that are highly relevant to the consumers and highly differentiated from the competition that will transform a product purchaser into a brand loyalist? Which touch points properly managed for which cohort framing what type of brand will optimize the transformation of purchasers into loyalists?

The answers will, in part, vary by the brand category, such as luxury, premium, masstige, and mass fashion. In addition, the model is dynamic, so as the competitive market changes, the attributes that drive brand loyalty will change as well. This puts an additional burden on the brand manager to be a story listener (as described in Chapter 2) and to be aware of consumer-driven market trends.

The Brand Loyalty Matrix

A useful starting point is a brand loyalty matrix featured in Figure 5.4. Here, the brand manager can begin to frame the degree of importance of various touch points to ascertain which warrant time, money, and managerial support. To read the matrix, begin in the upper left-hand quadrant, move down to the lower left-hand quadrant, move across to the lower right-hand quadrant, and then move up to the upper right-hand quadrant. This will provide a sequence, which culminates in the objective of determining the drivers of loyalty.

Relevancy and Differentiation

The matrix is bordered by its two key variables: relevance, as we saw in Chapter 3, is the importance of the brand to the consumer because it fits his or her lifestyle, and **differentiation**, the perception of comparative uniqueness that the consumer has of the brand and its products vis-à-vis its competitors.

Relevancy, sometimes described as salience, should be the point of departure in the formulation of the strategy. This is to ensure that the process of developing a strategy remains consumer-centric. If we begin with differentiation, we risk falling back to product and product-centric thinking. So relevance (what the consumer wants or needs) drives differentiation (what the competitive market may look like). This is especially operative in luxury products, where the competitive market does not drive brand experiences, the relevancy of the brand does. In either case, the relevancy dimension must be "meaningful" or, in the words of J.-N. Kapferer to whom we referred earlier, "*The new strategic brand management acknowledges the need for meaningfulness*"[26] or deeper values and emotional connections. Here are more granular expressions of meaningfulness: "*To rise above the pack and*

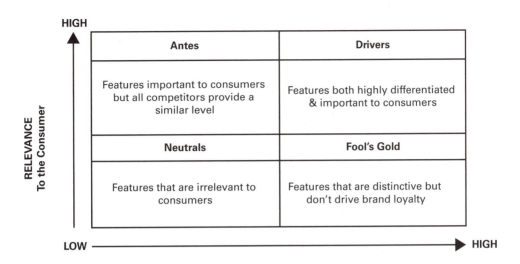

HIGH		
	Antes	**Drivers**
	Features important to consumers but all competitors provide a similar level	Features both highly differentiated & important to consumers
	Neutrals	**Fool's Gold**
	Features that are irrelevant to consumers	Features that are distinctive but don't drive brand loyalty
LOW		**HIGH**

RELEVANCE To the Consumer

DIFFERENTIATION
From your Competitors

figure 5.4

The brand loyalty matrix: Managing brands requires a permanent matrix for monitoring and analysis.

actually differentiate and win loyalty today, a brand has to meet consumers' emotional drivers and expectations . . . (which may include) a sense of personal connectivity, trust, or self-image."[27]

For non-luxury mass products, the intersection of relevancy and differentiation equals positioning. How do we present our identity as unique and compelling to a target consumer to whom we are appealing? At this point, it is critical that we accurately determine the competitive set since subsequent strategies will be built upon the accuracy of this assessment. Finally, as we've seen in our discussion of positioning, what applies for mass brands does not pertain to luxury brands. This is because luxury brands do not define themselves by determining their counter position to the competition but by their intrinsic and unique identity and by the loyal consumer who confirms that identity by the constant support for the brand and the business. This support also emanates from those

wanna-be consumers who partake in the brand experience through the brand's narrative elements and marketing communications and others who at times may make counterfeit brand purchases; this latter behavior dynamic will be revisited and explored in greater detail in Chapter 13.

Gathering Market Intelligence and Data

The competitors in your competitive set are not those whom you emulate or wish to be. This is often an error that start-up companies make, especially those with a strong designer-owner. When asked with whom they compete, they often mention a well-established luxury brand ("we're like Armani" or "our brand is a young Hermès"). This makes it impossible to determine the true competitive landscape upon which the brand must build its management strategy. Without knowing who you are up against, you lose vital information regarding items such as design details, pricing, and packaging.

In the absence of reliable competitive data, the brand manager can begin to collect market intelligence by asking pointed questions and making discrete inquiries. When speaking to store owners whom you might have targeted or whom you are currently calling on, you might ask, "Which brands would you consider we replace if they were not doing well?" Another question for a larger store such as a department store buyer might be, "With whom would we hang in your department?" A similar query to a customer would be, "If you couldn't find our brand, which might you buy as a substitute?" Speaking to independent sales representatives who carry products that represent your category is another sound approach to obtain current market intelligence. There are also various secondary research sources which can be obtained from libraries, especially articles from trade media. When all else fails, the web remains the first and last venue for information, and, if budgets and time permit, primary research should be the choice.

Although we'll discuss concrete examples in the next section, let's take a look inside each of the quadrants in Figure 5.4 and explore, in general, what touch point strategies they represent.

Determining Meaningful Touch Points

The upper left-hand quadrant, **antes**, is for those product or service features that are important to consumers but that all competitors offer at a similar level. Therefore, as in a poker game, this is the "ante," or the precondition for getting into the game. If you can't come up with the "entry fee," the consumer won't let you in the game. It also can be understood as what a brand needs "before" (or the word *antes* in Spanish) it can enter the competitive marketplace.

From a brand communications perspective, the features and benefits that are prerequisites for being in the competitive space should not be the message you communicate to your target audience because they do not differentiate you from your competitors. For example, stressing quality for an upscale or luxury product is a waste of time and suggests that you are "reselling" what is assumed by the consumer to be, in the light of price, image, and aspiration, a given. This raises the specter of credibility for the brand and can lead to uncertainty for the consumer and a reluctance to purchase.

In addition, we saw earlier in this chapter that generating emotional consumer experiences are becoming the paramount focus for brand managers. Meeting so-called rational expectations are what one analyst has called *"just the table stakes."*[28] In essence, the competitive perspective on determining the nature of your competition and the product-message-offers they are presenting to the consumer is necessary for brand management but not sufficient to generate brand loyalty. Here is how one industry pundit puts it: *"maintaining parity with category competitors in delivering on these rational expectations is simply the minimum for staying in the game."*[29]

Therefore, continuing to maintain this consumer-centric focus is a good way to avoid slipping back into a product-centric perspective. As an example, in a series of corporate training seminars with Brooks Brothers store managers, the challenge was how best to avoid their tendency to be overly product-centric.

The objective was to add to their already impressive skill sets by bringing a consumer-centric, brand-focused approach to their retail operations. One of the production-driven, product-centered mantras that was often heard in discussions between production managers and their associates regarding quality in the suits they manufactured was this: *"We put a lot of 'make' into our suits."* The expression "make" is a production/manufacturing term and a code word for quality in the men's tailored clothing business, and this was the type of expression likely to be heard by sales associates in their sales efforts.

The corporate training team reframed this expression to a consumer-centric perspective and contrasted it with the product-centric message it traditionally

Table 5.1 Product-centric versus Consumer-centric: How Descriptions Alter the Perception of the Product	
Manufacturing/Production Oriented	**Marketing/Consumer Oriented**
"We put lots of 'make' in our suits, for superior quality and value."	"Quality and Value are not determined by what the manufacturer puts into the garment but what the customer gets out of it."

conveyed. The two-panel comparison shown in Table 5.1 was presented in the seminars to the managers.

This shifted the focus and made the product mantra an "ante" rather than a "driver." It reemphasized that purchasing a suit is not only purchasing a garment but providing an emotional experience. Quality, given the Brooks Brothers brand and its stature, is a given, an expectation. To stress an ante not only wastes consumer time and marketing money on what is already assumed to be a given but could also raise some consumer doubts regarding brand credibility. In this instance, the learning outcome, given the clarity and commitment within the Brooks Brothers culture to the role of the brand, was readily achieved.

Neutrals, in the lower left-hand quadrant of Figure 5.4, have touch points that are often visually interesting or compelling but largely irrelevant for the lifestyle of the core consumer and insignificant as a competitive differentiator from similar brands. For example, marketing messages which communicate images on the updated styling of uniforms, even by designers of note, are interesting but lack seriousness as a driver of loyalty and are an insignificant competitive touch point. Together, low relevance and low differentiation have little or no effect on stimulating brand loyalty.

Fool's Gold, in the lower right quadrant of the matrix, is characterized by touch points that are highly differentiated from those of competing brands but are also of very low relevance to a consumer making a purchase decision among competing brands. These features or offers are often high in profile but low in staying power as brand preference drivers. They also cost more to implement and maintain, thus the reference to "fool's gold," or tactics that appear exciting or glamorous but whose return on investment (ROI) does not justify the expense. They do not drive a sustainable competitive advantage or a meaningful ROI, truly showing that all that glitters is not gold.

Last, drivers (the upper right quadrant of the matrix). Again, it is imperative that we determine the degree and the currency of the drivers as they will be subject to change. This dynamic reality requires our constant attention as brand managers. Consequently, we need tools and analytics that enable us to test and measure whether the drivers we are nurturing are still embraced by the most loyal of customers.

Some examples of these types of drivers are seen in the matrix in Figure 5.5. This includes a discussion of the tools and analytics needed to research and confirm which continue to be the operative drivers embraced by loyalists.

With the exception of the drivers, the examples in this matrix point to a failure to ask whether these features are both necessary and sufficient to influence customer choice and achieve consumer loyalty. Therefore, we should apply the following question as the test: "Is the touch point both *necessary* and *sufficient* to affect a loyalty outcome?"

Looking at the antes, both examples are preconditions for being competitive in the sector (hotels, airlines). Imagine an airline marketing its safety record as its main offer when safety is assumed by the consumer to be the brand promise. How about a hotel chain stressing in its advertising that its rooms are clean? In either case, the perception is likely to be that

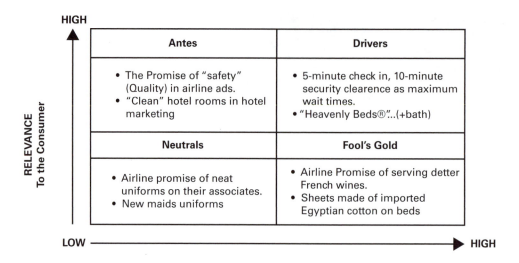

HIGH

Antes	Drivers
• The Promise of "safety" (Quality) in airline ads. • "Clean" hotel rooms in hotel marketing	• 5-minute check in, 10-minute security clearence as maximum wait times. • "Heavenly Beds®"...(+bath)
Neutrals	**Fool's Gold**
• Airline promise of neat uniforms on their associates. • New maids uniforms	• Airline Promise of serving detter French wines. • Sheets made of imported Egyptian cotton on beds

RELEVANCE
To the Consumer

LOW ——————————————————→ **HIGH**

DIFFERENTIATION
From your Competitors

figure 5.5
Applied insights for use in the brand loyalty matrix.

these are not brands that are to be trusted as serious competitors or as worthy of consideration as our "go-to" brand of choice. Safety and cleanliness are necessary preconditions for loyalty but are not sufficient to drive it.

By the same token, it's nice to have neat and new uniforms, but short of many of the industries' competitors' employees being shabby and sloppy, it is a stretch to believe that this can be a strategy with significant and long-term appeal as a loyalty influencer. In this instance, we would conclude that the touch point is neither necessary nor sufficient.

Fool's Gold presents us with another example of whether the touch points are both necessary and sufficient to command loyalty. The cost to locate appropriate vineyards, purchase, and maintain fine French wines is expensive. Each open bottle cannot be reused. For the hotels, Egyptian cotton with very high thread counts results in very delicate sheets and pillowcases which will still have to be laundered in an

industrial laundry. The fraying is likely to be extensive and replacement expensive. Even if maintaining the character of the wine and the suppleness of the sheets was solved, how compelling would it be for travelers to choose the airline and the hotel for these touch points? Almost everyone who can afford a hotel that features such sheets can own them, and few, if any, will choose an airline for its wines. These may be necessary differences but this is negated by whether they are sufficient as well.

As for the drivers, if you can find an airline that works with airport security and figures out how to significantly cut the waiting time in security lines and boarding times, all else being equal, you can be sure that company has found both the necessary and sufficient touch points that will guarantee it a lifetime customer.

But can a set of sheets and pillowcases become a driver? Westin Hotels figured out a way, which we will revisit later in the chapter.

Benchmark Brands

The first order of business, if we are to begin to think about how to identify drivers, is to obtain some **best practices** from those brands recognized as setting the bar of strategic excellence at the highest level of brand loyalty. As examples of those who have set the standard for achieving consumer brand loyalty (which I have labeled **benchmark brands**, or those by which we should measure our processes and our progress), we are going to review two brands that are truly industry leaders: the Walt Disney Company and Ritz-Carlton Hotels.

The Walt Disney Company and Ritz-Carlton

These brands and businesses were chosen first because they both are clearly benchmarks for consumer loyalty development. Both have taken their internal brand loyalty development programs and packaged them for outside resale and corporate training programs for other companies. Both programs have become acclaimed brand loyalty builders and successful enough to have become separate revenue streams for

their companies. Second, each has very strong repeat business from brand loyalists. Our objective is to see what we can learn from these brands for the purpose of managing the driver quadrant in the brand loyalty matrix. How do we go about identifying the experiential values that will constitute the drivers and sustain the relationship with the loyalists? Let's start with the Walt Disney archetype and brand values (Figure 5.6).

The Walt Disney Company is not in the business of theme parks or of movies; it is in the business of "magic." The theme park is called "The Magic Kingdom," one of the company's cruise ships is called "The Magic," and the firm has a history of magically turning cartoon figures into icons and memories, all reflections of magic and the main Disney archetype, **The Magician**. The magician can transform sadness into joy, a brand value that Roy Disney calls the company's mission: "Bringers of Joy." **The Jokester**, or the purveyor of joy and fun, is the second tier archetype for the Disney brand persona. The Magician creates the illusion wherein Fun and Joy appear.

For magic to work, there must be trust in the magician. In the opening statement on brand loyalty from the Disney Institute's "D'Think Your Way to

figure 5.6
A castle in Disney's Magic Kingdom theme park. Disney is not in the business of theme parks or movies—it is in the business of magic!

BRANDSTORMING SUCCESS: The Heavenly Bed®

An ongoing challenge that brand managers have is in avoiding dead-end touch points such as are found in Fool's Gold or in converting these dead-end touch points into something more positive. This is precisely what occurred with Starwood Hotels and its sub-brand, Westin Hotel.

The challenge of fancy sheets and pillowcases as outlined in our earlier example in the brand loyalty matrix was met and managed brilliantly by transforming a commodity (beds, linens, and pillowcases) into a brand. Managers developed a brand called Heavenly Beds® that became overwhelmingly popular. Here's how they did it.

Their staff had performed informal surveys of business travelers that resulted in an insight that became a business. What travelers discussed most was not their weekend clothes, their couch, or home-cooked meals, but their beds! In 1999, Westin Hotels embarked on a more formal consumer satisfaction survey. Again, they discovered that the features missed most by business travelers were, in fact, their beds.

It is important to emphasize that beds were an afterthought in most hotels and were seen as a disposable commodity that eventually would wear out and be replaced. Very little was invested in the category. The Heavenly Bed® changed all of that and moved a Fool's Gold touch point into a business opportunity and a brand loyalty driver.

The Heavenly Bed® was created and branded, and with it a differentiation that could not be copied because the brand promise was trademarked. In 2001, the Heavenly Crib® followed and garnished rave reviews from the National Safe Kids Campaign and its national director who lauded the brand for its concern for children. This rousing endorsement and the consumer buzz that followed led to more product extensions and even more customer kudos. Overall guest satisfaction ratings and loyalty indices increased as well.[33]

This experience was so relevant to consumers that Starwood began to offer the bed and other complementary products, all branded as Heavenly, for purchase. In the words of Barry Sternlicht, chairman and CEO, "*it helped our brand differentiate itself in a powerful way.*"[34]

By 2010, via the company's website, catalog, and Nordstrom, the firm had sold 30,000 Heavenly Beds® and over 100,000 Heavenly Pillows® and was voted number 1 in innovation at the National Business Travel Association; *The Wall Street Journal* also reported this with a tongue-in-cheek headline from Starwood's PR department: "*People Say Starwood's is Good in Bed.*"[35]

The brand extension strategy extended to bath, baby, and dogs and was poised to become a lifestyle brand. This would extend the circle of influence of the mother brand as its halo brightened and led the way to other business opportunities. "Heavenly" retail both direct and as a licensor followed. In the words of the vice

(continued on next page)

president of marketing: "*Since we launched the Heavenly Bed, we've strengthened our commitment . . . to Heavenly retail items and innovative wellness programs.*"[36]

New revenue streams from licensing extended the brand's reach into homes and transformed hotel guests into brand advocates. Again, guest satisfaction surveys continued to be strong. The transformation of a commodity into an iconic brand in an underserved category had become a reality.

As a concluding footnote, consumer satisfaction surveys from retail purchasers of the bed have been mixed. The bed appears, at retail, to be no more popular than many of its competitors. Is this a function of poor licensing oversight of the quality by the brand managers, or is it the perception of the bed in the hotel setting and the publicity it receives in that controlled environment that makes a difference? How would you go about determining the answer?

Success" program outline, we find this commitment: "*By building a bridge of trust, relationships (with consumers) are built . . . repeat business grows and the advance toward a sustainable future begins . . . the link to creating loyalty is established.*"[30]

A brand manager developing drivers for the brand loyalty matrix would, for Disney, focus on refining touch points of trust until they are confirmed by core customers and internal company metrics. Relationship building would be part of this and should be measured as well.

The Magician archetype serves as a conceptual metric against which both employee behavior and customer engagement and the engagement outcome, one of which would be "Joy," would be continuously measured. Another key metric would be the consumer's continual willingness to suspend reality and partake in the Magician's illusions whether they are the theme parks or movies. A measurement of this through sample surveys, focus groups, and/or in-depth interviews (all acceptable methodologies) would aid in continuous monitoring of the perceptions of the core consumers. Creation of an online consumer survey panel providing instant and continuous access to

current and relevant customer opinions would make sense here. Again, the rapid changes that are occurring in experiential loyalty dynamics and the fact that it is estimated to cost five times more to reclaim a customer than to retain one must create a sense of urgency on the part of brand managers; having a survey panel in readiness saves precious time and money. This is how a brand can maintain very high relevance and very clear differentiation.

The Ritz-Carlton's program is built around objectives similar to those of Disney's program, but it differs in that it is a luxury brand interacting with luxury brand consumers while Disney is a mass brand interacting with a mass customer base. Therefore, the drivers will differ. Let's begin by outlining the Ritz-Carlton Experience and the brand values (Figure 5.7).

The Ritz-Carlton staff are referred to as "*Ladies and Gentlemen in action!*"[31] As discussed earlier, in another training piece we find the Ritz-Carlton motto, "*We are Ladies and Gentlemen, serving Ladies and Gentlemen.*" The "20 Basics" are an additional source of brand values—in essence, the company's Ten Commandments—which every employee carries with her or him printed on heavy card stock. These

figure 5.7

A symbol of elegance on a Ritz-Carlton entrance: Elegance characterizes the brand and everything that employees do.

include calling guests by their names, escorting them to elevators rather than pointing, and "owning" a guest problem which each employee is empowered to solve irrespective of her or his position in the hotel. Every employee is authorized to spend up to $2,000 without authorization to solve a guest's problem. The Credo is another instrument by which the staff are guided toward the values of becoming engaged in experiential brand actions. Here is the opening statement: "*The Ritz-Carlton Experience enlivens the senses, instills well-being, and fulfills even the unexpressed wishes and needs of our guests.*"[32]

The archetypes for the brand are Caregiver and Creator. The first archetype, the Caregiver, or caring for others, is reflected in the mission statement (which opens with "*Provide genuine care*") and in all the other sources of the brand's values referenced above. The second archetype, the Creator, emanates from the actions of the first and is one who makes things of enduring value. Here that would be the relationships forged by extraordinary personal service and the confirmation of its success by the numbers of return guests confirming their brand loyalty.

These archetype values would serve as the basis for monitoring the drivers of brand loyalty. Given the various internal sources of brand values, one challenge for brand managers at Ritz-Carlton is to prioritize the various, although complementary, brand promises (The Motto, 20 Basics, The Credo, Mission Statement), all of which can be sources of touch points. Interviewing the guests also would occur and, contrary to the usual difficulties in obtaining the cooperation and participation of luxury consumers, the very intimacy of the relationship between the brand and the brand loyalists will make this less of an issue.

This intimacy and the relationship are, in part, reflected in the fact that each guest has access to the 20 Basics through in-room materials and can interface with any employee (which occurs) and question that employee's behavior in light of its standards. As the vice president of the Ritz-Carlton Leadership Center indicated when serving on a panel with the author in 2012, the phrase "*that's not very Ritz-Carlton*" is invoked to begin any such query and is known to both guests and employees alike. Guests therefore are accustomed, if they wish, to being engaged.

MEASURING AND LEVERAGING BRAND LOYALTY

Brand loyalty is a concept in need of both leveraging and measurement: leveraging loyalty in order to achieve business objectives such as market share or sales, and measurement to ascertain the degree to which, if any, it contributes to those business outcomes.

Emotional and Behavioral Loyalty

Consumer loyalty surveys are framed by four types of inquiries: emotional or sensory, affective, cognitive or rational, and behavioral. Each type or combination is designed to achieve different objectives, and research questionnaires should be written guided by those business objectives.

Emotional surveys pose questions that speak to feelings and are often driven by whether postexperience needs that motivated the purchase or visit were met. These are the standard satisfaction surveys (e.g., "How did you enjoy the restaurant?" "Was your experience with the salesman pleasant?"). The applications are for immediate corrective action, if needed, of the customer experience. There is no immediate or direct determination as to the impact of the respondent's answers on loyalty. It's assumed that a satisfied customer will become, at some point, a loyal customer. However, the assumption is flawed in that a loyal customer is certainly satisfied, but a satisfied customer is not necessarily loyal.[37]

This shortfall is partly due to the very nature of the metric, **satisfaction**, which is a short-term measure of a customer response to a survey question seeking to measure fulfillment. Satisfaction is most often a response to the immediacy of the need or the effect and therefore has no positive impact on future loyalty. As examples, the experience was satisfying because the outcome wasn't critical and/or the solution was immediate. It might also be a function of the fact that the store location was convenient which made the trip and the purchase a success. Satisfaction is fleeting, and later in this chapter, we are going to present and define its replacement, engagement, and in Chapter 11, we will present an in-depth look at how engagement can best serve brand management and help build brand equity.

Cognitive or **rational surveys** are those which capture the consumer's verbal expectations of products or services and are set up to mine utilities or practical outcomes that the consumer expected from the product attributes or benefits (e.g., questions of perceived quality based on product information: "Did the health food deliver as advertised?"). In this regard, such surveys are related to the "features and benefits" variables we discussed earlier in the chapter and would be used to assess satisfaction from product usage.

Affective/behavioral surveys are those which mine feelings of consumers toward products or services and ask questions regarding the experience in an attempt to mine feelings of engagement—that is, the relevancy to a consumer of the product or service experience on a deeper, more meaningful level. The questions are framed to mine the expectations of the consumer insofar as the brand is concerned and measure the degree to which there is an emotional relationship with the brand. In this regard, these surveys may serve as stronger predictors of loyalty. We'll explore this further in this chapter when we analyze this method's leading research proponent, Brand Keys.

Behavioral survey questionnaires are those which seek to determine future consumer actions or intent based upon current behavior, such as propensity to purchase or repurchase or to recommend to friends and family. This latter mode leads us to the leading proponent of this approach, Net Promoter Score.

Net Promoter Score

The Net Promoter System (NPS)[38] is one of the most widely used and controversial tools for measuring consumer satisfaction and, from that outcome, brand loyalty or the absence of it. The premise for the NPS process is based on the idea that the more you favor a brand and its products, the more likely you are to recommend it to others. And the converse is equally true: the less you favor a brand, the greater the likelihood you would not recommend it. This is captured by NPS by the answers to one simple measurement question that participants in an NPS survey are asked: "*How likely are you to recommend brand x to family and friends?*"

The questionnaire is organized on a 0 to 10 scale, with 10 being the highest. The results are scored by clustering the responses as follows: 0 to 6 responses are categorized as Detractors, those who are not brand or product supporters and would not recommend to family and friends; 7 and 8 responses are categorized as Passives, those without a strong brand commitment either way; 9 and 10 responses are categorized as Promoters and it is here where the brand advocates and loyalists reside.

A calculation of the survey results is then performed to arrive at a score. For example, if you have

45 percent of the respondents scored as Promoters, 30 percent as Passives, and 25 percent as Detractors, you would have an NPS of +20 (Promoters minus Detractors; Passives are considered neutral). This is considered to be a good score since it is a positive number and is higher than the score obtained by the average American company, which is less than +10.[39]

This number is not a percentage of supporters; it is simply a whole number that comes out of this methodology. There is also an open-ended question at the conclusion of the survey that asks "why" and which enables consumers to express their feelings rather than just responding to questions that seek only to solicit attitudes. Answers to this open-ended question often serve to generate more insights for a deeper understanding. Without this, the answers to the survey questions appear to some as a series of responses without much depth.

The proponents of the NPS process claim that the proof of the process is in its predictive capabilities. Survey results correlate with future business outcomes: low survey scores correlate with negative or slowing business results, high survey scores with more positive outcomes such as growth in sales and market share. Others feel the data from this are too sketchy and that one question is insufficient to capture the complexity of brand loyalty. The satisfaction measure is at issue here. Behavioral loyalty dynamics do not necessarily correlate with attitudinal responses gathered from sample surveys such as NPS since people often say one thing and do another!

There are some critiques of the measurement scales as well. The range from 0 to 6 is wide with various degrees of difference. To lump them together into one average number obscures what might be meaningful differences. The calculation of adding and subtracting also seems somewhat unsophisticated as it treats the averages as if they are all of the same qualitative value, which they are not, and as though they can capture the feelings and intensities expressed, which they cannot.

Its merit is that it is simple to use and understand as a company-wide metric. Also, it is a good point of departure for dealing with both positive and negative opinions.

NPS becomes a good point of departure because the questionnaire usually is administered from a telephone customer service group within the company as part of an overall move to better customer relations and it requires special sensitivity training (which is available from NPS trainers). This often results in gathering insightful nuggets of customer complaints and customer kudos. In both instances there is an opportunity to ask "why." Also, there is the opportunity to ask for the negatives and then convert them into positives. And for the positives, it is a chance to praise the loyalists for their commitment and for their advocacy. It also provides an opportunity to ask questions regarding competitors and obtain comparisons with your own brand and business.

Brand Keys

Brand Keys, a New York brand loyalty assessment research firm, has developed a method and a set of metrics for measuring brand loyalty and predicting within a twelve-to-eighteen-month future window related business outcomes such as sales and market share probabilities. Its key concept is the **brand loyalty engagement index** which measures how a brand of choice stacks up against the ideal that the consumer has for the brand in the category (e.g., autos, hotels, fast food) compared to the averages of a basket of competitive brands. The distance in responses from the competitive brands, compared with and measured against the proximity of the respondent's brand choice to her or his ideal brand, provides the index, or the measure of potential loyalty.

In each product or service category, four drivers are identified as the attributes and benefits and then are ranked higher or lower in importance per the consumer survey responses. For example, the key variables that are automobile behavioral drivers are fuel efficiency/environment, brand/design, quality/driveability, and safety/protection.

Although there are some rational or cognitive features and benefits questions (depending on the

CASE STUDY
Hyundai, USA

Prior to the financial crises of 2008, "*The Right Brand and Design for Me*" was the most important driver of loyalty to the Hyundai brand.[40] The crises did not change the variables but did change consumer priorities. The right brand and design became the second of four drivers of consumer loyalty, supplanted by "*Fuel Efficient and Environmentally Friendly*" which became number one. This shift underscores how brand managers need to be cognizant of shifting priorities driven by macro-economic factors. The fear of job loss and the costs of operating a car were paramount in consumers' emotional mind-sets.

Hyundai was a recent market entrant into the United States where it occupied the low-price sector of its competitive set with Toyota and similar low-price imports. The quest for a brand value proposition which transcended price and offered an emotional brand identity with which consumers could identify had eluded the brand managers.

The financial crises changed everything. In 2009, Hyundai announced that anyone who purchased or leased a Hyundai and lost his or her job could return the car for a full refund and without any worry of a negative credit report.

The offer resonated on an emotional level as the brand image moved from nondescript to a Caregiver/Rebel archetype, one who cared and cared enough to rebel against the time-honored rules of car financing. This is one of the most powerful archetypical combinations as it unifies two seemingly unrelated values into a complementary and more powerful single brand promise and dynamic brand persona.

Within a year, surveys confirmed that consumers' **consideration index**, their willingness to consider a purchase of a Hyundai, increased by 60 percent. And while the U.S. auto industry that year experienced a 22 percent decrease in sales, Hyundai enjoyed a 27 percent increase![41]

Clearly the brand managers had moved Hyundai's offers and promises beyond antes into drivers and repositioned the brand in the mind of the consumer as something special. It is this specialness, this unique transformation from a purely features-and-benefits brand to an emotional partner in life's journey, that put Hyundai and its core consumers on the road together to brand loyalty.

business sector), the overwhelming number of questions are written to capture emotional and experiential dimensions in consumers' feelings toward brands and purchasing. As a result, the index aligns better with the engagement metric that we feel is a better concept for understanding and predicting long-term outcomes such as loyalty.

Consumers are interviewed through a combination of phone, face-to-face, and online encounters; survey sample sizes are large (which suggests they cover a sufficient number of respondents to be valid) and cover all nine U.S. census regions (which suggest that they mirror regional differences in the United States).

The method has a high predictability index correlating high engagement rates with repeat purchases, which drive market share, increased sales, and brand loyalty. As an example, the Hyundai case study that follows shows how this method can be leveraged and the results measured.

Brand Loyalty Management Models

Once data have been gathered, there are several fundamental ways to organize them so that they can be managed for business applications. One way is the classic Pareto's 80/20 rule, and the other is the use of brand pyramids for structuring a consumer database.

Pareto's 80/20

In the early part of the twentieth century, Vilfredo Pareto, an Italian economist, discovered in his statistical analysis of certain social patterns a reoccurring quantitative distribution or tendency: 80 percent of various outcomes could be explained by or traced to 20 percent of the causes. For example, 80 percent of the wealth of societies tends to be owned by 20 percent of the population (in some more unequal social structures, 90/10). This theorem was applied to business and held up rather well. In analyzing sales or customer purchases, for example, 80 percent of the sales are usually generated by 20 percent of the customers. The same ratio applies to profits and other business variables.

The implications for managing data and confirming who are the potential brand loyalists becomes evident: once brand managers can identify the 20 percent, the ability to focus on and provide rewards for retaining those customers and nurturing them is now within reach.

Brand Loyalty Pyramids

Once the data from the 80/20 rule are discerned, they can be placed within a loyalty pyramid with the 20 percent at the apex (or 90/10) and other lower tiers with corresponding declining measures of sales and loyalty. This provides a good model for a general overview of how the business is maintaining its customer base and of whether there are any shifts upward or downward that need to be addressed.

Pyramids can be designed to reflect sales by tiers or types of customers, by frequency of shopping, or by the number of sales transactions by levels or customer

types. A pyramid also graphically keeps the brand manager focused on various metrics that constitute the basis for brand loyalty.

SUMMARY

Co-creation of brand value is a key dynamic in our consumer-centric world. It is anchored by the kinds of emotional perceptions and behavioral commitments made by consumers such as those framed by concepts like affective commitment: the more positive the experience over time, the deeper the loyalty quotient becomes.

Brand touch points are those moments and experiences when the customer interacts with significant aspects of a brand and its business operations. They are considered of prime importance because, over time, these experiences coalesce into brand loyalty (or its absence), and engendering loyalty is a key objective of every business. This interaction with brand elements is often encouraged by brand managements which create brand community centers. These facilities do not sell anything but offer interested consumers and loyalists a chance to interact with the brand in video and audio technology centers.

Managing the brand loyalty process requires a focus on touch points that are both relevant to the consumer and differentiated from those of the competitors. This requires market research to gather data on both consumers and competitors. As historical situations change, new cohorts of consumers, such as Gen Xers and Gen Yers, enter into the market, which requires shifts in touch point strategies to align with the newly identified values of such cohorts. Brand Essence can also be seen as a part of a brand's identity which also manifests itself in contagion, the psychological phenomenon whereby people perceive a brand's essence to be present in a brand's facilities, processes, and products. This associative identity tends to generate higher levels of loyalty.

For touch points to be meaningful to consumers, they need to be experiences that are both memorable and relevant. Brand loyalty is as much about this as it is about product or price, and for many brands and their customers, meaningful experiences are primary reasons for brand loyalty. In our study of brands such as the Walt Disney Company and Ritz-Carlton, we identified several archetypes that characterize these brands. Archetypes are important as anchors for maintaining a brand's identity and being consistent in interactions with consumers. The touch points that consumers want to experience when aligned with the brand archetypes serve to anchor these touch points. The Heavenly Bed® brand, for example, confirms that the need to listen with great care to customers and that a solutions response rather than an attempt to sell something can transform a Fool's Gold touch point into a driver.

Finally, the chapter explored two types of methodologies (Net Promoter System and Brand Keys) that help us understand the "why" behind consumer behavior. Knowing the "why" or the motives provides us with better insights than if we hear only consumers' reasons, which are often rationalizations. In both instances the common denominator is consumer-centricity, especially with Brand Keys, which focuses on how emotional "engagement" is a key variable to measure and predict consumer behavior. The case study of Hyundai points out how tapping into emotions through engagement helps the brand and the consumer. It's also important for a business to know its best customers and possible brand loyalists. The 80/20 rule and managing the data regarding them through the use of loyalty pyramids helps to achieve this.

KEY TERMS

Affective Commitment
Affective/Behavioral Surveys
Antes
Behavioral Survey
Benchmark Brands
Best Practices
Brand Essence
Brand Loyalty Engagement
  Index

Brand Touch Points
Cognitive or Rational Surveys
Connectivity
Consideration Index
Contagion
Customer Relationship
  Management (CRM)
Differentiation
Drivers

Emotional Surveys
Fool's Gold
High-Touch
Neutrals
Participatory Entertainment
Product Concierge
Satisfaction
The Jokester Archetype
The Magician Archetype
Utilities

CHAPTER CONVERSATIONS

- In what ways are experiential brand touch points different from features and benefits touch points?
- Why should relevancy drive differentiation and not the other way around?

- What do the Disney brand and the Ritz-Carlton brand have in common? How do they differ?

CHAPTER CHALLENGES

- Brand touch points and loyalty matrix management require monitoring, personnel, and big budgets and therefore are poor investments with low ROIs. How would you respond to this statement?

- You are the brand manager for a luxury brand and you are approached by Disney to co-brand a program for a Disney theme park. How would you go about assessing whether this is a good strategy for your brand?

- The Heavenly Bed® brand was a lucky fluke that is unlikely to happen again; therefore, it is not a good case study for guidance for a brand manager. Do you agree or disagree with this statement? Why or why not?

ENDNOTES

1. David A. Aker, "Five Steps to Getting Touchpoints Right," *Aaker On Brands*, January 9, 2013, www.Prophet.com.
2. For key discussions of the various ways brand loyalty manifests itself as both an attitudinal and behavioral dynamic, see David Aaker, *Managing Brand Equity: Capitalizing on the Value of a Brand Name* (New York: The Free Press, 1991); Kevin Lane Keller, *Strategic Brand Management* (Upper Saddle River, NJ: Prentice Hall, 2103), pp. 318–320; A. Chaudhuri and M. B. Holbrook, "The Chain Effects from Brand Trust and Brand Affect to Brand Performance: The Role of Brand Loyalty," *Journal of Marketing* 65 (April 2001).
3. See David A. Aker, *Building Strong Brands* (New York: The Free Press, 1999); see also A. I. Moolla and C. A. Bisschoff, "An Empirical Model That Measures Loyalty of Fast Moving Consumer Goods," *Journal of Economics* 4, no. 1 (2013): 1–9.
4. Alex Williams, "Move Over, Millennials, Here Comes Generation Z," *The New York Times*, September 15, 2015, www.nytimes.com/2015/09/02/fashion.
5. O. Iglesias, J. J. Singh, and J. M. Batista-Foqut, "The Role of Brand Experience and Affective Commitment in Determining Brand Loyalty," *Journal of Brand Management* 18, no. 8 (June 2011): 572; for additional confirmation that affective commitment is an important driver of brand loyalty, see V. Maheshwari, G. Logorfos, and S. Jacobsen, "Determinants of Brand Loyalty: A Study of the Experience-Commitment-Loyalty Constructs," *International Journal of Business Administration* 5, no. 6 (November 16, 2014).
6. Iglesias, Singh, and Batista-Foqut, "The Role of Brand Experience."
7. George E. Newman and Ravi Dhar, "Authenticity Is Contagious: Brand Essence and the Original Source of Production," *Journal of Marketing Research* 51 (June 2014), p. 373.
8. Ibid.
9. Ibid., p. 383.
10. Bernd H. Schmitt, *Experiential Marketing: How to Get Customers to Sense, Feel, Think, Act, Relate* (N.p.: The Free Press, 1999).
11. Paco Underhill, *Why We Buy: The Science of Shopping* (N.p.: Simon and Schuster, 1999).
12. Jack Mitchell, *Hug Your Customers: The Proven Way to Personalize Sales and Achieve Astounding Results* (N.p.: Hachette Books, 2003).

13. Caroline Tynan, Sally McKechnie, and Celine Chhuon, "Co-Creating Value for Luxury Brands," *Journal of Business Research* 63 (2010): 1161.
14. "Marketing the Mercedes Way," interview, *McKinsey Quarterly*, February 2015.
15. For more on the "co-creation" of the experience, see B. J. Pine II and J. H. Gilmore, *The Experience Economy* (Boston: Harvard Business School Press, 2011).
16. Jean-Noel Kapferer, *The New Strategic Brand Management: Advanced Insights and Strategic Thinking*, 5th ed. (N.p.: Kogan Page, 2012).
17. Edmund Lawler, "The Rise of Experiential Marketing." *Project Worldwide*, November 18, 2013, http://brandedcontent.adage.com/pdf/experientialmarketing.pdf.
18. Andrew Roberts, "Building Luxury Brand Loyalty via Exclusive Experiences," *Bloomberg Business*, January 31, 2013, http://www.bloomberg.com/bw/articles/2013-01-31/building -luxury-brand-loyalty-via-exclusive-experiences.
19. Ibid.
20. Ibid.
21. Tynan, McKechnie, and Chhuon, "Co-Creating Value for Luxury Brands."
22. Ibid., p.1160.
23. Ibid.
24. Piers Fawkes, "How IKEA Wins Business Through Co-creation and Collaboration," July 17, 2014, www.psfk.com.
25. "Marketing the Mercedes Way," interview, *McKinsey Quarterly*, February 2015.
26. Kapferer, *The New Strategic Brand Management*.
27. Karlene Lukovitz, "Emotional Expectations for Brands Reach New Highs," *Marketing Daily*, February 3, 2014, http://www.mediapost.com/publications/article/218607/emotional-expectations-for-brands-reach -new-highs.html.
28. Ibid.
29. Ibid.
30. "Program Content," Disney Institute, https://disneyinstitute.com/.
31. The Ritz-Carlton Leadership Center, http://ritzcarltonleadershipcenter.com/.
32. Ritz-Carlton, http://www.ritzcarlton.com.
33. "Barry Sternlicht: 'The Hotel Industry Thought We Were Nuts When We Introduced This Fluffy, All-white Bed,'" *Hotel Online*, August 30, 2004, http://www.hotel-online.com/News/PR2004_3rd /Aug04_WestinBed.html.
34. Ibid.
35. "Business Travelers Think Westin Is the Best in Bed," *Starwood News*, August 5, 2010, http://development .starwoodhotels.com/news/2/136-business_travelers_think_westin_is_the_best_in_bed.
36. Ibid.
37. For a further elaboration of the distance between brand satisfaction and brand loyalty, see A. Roustase-kehravani, A. B. A. Hamid, and A. A. Hamid, "The Effect of Brand Personality and Brand Satisfaction on Brand Loyalty: A Conceptual Paper," *Journal of Management Research* 7, no. 2 (2015), ISSN 1941-899X.
38. Fred Reichheld, *The Net Promoter Score* (Boston: Harvard University Press, 2003).
39. Gert Van Dessel, "Net Promoter Score (NPS)—Best Practice," *Check Market*, June 10, 2011, https://www. checkmarket.com/2011/06/net-promoter-score/.
40. Robert Passikoff, "Brand Loyalty/ U.S. Auto Sector," *Admap*, September 2010.
41. Ibid.

CHAPTER 6

The Brand Promise

AFTER COMPLETING THIS CHAPTER,
YOU WILL BE ABLE TO:

- Discuss how personas and archetypes inform brand promises.

- Compare and contrast luxury, non-luxury, and mass brand promises.

- Assess how brand promises differ in socially responsible company cultures.

"I'm not in the business of fashion, I'm in the business of dreams."

—Ralph Lauren

WHAT IS A BRAND PROMISE?

In the preceding chapter, we explored some of the antecedents and anchors of brand loyalty, including co-creation, brand experiences, and touch points. Now we extend this analysis and explore the concept of the brand promise, its relationship to brand identity, and the central role it plays in maintaining and optimizing consumer loyalty.[1]

A **brand promise** (sometimes referred to as the **brand mantra**[2]) is a promise to consistently deliver to a consumer a set of relevant, functional, and/or emotional experiences. The experiences can be **transactional**, which refers to purchases and the interaction with the brand's salespeople and selling platforms (both offline and online), and **existential**, those emotional takeaways that result from the latter and from the general everyday interaction with brand touch points (for example, the use of the merchandise or merchandise returns).

Because there is no central depository or authority which sets the definitions in brand management, the terms *promises*, *mantras*, *taglines*, and *slogans* are sometimes used interchangeably. For promises or mantras this is not a major issue as both marketing practitioners and marketing scholars often use them interchangeably. A brand promise, or mantra, is usually an internal company message (not to be confused with an advertising **tagline**, an external directive made to consumers) and is related to a positioning statement in that it says why the brand differs from its competitors and suggests its unique reason for being, or unique value proposition. It is a guideline that all internal members who interface with the brand should use as a guidepost in their everyday decision making. As an example, recall our discussion of the Ritz-Carlton Hotel in its internal marketing message which states,

"We are Ladies and Gentlemen serving Ladies and Gentlemen" and which provides such guidance.

The promise can, at times, be found in the **mission statement** (a company's expression of the brand promise) or in communiqués within the company. At Nike, for example, the essence of why the company is in business is to create athletic wear that promises to provide "Authentic Athletic Performance." You'll hear this mantra in internal exchanges among personnel. Again, it should not be confused with the company's tagline "*Just Do It*," which is consistent with and related to the promise but subject to change with a change in advertising direction. Think of the brand promise as a self-imposed directive to the people within the company, and a tagline, when it is consistent with the promise, made to its consumer outside the company. Taglines are usually found under a brand logo and show up in advertising.

A **slogan**, on the other hand, is more often found in the headline for an ad visual or ad copy or in the form of a **voice-over** (the verbal message played while the visual message is displayed) in a TV, radio, or online video which, if it's the headline, alerts the listener as to the purpose of the content, in effect prepping the consumer to be receptive to the message. If the slogan is at the conclusion of the advertisement, it's what the brand manager wishes the consumer to take away. As an example, think of the State Farm insurance company slogan, "Like a Good Neighbor, State Farm Is There," which is meant to evoke a sense of dependability but is not unique, different, or specific enough (in what way or how is it "dependable"?) to qualify as a brand promise. So, for example, the absence of uniqueness can be seen when compared with Allstate Insurance (a prime competitor to State Farm). Its ads have been using a similar slogan for several decades: "You're in Good Hands with Allstate." This effects a very similar association of the brand with dependable service and therefore doesn't work as a positioning statement.

Again, in some quarters, the words *slogan* and *tagline* are used interchangeably. We'll also see as we proceed in this chapter that luxury brands most often do not have taglines and when they do, those taglines are seldom changed (BMW's "The Ultimate Driving Machine" has been in place, under its logo, for over thirty years); mass brands, on the other hand, change taglines with great frequency as they respond to both market conditions and shifts in competitive positioning, something that luxury brands find contrary to their brand management strategy of timeless identity.

As brand promises become consumer experiences, they are transformed into consumer expectations. At this juncture, customers and brand managers develop an unwritten contractual obligation with each other. This obligation is contractual only in a metaphoric sense, but no less binding. Here, the venue that enforces this tacit agreement is the court of consumer opinion, dispensing "justice" by their support or rejection of the brand and its promise.

Each party to the contract, the manager and the consumer, obligates themselves in a **symbiotic** way, by serving and being mutually dependent upon each other for certain benefits and rewards.[3] The brand manager implicitly agrees to clearly and consistently provide the same relevant brand experience while consumers implicitly agree to behave at some point as loyal customers.

The definition of relevancy in the brand promise includes large measures of **authenticity**, seen as genuine concern for consumers' well-being along with the alignment of the brand's identity and business practices with this concern. Due to macro socioeconomic trends detailed later in this chapter, authenticity becomes a major standard to abide by in the "contract."[4] When the parties to the contract perform accordingly, both benefit. When either party fails to perform, repercussions follow. Both of these effects—benefits and repercussions—are discussed in the sections that follow.

For brand managers, the key to fulfilling the promise is to be clear about the brand's essence—that is, its unique identity by which it differentiates itself from the competition and makes itself relevant to its key consumer cohort. So, for example, for Starbucks it's "The Third Place," for Volvo it's "Driver Safety," and for Disney it's "Magical Family Entertainment."

We can also drill down past the concept of brand essence into archetype—that is, those deeply held, subconscious dispositions discussed in Chapters 4 and 5 which anchor the brand essence and which each culture develops and each individual in the culture subconsciously absorbs. In the Disney example, the archetypes are, as we discussed, the Jokester and the Magician. Both of these are clearly in evidence in the company's marketing (the fun cartoons and the Magic Kingdom) and, by referencing them internally through training and in meetings, enable their brand managers to stay on-brand (Figure 6.1). The brand promises are found in those communication elements

figure 6.1
Disney's Magic Kingdom and archetypes:
Here the cartoon characters capture the Jokester archetype.

(e.g., taglines) which are intended for the target audience and which capture and convey the spirit of the archetype.

Brand Promises, Personas, and Archetypes

Brand promises are anchored in brand archetypes and brought to life by brand personas. The **personality** (its identity over time) attributes of the brand persona humanize the promise and serve as a metaphor for a more personal communication between consumers and the brand.[5] It's part of the brand experience.

How Archetypes Inform Brand Promises

"When you connect an archetype to your brand promise, you have a better chance of delivering brand experiences that are . . . in-voice," the brand narrative which expresses the brand personality,[6] who it is for, and why it matters.[7]

The archetype provides an example of and a reference point for the behavior one can imagine the archetype would display in any situation, if the archetype were an actual person. This expected brand "behavior" can guide brand managers in ensuring that their decisions are "on brand" and thereby aligned with consumer expectations. Here is how one writer describes this effect: *"These archetypical expectations help people on the inside of a brand understand what is required to bring the brand to life . . . (and) they cue customers on what to expect in the brand experience."*[8]

As examples, if we look at Apple compared with Microsoft or IBM, what does the brand as a personality say to us? What might be our assumptions as to which archetypes are in play?

We might say that Apple is "cool," "approachable," a leader without being autocratic. We could agree that Microsoft and surely IBM are perceived, to one degree or another, as the opposite types of brand personas. Beginning with the iconic Super Bowl ad in 1984 and the rebellious message which promised to launch a new era in consumer-friendly computers,

figure 6.2
Steve Jobs in jeans and a mock turtleneck—the Approachable/Democratic brand archetype.

along with its energizing "Think Different" tagline as a challenge to PC users, Apple's personality is immediately seen as different from that of the other competitors.[9] First, look at its logo, an apple with a bite taken out of it. It is a logo with a "down to earth" feel. Then look at the structure of an Apple retail store—it is very democratic, easy to navigate, and no one tries to sell you anything; it's considered "friendly." Finally, Steve Jobs, the former CEO, would appear publicly in jeans and turtleneck shirts, creating an unpretentious image (Figure 6.2).

Contrast that with IBM's CEO in blue suits, white shirts, and ties. His persona is clearly more autocratic

figure 6.3
Sam Palisano, in suit and tie when CEO of IBM—
the Unapproachable/Authoritarian archetype.

and a reflection of the Ruler archetype—in control, follows the rules, must run the show (Figure 6.3).

We could go on, but what begins to emerge is that seemingly disparate touch points (logos, store environments, the image of the CEO) are all consistently aligned with the values and the promise of the brand and anchored by archetypes which help ensure its consistent execution; the **Creator archetype** (for solutions innovation) and the **Rebel archetype** (for disruption of the status quo, breaking the rules of the game) are the two that provide the underpinnings for the Apple brand persona and its personality. Although some might argue that Steve Jobs's personality was controlling and autocratic, we must separate the private persona of the firm's leadership from the public persona of its brand personality. This archetypical foundation and the expression of its value propositions serve as the guardrails keeping the brand promise and the brand persona in sync and on the same path with each other and with the brand's values.

The original Apple tagline "Think Different" gives permission to the consumer to be innovative, to

break the rules, and to join the brand in a contract whose promise is that it is okay to "think different." Apple promises that it will be with you as it thinks differently as well. This proposition is the very definition of an authentic brand.

Taglines as Brand Promises

Although brand promises appear in various marketing sources (such as content in company blogs and quoted commentaries of brand managers), they are most often found in company mission statements (which we'll revisit later in the chapter). They are condensed into advertising taglines and are usually found just below the brand logo. Taglines are most effective when they are condensed brand promises designed to inform the target consumer. This is in part because they then align with internal brand promises and employee brand advocates, creating a seamless communication effect with less chance of disparities between what is valued inside the company and what is communicated outside the company.

Successful taglines, when they present a brand promise, follow the three fundamental principles of sound brand management which inform this book:

1. They are highly relevant to the target customers' values.
2. They capture and convey a "solutions" rather than a "product" promise.
3. They contain an implicit archetype anchoring the promise.

Using these as benchmarks, let's take a look at two competitors in the same service space and see how each meets the listed criteria: United Parcel Service and Federal Express.

Aligning the Brand Promise with Consumer Relevancy

The importance of aligning brand promises with targeted consumer segments is not merely an exercise in communications but a fundamental business activity of brand management. It is made all the more

UPS and Fed Ex:
Comparative Taglines

We've chosen to compare United Parcel Service (UPS) with Federal Express (FedEx). Both are global businesses that operate in the same competitive space—package delivery, often with a targeted time or guaranteed delivery window. The following lists show the taglines each has used since the companies began until 2015.

UPS

"We run the tightest ship in the shipping industry"

"Moving at the speed of business"

"Synchronizing the world of Commerce"

"What can 'Brown' do for you?"

"We love logistics"

FedEx

"When it absolutely, positively has to be there overnight"

"Relax, it's FedEx"

"The world, on time"

The FedEx taglines follow a consistent, clear, compelling, and memorable emotional promise that recognizes the very anxiety that generated the overnight delivery solution. Its first tagline put it on the map. But notice that all the taglines reflect this original promise; they promise the relief of anxiety as to whether your delivery will arrive as planned. FedEx is not in the package delivery business, it is in the business of peace of mind, and its tagline delivers that highly relevant consumer message.

UPS, on the other hand, apart from the easy to remember alliteration of the "ship/shipping" metaphor, presents a series of uncertain promises. The first tagline suggests that the company doesn't waste money, but that isn't obvious; perhaps it's a statement about efficiency. The second tagline references "moving," but moving what at the speed of business? And how do I benefit from this? In the third tagline, "synchronizing" (much too long a word!) sounds like the company is in the master clock setting business. Without beating the point to death, the other taglines are equally without internal consistency as to the problem recognized and the solution offered. This is the result of the company's focusing on what it does, rather than on what it can do for you. Without this consumer relevancy, the purpose and effect of the brand promise—which is to inform and create a consumer expectation—are lost.

challenging when there is a portfolio of many brands that need to be managed. Often some of the brands in the portfolio are underperforming or no longer fit comfortably within the overall corporation's core competencies, or what it does best. We saw this in our discussion of Kering in Chapter 3 when we discussed how brand portfolio management is critical to successful luxury brand business outcomes.

This challenge is not confined to luxury brands. Mass brands are also managed in this way. Procter and Gamble (P&G), the household and personal care mass brand giant, has undertaken, from time to time, brand portfolio reviews. The most recent one by P&G offers us a look at just how strategic the relationship is between the brand promise and its targeted consumer. Here is what transpired.

In February 2015, A. G. Lafley, Procter and Gamble's CEO, reported at a Wall Street analysts meeting that P&G was continuing the dramatic overhaul of its brand portfolio which it had begun in the summer of 2014. This had been in response to falling stock prices and declining profits. As we've discussed, under review for possible selling or downsizing were as many as 100 brands in the portfolio of household and personal care brands! Here is a quote from the February meeting regarding Lafley's concerns and his strategy for meeting the challenge he was facing: "*We have to understand . . . the different consumer needs and wants. We have to nail it with the brand promise.*"[10]

With over $84 billion in revenue, Procter and Gamble (P&G) is the oldest, largest, and most successful consumer packaged goods company in the world. Yet the CEO himself, apart from the brand managers, displays in the above quote both sensitivity to, and a struggle with, how to create and communicate the brand promise so it meets "*the different consumer needs and wants*"! What makes this even more compelling is that it would be for a multitude of brands and therefore not simply one brand and one promise. Each brand and its corresponding brand promise must be tailored to, and aligned with, appropriate consumer segments and their "needs and wants." Only then will each brand earn its place within the portfolio.

This is added confirmation of the strategic commitment to consumer-centricity reflected in Lafley's edict issued to the entire company (which we explored in Chapter 4) that "*The Customer is the Boss*"!

This is quite extraordinary, and it points to our need to carefully analyze the challenges in this dimension of brand management. By examining successful, and not so successful, iterations of brand promises, we can learn what is a winning approach, and what is not.

Successful Alignments

Brand promises in brand taglines are successful alignments when they meet two general criteria: the first is that they are clear, concise, compelling, and memorable because they strike an emotional chord; and the second, and most critical, is that they align with the relevancy of the values of the targeted consumer. We need both standards.

The taglines that follow have stood the test of time. The companies that use them—Nike, Allstate Insurance, and DeBeers—have been using these taglines since each company's beginnings and/or from the taglines' inception.

Nike's "Just Do It!" is both a challenge and a promise. It provokes the amateur athlete to act and to do so, of course, in Nike gear. It addresses the anxiety that athletes feel when they are about to compete or to begin the physical commitment to the activity. But it carries an implied promise that it's not that hard, once you do it (Figure 6.4).

Like Nike, Allstate Insurance, as noted earlier in this chapter, has a tagline that has been from its inception the company's only brand promise: "You're in Good Hands with Allstate." Insurance and insurance claims are uncertain landscapes for most consumers. So again, levels of discomfort and the need for a sense of security are constants that need brand promises that will allay the anxiety associated with accidents, damages, and life's travails. Here, the promise is reassuring, but it is more a slogan as competitors entering the market (such as State Farm discussed earlier) have

figure 6.4
Nike's "Just Do It" tagline so resonates with consumers that its message even works on apparel.

erased, through co-opting or copying the association with the promise of reducing anxiety, any clear delineation of uniqueness in Allstate's claim.

Finally, DeBeers, the world's leading merchant and purveyor of diamonds, has tapped into a deep emotional channel with its tagline "Diamonds are Forever." This plays on two levels: first, the diamond as something of value that doesn't change in a changing world, and second, the association of diamonds with engagement and marriage and the hope and dream that it will be forever. Here the diamond, and by implication the ring, is presented as the seal of commitment, symbolizing and validating entry into a timeless relationship.

Unsuccessful Alignments

An example of a misalignment is Coors beer. Coors has been using the tagline "The World's Most Refreshing Beer" for some time. It is part of a more general campaign theme that attempts to anchor the brand in Colorado's mountains and its allegedly clearer, crisper mountain streams that are drawn upon to make the beer. Besides being flat (no pun intended)—that is, less than a memorable or an emotionally charged promise—is it relevant? Do beer drinkers drink beer to be refreshed?

In reviewing the Coors TV commercials, they display a certain consistency: young, 30-something, handsome guys and pretty gals at a bar, party, or event having fun and drinking Coors. The link to "refreshing" is not in evidence. In addition, there is no apparent archetype driving the brand persona or its promise. The absence of an archetype is often a sign that the brand persona, and therefore the promise, is either unclear or not relevant to the targeted consumer.

Volkswagen provides us with another example of a tagline which fails to communicate a promise of any consequence. "Das Auto" is the tagline appearing at the end of each ad in the brand's 2015 television campaign (Figure 6.5). In German, the phrase means "The Car." One assumes that the intention is to suggest that a VW is *the* car! First, not everyone knows the

figure 6.5
Volkswagen's Das Auto tagline message:
The promise is unclear.

translation (there is no voice-over explaining it even in TV ads). Second, how does this specifically meet the relevancy criterion? What is being promised?

Finally, Circuit City (at one time a prime competitor of Best Buy in the electronics space) devised the following taglines, replete with similar shortcomings: "Imagine That!," "Just What I Needed," and "Circuit City Makes it Simple." These are three of the taglines that were used from 2000 to 2007. There is an absence of any connection with the challenges that consumers have with electronics. "Circuit City Makes it Simple" comes closest, but we never know what is simple. Is it the purchasing process? The usage of the equipment (does the company have a consumer education program)? Credit availability? All of these? Does "Just What I Needed" refer to the consumer or to the store?! And, if the consumer, what is it that's needed that Circuit City would provide? Consumer relevancy again left curbside! (As a footnote, in 2008, Circuit City filed for bankruptcy and in early 2009 closed all 569 retail outlets in the U.S.)

MANAGING THE BRAND PROMISE IN LUXURY, NON-LUXURY, AND MASS BRANDS

As we indicated earlier, brand promises are most often found in company mission statements and presented through advertising taglines. However, today they can also be found on websites, in interviews, and in other public speeches by CEOs and brand managers.

Whatever the source, brand promises must be managed to ensure that they are consistent with brand personas and archetypes. This applies to both luxury and non-luxury brands.

When we look at luxury brands we discover an added dimension than isn't found in non-luxury brands. In the creation of brand promises, luxury brands reach back to their heritage to find the values that will inform the mission and, therefore, the brand promise. Non-luxury brands look to their history. This may seem like a small difference, but heritage is not at the mercy of history; in fact, it frames and animates history. History is subject to interpretation and to the opinions of the many; heritage is not. This tends to make luxury brands more grounded.

The Luxury Brand Promise

One outcome of being grounded is that luxury brand promises eschew the features and benefits strategy which animates most non-luxury brands. Here are some examples of luxury brands and how they construct their brand promises.

The highly successful luxury handbag and accessories brand Bottega Veneta has as its tagline this brand promise: "When your own initials are enough." This alludes to the artisanship in the product and heritage in the brand; therefore, the fact that you have chosen it is proof of your discriminating taste. This captures the need for luxury brands to create a *griffe* (from the French word for "scratch") or "*a set of special signatures . . . subtle cues that identify their products as their own even in the absence of an explicit logo or brand name.*"[11] The design and unique artistry of each bag conveys the brand identity. There is no need for displays of logos or icons to show off to others that you "have arrived" (a disposition of the Patrician luxury consumer which we presented in Chapter 4).

In a similar vein, Patek Phillipe, mentioned in an earlier chapter, is one of the most successful timepiece brands in the world. On its website is an invitation to "Begin your own tradition." This suggests that your purchase will align you with what the brand promises, a heralded tradition of excellence which the brand now shares with you. As a result, you have begun your own tradition and perhaps it will become for you, through additional purchases, a time-honored one.

Taking these experiential and emotional promises to an even more profound promissory level is Montblanc. The luxury writing instrument and professional accessories brand honors these aforementioned promises and goes beyond them to forge an even deeper meaning of the luxury ideal. Here is a quote from Lutz Bethke, the CEO, about the experiential effect of ownership. When interviewed by Forbes, he spoke of both giving a gift to yourself and receiving Montblanc as a gift from someone else: "*As a gift to you . . . it becomes a lifetime companion worthy to be handed down to the next generation.*"[12] The brand is an affirmation of how you are perceived and a confirmation, without the conspicuous symbols, that you own something of value that transcends time and place—a lifetime companion and an heirloom for generations to come.

Taken together, these luxury brand promises reflect the **Ruler/Creator archetype**—one who has the power to create an experience of lasting consequence. This archetypical combination is, psychologically, very powerful and helps to explain the staying power of luxury brands. The brand promise is that you will be able to create a world that is of your own doing and be elevated in the process. This strategy, which is elegantly presented and persistently managed by luxury brands, builds upon profound insights that consumer science research has discovered regarding the link between brand identities and personal identities and how they congeal into becoming our social identities.[13]

Empirical research confirms that we choose the brands that are like ourselves, or as we believe we are, or as we wish ourselves to be. The bridge, in this dynamic, which joins the brand to the consumer and the consumer to the brand is the brand persona; whether its Burger King's cartoon character crown prince or Armani's understated elegance, by putting a human "face" on the brand identity, it transforms an abstract word into a concrete image and, with our psychological consent, into someone like ourselves or whom we wish ourselves to be. We will explore this in greater depth in Chapter 11.

Brand Character

One significant outcome of this is that a luxury brand has a more clearly defined **character**, or invariable identity over time; non-luxury brands have a more clearly defined personality, or variable identity over time. The former provides a more solid foundation for developing a brand promise because, coming from its heritage, it has deeper roots which resonate with authenticity. And it is authenticity, as we will see below, that is a key consumer value in the internet age (Figure 6.6).

Character is meaningful because it goes to the essence of what a brand is (its being) and is defined by its unalterable DNA. This quality manifests itself in action, or what it does for others and how it forges relationships with them. Personality goes to the essence of who a brand is and is defined by its social self. It manifests its identity in words, or what it says to others. To a large degree, it is based on traits that others perceive in the brand (brand image) that the

brand has internalized (brand identity). Therefore, it tends to be less definitive and more subject to the changing dynamics of market pressures.

One set of outcomes from this distinction is that luxury brands do not chase trends or do consumer research prior to the launch of a new line. Non-luxury brands do both. Luxury brands have personalities, but these are based on their character because they emanate from their heritage wherein their character resides; non-luxury brands are in search of character that they hope will develop over time through consistent behavior confirmed by consumer loyalty. Time and consistency will result in defining who they are (the brand image) and can create a more solid foundation for defining what they are (the brand identity), or wherein character resides. The brand promise, once you know your character, is clearer and its impact on business practices more direct and immediate.

One reason for this impact is that its pronouncements and identity are seen as more authentic by target audiences and core consumers. Authenticity is, and will continue to become, a key dynamic in driving business outcomes in both luxury and non-luxury brands. This is the result of the intersection of two macro-social events: the first is the dominance of the internet in commerce and communications and how

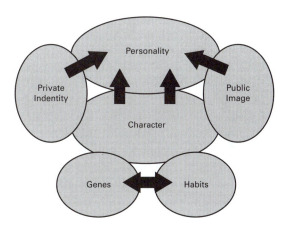

figure 6.6
Human character and personality: A model for understanding how brands develop personalities.

The key to a successful implementation of the brand promise is to pronounce the purpose for which the company is in business. It should be inspiring and uplifting but without the standard platitudes as to how "concerned" with their employees the company is or how focused on "quality" or "shareholder value" and the like. In essence, it should avoid the type of statements that might be found in the Antes quadrant of the brand loyalty matrix in Chapter 5. It should take its cue from the values found in the Driver quadrant, where the high degrees of consumer relevancy and competitive differentiation reside.

The importance of engaging company personnel should not be underestimated. Successful brand marketing begins from inside the company first and foremost. The employees, being the best potential brand advocates, can only begin to be so when they are clear as to what the company stands for; that is, what is its unique purpose as formulated in the brand promise and captured in its mission statement? This employee engagement is essential to the internal integration of all into a team and to the realization of the everyday objective of motivating each and every employee.

BMW (aka Bavarian Motor Works) is another example of a highly successful luxury brand that has integrated its mission with its tagline and brand promise. The clarity and character of the content is confirmed by the fact that BMW's mission statement and tagline have never been changed in over thirty years! The logo and the accompanying four-word tagline are shown in Figure 6.7. Besides the fact that

figure 6.7
The BMW logo imparts the feeling of a racing car with a blue-and-white rally flag motif.

a concise tagline is easier to remember, as a practical matter it should not be too long as it often needs to fit under the logo in advertising layouts.

Here is BMW's mission statement:
"*The BMW Group is the world's leading provider of premium products and premium services for individual mobility.*"

Here is the tagline:
"*The Ultimate Driving Machine.*"

What is so powerful about the value propositions in these two sources of the brand promise is that there is no mention of any products but only the brand experience. Had the copy referenced motorcars, it would have kept BMW from readily marketing motorcycles, snowmobiles, and the like, thereby falling into the trap of marketing myopia. The brand promise clearly

(continued on next page)

aligns with the relevancy of a target segment that longs for the exhilaration of driving a premium motorcar but speaks to the psychological dynamic of an individual's experiencing a certain "mobility" that the brand promises to deliver. This mobility conjures up the idea of "freedom" and, as a result, it resonates on several levels. On the one hand, it corresponds to the open road and the exhilaration of the "ultimate" driving experience. On the other hand, it hints at a confirmation of social mobility, for which the reference to "premium" serves as a code word, in this context, for luxury, promising the consumer will experience that as well.

The takeaway here is that the messaging is truly an example of **relevant differentiation**, or the successful integration and optimization of the two variables which frame the brand loyalty matrix.

Not every brand has a tagline that accompanies its logo in ads and on homepages. Some, such as Polo Ralph Lauren (PRL), express their brand promise through advertising copy and expressions of values which accompany fashion shows and online postings. The opening quote for this chapter, for example, comes from Ralph Lauren's 2008 brand **look book**, which is a compilation of images and pictures of that season's collection.

The test of a mission and a promise, therefore, is not necessarily in the creation of formal vision communications. As an example, here is copy of the voice-over from a series of sumptuous television ads run by PRL that ran as an introduction to *Downton Abbey*, which has aired from time to time on PBS's *Masterpiece Theatre*: "*I create a world beyond fashion. I want to conjure a feeling of romance and vintage glamour. This is how fashion becomes timeless and tradition becomes forever.*" This voice-over copy, produced in 2014, is remarkably consistent with the quote at the beginning of this chapter and composed some six years prior. The same brand promise, as literally expressed by the "brand voice" Ralph Lauren in 2014, is exactly as it was in 2008: "*I'm not in the business of fashion, I'm in the business of dreams.*" The preceding quotations are expressions of character born of a clear brand heritage and identity.

brands are subject to an ever-increasing scrutiny, and the second is the advent and ascendency of Millennials as the largest and most aggressively engaged cohort. With them comes a preference for acting over speaking and for the authentic over the contrived.[14]

The exception to the challenge that non-luxury brands face regarding character is found in those companies which are socially responsible and whose cultures of social concern are intensely authentic.

These companies are able to operate in a different way. They don't pander to public opinion, and they tend to behave in ways that are counterintuitive to conventional business wisdom. Later in this chapter we'll look at socially responsible companies that have seamlessly woven authenticity into their business cultures and business objectives, creating a new source of brand character. As they do so, they begin to mimic luxury brands.

Mission Statements

As mentioned earlier in the chapter, mission statements are often the ultimate source of a brand promise and the consumer-centric tagline. In addition, well-crafted and consistently communicated mission statements are the first steps toward internal brand awareness, which is a precondition for successfully building external brand awareness.

Luxury brands tend to show a greater consistency in aligning missions with internal operations and building internal brand awareness. Once again, this is the result of a clearer connection between the heritage, the mission, and its brand promise, which we've labeled "character."

But to be effective, the mission has to be part of a brand management strategy which integrates the mission into everyday operations; it must be something more than just a poster of promises pinned up in the stock room or posted in an employee's locker. What follows are several examples of luxury brands that consistently execute their missions and operationalize the brand promise.

Delivering Brand Promises in Social Media

"The promise of content marketing is that we can directly connect with our customers (but) . . . customers want to hear about what you can do for them. The smartest brands are aligning their content to something greater than themselves."[15]

With this vision of **content marketing**, and its focus on relevant communications for and alignment with core consumers, we return again to the notion of experiential brand management. The brand promise can be as key a strategic element online as it is offline and deliver brand values providing a seamless consumer experience between the two. The most successful brands online understand that the business they are really in is not about the product or about self-promotion but about the consumer and emotional needs, and they follow this vision accordingly.

Non-Luxury Mass Brands

Let's begin with the Subway food and sandwich brand. A visit to Subway's website shows strong, health-focused content with suggestions from experts such as nutritionists and trainers on how to live healthily. There is no suggestion that Subway sandwiches can help in this endeavor. In fact, recipes for cooking at home are featured! Subway also sponsors American Heart Association walks and contests for weight loss. The business the company is really in is *"helping you live a healthier life."*[16]

A stop on the LinkedIn site proves as insightful as Subway's site. Beginning as a platform for job seekers, LinkedIn has evolved into something more comprehensive. Its "Influencers" programs, for example, has inspirational commentary and informational anecdotes from high achievers like Bill Gates as well as everyday people regarding their own experiences. It positions the brand as a place for people who are ambitious and want to get ahead. Very often, the tactics used to build careers are innovative and are posted as learning opportunities. *"LinkedIn is now for anyone who has ambition."*[17] This is the business the company is really in—the business of encouraging ambition.

Where LinkedIn has succeeded, Facebook has not. Facebook's content strategy began on a solid footing, but the company soon found itself on a slippery slope. Its "Facebook Stories" was devised to be a content platform for how people used Facebook in imaginative ways with extraordinary results. The problem that emerged was twofold: first, there was no thematic structure as to what might be posted, so the site suffered from a lack of congruity, and second, the Facebook posting policy required that the stories had to be about how Facebook helped, something that is not required on LinkedIn. This invariably leads to a kind of censorship in the interest of brand promotion. It is the very opposite of what the **connective online community**, those who participate in and identify with social media groups, seeks from online content—objectivity and authenticity.

In a similar scenario, where Subway succeeded, McDonald's has not. Its content platform is labeled

"Mom's Quality Correspondents" and raises concern as it implies that real moms are writing real stories, which they apparently are not. The stories are crafted by McDonald's PR people and seem unable to tell a tale that is relevant to its customer base and one that isn't a promotion of the brand and its products. For instance, articles on McCafé coffee suggest that the company holds coffee growers to a higher standard. Why this would be something of such high relevancy to a mom that she would comment on it is unclear. Another article talks about how a Happy Meal toy is part of the brand experience and, by implication, is what concerned moms think about when they plan a trip to McDonald's. How this is factored in to mom's plan is never explained.[18]

We come back to our standard of relevancy which, given the transparency of all content on the web and its wide availability (including repostings of all stories), imposes an even greater responsibility on brand managers to abide by objectivity and authenticity and to align content with real needs of actual consumers. In this instance, finding out the real concerns of real parents who come to McDonald's for a family meal and clean restrooms would have been a proper start toward aligning content with community.

Luxury Brands

The Louis Vuitton (LV) blog entitled *Nowness* has been heralded as a model for a luxury brand's online content creation.[19] The story content was about those who created the online story, a kind of story within a story, and as a result it became experiential without promoting the brand itself.

Thematically, the story lines continued to play off the Louis Vuitton "Art of Travel" video with whimsical tours of Paris, New York, and other cities. It had broad viewership on YouTube and on its Art of Travel page on Facebook, where it had over 1,750,000 "likes." This content reflects LV's identity with the **Explorer archetype** (risk taking and innovation) and continues a seamless transition from the brand's first content offering in "City Guides," with its insiders' travel tips, to its travel journals; these journals are written by actual LV travelers as reflections of their feelings and their actual travel adventures which LV makes available for sale. There are no pictures of "best" vacation destinations or a travelogue of recommended hotels and restaurants. These are actual journals created by the experiential journaling of actual LV consumers and travelers. They are living examples of the archetype and anchor the brand solidly in authenticity and relevancy. Since there are no LV travel accessories featured, the brand is in the experience.

The LV heritage of indestructible steamer trunks and elegant travel accessories supports and guides the brand's character, which becomes apparent from the internal consistency of the content. The LV brand promise is that with LV, your travel experience will be like none other, even if that experience is virtual. Now anyone can experience the LV lifestyle. "*The beauty of Nowness is that it doesn't feel like branded content . . . it's a distinct, independent point of view that you can't get anywhere else—and that's what consumers are craving. A good example of how luxury brands can participate in the social digital space and keep their brand cachet intact.*"[20]

Another example of how branded content can be successfully packaged and presented is Burberry's "*The Art of the Trench.*" Again, anchored in the heritage of the brand and its iconic trench coat (and the Haymarket Plaid that came with it), the very name continues the tradition while the new media bring it into today's modern brand experience. The plaid is nowhere to be seen, but trench coats show up everywhere! As a nod to modernity, they are now designed to be shorter and are presented in ads as appropriate for rain or shine! They are fashion accessories worn by attendees at the various events (usually store openings and the parties that come with those openings). The videos are shot in Seoul, Tokyo, New York, Shanghai, and other cool fashion markets. The consumer is decidedly young—30-something men and women—the mood is fun, and the wearing is easy.

This content honors the brand's heritage while bringing it into a modern sensibility. There is no posing, and the product is not the centerpiece of the photography, but the lifestyle is, and that's the message and the brand promise.

BRAND PROMISES IN SOCIALLY RESPONSIBLE COMPANY CULTURES

Cone Communications, a think tank and research organization that tracks charitable giving by corporations and consumer response, has concluded that brand loyalty is increased by corporate charitable giving.[21]

In a 2013 consumer opinion survey, Cone Communications found the following:

1. 93 percent of U.S. consumers say that they have a more positive image of a company that supports a cause.
2. 90 percent of Americans say they are more likely to trust companies that support a cause.
3. 92 percent of Americans if given the opportunity would buy a product with social and/or environmental benefits.
4. 90 percent of Americans said they would be more loyal to companies that back a cause.

Authenticity in Brand Promises and Charitable Giving

The preceding data are further confirmation that consumers embrace brands that display character and authenticity. These brand promises, in turn, become part of consumer expectations of the brand experience as brand managers seek ways to embed these emotional drivers into the brand promise without compromising brand integrity.

In light of these findings, the brand promise has taken on new ways to express itself and new platforms upon which to do so. Corporate charitable giving, often to nonprofit organizations, has emerged as an essential expression of the brand promise. This giving back takes several institutional and organizational forms which have different impacts on consumer perceptions of the brand promise.

Cause Marketing, Philanthropic Giving, and Social Consciousness

Of these three approaches to charitable giving, Cause Marketing has the widest corporate involvement and the greatest exposure to consumer criticism.

It might take the form of annual contributions or an event such as Yoplait Yogurt's "Save Lids to Save Lives" campaign. In this campaign, for each yogurt lid sent in to the company, Yoplait contributes a fixed amount to the Susan G. Komen for the Cure foundation to fight breast cancer. Another example is P&G's support for the Special Olympics through its Brand Saver coupon, a special discount for certain product purchases. P&G then contributes a percentage of those sales made within a specific time frame. In each of these promotions, the programs are win-wins for both the charities and the corporations. The former enjoy the revenue from the corporate contribution, while the latter experience sales plus the strong possibility of building consumer loyalty to the brand driving the promotion.

The challenge is to remain socially responsible and create **social value**—that is, a measurable increase in realizing the objectives of the charity without exploiting the opportunity to turn the giving into a public relations coup by trumpeting the donations. In a study published in the *Harvard Business Review*, Michael Porter and Arnold Kramer concluded that *"as long as companies remain focused on the public relations benefit of their contributions instead of impact achieved, they will sacrifice opportunities to create social value."*[22]

However, there is risk in this type of giving. Yoplait as a brand has no intrinsic or organic relationship between eliminating breast cancer and its brand identity. There is no necessary connection other than that women may be the core consumer of the brand; the question can arise as to whether the charitable giving is an expediency. The promise of the brand, as presented in its ads, is that Yoplait is a low-calorie, delicious snack. The promise is not primarily tied to better health.

This is not to say that the corporate objective is not a noble one; certainly eliminating breast cancer is a goal we all would welcome. But what is the consumer perception of the giving? If the charity is not aligned with the brand promise and its identity, does it not run the risk of being questioned by the consumer as to its motives? Is it charity or commerce that is driving the giving?

A similar and perhaps more disparate connection exists between P&G and the Special Olympics. Apart from general use, how do Crest, Tide, and other brands in the P&G portfolio align with the Special Olympics? Again, the further the distance between the brand identity and the charitable cause, the greater the possibility of consumer disengagement. In the words of one observer of charitable giving and its impact on brand loyalty, "*While consumers seem likely to support causes with their purchases, Cone Communications also found that they are willing to boycott companies that behave irresponsibly.*"[23]

This is not to say that these charitable givings should end because they jeopardize the brand promise. It is saying, however, that the greater the distance between the brand promise and the charitable solution, the more cautious brand managers must be. When posting web content, for example, they need to be cautious and to avoid fostering the perception that they are promoting the charitable giving. In the words of another observer who follows corporate giving as Cause Marketing, "*Cause Marketing can be a tricky business . . . consumer perception can quickly lead to success or failure—to a positive brand association or a negative one that impacts your organization long-term.*"[24]

Corporate philanthropic giving is also a widely used method of major brands for giving back to their communities. This is less subject to the consumer scrutiny found in Cause Marketing. Again, the charities involved are most often not directly aligned with the brand promise, but philanthropic giving is almost always nonpromotional and without ties to an immediate sales and revenue benefit. This insulates the brand from some of the possible criticism that the giving is self-serving.

A good example of this is found in Brooks Brothers and its Golden Fleece foundation. Here, the philanthropic giving is viewed as an extension of the Brooks Brothers' brand value of relationship building. The giving is usually back to communities that are close to the business locations, but the public pronouncements of the donations, apart from a section on the company's website, are almost nonexistent.

The Golden Fleece is, however, well understood inside the corporate culture. In terms of heritage, as you'll recall from our discussion in Chapter 2, the Golden Fleece was a symbol of quality and integrity, something the Brooks Brothers brand strenuously adheres to. This connection is clearly referenced in the company's mission statement: "*To make and deal only in merchandise of the best quality, to sell it at a fair profit only, and to deal only with people who seek and are capable of appreciating such merchandise*" (Henry Sands Brooks, 1818).

This implies a culture of privilege and with it often comes the inferred responsibility to give back to the less fortunate. This mission helps to integrate the various functional teams inside the company as an internal brand promise of which they are justly proud and which has the effect of uniting and motivating the employees to be brand advocates.

Aligning Internal Company Values with Social Causes

The most successful Cause Marketing undertakings are those that integrate the cause with the brand's heritage and everyday operations. In these cases, social causes become company policy rather than afterthoughts.

Levi's commitment to saving water in the production of denim products is a case in point. The amount of water used in producing a single pair of jeans could serve as drinking water in a village for days. In fact, Levi's has joined with villages and NGOs (nongovernment organizations) in India to bring better irrigation methods to a sweeping number of villages in

India. The company has tied this back to intensive research on developing denim without heavy usage of water in the process.[25] From this social cause commitment it created a Levi's jean that does not need washing and resists dirt, odors, and stains. In one of many testimonials from satisfied users, a customer claims that he has not cleaned his Levi's jeans made with this process in almost a year![26] Levi's has created a separate merchandise presentation for this collection based in the idea of water conservation and garment durability, including special hangtags on each garment which explain the process and the social benefits. This commitment to sustainability was extended to the company's Dockers division with its Wellthread initiative in which the integration of saving water, educating workers, and creating more durable and less disposable products was continued.

This brings Levi's back to its Explorer heritage and the archetypal values and behavior of risk taking and innovation that accompany it. For some time, it had oscillated from Rebel to Lover to Innocent archetypes in different marketing campaigns in search of its brand identity. The brand promise became muddled.

With this new social cause, Levi's returns to its roots in the innovation space from which it originated. This anchoring in the Explorer archetype lends character and authenticity to this undertaking and has helped catapult Levi's back into market prominence. Having literally invented the category (denim jeans), the company has now returned and reclaimed its heritage. Levi's brand promise that it will be the Explorer is back. Here is the brand promise restated by Michael Kobori, vice president of social and environmental sustainability at Levi Strauss: *"Our company has been guided by the same principles since its founding 160 years ago . . . We believe that we can use our iconic brands to drive positive sustainable change and profitable results. Progress is in our DNA. We invented a category and with that comes the responsibility to continually innovate for each new generation of consumers."*[27]

The movement toward sustainability finds some companies that were launched not from an original product or service perspective but from a social responsibility consciousness. Two such companies are TOMS shoes and Warby Parker eyeglasses.

The impetus for TOMS shoes began in 2006, when its founder, traveling in South America, became aware of how essential basic footwear was and how often it was beyond affordability for many children. TOMS donates a pair of shoes to needy children around the world with each pair that is sold. To date (2015) that comes to over 35 million pairs of shoes in over seventy countries! Other product categories have been added to this charitable giving.

The degree to which this brand promise of giving is embedded in the culture is reflected in the company's website, which has updated versions of TOMS "Giving Story," and in the creation of a "C"-level position within the company, a Chief Giving Officer! Here is how this is described on the website: *"At TOMS, giving is our DNA and has been from the start! As perhaps the only company with a Chief Giving Officer, giving will always be core to our work as a responsible company."*[28]

Warby Parker (WP) does with eyeglasses what TOMS does with footwear, making them affordable and accessible to a broader population. As with TOMS, the impetus for the business was to be as socially conscious as the brand promise. For WP, this included becoming a **B Corporation**, a for-profit company that pledges to achieve social goals as well as business ones.[29] A B Corporation commits the business to pursue its self-imposed social responsibilities and requires compliance with this commitment or be subject to shareholder reaction and possible legal proceedings. This is the ultimate confirmation of the company's commitment to the brand promise.

The firm's social responsibility actions are seen as authentic by the core consumer because they have become the reason for the company's being. The brand promise is the social cause.

Of all these examples, the one brand that leads the way in the total seamless integration of social responsibility with its brand identity and brand promise is Patagonia.

CASE STUDY
Patagonia

Patagonia was founded by Yvon Chouinard, an avid rock climber, hiker, and outdoorsman. When he could not find high-quality steel climbing pins used for ascending a rock climb that were reasonably priced and did not damage the rock formations, he developed his own, and Patagonia was created.

This respect for the environment and quest for the innovative high-quality solution became the brand mission of Patagonia. Here is the company's mission statement from its website: "*Build the best product, cause no unnecessary harm, use business to inspire and implement solutions to our environmental crises.*"[30]

The company gradually added apparel and other equipment (e.g., for fly rod fishing). It also made the commitment early on to give back to environmental causes. The give-back formula was, and thirty years later still is, 1 percent of sales or 10 percent of profits, whichever is greater. Today, the company generates over $650 million in sales and is a B Corporation.[31]

The company culture expresses the company brand promise. Leaving work early to surf or hike or rock climb is encouraged without any reduction in pay. There is no punching in or signing out, and the company supports charitable work by offering flextime for it as well.

The company does little advertising. When it does, the advertising is thematically consistent with the company's brand promise of safeguarding the environment. Several promotional movies have been made (and more are on the drawing board) which provide hard facts on environmental challenges.

When traditional ads are run, they are environmentally charged. In an unparalleled ad in the

New York Times just before Christmas 2011, a Patagonia jacket was shown with the headline "Don't Buy This Jacket," admonishing consumers to make purchases of only what they really needed. This was reinforced on the website with the company's "Common Threads" and "The Footprint Chronicles" pages. The former advocates sustainability by asking consumers not to buy what they can't use or don't need. The latter presents, in sobering details, the amounts of water, toxic waste, and carbon dioxide expended to make and distribute a Patagonia jacket.[32]

The theme that "disposable" apparel was a threat to the environment was reinforced by a three-part company policy still in effect:

1. Develop products from recycled plastic bottles.
2. Allow consumers to return worn Patagonia products to the company for resale.
3. Open "Worn Wear" facilities for receiving, refurbishing, and reselling apparel.

In fiscal year 2012, when apparel companies were struggling with sales and bottom-line results, Patagonia experienced a 30 percent increase in revenues![33] "*The company is making money by living its brand promise.*"[34]

As a further commitment to abiding by its brand promise "*to inspire and implement solutions to our environmental crises,*" Patagonia's CEO Rose Marcario announced in early March of 2016 its role in creating a $27 million fund along with three other B Corporations, including two banks and a solar panel energy company, to install solar panels in 1,000 homes in Hawaii free of charge with more plans for other states as well. This outreach to private homes is a first for the company and extends its brand promise beyond sustainable practices which are in effect within Patagonia's organization.[35] This is another example of how, in authentic ways, Patagonia continues to express its brand identity and increase its engagement with brand loyalists.

SUMMARY

Brand promises are key aspects of consumer information that brand managers need to develop and manage. A brand promise or mantra is usually an internal company message (not to be confused with an advertising tagline) and is related to a positioning statement in that it says why the brand differs from competitors and suggests its unique reason for being, or its unique value proposition. It is a guideline that all internal members who interface with the brand should use as a guidepost in their everyday decision making. Brand promises differentiate a brand from its competitors and generate consumer expectations as to what experience the brand will deliver. Brand promises need to identify their archetype. These create the foundation for the brand identity. Brand personas complete the communication strategy by delivering the message in the form of a brand personality.

Taglines are the major means of communicating these promises. To be effective, they need to be concise, clear, and compelling and aligned with what the core consumer values and why she or he purchases the brand. When there are constant changes in the tagline message and a change in the consistency of the content, an opportunity to engage the consumer is reduced or lost.

The brand promise has to execute its purpose with integrity. That is, what is promised is delivered. For luxury brands steeped in heritage, it is often much easier to locate the brand's DNA or its character and identity which creates a clearer idea of what the timeless promise is. Non-luxury brands need to be more diligent in determining their identity and maintaining their character.

Mission statements are a good starting point for finding the principles and values of a brand's promise. They should guide the creation of the tagline, which should capture the spirit of the mission in condensed content. However, especially with luxury brands, often the brand narrative and the heritage contain the promise.

The very same principles just discussed should guide luxury and non-luxury brands online.

Finally, as consumers seek more and more authenticity in brand promises, socially responsible charitable giving becomes an important part of brand management. Those companies that have aligned their everyday operations and cultural values with the social cause are most likely to be seen as authentic. This is especially so when companies such as Patagonia engage problems and implement solutions to sustainability issues that are aligned with their core business competencies and brand identity.

KEY TERMS

Authenticity
B Corporation
Brand Mantra
Brand Promise
Character
Connective Online Community
Content Marketing
Creator Archetype

Existential
Explorer Archetype
In-voice
Look Book
Mission Statement
Personality
Rebel Archetype
Relevant Differentiation

Ruler/Creator Archetype
Slogan
Social Value
Symbiotic
Tagline
Transactional
Voice-over

CHAPTER CONVERSATIONS

- How do brand promises align with personas and archetypes?
- In what ways do luxury brands have a stronger foundation for their brand promise than non-luxury brands?

- Why is authenticity an important value for brand managers in B Corporations?

CHAPTER CHALLENGES

- You're the brand manager. Your chief marketing officer has been approached by a marketing agency to change your tagline. She's asked for your opinion and guidance. How would you answer her?
- "Social media and traditional media are two separate worlds and therefore need two brand promises." How would you respond to this assertion?

- Your CEO is thinking of changing the company's legal status to a B Corporation. What would be the key questions that the CEO should be thinking about?

ENDNOTES

1. For a detailed exploration of this linkage, see David A. Aaker and Eric Joachimsthaler, *Brand Leadership* (New York: The Free Press, 2000).

2. Kevin Lane Keller references the "brand promise" as the "brand mantra" in *Strategic Brand Management*, 5th ed. (Upper Saddle River, NJ: Prentice Hall, 2103).

3. Jean-Noel Kapferer, *The New Strategic Brand Management: Advanced Insights and Strategic Thinking* (N.p.: Kogan Page, 2012).

4. George E. Newman and Ravi Dhar, "Authenticity Is Contagious: Brand Essence and the Original Source of Production," *Journal of Marketing* 51 (June 2014).

5. Susan Fournier, "Consumers and Their Brands: Developing Relationship Theory in Consumer Research," *Journal of Consumer Research* 24 (March 1998).

6. For a more in-depth exploration of the brand personality concept, see Jennifer L. Aaker, "Dimensions of Brand Personality," *Journal of Marketing Research* 34 (August 1997): 347–356.

7. Laurence Vincent, "How to Bind Customers to Your Brand," *Inc.*, February 21, 2015, http://www.inc.com/inc.

8. Ibid.

9. Rob Siltanen, "The Real Story Behind Apple's 'Think Different' Campaign," *Forbes*, February 14, 2012, http://www.forbes.com/sites/onmarketing/2011/12/14/the-real-story-behind-apples-think-different -campaign/.

10. The Procter and Gamble Company, "The Procter & Gamble's (PG) CEO Alan Lafley Presents at Consumer Analyst Group of New York Conference Call (Transcript)," *Seeking Alpha*, February 19, 2015, http://seekingalpha.com/article/2932656-the-procter-and-gambles-pg-ceo -alan-lafley-presents-at-consumer-analyst-group-of-new-york-conference-call-transcript.

11. For an empirical study confirming this phenomenon, see Y. J. Han, J. C. Nunes, and X. Dreze, "Signaling Status with Luxury Goods: The Role of Brand Prominence," *Journal of Marketing* 74 (July 2010): 27.

12. Ariel Adams, "Montblanc on How to Be a Luxury Brand for Many," *Forbes*, March 14, 2013, http://www.forbes.com/sites/arieladams/2013/03/14/montblanc-on-how-to-be-a-luxury-brand-for-many/.

13. For an additional look at brands and relationship theory, see Hazel H. Huang, "The Role of Imagination and Brand Personification in Brand Relationships," *Psychology & Marketing* (January 2014).

14. Christie Garton, "3 Brand Experience Strategies to Attract Millennials," April 20, 2015, www.entrepreneur.com/article.

15. Ryan Johnson, "Content Lessons from Three Brands That Kept Their Brand Promise (and Three That Didn't)," *MarketingProfs*, January 8, 2015, http://www.marketingprofs.com/opinions/2015/26774/content -lessons-from-three-brands-that-kept-their-brand-promise-and-three-that-didnt.

16. Ibid.

17. Ibid.

18. Ibid.

19. Macala Wright, "7 Stellar Examples of Branded Content from the Fashion Industry," *Mashable*, January 3, 2011, http://mashable.com/ 2011/01/03/fashion-industry-branded-content/.

20. Ibid.

21. Cone Communications, "2013 Cone Communications Social Impact Study: The Next Cause Evolution," *Cone Communications*, 2013, http://www.conecomm.com/stuff/contentmgr/files/0/e3d2eec1e15e858867a5c2b1a22c4cfb/files/2013_cone_comm_social_impact_study.pdf.

22. Michael E. Porter and Mark R. Kramer, "Creating Shared Value," *Harvard Business Review* (January 2011).

23. Ibid.

24. Melanie Negrin, "Corporate Philanthropy, Corporate Sponsorship, Cause Marketing, and Corporate Social Responsibility," *For GrantWriters Only* (blog), April 27, 2011, http://blog.forgrantwritersonly.com/2011/04/27/corporate-philanthropy-corporate-sponsorship-cause-marketing-and-corporate-social-responsibility-csr/.

25. Leslie Kaufman, "Stone-Washed Blue Jeans (Minus the Washed)," *New York Times*, November 1, 2011, http://www.nytimes.com/2011/11/02/science/earth/levi-strauss-tries-to-minimize-water-use.html?pagewanted=all&_r=0.

26. Ibid.

27. "Levi Strauss Invests in Sustainable Design with Dockers Wellthread," *Apparel*, November 8, 2013, http://apparel.edgl.com/news/Levi-Strauss-Invests-in-Sustainable-Design-with-Dockers-Wellthread-89337.

28. "About TOMS: One for One," *TOMS*, February 27, 2015, http://www.toms.com/corporate-responsibility.

29. James Surowiecki, "Companies with Benefits," *New Yorker*, August 4, 2014, http://www.newyorker.com/magazine/2014/08/04/companies-benefits.

30. Patagonia, http://www.patagonia.com/us/home.

31. Meredith Derby Berg, "Why Advertising Is 'Dead Last' Priority at Outerwear Marketer Patagonia," *Advertising Age*, December 17, 2013, http://adage.com/article/cmo-strategy/advertising-dead-priority-patagonia/245712/; Patagonia, http://www.patagonia.com/us/home.

32. Jeff Rosenblum, "How Patagonia Makes More Money by Trying to Make Less," *Fast Company*, December 6, 2012, http://www.fastcoexist.com/1681023/how-patagonia-makes-more-money-by-trying-to-make-less.

33. Hugo Martin, "Outdoor Retailer Patagonia Puts Environment Ahead of Sales Growth," *Los Angeles Times*, May 24, 2012, http://articles.latimes.com/2012/may/24/business/la-fi-patagonia-20120525.

34. Ibid.

35. See Diane Cardwell, "Patagonia to Help Fund Residential Solar Installations," *New York Times*, March 10, 2016, http://www.nytimes.com/2016/03/11/business/energy-environment/patagonia-to-help-fund-residential-solar-installations.html?_r=0.

CHAPTER 7

Measuring Brand Value

AFTER COMPLETING THIS CHAPTER, YOU WILL BE ABLE TO:

- Distinguish brand equity from brand valuation and derive brand value.

- Discuss and assess the various methods for measuring brand value.

- Understand how to manage brand value in Luxury and Mass brands.

"What Gets Measured, Gets Managed."

—Peter Drucker

DERIVING BRAND VALUE FROM BRAND EQUITY AND BRAND VALUATION

Implicit in our prior chapter's discussion of the brand promise is the notion that external brand marketing, to be successful, must first be anchored by internal brand management. This includes not only the commitment and internalization of the brand's promise by its employees but also the management of **brand value**, which holds that every tangible and intangible brand asset that a company owns can be given an estimated monetary value.[1] This sets the stage for introducing the **brand value chain**, which frames the connection and the interdependency between the value of a brand as a marketing asset (brand equity)[2] and the value of a brand as a financial asset (shareholder valuations)[3] and calls for quantitative methods to measure their value.[4]

The quest to quantify brands as measurable assets emerged in business in the United States in the early 1990s.[5] It was driven by the emergence of brands, as we discussed in Chapter 1, as essential drivers of business value in Wave III of the evolution of American business.

This evolution helped foster the introduction of the concept of **brand equity**, a measurement that could provide a means of assessing how much value brands might be contributing to business development. Here's how one leading scholar has described this measurement concept: *"The act of combining a financial concept (equity) with a marketing notion (brand) is symptomatic of a growing awareness of the financial value of brands. . ."*[6]

The challenge that emerged, and continues, is to establish an agreed-upon definition and measurement of brand equity, brand valuation, or brand value as there is no central authoritative source for doing so.

Brand equity and terms such as brand value and brand valuation are used interchangeably. For example, one subject matter expert uses the concept of brand equity to describe every facet of value that characterizes a brand.[7] As there is no single, universally accepted concept, meaning, or metric, various scholars continue to present various approaches as there continues to be *"a disagreement within the community of experts."*[8]

Drawing distinctions between different aspects of brand value is important because they impact brand management strategies, some which are clearly consumer-centric while others are clearly finance-centric. Each would be better served through two separate concepts. By describing every brand value as brand equity we homogenize meaningful differences and fail to see meaningful nuances. This is something this chapter addresses. Hopefully the result is a more granular conceptual framework which is more reflective of how managers manage.

We will approach the challenge, as we have done in other parts of this book, from a commonsense market perspective and how words are used and understood in that context. We'll begin by suggesting several simple conceptual distinctions.

How Brand Equity and Brand Valuation Are Complementary

Our objective is to determine the elements that constitute brand value—how much or how little the brand contributes to financial outcomes and business objectives.

Brand value has two dimensions: brand equity, or the influence of consumer markets' perceptions on the value of the brand (which would include, for example, consumers, suppliers, retailers/distributors, fashion media, etc.), and **brand valuation**, or the influence of financial markets' perceptions of the value of the brand (which would include, for example, investors, stock markets, financial media analysts, banks, etc.).[9]

The distinction here is important because it enables us to focus on the fact that we have two separate but interdependent streams of influence—brand equity and brand valuation—both of which have to be managed. "*Positive brand equity drives* customer value (*or the lifetime monetary return on investment from each customer to a brand) which in turn drives* shareholder value or the increase in price of a stock, its dividends and other monetary benefits derived from stock ownership."[10] The distinctions that we've made, and the use of the term *equity* for consumer-driven value and the term *valuations* for financial-driven value, fit with the ordinary usage of the words in the marketplace.

Brand Valuation and Financial Markets

Brand valuation is the assessment of the brand by financial markets in terms of its contribution to the business at hand. Financial markets, such as the stock market, investment banks, and private equity funds, drive brand valuation. The word **valuation** is most commonly used as a metric to describe the value of financial instruments such as certain aspects of stocks traded on the stock exchange. For example, **price/ earnings multiples** or ratios, or the relationship between a stock's price and what it earns per share, is a widely recognized valuation formula used to assess the attractiveness or the lack thereof of a stock. So we have chosen this word to describe the financial value of a brand. Later in the chapter we'll present and evaluate a variety of brand valuation methods and formulas currently in use in financial markets.

Brand Equity and Consumer Markets

We have chosen to describe consumer market impact on brand value as brand equity. By **market impact** we mean how consumer behavior and the behavior of consumer-oriented players, such as retailers, impact brand value. Actions such as consumer purchases, brand loyalty, and the distribution of the brand in appropriate channels drive brand equity.

The word *equity* is often associated with the added value created by market demand. So, for example, the equity you have in your home is the amount of value that remains above its assessed value after deducting the amount that remains on your mortgage. Brand equity is similar. It represents the amount of value that remains after subtracting the value of the product from the value of an overall transaction; what remains is brand equity. Later in the chapter, we'll present and evaluate a variety of brand equity metrics currently in use in consumer markets.

Strategies for Optimizing Brand Value

Brand value, in its simplest form, is best understood as what your brand assets might be worth if you sold them in the marketplace. These assets may include your logos, icons, taglines, and intellectual property. They would include the degree of value that the consumer marketplace has embedded in the brand, plus what the financial marketplace perceives the value of those brands to be.

For example, you also would get an idea of brand value if you were a publicly traded company and sought to license your brand for product categories that you yourself did not produce. The strength of the brand and its association with the product category and the category's growth in the consumer market together with the stock price and its performance (has it been on a steady rise in market value?) would combine to create a brand value. As we will explore later in the chapter, this method is not adequate for a final valuation but does provide a starting point from which a value calculus can be determined. What we can conclude is that brand managers need to be conversant with both consumer market dynamics and financial market dynamics because the measure of a brand's overall strength tends to fluctuate with market conditions and the interplay of financial and consumer perceptions of value. These include identifying and **benchmarking** the competition, which provides a means of assessing the progress of your brand in the space where you compete.

The commitment to benchmarking recognizes the reality that all assessments, whether of brand equity or brand valuation, do not occur in a vacuum. They are meaningful only when they are benchmarked against what your rivals are doing. The standards of business achievement or shortfall are relative to the achievements or shortfalls of the competitors in the market in which you operate. This market is defined by its **parameters**, or its size, growth patterns, geography, and consumers, and it fluctuates in its dimensions and in its players who enter and exit, rise and fall.

Determining the Market Value of a Brand

Brands are intangible assets whose value is a function of perceptions. To capture the essence of an intangible, and then to quantify it, is a complex undertaking requiring knowledge of consumer behavior and survey research techniques as well as some rudimentary experience with statistics. To begin our exposition, we'll first turn to the two fundamental approaches to framing the research that will lead to a deeper understanding as to what drives consumer behavior. The two leading figures here are David Aaker and Kevin Lane Keller.

Determining Brand Equity

David Aaker's view of brand equity begins by positing four variables which must be researched and weighed; these include perceived quality; **brand awareness**, or the ability to recall and recognize aspects of the brand's position in the market such as the products; brand loyalty; and **brand associations,** or the feelings that the brand conjures in the minds of the consumer; and adds proprietary brand assets such as trademarks and patents (the latter are considered less connected to driving brand equity).[11] Aaker's study concluded that the strongest correlation was between brand loyalty and brand equity.

Lane Keller tends to focus on similar but different variables to explain brand equity. For him, it is a function of brand knowledge held by the consumer which is driven by the consumer's awareness of the brand. The level of awareness is confirmed by **brand recall**, or the ability to recollect certain messages or images

in marketing materials. This recall data and brand recognition are gathered by consumer research. This is often conducted in small theaters where a sample of targeted consumers is recruited to participate in the recall review.

Other research approaches are **aided awareness** (whereby consumers are shown the brand and asked for the appropriate associated product) and **unaided awareness** (whereby consumers are asked to recall and/or associate attributes which are in ads and which characterize the brand). Strong brand equity is, therefore, the degree to which these outcomes correlate positively with recall and recognition or the elements of brand association. These have been shown to correlate very strongly with high degrees of satisfaction and brand loyalty. Although we disagree with the linkage between satisfaction and loyalty (which we examined in Chapter 5), the evidence from both Aaker and Keller and others strongly confirms that brand loyalty is the major driver of brand equity. The **degree of equity**, or the strength of the brand, helps determine the degree to which the brand can withstand competitive forces, disruptive innovations, and shifting trends and continue to be a market leader.

Later in the chapter, when we examine brand value, we'll see the degree to which loyalty plays a seminal role in driving **brand strength** (based on relevance and differentiation in the brand loyalty matrix) and further adding to brand value.

Determining Brand Valuation

Determining and increasing brand valuations are essential for successfully executing a variety of brand management strategies. For starters, high brand valuations are important financial assets. They are used to estimate the degree of value that the brand contributes to the stock price. For instance, it is estimated that upward of 50 percent of Coca-Cola's market price is a function of the brand's equity and its contribution to it; McDonald's has been estimated at around 70 percent. Another estimate has the Google brand contributing 80 percent of its value as reflected in its market capitalization![12] Therefore, tracking changes in brand valuations is a way for brand managers to anticipate changes in stock market prices and overall **capitalization** (or the value of the company as a function of the number of outstanding shares multiplied by the stock price).

The impact of this tracing and tracking is significant financially. It can lead to lower interest rates and better terms when going to a bank for a line of credit since the higher the stock market capitalization, the more valuable the company, at least as potential **collateral** as security for a loan. Another effect from a higher value in stock market prices is that the highly valued brands have a halo effect on the overall perception of the company's financial well-being. One example of this is the change in the perception of value of Supreme International, a Miami, Florida, apparel company.

Supreme had begun as a private label manufacturer and distributor of moderately priced products, and was publicly traded on the NASDAQ stock exchange under this name, when in 1999 it purchased the intellectual property assets associated with the Perry Ellis International (PEI) brand from the Perry Ellis estate.

Perry Ellis was a very successful young designer who changed how men's apparel was perceived; his designs were both casual and elegant and easy to wear (this carried over into women's apparel as well), and, until his death in 1986, his business had flourished. The brand continued to have **cachet** as it was viewed by the market as having a distinctive and authentic look. At the time of purchase, the brand had been licensed to the Salant Corporation for various men's and women's product categories, and PEI did not manufacture any Perry Ellis products. Shortly after the acquisition of the Perry Ellis name, Supreme changed its corporate name to Perry Ellis International and its stock symbol from SI to PERY. George Feldenkreis, the CEO at the time, commented that it changed the company, or, in the words of one commentator, "*It elevated the Miami company to major status in the international fashion industry.*"[13] This is indicative of a high degree of brand equity which still resided in the brand, although its most successful years, from a sales

growth and profit perspective, were behind it and the Salant Corporation was struggling with the licensed businesses. The consumer markets responded to the perceived value of the brand.

In June 2003, PEI acquired Salant, the Perry Ellis brand licensee, and with it the Perry Ellis licenses that were still active. This now gave PEI control over manufacturing the product and distribution of the brand as well as the prior ownership of the name.

Here is where the financial markets come into play in the creation of value: "*The market responded favorably to PEI's acquisition of Salant. PEI stock price increased over 40 percent . . . six months after the announcement.*"[14] We should add that there were no increases in PEI's business from the consumer markets to explain the positive uptick in the stock price (in fact, PEI had a drop in corporate revenue that year), and this stock price increase occurred in a challenging retail environment and economy.

Such changes in the perception of value also have the benefit of becoming important drawing cards for recruiting managers, who are drawn to the company by the power and prestige of the brand. This carries over into pride of workplace, which is a motivator for the personnel of a company to work more diligently and to show higher degrees of loyalty. For those senior executives, recruitment incentives often include stock and related financial assets; thus, the value of the stock directly impacts their initial and future compensation.

Finally, in terms of brand portfolio management, knowing the value of brands within the portfolio enables managers to decide whether brands are undervalued or are not generating sufficient value vis-à-vis those of competitors. Managers can decide whether additional investments of time, money, and talent are required or whether brands should be sold off to strengthen the remaining brand assets in the portfolio.

The financial benefits of strong brands can also be seen in what is called **securitization** of brand assets wherein strong brands can be used as collateral to secure a loan against future earnings and/or cash flow from operations or licenses. Besides direct borrowing and using brands as collateral, the portfolio of brands in a licensing packet can provide a way for a company to transition from an active brand management company to a passive participant. An example is the Bill Blass brand that, for many years, was part of the American Big Three designer names on Seventh Avenue (Oscar de la Renta, Geoffrey Beene, Bill Blass). By 2000, Blass had a business that consisted of over fifteen licenses generating over $25 million in **royalty** revenues (a percentage of the selling price of each item sold and shipped) per year. Blass himself wanted to retire. The licensees were solid companies with long-term agreements to license the Bill Blass brand. He opted to take a monthly income, guaranteed from an investment group, backed by a bank, and secured with the royalty revenues and licensing contracts.[15]

Finally, brand valuations are important to support claims made by brand owners and managers during litigation proceedings. These valuations could be brought as evidence in court cases relating to improper usage or infringement of brand names and assets (we explore this in greater detail in Chapter 8) where brand valuations would play a role in the determination of damages.

The valuation of brands, especially in the U.S., began with the need to evaluate mergers and acquisitions transactions. As no business is ever sold solely on **book value** (or assets minus liabilities found on its balance sheet), the value of a business is not simply the tangible assets as found on that balance sheet. There are intangible assets found there as well under "goodwill":

"when Rupert Murdoch (current Chairman and CEO of News Corp, owner of the Wall Street Journal and Fox News) bought The Times of London, the first thing he did was to enter on its balance sheet a goodwill item of as much as 50 million (English pounds); when his solicitors said he couldn't do that, Murdoch asked why not? '. . . why do you think I paid 27,000,000 for it? . . . for the printing plant? . . . I'm shutting that down. . . . for its staff? . . . talent is for hire. . . . I bought it for its name.'"[16]

Goodwill is the catchall bucket wherein brand value can be found. Brands themselves are not listed, but their cumulative value is. Also included, although not spelled out, are trademarks, patents, and customer lists as well as "superstar" members of the management team whose names are not mentioned but who bring value to the company. All of the above add value to merger or acquisition transactions. One hidden value lies in those brands not included, which are those that were developed in-house; for now, only purchased brands, which is an accounting practice, find their way to the goodwill bucket as an asset.

Having introduced book value, let's look at what role it plays in valuations. A metric called **book-to-market** has been used to derive brand valuation by subtracting the book value of the company as found on the balance sheet from stock market prices and then multiplying by the number of shares outstanding. The result derived from this calculation is thought to provide a good approximation of brand valuation. The challenge here is to decide what is being measured. Does the stock market price reflect the market's perception of the corporation as a brand or of its products? Also, if there is a portfolio of brands that sit under the corporation's stock listing, then which brand are we measuring against?

Licensing is another source by which brand valuations are benchmarked and measured. If you recall our discussion in Chapter 2, licensing is basically renting the brand's intellectual property (brand name, logo, etc.) for a period of time and for a specific product category, and then manufacturing and distributing the product under the licensor's brand. For this, the licensor receives a royalty. The amount of royalty that the market will bear is used by some to ascertain brand valuations. This is called the **relief from royalty** method of brand valuation. Here the royalty rate is used as a proxy or a parallel measure for brand value. This is termed "relief" because owning the brand relieves firms of incurring the cost of licensing it themselves. This rate will vary among competitors in the same competitive space with the same product category. Therefore, the royalty rate is the value

The Coca-Cola brand has consistently ranked as the highest valuation brand in the world for thirteen years running, ever since Interbrand launched its valuation process (which we'll look at in detail later on in the chapter).[19] Although in 2014 it fell to third place, Coca-Cola continued to be the number one soft drink brand in the world. It is also a brand whose tangible assets are very limited. For many years the company did not own any of its manufacturing or distributing plants or equipment because the product manufacturing and distribution was franchised to bottlers. Coca-Cola had no inventory or raw materials to count as assets. Its asset base, and therefore its valuation, was almost entirely based upon its intangible assets derived from brand identity and market image. Consumer associations with the brand's archetype (the Innocent) and its brand persona were forged from over 125 years of being part of American life. The brand has created what has been referred to as an *affinity brand*, one that consumers have intimately embraced and are passionately loyal to because they believe the brand shares their most important values (Figure 7.1).

For decades, Coca-Cola's main competitor has been Pepsi-Cola. It still is. In the early 1980s, Pepsi slowly began eroding Coca-Cola's market share, and the trend downward seemed to have no bottom. This was impacting the Coca-Cola stock price as well.

In 1987, Pepsi, emboldened by its progress against its rival, embarked on a marketing and ad campaign called "The Pepsi Challenge." This was a series of "blind" taste tests wherein Coca-Cola drinkers were asked to try both sodas, not knowing which brand was which, and then decide which they liked better. Over 50 percent of the Coca-Cola drinkers preferred the Pepsi taste! Coca-Cola's management replicated these tests and again, over 50 percent of the participants (more than 200,000) preferred the taste of Pepsi! It was decided that the syrup formula needed to

figure 7.1
A classic Coca-Cola print ad reflecting the brand's image of good times and "Americana."

be changed and brought in line with the sweeter taste of Pepsi. A sub-brand, "New Coke," was launched in April of that year (Figure 7.2).

The reaction from affinity loyalists was overwhelmingly negative. The graphics on the "New Coke" can did away with some of the old imagery that had become so associated with the brand. Though over 200,000 taste testers seemingly confirmed the opposite, the new sweeter taste was rejected by loyal drinkers of the old formula. The Coca-Cola headquarters in Atlanta was bombarded with over 1,500 phone calls of protest a day; this peaked to 8,000 a day in June. In July, some eighty days after the launch, Coca-Cola announced that it was restoring the old formula and relaunching it as "Classic Coca-Cola." Shortly thereafter, Coca-Cola sales skyrocketed and continued their upward trajectory for some

figure 7.2
**Graphics on
a can of the
"New Coke":**
The classic Coke
logo and colors
draw on the
brand's equity.

time. The stock price, which had been hovering around the mid-$60 range, hit $87 by September and by January was at $101![20]

There are a few questions regarding brand valuation that emerge. First, how could anyone have predicted such volatility and how would this have impacted any estimates based on prior historical patterns?

Second, it raises the question as to whether the corporation or the product was being evaluated. In hindsight, it was clear that the taste was not the issue. It was the way in which the company leadership went about it; they never asked the consumers if they wanted a change of any kind! This places another major variable, the lack of consumer-centricity, in the valuation path that becomes a barrier to predictability.

Third, how does one factor in the relationship to the brand's affinity drivers, namely, the logo, the graphics, the colors, the name, the iconic shape of the Coke bottle, none of which was seen by the participants in the taste tests as they compared the two drinks from plastic cups! As we will explore in a later chapter on the neuropsychology of consumer decision making, the exercise of the sensation of taste is affected by the expectations of what it might be like. So-called taste buds do not operate in a vacuum, especially with iconic brands with deep degrees of affinity loyalists who are emotionally attached to the brands which in turn are attached to associated experiences and expectations.

And finally, the role of these brand affinity loyalists who are committed opinion leaders in driving a consumer definition of brand value is markedly different from the general public's short-term assent to the proposed change in the formula. The intensity and velocity of the outcry could not be measured or predicted by traditional sample surveys which in hindsight asked the wrong question to the wrong cohort.

In the words of the current CMO of Coca-Cola on the business it is really in and what should have informed its decision in 1987, "*the lasting power of our brand is built on the social moment of sharing a Coca-Cola with friends and family . . . creating these simple moments, delivering on our brand promise each and every day, remains our focus. . .*"[21]

This raises the question of what type of methodology works best in deriving brand value. As we will see in the next section, some models are based more heavily on financial variables and some on consumer variables as predictors.

The above case analysis suggests that assessing brand value from the financial analytics approach (stock price and market share) is by no means sufficient to explain the dynamics of value in deeply consumer-driven brand businesses. A closer look at the Millward Brown methodology based more on consumer dynamics, and discussed in the next section, will suggest that these types of models are better assessment tools and predictors of value than those heavily dependent on financial data. For example, in its "BrandZ" methodology, the company focuses on a definition of brand value as "*the dollar amount a brand contributes to the overall value of a corporation which provides us with a more relevant approach.*"[22]

generated by the brand and, thus, reflects the brand value. Also, by comparing what your brand can command with what the competition can command, you can also get an idea of how much more your brand is worth. The challenge with this method is that it looks down a narrow corridor wherein licensing is found. Not all companies are licensing all product categories, and some do little or none at all. Therefore, those competitive comparisons may be either incomplete or nonexistent.

Another approach to establishing a valuation is the **cost to replace** method (sometimes referred to as the **historical method**) by confirming what it costs to re-create a brand. This never bears the fruit that it seems to promise. Brands that have been around for some time now operate under a different cost structure as well as a different set of historical additives (such as the impact of inflation on cost estimates and the perception of the brand's importance). For example, changes in the competitive landscape might increase the value of the brand over time because it was able to withstand competitive assaults on its image and market position. Or, which may also be the case, the brand may lose value because it cannot compete, which reduces the "cost" of creating a brand. In both instances, there are too many variables that can't be weighted or held constant. These impact a reasonable valuation. So even if you were able to calculate the costs which are distributed over so many time periods, and with so many factors of so many campaigns and monetary investments, and even metrics which vary over time and place, estimating the cost would likely be an exercise in futility. Additionally, hidden dynamics, such as employee motivation, the "climate" of the times, and changes in the perception of brand value, make this an uncertain metric. Finally, we can add and conclude that "*there is no direct correlation between the financial investment made and the value added by a brand. Financial investment is an important component in building brand value, provided it is effectively targeted.*"[17]

The **premium price** method is another attempt to valuate brands. Here the calculation is based on the **net present value** (the value over a designated period of time less the cost of capital) or the price differential in the market that the brand will command over time in comparison with an unbranded or generic product against which it competes in the product category. This is also referred to as **gross profit differential**.[18] The first problem here is that many commodity brands seek volume for generating revenues and profits rather than premium pricing. Second, there may not be comparative competitors and when there are, there are variables other than price which generate brand strength.

It is important that we introduce at this stage the notion of risk. Almost all of the models and formulas that follow in this section factor in some degree of future risk in determining valuations. This is because most of the methods are concerned with estimating future value, so to be realistic they have to come up with some measure of future risk as a measure of uncertainty. As a cautionary note, do not expect these estimates and metrics to arrive at a set of absolute risks and/or revenues. What is important is that we see these as reasonable projections and guidelines for managing brand value.

Two methods that have stood the test of time include **beta benchmarking** and **discounted cash flow**. In beta benchmarking, the objective is to estimate the level of risk and how that might impact the brand strength. We want to understand the impact of market uncertainties on the brand's resiliencies. Here is the process:

1. Begin with determining the brand's **competitive set** (*set* means more than one competitor in the sector).
2. Create a basket of the same core products and pricing and measure the variation in pricing over time. For example, what are brands' pricing strategies which require discounts and to what degree in order to remain competitive?
3. Derive a value for your brand plus or minus the market average.

The other widely used methodology is discounted cash flow. The ability of a brand in a company to generate cash flow is often said to be the best sign of a brand's contribution and a company's financial health. This is because a high amount of cash generated over a reasonably even monthly distribution is a sign that the business is able to pay its bills out of daily revenues and operations and, hopefully, to generate a profit. No need to scramble to keep the lights on or to borrow against a credit line and pay interest. The word *discounted* refers to the beta benchmarking results or the risk. The beta result would be subtracted from the calculation and become the final brand valuation. A key variable here is the time line. How long do you project the cash flow? Is it five years? Ten years? Fifteen years? This is important. Too far out is unrealistic as circumstances in business often change so suddenly. The decision should be based on the volatility of your specific industry sector. The key is to ascertain a risk factor and a meaningful time line upon which to place it.

Several of the key measurement issues just discussed can be found in various marketing challenges experienced in Coca-Cola's history. Let's explore some of these in the context of a brief review of its history, brand identity, and brand value.

MEASURING BRAND VALUE

The measurement of brand equity and brand valuation is important not only because together they constitute brand value, but because they also lead us to the means of measuring consumer engagement and brand loyalty. These remain the ultimate objectives and goals of brand management. Brand value is, in our view, driven more by these consumer dimensions than it is by financial benchmarks.

All of the research models that we'll discuss gather their data from extensive consumer survey research, literally tens of thousands of interviews and questionnaires regarding a multitude of brands and broad global markets. This gives their methods a high degree of **reliability** that they are capturing a picture that is consistent and transmitting it to us in their research findings. Because they have correlated their assessments with measurable business outcomes, such as sales and profits, the methods used also pass the test of **validity**—that is, they are measuring what they claim to be measuring.

Proprietary Research Models

Consequently, as indicated above, it's essential that we look at the frame of research reference—is it consumer focused or is it financial focused? We are looking for a combination of the two, with a decided emphasis on consumer-centricity. Below are the leading methods and models currently in use that approach the value measurements in different ways:

1. Young & Rubicam's Brand Asset Evaluator
2. Millward Brown's Brand Dynamics
3. Interbrand's Brand Valuation
4. Brand Key's Brand Engagement

Young & Rubicam (Y&R)

Young & Rubicam's methodology is based upon the assumption that consumer awareness is the key to brand value. It is one of the most popular and widely used frameworks in the age of experiential brand management as it looks to consumers' feelings and their emotions to ascertain which brands are optimizing their value potential and which are not. The model measures two brand dimensions—brand strength and **brand stature** (consumers' regard for and knowledge of the brand). Brand Strength is based upon how fully realized relevance and differentiation are in the brand loyalty matrix discussed in earlier chapters. Optimizing relevant differentiation—the confluence of being highly relevant to the consumer and highly differentiated from the competitors—is the objective. Brand Stature is the degree to which the brand is held in high Esteem by consumers and the degree of Knowledge they have about the brand's identity. Brand building in the form of high degrees of these variables being in play in the consumer mindset results in the retention of brand value (Figure 7.3).

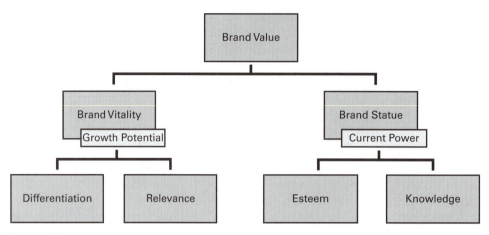

figure 7.3
Young & Rubicam's Brand Asset Evaluator: Outline of a model for measuring brand values.

Y&R's Brand Asset Evaluator asks a series of highly correlated questions of consumers concerning measuring the degree of intensity regarding

a. Relevance
b. Differentiation
c. Knowledge
d. Esteem

The objective is to separate the influence of product from the influence of the brand as a measure of the degree of leverage the brand has in affecting the purchase outcome. Two dimensions are set up to funnel the answers according to which dimension is operative:

$$Strength = Differentiation + Relevance$$

$$Stature = Knowledge + Esteem$$

The highest scoring of both Strength + Stature = Brand Equity is a highly consistent predictor of loyalty and sales.

Although the Y&R model argues that Differentiation should drive Relevance in order to avoid the brand's becoming a commodity with less perceived value, we believe the relationship should be reversed. Relevance (as discussed in Chapter 5 in our loyalty matrix) is the consumer-centric variable, and the need to focus on it stems from the emergence of the web and the power of the consumer to influence the brand promise. This does not mean that Differentiation or uniqueness isn't important—it is. However, it may need to find its identity as evolutionary, in that it is driven by the new cohorts who, over time, come to embrace the brand with a new vision as to its possibilities.

Millward Brown

Millward Brown combines financial and consumer data to derive a brand value index. As a result, it is a more comprehensive methodology than that of Young & Rubicam. One should consider using the Y&R model if the objective is to devise a consumer-oriented market strategy (e.g., build brand awareness). If the research objectives include financial objectives (i.e., increase market capitalization), then Millward Brown should be considered. Analyses, over time, have confirmed that brands which are successful exhibit the following attributes:

1. Consumer affinity
2. Relevance to consumer needs
3. An identity which is unique
4. Sector trend leader
5. Top-of-mind consumer awareness

The factors that drive the above attributes are the following:

a. The brand is meaningful, delivering on emotional and functional needs.

b. The brand is different, a sector or category leader, both unique and dynamic.

c. The brand is salient, displaying high top-of-mind consumer awareness.

"*These three qualities, in various combinations, are present in brands that sell the most, command the highest price premium and generate the most value (market) share growth the following year.*"[23]

The Millward Brown model, similar to those of Young & Rubicam and Interbrand, seeks to measure the degree of Presence and Bonding the brand generates in questionnaire surveys to a Share of Wallet metric. This metric may be thought of as a variation of "putting your money where your mouth is."

In all these instances, the shift to measure *feelings* as opposed to *attitudes* is paramount. This is driven by the desire to measure behavior and to find the drivers of actual purchasing activity rather than just building attitude-based preference or propensity surveys which too often have low predictive value (Figure 7.4).

The researchers at Millward Brown have also embedded into their assumptions, questionnaires, and research designs some of the more dynamic findings of neuropsychology and decision making. Although we will discuss this in more detail in Chapter 15, here is one way in which the approach lends richness to the researchers' inquiries not found in the other methods. For example, they explore the affect heuristic and how it impacts the concept of saliency.

The **affect heuristic** postulates that if we think of something, it must be important. The classic concept of top-of-mind awareness now takes on additional meaning and therefore becomes a critical dimension in brand management. The affect heuristic is a shortcut that the mind engages in when it makes decisions. It looks for more immediately accessible images and data that have been stored in memory. Thus, more salient brands have an advantage over those that are not as readily available and easy to access for the human mind.

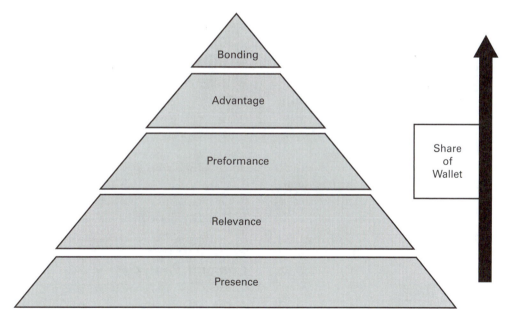

figure 7.4
Millward Brown's Bonding Model: How brands create emotional consumer bonding.

Interbrand

Interbrand is a financially driven method which has wide usage and application for research and management that have strong financial objectives. This means that its focus tends to be more on generating shareholder value, or the measures of value as reflected in higher stock prices, dividends, and more robust balance sheets. Its methodology revolves around three key components to measure brand strength:

1. An in-depth segmentation model delineated by financial performance, the role of the brand, and its strength in its sector.
2. A financial analysis which is based on the brand's generating a "*fair return on working capital*."[24]
3. The role of the brand in purchase outcomes.

Brand Strength is measured against ten major factors both within and outside the company. The internal variables are Clarity, Commitment, Protection (Brand), and Responsiveness. The external variables are Authenticity, Relevance, Differentiation, Consistency, Presence, and Understanding.

Upon reflection, it becomes apparent that the various factors framing the research as variables that affect value outcomes are often the same or very similar across the differing methodologies. For example, Relevance and Differentiation, which are key drivers of value, are found in Young & Rubicam, Millward Brown, and Interbrand, and as we will see and review below, Brand Keys. This is an important awareness since it points to a universally agreed-upon set of key concepts, which, given the global reach of these firms, establish the cross-border and cross-cultural application for data analysis and brand management of these concepts. This makes for a more unified strategic approach, which we will examine in greater detail in Chapter 11.

Brand Keys

For Brand Keys, Brand Engagement (BE) is introduced (as opposed to brand satisfaction) as the key independent variable to be measured. The higher the degree of BE, the greater the degree of loyalty and all the benefits that go with it. The essence of BE, and why it is preferred as the key metric, is that it is based upon a psychological model of human behavior that looks toward *expectations* as the essential explanation of loyalty. It asks a series of questions as to whether the brand meets or exceeds target customers' expectations versus expectations held for the product category in general and in which the brand competes. The distance between the two outcomes, measured against the Ideal Brand metric as the benchmark, generates a quantitative value or the degree of equity within the three brand sets and their relative distance. The expectation outcome calculated within each of the three brand sets is derived from the intersection of four primary psychological drivers—Awareness, Differentiation, Accessibility, and Connectivity.

Brand Keys claims that its data sets correlate at .85 (1.00 is considered a perfect score) "as a predictor of purchase behavior and loyalty to the brand." This .85 correlation coefficient is considered a very strong confirmation that the research findings are, in fact, measuring with a high degree of statistical validity that which they claim to be measuring and predicting.

Quantitative Methods for Measuring Brand Equity

Market researchers seek ways to mimic how consumers might go about making purchase choices. We know that a lot of it has to do with trade-offs between price, product, and brand. Part of this has to do with the affect of the brand as a variable in that decision. The idea is that if we can determine what the priorities and trade-offs are, we can also offer products and services that more effectively meet consumer wants and needs (Figure 7.5).

Conjoint Analysis

Conjoint analysis is one of the research techniques that present choice models to a brand's targeted audience. Through a series of both real and hypothetical trade-offs of features and benefits, the researcher is

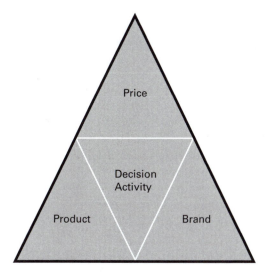

figure 7.5
Basic decision-making model factors that combine to affect consumer purchasing and loyalty.

able to hone in on consumers' priorities or what they are willing to give up in order to have something of net benefit to them. Used in conjunction with a segmentation model, the results can be aligned with different consumer types leading to different product extensions.

For instance, if Nike was considering a new athletic sock that had some special features and wanted to know which features were paramount drivers and which did not pique purchase interest, conjoint analysis would be a way to measure. Let's say the brand manager wanted to know if antibacterial was a more important feature than **wicking** (keeping perspiration from affecting the socks' performance). Let's also say that the manager wondered if the sock would be received as well if it were a private brand or the Nike brand. That is, was there some question as to whether the features were more or less credible given the brand as a feature? By alternating the features mix and then measuring the degree of purchase interest, conjoint analysis generates a good idea of which combinations are likely to be solid sellers and to which consumer cohorts.

Measuring brand equity would work here as well. The approach would include presenting the product with various combinations of features and benefits to see which combinations the consumers found preferable. Mixing price levels with the Nike brand, and then alternating lower pricing and testing the private brand, one gets an idea of how much equity is in the Nike brand that enables a higher retail price to be charged (and with what latitude) and either all the new features or some to be retained in the product and the resulting degree of preference.

An important caveat here is that conjoint analysis predicts preferences, not market share. It cannot tell you how much you're likely to sell, only what combinations are likely to work best. In addition, it assumes availability in the market and awareness of that availability on the part of the target consumer.[25]

Discrete Choice Models

Brand equity exists as a function of consumer choice. Brand management is concerned with communicating the brand identity and building a brand image in the mind of the consumer, leading to a purchase choice. But what is that brand image worth? Do we know how much "equity" in the brand drove the purchase decision? In this instance, price is one variable driving choice; others may be the stature of the brand and its brand image. The distinction between conjoint analysis and discrete choice is that the latter deals with real competitive products, prices, and brands all shown together, simulating a real purchase scenario. Price levels and brands are alternated and consumers "vote" their preference and likelihood to purchase. Brands can be removed and prices adjusted until an optimized brand/product/price is derived. Because it is a comparison with real competitors, a market share percentage can be generated as one of the outcomes. Pricing and promotion strategies become available and provide a good read on how changes in pricing and margins are likely to impact sales and market share. We can see how much price elasticity there is relative to the brand strength. The distance provides the measure of brand equity.

In 2007 Walmart contacted WDA's Apparel Analytics™ and asked if it could temporarily partner with one of the leading research companies in the U.S. The objective was to revive Walmart's ailing apparel business. A research project was in order to ascertain the root of the problem and to offer meaningful remedies.

Management at the world's largest retailer felt that, in certain product categories such as denim and casual weekend wear, they could and should command a larger share of the market. Second, margins were much lower than industry norms and there was a sense that perhaps the inventory levels and assortments were excessive in relationship to demand and, therefore, a **less is more** strategy (an evaluation of whether inventory levels and assortments are excessive relative to consumers' purchase patterns whereby smaller inventories can still serve most consumers' needs) should be explored.

The research proposal submitted to Walmart was designed to elicit the following information, which became the research objectives:

1. What degrees of brand equity, if any, resided in the house brands that would enable management to increase prices without decreasing sales or the velocity at which the merchandise "**turned**" (that is, the pace at which it sold each week within a predefined seasonal window)?
2. Are there certain brands that command sufficient loyalty that a paring down of the range of colors and styles would only marginally impact choice and customer satisfaction?
3. How did brands owned by Walmart stack up to, and compete with, the major national brands in value? What factors made the higher priced national brands more likely to be chosen than the Walmart brands or vice versa. in the same product categories? What is the **price elasticity of demand**, or the degree to which the equity in the national brand supersedes the perception of lower price as the driver of a consumer choice?

The method chosen to conduct this research was Discrete Choice. Walmart management had identified two cohorts that were steady Walmart shoppers in the departments where the apparel was being studied. Management also believed, given the cohorts' shopping habits and patterns which had been charted over time, that they were the target consumers. Their internal cohort designations were Brand Aspirationals and Price Value Shoppers.

The samples of over 1,000 shoppers from each of these cohorts were drawn from Walmart's database. The survey was conducted online. Participants were subjected to visual and verbal stimuli mining their opinions and perceptions. For example, animated avatars wearing the products were shown and brands and associated pricing were presented while preference and the degree of commitment were solicited from the shoppers. In classic Discrete Choice manner, attributes (in this instance, brand and price) were adjusted until the highest quotient of positive responses

(continued on next page)

was obtained and the brand equities recorded. *"Testing the styles with different brands in separate samples allowed us to identify whether styles are driving prices or if brands are driving prices."* [26]

Here are two of the major findings:

1. Brand equity in the denim category of Walmart house brands was 10 percent more than expected; this provided an opportunity to increase margins without losing sales.
2. Style preference was such that when aligned with some house brands, the equity in the brand supported the "less is

more" merchandising strategy. Specifically, **SKUs** (stock counting units) from selected assortments could be reduced by up to one-third and it would still satisfy 90 percent of consumer choices in the category. This leads to an enormous savings in inventory while maintaining close to a 100 percent choice assortment for consumers.

These conclusions from the research provide a solid example of how Discrete Choice can be used to identify brand value in competitive scenarios and apply brand equity measures to devise a strategy that can eventually add valuation to the brand as well.

MANAGING BRAND VALUE: LUXURY AND MASS

The irony of the Coca-Cola taste test debacle was that in managers' rush to protect the value of the brand, they momentarily forgot the value in the brand; they were reminded by their loyalists. There is also the question of leadership. When Roberto Goizueta became CEO and chairman in 1982, he vowed to be the "Chairman of Change." Within two years of his taking office, he oversaw the launch of Diet Coke, Cherry Coke, and "New Coke" in 1985. Was this search for market share more a reaction to Pepsi's inroads than it was to sound brand management? Was his personal pledge to shake up a conservative company culture stronger than the brand promise?

Brand Value Management

In luxury brands, there is always less chance of this kind of failure occurring. First, they are not reactors to consumer trends but trendsetters. Second, they often have brand guardian teams. These teams are a balance of creativity and business instincts and are, first and foremost, brand guardians. We have seen this with Tom Ford and Domenico De Sole at Gucci, Marc Jacobs and Robert Duffy at Yves Saint Laurent and later Louis Vuitton, and Patrizio Bertelli and Miuccia Prada at Prada. These teams have generated margins for their luxury brands far greater than those of mass or fashion or premium brands and thus can afford to take more time to make any corrections that they deem necessary. As a result, they are not driven by stock market prices or such valuations but take a longer view. Of course, when they are part of an international conglomerate such as LVMH, some of these considerations give way to corporate realities such as balancing **brand portfolio yields** so each brand is contributing to the overall financial health of the corporation. Still, the strong managers hold on to their guardian responsibilities, and insightful corporate leaders such as LVMH's Bernard Arnault allow them the latitude to do so.

Luxury Strategies

Although luxury brands are known to undertake awareness research, they are more concerned with brand identity—that is, what constitutes the awareness, and is it in line with the brand's DNA?[27] The reason for this approach is that the value of the brand is key to strategic decisions and is therefore anchored, for luxury, more in the brand's essence. This is all part of a value strategy that is uniquely luxury's: "*the financial strategy of a luxury brand will be to maximize not the net profit, but the brand's value and this is very different from traditional strategies.*"[28]

This is made possible by very high margins (often around 80 percent) and the avoidance of seeking **economies of scale**, or increasing production to where the greatest cost savings are realized relative to the highest output of units. This too often leads to reducing the intrinsic craftsmanship of luxury and risks as well eliminating the mystique of rarity which generates the perception of value.

Looking at Interbrand's valuation rankings, luxury brands are ranked with other brands whose revenues are significantly higher but whose brand value is relatively low. The strategy of luxury is always to appear much larger than it is yet to behave in ways that are quite intimate. This juxtaposition is part of the eternal yin and yang that keeps luxury brands so enticing. They seemingly have resolved the long-awaited integration of cosmic opposites!

Mass Strategies

Brand such as Coca-Cola always tend to be at the mercy of market dynamics and display reactive brand management. However, there are brands that are not luxury brands but abide by some of the major rules of luxury and prosper by avoiding reactive brand management. These would include Apple and the Mini Cooper.[29] The characteristics displayed by the brand that create brand value include a founding story that has authenticity (often a founder as well), a specific product uniqueness that usually goes against the tide and trends, the opportunity for the consumer to personalize the product so it becomes her own, a firm pricing strategy (few if any sales, discounts, or promotions), controlled distribution, and a community bonded together in their lifestyle and value by the brand.

SUMMARY

Brand Value is the sum total of what a brand contributes to a company's business worth. This includes both its contribution as a financial asset and its contribution as a market asset. It is derived from the interplay of Brand Equity (BE) and Brand Valuation (BV), which are distinctive concepts but interdependent business dimensions. BE is driven by consumer perceptions of the brand, and BV is driven by financial stakeholders' perceptions of the brand. Each influences the value of the other. Although there is no agreed-upon definition of these concepts, we believe our common-usage method of defining them is a useful approach to helping resolve long-standing differences among experts.

Determining the market value of a brand is necessary to assess how the brand is performing relative to its competitors. Both BE and BV have a variety of formulas for determining value. Some, such as "Book to Market," are simple and direct and widely used. Others, such as cost to replace, are a bit more difficult to apply.

Nonetheless, there are major global research and brand assessment companies that have created tools to measure Brand Value (BV). These are used to ascertain a brand's health and a brand value from an asset perspective. Although their models differ somewhat with some emphasizing consumer perceptions more than those in financial markets, all use sophisticated and time-tested survey and statistical techniques. We also looked at some research methods that any company could use to determine brand value; a real case (Walmart) provided a scenario as to how these techniques could contribute to understanding BV.

Finally, BV management differs in luxury and mass brands. However, there are some hybrid brands that mirror and successfully manage their brands by the rules of luxury.

CHAPTER CONVERSATIONS

- How is brand equity different from brand valuation? How do they contribute to brand value?
- Of the various formulas in use for determining various dimensions of BV, which do you think is most useful and why?
- What makes luxury brand valuations so much greater than luxury brand tangible assets?

CHAPTER CHALLENGES

- If you were the brand manager in charge of Coke, what steps might you have taken to avoid the decision-making mistakes associated with the taste test scenario?
- You are the chief marketing officer of a fashion apparel company. Your CFO has asked for your assessment of the future earnings potential of one of the brands in the company. Which methods and/or research models would you recommend and why? Which would you advise not be used?
- The CEO and CFO want to launch a new product. Which quantitative measure would you use to test its best attributes for successful market entry? Why was this your choice?

ENDNOTES

1. For a compact discussion of tools and methodologies for developing and assessing brand value, see Pedro Laboy, "The Importance of Measuring Brand Value and Brand Equity," April 6, 2006, www.tocquigny.com.

2. For the classic definition and applications of brand equity, see Kevin Lane Keller, "Conceptualizing, Measuring and Managing Customer-Based Brand Equity," *Journal of Marketing* 57 (1997): 1–22.

3. K. L Keller and D. R. Lehmann, "The Brand Value Chain: Optimizing Strategic and Financial Brand Performance," *Journal of Marketing Management* 12, no. 3 (May/June 2003): 26–31; see also K. L Keller and D. R. Lehmann, *Brands and Branding: REsearch Findings and Future Priorities*, Marketing Science Institute Research Conference, May 2005, pp. 34–35.

4. For a comprehensive analysis of various approaches to brand valuations, see David Haigh and Jonathon Knowles, "Brand Valuation: What It Means and Why It Matters," *Brand Finance* (May 2004); see also Special Issue on Valuations, *Journal of Brand Management*, 5, no. 4 (April 1998).

5. David A. Aaker, *Managing Brand Equity* (New York, NY: The Free Press, 1991); see also Kevin Lane Keller, *Strategic Brand Management: Building, Measuring, and Managing Brand Equity* (New York, NY: Prentice Hall, 1998).

6. Jean-Noel Kapferer, *The New Strategic Brand Management: Advanced Insights and Strategic Thinking* (N.p.: Kogan Page, 2012).

7. Ibid.

8. Ibid.

9. Tocquigny Staff, "The Importance of Measuring Brand Value and Brand Equity," *Tocquigny*, November 10, 2013, http://www.tocquigny.com/news/white-papers/importance-measuring-brand-value-brand-equity/

10. Ibid.

11. Xiao Tong and Jana Hawley, "Measuring Customer Based Brand Equity: Empirical Evidence from Sportswear Market in China," *Journal of Product and Brand Management* (April 18, 2009): 262–71.

12. Patrick Collings, "Measuring Brand Value," *Slideshare*, April 3, 2010, http://www.slideshare.net/pjcollings/measuring-brand-value-patrick-collings.

13. *International Directory of Company Histories* (Thomas Gale, 2006), www.encyclopedia.com/doc/!=IG2.

14. "Dressed for Success," Perry Ellis Case Study, www.sawayasegalas.com/resources/casestudy/20030619.

15. Lindsay Moore, "Monetize Intellectual Property Assets with Securitization Finance," *Newhope 360*, October 1, 2008, http://newhope360.com/supply-news-amp-analysis/monetize-intellectual-property-assets-securitization-finance.

16. "Brand Valuation—Introduction to the Special Edition"/Editorial, *Journal of Brand Management* 5, no. 4 (April 1998): 222.

17. Interbrand, "Brand Valuation: The Financial Value of Brands," *Brand Channel*, September 24, 2006, http://www.brandchannel.com/papers_review.asp?sp_id=357.

18. Ibid.

19. Interbrand, *Rankings*, 2013, http://www.bestglobalbrands.com/previous-years/2013.

20. For empirical research confirming the correlation between product performance in the marketplace, high-profile "glamour" brands, and shareholder value, see T. T. Madden, F. R. Fehele, and S. Fournier, "Brands Matter: An Empirical Investigation of Brand Building Activities and the Creation of Shareholder Value," *Journal of the Academy of Marketing Science* 34, no. 2 (2006): 225–235; see also Matthew T. Billett, Zhan Jiang, and Lopo L. Rego, "Glamour Brands and Glamour Stocks," *Journal of Economic Behavior* (April 2012): 107, where they wrote, "*overall we conclude that glamour in the product market appears to partially drive glamour in the stock market.*"

21. Stuart Elliot, "Apple Passes Coca-Cola as Most Valuable Brand," *New York Times*, September 29, 2013, http://www.nytimes.com/2013/09/30/business/media/apple-passes-coca-cola-as-most-valuable-brand.html?_r=0.

22. Eric Schroeder, "Coca-Cola, Red Bull Prop Up Beverage Brand Value," *Food Business News*, June 19, 2013, http://www.foodbusinessnews.net/articles/news_home/Consumer_Trends/2013/06/Coca-Cola_Red_Bull_prop_up_bev.aspx?ID=%7BFC0E8BD0-D851-4561-9F24-0702585DBA4E%7D&cck=1.

23. Jorge Alagon and Josh Samuel, "The Meaningfully Different Framework," *Millward Brown*, 2011, http://www.millwardbrown.com/docs/default-source/insight-documents/articles-and-reports/MillwardBrown_MeaningfullyDifferentFramework_April2013.pdf.

24. Mike Rocha, "Brand Valuation: A Versatile Strategic Tool for Business," *Interbrand*, May 20, 2014, http://interbrand.com/en/views/31/brand-valuation-a-versatile-strategic-tool-for-business.

25. B. Orme, "Understanding the Value of Conjoint Analysis," in *Getting Started with Conjoint Analysis* (N.p.: Research Publishers, 2010).

26. These are proprietary Walmart cohorts developed from internal market research.

27. Michel Chevalier and Gerald Mazzalovo, *Luxury Brand Management: A World of Privilege* (Hoboken, NJ: John Wiley and Sons, 2012).

28. Jean-Noel Kapferer and Vincent Bastien, *The Luxury Strategy: Break the Rules of Marketing to Build Luxury Brands* (N.p.: Kogan Page, 2012).

29. Ibid.

CHAPTER 8

Creating Brand Names and Protecting Trademarks

AFTER COMPLETING THIS CHAPTER,
YOU WILL BE ABLE TO:

- Identify various approaches to generating an effective brand name and other intellectual property (IP) assets.

- Develop strategies to promote and protect brand value, including out-of-court settlements.

- Assess how legal outcomes vary in different countries and courts.

"Going to court to defend your trademark should be a strategy of last resort."

—Tiffany & Co. v. Costco Wholesale

THE BRAND ASSETS

Chapter 7 focused on the brand as a marketing and financial asset. The value of a brand's contribution was underscored by the various strategies that strong brands can support for sustainable business development. Given this, it seems reasonable that creating and protecting brand names and supporting elements need to be approached strategically. Chapter 8 focuses on these three components and their dynamic and interdependent relationship.

Brand elements, including logos, icons, taglines, and any other identifiable and trademarkable brand attributes (i.e., color), are called **Intellectual Property (IP)**. These items are assets that can be given a valuation and need protection much like physical property that one might own. Consequently, the age-old question that Shakespeare posited—"What's in a name?"—can now be answered. In brand naming and in its counterpart, trademark law, quite a lot is in a name![1] This section explores this value proposition.

Generating an Effective Brand Name and Other IP Assets

Generating a name, logo, tagline, or icon (IP asset) that conveys a brand's unique identity needs to be a strategic undertaking.[2] Begin by asking, *who are your core consumers?*

- What do they value in their life and lifestyle?
- What problem are you solving for them?
- What concrete need or aspirational desire will be served?
- What core business competencies can you bring to help realize this?
- How can you, as an enterprise, do it best?

Then, think of what solution to wants or needs you are offering your target consumers; combine that with a consumer profile and factor in your company's competencies. The consumer profile should be derived from your target customers' lifestyles (how they live and their priorities) and your core competency, which is what your company does best (this could be an aspirational or a functional solution). So, for example, if you know your customer's lifestyle is as an avid outdoorsman and your product specialty is rugged raingear (your competency), what special solution can you offer? How can you be highly relevant to this lifestyle and highly different from your competitors? As you begin to answer these questions, names will emerge for this solution; mixing in prompting questions (e.g., "What is it called when . . . ?" "When he uses it, how will he feel?" "How might our customer refer to it?" "How might he describe it to his friends?" etc.) will generate added names.

This line of thinking will set the stage not only for an appropriate brand name but also for a tagline that states the promise you wish to make to your consumer. As you begin to gather these IP assets, revisit our discussion of the brand promise in Chapter 6 and be aware that the tagline will have to be concise enough to fit under the logo. Also, you'll recall, if you already have a mission statement, the tagline should be consistent with the values and promise of the mission. Assembling and unifying these elements (name, tagline, and icon) are what creates the brand architecture, again which we first presented in Chapter 6.

Although we tend to think of the above as a linear thought process (mission first, then the other assets), this isn't always the case. Often a more random process prevails; what's important is the organic consistency in image and meaning among all the elements.

Although brand architecture is usually thought of as a framework for brand portfolio management, it also can serve as a metaphor for integrating and building the IP assets of a single brand. It also is a reminder to maintain the internal integrity of its structure.[3]

There is an abundance of evidence, confirmed by empirical research,[4] that names that are easy to recall and easy to say correlate more positively with business success.[5] All things being equal, this is the result of human perception as people's cognitive assessment biases kick in. Later in this chapter, we'll present a framework for assessing which brand names are the most salient and we'll offer a way to rank their differences.[6]

Brainstorming

Another approach to name generation is a classic **brainstorming** session (a process of group idea generation where concepts and strategies are subjected to critical assessment until a consensus is reached). Here, key members of the organization are brought together to participate in a name generation process, which is preceded by the distribution of a brainstorming workbook (for an actual workbook, see your ancillaries at chapter end). The workbook has a variety of exercises designed to trigger ideas, and each workbook is customized for the particular company (given the product and the positioning); all are filled out prior to the meeting of the group and returned to the brainstorming moderator prior to the meeting, who will then use them to frame and conduct the meeting that follows. In order to engender the most creative results, all participants are instructed not to share their thoughts with their colleagues prior to the meeting.

This process begins by taking a market perspective. How is the product or service positioned as a solution vis-à-vis the competition? What attribute and/or benefit drivers have we decided defines the essential value of the product/service offer? Here are some examples of what might be the "essential value":

- A "convenience" service
- A "comfort" product
- An "aspirational" service
- An "affordable luxury" experience

Next, the focus is on the target consumer. Demographics, lifestyle values, and psychographic attitudes all combine to provide a backdrop for the new brand name's creation. How, where, and why would the typical consumer use your product or service? Write these profiles as "personas"—that is, people profiles that bring the target customer to life. Include names, types of shoppers, and even pictures of

what the personas might look like. The brand name is one that will appeal to the people it serves as well as reflect them. What might they call such a product? Here, in the absence of market research findings, we turn to a **jury of executive opinion**, or the experience of senior managers, and draw upon their insights.

Finally, think of which product attributes align with which product benefits and set up a grid which reflects this. For example, if your product is a new soft drink positioned as a weight-loss drink, you might graph the dynamic as follows:

> Attribute: *Benefit*
> Tastes great chilled or warm: *Convenient Refreshment*
> Can't spoil: *Low Maintenance*
> Works while you drink it: *Instant Gratification*
> Tested for optimum results: *Peace of Mind*

In all three of the preceding approaches, you will be building an inventory of words that you'll be writing on a flip chart or whiteboard. Hopefully, this will help you see word combinations that relate to appropriate brand meaning. If, at this stage of the brainstorming, you find that you are not generating enough fresh, relevant ideas, reverse the process by generating antonyms which then will enable you to search for their opposites or new synonyms—we call this "reversing your engines." It allows you to get rid of "seaweed" obstructing the free flow of ideas so you can move forward by freeing your creative propeller! Throughout this process you should practice using analogies and metaphors. **Associative Projective Techniques** (methods using word or image stimuli which generate creative thinking) are also employed. For example, you might ask, "If the brand were an animal, which would it be and why?"

The Volkswagen Beatle, the iconic brand from the 1960s and 1970s, could be thought to have followed this path. A name generation exchange might have sounded like this: "The car looks like and seems to scurry along as if it were a . . . and our target customer, who is probably a bit whimsical and counterculture, might call it a . . ." Well, you get the idea.

In the cases that follow, the brainstorming method was used to generate brand names which were trademarked and found their way into their respective markets. The cases provide two distinct approaches to brand naming. The first combines brainstorming with focus groups and provides a snapshot as to how a business strategy can animate and inform the naming process. The second provides a look at a classic brainstorming process and offers insights into how a well-functioning session can generate brand naming solutions even when it appears that the team has been stymied.

A name generation strategy that resulted in the creation of a multimillion-dollar hosiery business at a leading U.S. department store combined idea generation techniques with consumer-centric focus groups to test the name's viability. Our client had developed a sock with a unique silicon ring inside that solved a major dress hosiery problem faced by men, socks that don't stay up. With this new silicon ring, socks that wouldn't stay up now effortlessly remained neatly in place. But what to name it? First, a brainstorming session was held at the client's headquarters attended by the key design, merchandising, and marketing managers plus the CEO and COO. Sets of possible names were proposed. Others were generated from the process described earlier. The top four were agreed on and a series of taglines developed that could have organically been part of any of the four. It was agreed to let the consumer be the final arbiter.

A focus group was facilitated with men and women who met two criteria: they were men's hosiery customers who frequently shopped in the department store in question, and they had purchased men's hosiery there in the last six months. The following names and taglines were proposed:

Always Up Hosiery: "The stays up sock"
The Smart Sock: "The sock that knows its place"
EverStay: "The sock that won't let you down"
ComfortPlus: "Staying up with fashion"
    (generated by one of the consumers in the
    focus group)

The product was positioned as both a fashion and dress-up product and didn't hint at any remedial health solution. We wanted to deal preemptively with any possible consumer misinterpretation that the sock stood up because of its heavy construction, thereby suggesting that it was really an orthopedic solution masquerading as fashion hosiery; this would have been its death knell. The name and tagline together had to clearly convey its benefits. In the end, the overwhelming choice of the focus group was EverStay,® "*The sock that won't let you down.*"

The group also liked the taglines "*staying up with fashion*" and "*the sock that knows its place.*" The multiple taglines all conveyed the same brand promise so the variety did not compromise the brand's positioning. From a brand management perspective, having multiple taglines opens up a channel distribution strategy of offering a type of **exclusive brand** (one that is not offered to competing department stores) by retaining the newly minted brand name, logo, and font yet changing its colors and taglines. This preserved the identity of the brand while opening up the possibilities of much wider distribution and sales to competing department stores, each of which could have its own particular and unique EverStay® iteration and packaging.

Another successful example of how the brainstorming method works occurred while I was consulting for a men's tailored clothing company. The client had developed a strategy to capitalize on the casual dressing trend that Dockers® and others had successfully enjoyed. The company had developed a great tailored sportswear product and now needed a name and a positioning strategy. We began by agreeing on the following target consumer parameters:

- The core consumer is a modern young creative and/or middle manager, ages 25 to 39.
- His sensibilities in dressing are cool but not edgy, not overly formal or too casual.
- He may be married and helps equally with the kids and the house, especially if his wife works. He's modern.

- He wants to be able to attend a business meeting at work and go out at night socially wearing the same outfit.

We wanted to convey "tailored" as a differentiator from other sportswear brands, so we looked for words which could suggest tradition and modernity. "Heritage" as a brand name came up, but we felt it was too traditional and probably unavailable to trademark. There were many other suggestions such as "Genealogy" and "Classic Softwear" in an attempt to capture both tailored as a benefit with a modern twist. We had agreed that the tagline that would accompany the name would be *"Modern Clothing."* Here was an example of nonlinear creative development of the IP assets as referenced earlier in this chapter, as we determined the tagline prior to the brand name.

For several days we tried to discover the new brand name. During one long day, we took an early recess and agreed to reconvene the next day. At about 2:00 a.m. that morning, the name came to me and I wrote it down (I always keep pen and paper on my night table). The next morning, the merchandiser came in to my temporary office and exclaimed, "I've got it!" He showed a name on a sheet of paper. I just smiled and opened my sheet from the previous night. The name on both sheets of paper was exactly the same, and perfect for the brand imaging and product positioning: Lineage!

The merchandiser and I had not been in contact either by phone or email since the previous day. The method had generated in each of our minds, given the positioning and imaging, the right name!

Next we needed to transform this into a logo that could be trademarked and that mirrored the positioning and differentiation strategy. Enter the creative or "branding" side of the equation. The final logo/brand rendering and the reasons for choosing it appear in Figure 8.1.

We agreed that the font should be clean and somewhat angular and architectural, and the color should be a steel cadet blue. Combining these produced a strong masculine tone and conveyed a modern sensibility.

LINEAGE
collection
MODERN CLOTHING

figure 8.1
Rendering of the Lineage logo with its tagline "Modern Clothing." The color, font, and name for the brand capture the positioning of the product and the relevancy/lifestyle of the target customer.

The name "Lineage" clearly captured the continuity with the past, and thereby paid homage to the tailored dimension of the collection, and it was available for trademark.

Initial market entry resulted in opening over 200 men's better specialty stores across the U.S. and exceeding the sales plan. The brand was later purchased with other brands from the 500 Fashion Group and is now owned by the largest men's tailored clothing retailer in America, Men's Wearhouse! Figure 8.2 summarizes things to consider when creating a brand name.

Random Name Generation

Brand names can also be generated by other approaches. Sounds, myths, or just the name of the founder have all been used as sources for brand names. Here are some actual brand names and the reasons they were chosen:

Yahoo!: Meaning a rude, uncouth person, this name was the choice of its founders for its irreverent tone, suggesting a break with traditions and conventions.

Nike: The name of the ancient Greek god of victory, it captures the idea of competing and winning in sports and life.

Verizon: This telecommunications company was born from the merger of several companies. Managers wished to suggest and position the new

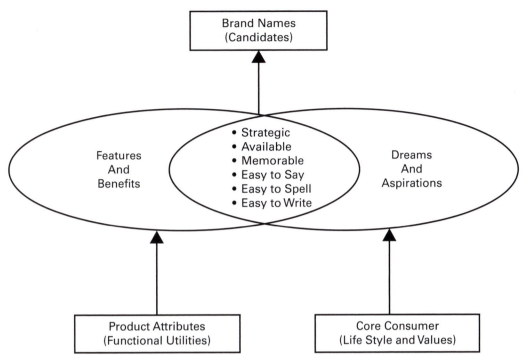

figure 8.2
A model for brand naming: What needs to be considered to effectively work the process.

company as groundbreaking in its sector. They combined *veritas* and *horizon* for "True"/"New Directions."

Pop-Tarts: This descriptive approach tells the consumer about the product's main attribute. It's a frozen breakfast tart that can be put in a toaster (thus the "pop") and toasted for a quick, convenient snack or breakfast.

Kodak: This name was created by the inventor of the camera, George Eastman, because he liked the strong sound of *k* and was more concerned with creating a name that was easy to say, pronounce, and remember.

Apple: The name might have come from Steve Jobs's love of the Beatles and their record label name "Apple" or from his satisfying work in the apple orchards of Oregon! However, what we do know is that the iconic logo, the apple with the bite taken out, directly captures the brand essence and positioning: the forbidden fruit, taken from the tree of knowledge, from a lust to know, which opened up unimaginable beginnings for humankind.

Brand Registration Strategies

When generating possible brand names, you should have a minimum of two to three choices that align with the Relevance/Differentiation brand loyalty positioning matrix discussed in Chapter 5. This will give you more options, and save you time and money, if you find that one of your names is already registered in your class of trade (business sector) because initial searches often do not uncover this. Also, "ownership" may be pending or may be claimed by usage awaiting official registration.

BRANDSTORMING SUCCESS: PPR Becomes Kering

Brand strategies apply to entities other than products or services; countries and corporations themselves often develop a brand architecture for business development.

An excellent example of the process of renaming and reimaging a corporate brand can be found in the recent change in the company name of Pinault- Printemps-Redoute to Kering, the luxury **conglomerate** which owns and markets multiple brands and which we've mentioned in several earlier chapters. Here are the details.[7]

The corporate business model of Pinault- Printemps-Redoute (known by its brand call letters as PPR) had changed over time. Beginning as a financial holding company in 1967, it grew by adding retail and luxury brands to its portfolio, but by 2013 only luxury brands (such as Gucci and Saint Laurent) and premium sports brands (such as Puma) remained. This raised the question as to whether the current corporate brand reflected the business that PPR was really in. It became clear that it had evolved into being "a world leader in apparel and accessories" and was no longer a conglomerate of unrelated business units. This disconnect was seen as both projecting a lack of clarity of the corporate mission and reducing a sense of common purpose. This could fail to encourage cross-pollination and the sharing of ideas and experiences among brand managers. Led by François-Henri Pinault (chairman and CEO), the process of renaming/rebranding the company began.[8]

Beginning with internal brainstorming sessions and culminating in the hiring of several global brand development agencies (TBWA, Havas, and Dragon Rouge), PPR explored ideas and names that optimized both brand relevancy and differentiation. The idea emerged that PPR was in the business of "empowering imagination" by taking something immaterial—imagination—and turning it into something tangible—luxury and premium brand experiences. This reflected the corporate values of combining caring and action, and fulfilled the relevancy/differentiation benchmark. The phrase "*empowering imagination*" became the corporate tagline.

The new corporate name that emerged, Kering,® is pronounced as the English word *caring*. It was also mentioned that the root word *Ker* means "home" in Breton, the local dialect of the French province of Brittany where the business began! The new name was symbolized by a new logo, a modern rendering of an owl to convey both vision and wisdom. It reflected the idea of both craftsmanship in product development and concern with employees and their lives, a hallmark of this originally family-owned company.

A major communications campaign followed both within and outside the company, including partnering with a fashion blogger to explain the vision and the change. Some have questioned whether the expense was worth the outcome. How do we measure whether all stakeholders benefited or will benefit from this change?[9] How would you go about answering this question?

"In Commerce"

This points to what is often referred to as an **in commerce** strategy. The patent and trademark laws were written to encourage commerce and business, and courts will often protect those who have active trademarks, or are using them "in commerce," rather than those who may sequester marks for future use or as saleable assets.

Thus, first and steady usage, all things being equal, may establish a claim on a mark. It is strongly recommended that new businesses with new brands, while seeking registration, establish that they are in commerce with the brand by creating invoices and effecting a sales transaction as early as possible. Adding a ™ next to the brand assets (name, logo, and/or icon) symbolically states your claim, as you await the arrival of ®. For taglines, a service mark (SM) can serve the same function. Continuing the brand market presence through creating websites, attending tradeshows, and the like can also help establish the intent to own the brand assets. Sending and keeping a sealed, postmarked envelope containing a paid invoice is a simple backup to establishing a date when your brand entered the market.

Classes of Trade

Your **class of trade** is also important here as it will, in part, determine the availability of the mark. Different claimants can register the same name so long as they are in different business sectors or classes of trade. These classes or sectors are written in intellectual property regulations and international agreements such as the NICE Agreement, which officially demarcates and then defines the sectors of commerce and the class of product and or service within each and which many countries especially in the European Union have signed on to. The U.S. Patent and Trademark Office has a similar listing for U.S. markets, which can be accessed online. The use of the same or similar IP assets is, however, circumscribed by many legal venues which restrict unfair or negative usage no matter the class of trade.

Evaluating and Managing Brand Names

Once you have agreed on several possible names and they have cleared a preliminary search, it pays to put them to an attribute ranking test to ascertain which are the strongest. Table 8.1 can help you assess which pending brand names that you've identified have strategic priority over others. Use one table for each brand name that you have established as a candidate for registration. This will move your team from using different language and words in describing their preferences to the more universal language of numbers. With this, a faster consensus will emerge on which of the top two or three to continue to invest your company's costly resources of time, money, and creative energy.

Ranking and Scoring Available Brand Names

Once you have the names, review your mission statement. Deconstructing a well-constructed mission statement as we did with the Ritz-Carlton Credo in Chapter 5 can help by identifying the values in the statement that, taken together, constitute the brand promise and other aspects of a good name.

Add to this a strategic marketing plan that details geographic markets, product categories, and the channels of distribution strategies where the brand will compete. All of these elements will provide the " guardrails" to keep you "on brand." Finally, if the new brand is part of a portfolio of existing brands such as diffusion brands (those that extend some aspect of the flagship brand to the brand names of other product categories), complementary positioning (i.e., avoiding cannibalizing/encroaching on the other brands in the portfolio) must be factored in to maintain the corporate strategic brand architecture.

Brand Portfolio Management[10]

An excellent example of a consistent corporate strategy of diffusion, or brand extension, and **complementary positioning**, whereby the brands cumulatively

"Brand Name"	Low 1	2	3	4	High 5	Total
Table 8.1 Evaluating Potential Brand Names What gets measured has a better chance of getting effectively managed. This table provides a way to quantify the assessment process and the results.						
Strategic						
Different						
Inspiring						
Enduring						
Believable						
Consumer-Friendly						Total:
Short and Simple						
Easy to Say						
Easy to Read						
Easy to Remember						
Fits into Our Brand Portfolio						Total:
Available						Total:
						Grand Total:

add to the vision of the corporate brand, can be found in Polo Ralph Lauren® (PRL). At PRL, **diffusion brands** allow the business to expand not only the corporate brand awareness but the client base as well. Expanding from the core Polo® brand (better price points), Ralph Lauren® has added diffusion brands, including Lauren Ralph Lauren® (upper moderate prices) and Ralph Lauren Black Label® (designer prices/product) and, at the apex, Ralph Lauren Purple Label® (couture product/prices). This creates complementary positioning and businesses and avoids cannibalization.[11]

Coupled with different channels of distribution, this strategy creates distinctiveness in price and design but ensures that the image, quality, and luxury that are the hallmark of the Ralph Lauren brand are maintained.

Approaches to Brand Management Cases[12]

Once you have secured the legal right to market your business through your brand assets, the importance of managing the brand now becomes paramount. Managing has two dimensions to it: first, strategizing how best to realize the business potential in the brand, and second, when and how to protect and defend it from improper and/or illegal usage. These two responsibilities of the brand manager coalesce in the legal environment in statutes, case law, and courts.

Luxury brands, although at times in **co-branding** relations with mass brands (think, for example, of Karl Lagerfeld and H&M retail stores where both brands join together in a project or product launch to the benefit of each, which we discuss in more detail in

Chapter 9), often find themselves at odds with both their luxury competitors and their mass associates. This points to the extraordinary equity value of brands as business drivers in general and in luxury brands in particular. As we shall see, the deep well of consumer equity residing in luxury brands often seems too tempting to resist.

FUNDAMENTAL LEGAL PRINCIPLES IN TRADEMARK LAW

The trademark cases that we are going to review represent a growing field of brand strategies that are suddenly in conflict and find themselves locked in litigation. As we will see, going to court even if the law appears to be on your side is always risky business, especially in our global economy. Nations, treaties, and foreign courts often have differing interpretations of the same law. Brand managers should think of courts as venues of last resort, not as strategic fallback positions, and act preemptively rather than react defensively in their guardianship of the brand.

Prevailing Types of Transgressions

The goal of trademark law is to protect the ownership rights in intellectual property (IP). In general, there are two main transgressions that the law addresses. The first is **infringement**, or the unauthorized use or copying by a business of any part of a brand's trademark assets owned by another. The second is **dilution**, or the trivializing of a mark, thereby lessening its IP value through improper reference or use. Dilution can show up in two ways: one is **tarnishment**, or injury to reputation via negative/unfounded associations, and the other is **diminishment** to its distinctive quality by which the IP asset has become known in the marketplace.

Standards for Legal Action

The standards used to determine if these transgressions are actionable at law are confusion by the ordinary consumer in their day-to-day shopping experience and a dilution of the equity in the brand when lower-priced look-alike products trade/present themselves as if they were the higher-priced brand.

Prevailing Types of Defenses

The legal defenses most often launched against the accusation of infringement include **generification**, which most often takes the form of the **acquiescence** defense. Here it is argued that failure to claim a mark or properly file and/or the everyday use of the mark as a word to describe a category (e.g., "Escalator") renders the mark null and void (i.e., the "owner" has "acquiesced" or has abandoned the mark through improper or untimely inaction).

The **First Usage** defense holds that first usage—that is, which company used the brand first in a business situation or transaction rather than formal registration—establishes ownership. Finally, the **Parody Defense** protects the right to ridicule, caricature, or make fun of a brand as part of a country's commitment to the protection of freedom of speech.

Generification and the Acquiescence Defense

Trademark dilution can also occur, ironically, from too much success. For example, as noted earlier, when the brand name slips into the daily language of a culture and becomes synonymous with the product category, such as Vaseline®, Xerox®, and Band-Aid®, it risks the product it represents being perceived as a commodity rather than as unique and distinctive. The aforementioned brands have all become part of our everyday language and thereby risk the reduction in value and possibly in premium pricing. They are all examples of generification. One of the leading brands that has mounted a counterattack on this erosion of its brand equity by generification is Kleenex®.

CASE STUDY
Tiffany Inc. v. Costco Stores Inc.

Tiffany Inc. v. Costco Stores Inc.[14] is a good example of the acquiescence challenge and defense. Here the iconic Tiffany® brand sued Costco® stores for **unfair trade** practices (falsely presenting diamond rings as "Tiffany's") and **trademark infringement** (the unauthorized use of the trademarked name). Tiffany, a luxury retail brand where limited availability and rarity are the rule, and **Costco**, a warehouse club that emphasizes low prices and high volume as its business model, could not be any farther apart in their business philosophies.

The facts in the case were that Costco had been selling so-called Tiffany setting rings at below-market prices. Tiffany Inc. claimed that they were "Tiffany" rings, not "Tiffany settings." The rings were advertised in Costco's in-store advertising and by its sales associates. No ads were on the web or in public media. Costco argued that "Tiffany setting" is a general jeweler's term (which is true) that describes a popular type of setting for engagement rings (created by the founder of Tiffany). Tiffany countered that it had trademarked "Tiffany Setting" separately from the Tiffany® iconic mark in 2003. Costco's defense was that registration at this late date was tantamount to "Acquiescence," or the acceptance that the term "Tiffany setting" had crept into jewelers' and society's lexicons. Costco's position was that the term was widely used for years before

2003 and therefore was given up as a defensible mark (became generic) and was open to whomever wished to use it.[15]

The strategic issue for a brand manager is not whether to defend the mark but whether to do so in court. Once a challenge becomes part of the public record, this could open the door to more challenges and further erosion of the brand's distinctiveness; a brand manager needs to weigh the possible outcome and what the definition of "winning" really means.

Here the key issue was the in-store references to the brand "Tiffany" to describe the rings. This is clearly a violation of the mark. However, the brand guardians opted to settle out of court and to avoid further possible incursions and erosions of the brand's equity. Costco agreed to police sales pitches and change its in-store advertising. The case was ended.[16]

As we have seen, the two general benchmarks that courts apply in most venues to determine whether a breach in trademark rights might have occurred are:

- Is the competing mark so similar to the established mark that it is likely to be confused by the everyday consumer?
- Is the similarity so close that the competing mark can be said to be diluting the investment and equity in the challenging mark?

The cases that follow provide us with some of the key court decisions applying the preceding benchmarks.

Kleenex®, the soft facial tissue and consumer pack-aged goods company, has aggressively fought that tendency by posting ads online and in other venues indicating that Kleenex is a brand and should not be used as a generic word to describe facial tissues. The ads further state how to properly use the brand name (correct font, registration mark ®, etc.) and warn those who may misuse the brand name of a "vigorous" legal defense of the brand's equity.[13]

Brand managers are advised to be on watch as to how a brand is spoken of in ads, in daily conversation, and within the organization. Online venues such as blogs, postings, and the like, being difficult to mon-itor, have increased the possible erosion of equity or the commoditizing of a brand name. A good rule of thumb is that brands are adjectives, not nouns or verbs, and when they begin to be used as such, imme-diate action is required (e.g., "Shoprite Kleenex on sale" or "Xeroxing: 5 cents a copy"). Failure to defend has been grounds for claims of abandonment or acquiescence, allowing others to lay claim to the right to use the mark.

The First Usage Defense

Polo Ralph Lauren v. United States Polo Association: The Battle of the "Horsemen" (or is it the "Polo Players"?). This distinction points to the fundamental differences in the two brands' positioning: Polo Ralph Lauren (PRL), in its marketing communications, never refers to its logo as a "polo player" but always as a "horseman." This reflects and supports its assertion that its use of "Polo" is not a reference to the sport but to a lifestyle and a lifestyle brand. For the U.S. Polo Association (USPA), it refers to its logo as "polo players" for it is about a sport wanting to become a lifestyle brand. Herein lies the essence of their legal conflicts that date back to 1984 and continued with a filing in October 2013 by Polo Ralph Lauren of a suit against Arvind Ltd., a major vertical apparel company which is USPA's licensee in India.

In a series of court decisions covering apparel and fragrances, courts have concluded the following

regarding the usage of different logos and brand reg-istered names:

- The U.S. Polo Association logo of two polo horsemen and players does not necessarily infringe on Ralph Lauren's single player and Polo's horseman logo.
- The use of the word "Polo®" by Ralph Lauren when established over time with a lifestyle/product category is protected and cannot be used by the U.S. Polo Association in that category.

Here is the background and the nuanced legal reasoning. USPA® is a not-for-profit organization founded in 1890 to govern and grow polo as a sport. It oversees competitive rules and standards and encour-ages the growth of the sport. One advertising head-line, as shown on the organization's website, captures the essence of this charge: "Before fashion, polo was a sport."

USPA Properties LLC is the division within the USPA responsible for licensing the brand in its various iterations and registrations and generating revenue for the sport. Licensing has been largely in apparel, footwear, accessories, and fragrances. The licensing effort has been very successful both in the United States and globally, with major mono-brand store groups in Turkey, India, and other foreign markets.

In 1988, USPA licensed the brand to Jordache® Enterprises, which began to develop an apparel col-lection distributed to department stores, raising the brand name awareness and possible conflicts. The horseman logo and other marks were owned, regis-tered, and in commerce from Polo Ralph Lauren®, the iconic American lifestyle brand and fashion house, which first used and registered the Polo player/Polo horse logo in 1972.

USPA had been using a similar symbol (the double horsemen players) on its official polo outfits, which resulted in the first lawsuit in 1984. Here, USPA pre-vailed in its right to use three of the four logos that were in circulation, the exception being the solid double horsemen players. This logo could be used so long as it was "distinctive" from the Polo Ralph Lauren® logo to avoid **consumer confusion** (the benchmark by which courts ask if everyday consumers in the process of shopping are likely to confuse two similar logos). To adhere to this, USPA designed the double horsemen logo with the second or rear image in outline form and the front image in a solid rendering.

All other marks of the USPA were held to be valid and did not violate Polo Ralph Lauren® trademark rights (Figure 8.3). What was clear was that the licensee's brand management strategy was to copycat Polo Ralph Lauren® whenever possible (Figure 8.4).

An email from an executive at Jordache (the licensee) was offered into evidence by Polo Ralph Lauren® in an attempt to prove **unfair competition**, which requires that competitors in their advertising and public promotions avoid intentionally misrepresenting the business practices of competitors or falsely accusing them of poor performance or behavior. It became known in the industry as the "Ralph Rip-Off" email and here is the text: *"Everyone knows we're ripping off Ralph including us. It is the mission of our advertising to deny it by appearing to be true to the sport. After all, Ralph did rip off the sport."* The court did not factor the email into its decision as it does not go to the issue of asset ownership.[17]

figure 8.3
U.S. Polo Association storefront logo: USPA is adhering to the court's decision with a larger-than-life logo!

figure 8.4
Polo Ralph Lauren storefront "Horseman" logo: To avoid any suggestion that Ralph Lauren is knocking off the sport of polo, the logo is referred to within the company as "The Horseman."

A second major trademark confrontation occurred in 2011 when USPA launched a fragrance collection. The court ruled against USPA, stating that Polo Ralph Lauren® had created a long-standing link to the fragrance category (launched in 1978) with the Polo horseman (Polo Ralph Lauren®, the court, and media never refer to the logo as a "Polo Player" but as a "Horseman"!) and the word *Polo*®. The court barred USPA from using this for fragrance but all other USPA marks were available and could be used accordingly. The court rejected the argument that Polo Ralph Lauren® was attempting to corner the sport of polo for its own use. This is where brand strategies and legal reasoning intersect. For Polo Ralph Lauren®, the IP assets are not meant to convey polo as a sport but as a lifestyle and a set of attitudes and values . . . and the court agreed![18] The logo for the Polo Ralph Lauren® fragrance is shown in Figure 8.5.

figure 8.5
Polo Ralph Lauren fragrance bottle logo:
Again, the argument made in court which was upheld was that Ralph Lauren was projecting a lifestyle, not a sport.

The court did not restrict USPA from licensing in the fragrance sector, but certain marks were circumscribed and unavailable to USPA—for example, the use of the word *Polo*. This was the brand name claimed by PRL and agreed to by the court to be a separate and defensible mark.[19]

Although court cases and out-of-court settlements appear to resolve legal issues, without goodwill the issues remain. In May 2013 while in Shanghai on business, I was traveling down an escalator in an upscale mall. I happened to glance up to my left and caught a glimpse of a USPA storefront with a large polo player logo over the entrance. It was a double *solid* player and not the variation that courts in the United States had ruled on and that the USPA ostensibly agreed to abide by to avoid infringement and consumer confusion. This points to the absence of a global trademark court whose jurisdiction would enforce decisions from nation-state courts. In addition, in spite of treaties unifying principles of law, actual case law can differ from country to country. The U.S. decision is neither binding nor necessarily guiding in Chinese courts and neither is it binding nor a guideline in many other countries as well.

The Parody Defense: Confusion/Dilution

The first amendment to the U.S. Constitution provides protection for political speech, however vitriolic, and for social parody, however mocking or irreverent. This has found its way into court cases in the luxury sector, most notably in *Louis Vuitton v. Haute Diggity Dog*![20]

Here a small manufacturer marketed a chew toy for dogs that it branded Chewy Vuitton® (Figure 8.6). A lawsuit followed and the defendant prevailed. The case hinged on whether there was any chance of confusion with the luxury mark of Louis Vuitton (LV) or if the distance between the two brands was so great that the name was clearly a parody. This decision was rendered by the court even though LV had sold dog products in the past, albeit very expense ones. However, it is the very connection with the brand's

figure 8.6

A Chewy Vuitton bag. The key question was whether this was a parody or infringement. What do you think?

and owned by the largest apparel company in the world, VF Corporation (VFC), sued South Butt, a very small company with revenues of around $20,000 per year. In 2009, VFC attorneys discovered online a website selling hoodies, T-shirts, and the like with the name South Butt and with a logo seeming to mock the North Face registered logo (Figure 8.7) and brand name. This included the tagline *"never stop relaxing"* as a counter to North Face's *"never stop exploring."*[22]

A **cease and desist letter**, which stated the alleged infraction and threatened legal action if the recipient did not immediately cease the alleged infraction, was immediately sent to the owner, a college student, whose only other product distribution was in a local drugstore near the university he attended. The revenues were minimal. The student claimed that he was mocking the brand and sending a message to his fellow students to stop being so infatuated with the North Face brand. Thus, the parody claim as their legal argument and the exercise of the parody defense by the student and his attorney were based upon this.[23]

The parody defense works best when the plaintiff owns a well-known or iconic brand and when other factors, such as clear differences in the type of retail distribution, complement this. This seems counterintuitive, but the degree of fame of the mark works against the plaintiff. The courts tend to hold that because of the mark's iconic stature, the consumer can clearly see that the "competing" mark is a parody of the iconic one, and, thus, there is no real possibility of confusing one with the other. This was clearly one of the principles guiding the Louis Vuitton case.

Also, if the products are unrelated, the price points disparate, and the channels of distribution in no way parallel, a critical mass of distinctiveness emerges, resulting in a protected class of permissible trademark and product design based on the right to parody social icons and institutions. This was the situation with Louis Vuitton. Even if the dog toy mimicked the Louis Vuitton® handbag (which it did), the product, customer, price, and channel of distribution (pet stores) insulated it from the plaintiff's claim.

famous product offering (high-priced accessories) that, by accentuating the distance between the two brands, makes the parody defense work. Also, consumers know that brand owners are not inclined to make fun of their own brand. So two questions of brand management arise: What would have been gained with a "victory" in court? And what costs were incurred to bring the litigation?[21]

In another parody case, a similar David and Goliath confrontation occurred. North Face® Apparel Company, a brand generating $1 billion in revenues

figure 8.7
The North Face logo. The South Butt logo that precipitated the lawsuit reversed the brand elements in the North Face logo.

Here, however insignificant the South Butt business was, the products were similar to what North Face marketed (especially the famous Denali jacket). The South Butt brand logo appears to be simply a copycat of North Face in reverse. This led the judge to reject the defense's call for a dismissal, and the case went to settlement. Had there been no attempt to sell garments, the parody defense here probably would have prevailed. The results of the settlement were never made public, but by 2011, South Butt had closed its website and its owner had moved on to other interests.[24]

The possibility of a lost opportunity to turn parody into a marketing positive by engaging the owner and the consumer in a contest or a creative undertaking seems never to have been considered. Although dilution was argued as grounds for challenging South Butt, VFC could not show revenue or market share losses, or any real diminution of the North Face brand. Consequently, it raises the question of what strategic business advantage, if any, was realized and what consumer-centered brand-building opportunities were lost.[25]

Alternative Brand Management Strategies: Publicity and Collaborative Opportunities

The ultimate objective in defending IP assets from improper use is not to realize a monetary gain or to punish offenders but to ensure the brand's effectiveness in marketing communications. This is the classic divide that most often separates brand managers from their attorney counterparts in corporations. The latter tend to be punitive in their strategic perspective, while brand managers seek to be collaborative.

Let's think of what could have been in the North Face case. Jimmy Winkelman, the creator of South Butt, was a student at the University of Missouri when the case occurred. It's hard not to admire Jimmy for his creativity and for his courage in taking on the big guy; it is also hard not to feel a degree of "shame-on-you" for North Face and VFC (the largest apparel company in the world)! America loves the underdog, and VFC failed to capitalize on this. The University of Missouri has a very successful fashion and apparel merchandising program, seemingly low-hanging fruit for an imaginative brand manager to build upon. What if VFC had set up an annual scholarship for a creative brand development contest on campus in fashion and apparel? Jimmy could have been one of the judges in a mixed team of faculty, students, and North Face/VFC managers. This would have been much less expensive and a much better brand-building opportunity for North Face, to say nothing of the twenty-five or so other brands in the VFC portfolio. Sounds like a better ROI than the foolish jaunt into court!

If the North Face versus South Butt case is about publicity as an alternative, *Stevens Aviation v. Southwest Airlines* is about collaboration—leading to an over-the-top dose of publicity!

Southwest, known for its zany culture and quirky flight attendants, introduced the new tagline "*Just*

Plane Smart" as a perfect brand promise. Unbeknownst to CEO Herb Kelleher, Stevens Airlines in South Carolina, a much smaller commuter airline, claimed first dibs fifteen months prior with "*Plane Smart*" as its publicly disseminated tagline and brand promise in its advertising. A cease and desist letter went out from Stevens to Southwest. But wait a minute, here is where leadership comes in to drive brand management in its proper direction. The two CEOs got on the phone and agreed to a contest—an arm wrestling match—the winner of which would claim the tagline! They dubbed the event "Malice in Dallas."

The newspapers and TV and radio stations could not get enough of this and covered it from beginning to end. The CEOs rented out the Dallas Sportatorium; Kelleher showed up in a white silk robe with cheerleaders, Stevens ran into the arena in a red robe, and the *Rocky* theme song blared on the loudspeakers. Stevens won the arm wrestling contest, but Kelleher didn't lose. Stevens agreed they could both use the tagline! Kelleher later estimated that avoiding litigation saved Southwest a minimum of $500,000. Brand image–building value? Incalculable!

INTERNATIONAL TRADEMARK LAW

In this section, we discuss some of these issues of infringement and registration in trademark law in international markets, with a focus on global fashion brands and their unique relationship to color as an IP asset. We then take a brief look at some of the prevailing issues in litigating in foreign courts with an added focus on China.

Can You Trademark a Color?

The immediate answer is yes, witness Tiffany's "Robin's Egg Blue," UPS's "Pullman Brown," and Coca Cola's Red and White. We could add Owens Corning® and the registration of "Pink Panther Pink" and a Pink Panther, as the company capitalized on the globally popular *Pink Panther* movie series here! A Pink Panther cartoon character introduced each sequence in the hugely popular motion pictures starring Peter Sellers as the comic bungler, French Chief Inspector Clouseau. The company then used both the Panther and the Pink on packaging and product. By doing so, it transformed a commodity (rolls of asbestos insulation for homes) into a trademark-protected and clearly distinctive product and brand. By coloring the asbestos fiber "Pink Panther Pink," a registered mark, the brand manager ensured that no competitor could copy it. This would allow the product to stand out and receive prime shelf space at retail.

When we turn to fashion brands, color trademark protection is a bird of a different, well, color![26] This is underscored by the recent court cases of Christian Louboutin (CL), the French fashion footwear designer with a luxury brand and an upscale, fiercely loyal international global following and business. His signature red-colored sole, which is registered, is found on every pair of shoes he brings to market (Figure 8.8). This, in the trade and for consumers who make a purchase, immediately identifies the shoe as his brand and as expensive, a kind of "mark" of having arrived.[27]

Louboutin had the presence of mind to register red soles as a trademark. In 2010, along comes Yves

figure 8.8
Christian Louboutin's shoes: The "trademark" red sole by which the brand is widely recognized, engendering the secondary meaning claim which helped the brand win most cases.

Saint Laurent (YSL) and in his 2011 footwear collection is a red shoe with a red sole! CL sued YSL for trademark infringement.

The decision in the case hinges upon the unique standing that fashion has before the law. First, a color, to be protected, must serve to identify the source or maker of the product. Second, however, if the color is a useful feature (i.e., functional), it is not subject to trademark protection because the purpose of trademark law is not to sequester ownership of things but first and foremost to encourage competition. This pertains in the United States and in most European Union (EU) jurisdictions. In fashion, color is central and is always a "useful feature" of aesthetic design; thus, all should have access. In the words of Judge Victor Marrero who handed down the decision in favor of YSL in January 2012, *"in the fashion industry, color serves ornamental and aesthetic functions vital to robust competition."*[28]

A similar case occurred in 2014 in French courts where Louboutin sued ZARA® for identical trademark infringement. Here the French court ruled that the CL mark was "too vague" to be protected and defensible and intimated the registration should never have been permitted and should be withdrawn. The suggestions abound that if Louboutin had trademarked a particular shade of red (let's call it "China Red") with a designated Pantone® color number and filed these together in the registration, it most probably would have been protected (assuming that the particular trademarked red was on every CL shoe sole). It appears that Louboutin's error was in being too general in his designation of red.

The widely recognized exception to this rule of law in the fashion industry is the "Secondary Meaning" defense, which looks to the market for consumer, trade, fashion media, and/or celebrity confirmation of the distinctiveness of the brand. If the consumer and trade publics behave toward the brand color in ways that signify its "distinctiveness" and if this is so consistent and broad-based that it stands in as the brand DNA, this could provide Louboutin and others with a defensible mark.[29]

Color, Secondary Meaning, and Limited Protection

In September 2012, a U.S. Court of Appeals decision settled the issue for the U.S. market; it found Louboutin's red sole trademark valid and protectable in the United States so long as the red sole contrasted with the color of the remainder of the shoe. The argument was made that the red sole had **secondary meaning**, or that the market had established that it held the distinctiveness of a trademark. The evidence presented to confirm this included marketing expenditures, media coverage, and celebrity sightings, all of which provided overwhelming evidence that the red sole conveyed and maintained the brand's distinctiveness. Therefore, the notion of distinctiveness can be thought of as an acquired characteristic of a mark and can be built into the early stages of brand management strategies. Louboutin has now embarked on a global branding strategy seeking to establish red sole marks in multiple markets and jurisdictions.[30]

Similar protections based on establishing distinctiveness can be found in *Cadbury v. Nestle*. In contention was the use of the color purple in food packaging. Cadbury® argued that years of market exposure had created identification between purple and chocolate products. Consumer surveys and other such data were presented. The court agreed with the plaintiff yet limited the protection to chocolate bars, tablets, Easter eggs, and drinks. Chocolate cake mix and the like would not be protected.[31]

However, the decision was reversed on appeal. The appeals court argued that color alone was too vague and did not constitute a "sign" or "symbol"; it suggested that if a Pantone of the color had been registered, together with greater descriptive clarity and specificity, the original ruling may have been confirmed. This is in spite of the fact that Cadbury had filed a Pantone reference for its purple and the registration office in the UK has accepted it!

Our final case on color as an IP asset presents a classic confrontation between luxury and mass brands. Here, a UK court ruled in 2013 that Victoria's Secret's

Pink®, it's very successful diffusion brand, infringes on luxury brand Thomas Pink®, citing consumer confusion regarding "Pink" and dilution of its iconic mark.[32] Again, the issue of brand management becomes paramount. It is reasonable to assume that if the case had been brought in U.S. District Court in New York City, the outcome would have not been the same. The iconic stature of the Thomas Pink brand in the UK changes the legal landscape, but this is precisely what brand managers must factor into their "what if" analysis of best market entry strategies and possible challenges from local case law and/or practice. In this case, finding a registration approach coupled with disclaimers on "Pink" packaging might have avoided this costly confrontation. As of this writing, the case is pending on appeal in the British courts.

Trademark Law in China

With China as the second-largest global economy, a brief survey of key case law outcomes is in order. This offers insights into how a nation's legal culture can follow consumer-centricity in its laws and trademark principles yet render court decisions which differ in significant ways from those of its major trading partners (such as China and the United States, and China and the European Union).

The Crocodile Wars (Lacoste® v. CGL)[33]

Founded in Hong Kong in 1952, Crocodile Garments Ltd. (CGL) is a major manufacturer and retailer of men's, women's, and children's fashions. Distribution is in China and other Asian markets. The d/b/a (doing business as) name found on some of its labels and on all of its storefronts is "Crocodile"and Cartelo. Product was, and is often, branded with the combination of language and logo as shown in Figure 8.9. The classic Lacoste® crocodile, shown in Figure 8.10, sets the stage for the trademark confrontations and cases that follow.

Prior to becoming Crocodile Garments Ltd. (CGL), the original company was founded in Singa-pore in 1943 and filed the crocodile logo in 1949 in Singapore, Hong Kong, and many other Asian countries. Lacoste, founded in 1933, registered a crocodile at that time in France and later in the late 1970s in China.

The first "war" occurred in Japan when CGL sued Lacoste for trademark infringement. The case was settled amicably with Lacoste permitted to use the logos but having to pay CGL for past usage.

The more current China case began in 2001 and continued through 2009. Lacoste argued that CGL's

figure 8.9
Cartelo's Crocodile Logo: Registered in Asia well before Lacoste, it became the grounds for several lawsuits by Lacoste.

figure 8.10
Lacoste logo: Notice the alligator faces in the opposite direction from the Cartelo logo; Chinese courts have pointed to this and to the shape of the nose as discerning differences, giving some winning cases to Cartelo.

use of "Cartelo" in China did not differentiate Lacoste products from CGL products because CGL still used a crocodile, and "Cartelo" was only on the packaging and hangtags, which would be thrown away after purchase. Also, because "Cartelo" was in English, the crocodile logo would mean more to Chinese consumers than would the co-brand name Cartelo.

The court held that the long history of mutual usage of this crocodile logo entitled both to continue. This was especially so because the Lacoste icon faced right while CGL's faced left. CGL agreed to elevate the tail and to use heavier scales on the crocodile's body to further differentiate from Lacoste.

What seems to be absent as evidence underscoring the decision is any Chinese consumer surveys or research that explored the likelihood of logo confusion on the part of consumers. Such research could well have resulted in a more favorable decision for Lacoste.

The case may have been influenced by an added consideration. A major sidebar was that CGL manufactured for Lacoste for Asian distribution. There is no direct mention in the transcript of this influencing the judge's decision, but given the Chinese sensibility to find a Solomon-like common ground as mediator, this may have had some effect on the outcome.[34]

Luxury Brands versus Mass Market Brands: Hermès, Burberry, and Their Trademark Challenges in China[35]

In China, foreign brands are often faced with registrations that require brand managers to file in ideograms (Chinese characters), pinyin (Chinese in Romance language lettering), and in English or the name of their brand in their language. An added challenge is that a brand name in pinyin is formulated by how the lettering sounds phonetically when pronounced in Mandarin! This has led to several high-profile infringement cases in Chinese courts.

Infringement cases are often countered with the abandonment defense. In two related but somewhat

different cases, *Burberry v. Polo Santa Roberta* and *Hermès v. Foshan*, we encounter this defense and some important lessons for brand managers.

In the Hermès case, the venerable French house found itself in an unlikely situation. It had registered "Hermès" in China but had not thought of doing so with the Mandarin name. Foshan (Guangdong Foshan Dafeng Garment Company) had done so shortly after Hermès, using a phonetic spelling in pinyin, Ai Ma Shi, sounding much like "Hermès" when pronounced. Hermès sued, arguing infringement. Foshan countered by claiming that the Chinese mark, not having been registered, was abandoned. The courts have agreed with the defendant and an appeals court agreed; the final outcome is still pending.

In a related but different case, Burberry had made a strategic shift in its brand merchandising by moving away from the iconic "Haymarket Plaid" as its standard global mark. It was less prominent in advertising and on products, as the company sought to move to a wider and more fashion-driven identity. Polo Santa Roberta developed and marketed handbags in China with the plaid clearly displayed. The company argued that this mark had been abandoned in China as it had not been reregistered within three years as required by Chinese law (in the United States it is every five years). Burberry countered that the mark was globally recognized by the media and consumers everywhere and submitted evidence of this from Hong Kong sources as well as evidence of the registration in Hong Kong. The Chinese court rejected the argument, saying that Polo Santa Roberta had followed the law by adhering to the proper registration procedure in China which Burberry hadn't and that Burberry did not present any evidence of brand awareness in China from Chinese sources.

Again, here is a strong lesson for brand managers that foreign courts, although operating in a global brand marketplace, should be the venue of last resort in resolving trademark disputes. If possible, a collaborative approach should prevail, or think local when managing global! A summary of cases and lessons for managers can be found in Table 8.2.

Table 8.2 Comparative Legal Issues and Outcomes: Summary of Main Cases and What Brand Management Strategy Is Needed

Case (Main Question)	Issues and Plaintiff's Argument	Issues and Defendant's Argument	Outcomes and Brand Management Takeaway
PRL v. USPA (How does lifestyle positioning establish a mark?)	Consumer confusion/logo infringement	Prior use + different class of trade; proper usage of the mark	Brand managers need to police foreign and domestic markets, packaging, and retail, not just products
CL v. YSL (Can color be trademarked?)	Color can be and become a mark; register with Pantone + secondary meaning	Color is functional; functional in fashion not protected	Use of Pantone in filing + consumer perception critical; managers need to engage core consumers over time
Lacoste v. CGL (How can marks be similar yet distinctive?)	Consumer confusion; logo infringement; dilution of equity	Prior use + fair use	Similar logo can be made to look different if parties agree; save money by agreement outside courts
LVMH v. Haute Diggity Dog (When is reference to a mark acceptable?)	Dilution as tarnishment	Parody + different class of trade + different consumer	Reference to your mark is not always infringement or dilution; tarnishment requires negative impact on mark
Hermès v. Foshan (Can the sound of a mark be trademarked?)	Sound of competing mark if similar in another language equals infringement	Acquiescence + failure to register mark in Mandarin in China equal abandonment	Registration rules in foreign markets differ; what and how often to reregister are critical
Burberry v. PSR (Is failure to reregister online equal to abandonment?)	Unfair competition; plaid has worldwide recognition as Burberry mark	Abandonment of mark over time by nonusage in China market	Awareness of a mark needs to be established in market where it is challenged change in product can affect the mark
Tiffany v. Costco (When does a mark through popular usage risk generic standing?)	Infringement/consumer confusion; mark is "incontestable"—use of name "Tiffany" protected from unfair competition	"Tiffany setting" is a generic term in jewelry industry; filing by Tiffany of phrase in 2003 is too late—inaction equals acquiescence	May be safer to settle out of court and avoid mark being ruled "generic"; prior policing of jewelry industry needed

SUMMARY

Brand naming is both science and art; it requires both analytic and creative thinking and should be generated and owned by all major brand influencers in the organization. Names can also be generated from the founder's vision or from the solution that the brand owner brings to the market. When it's the latter, the lifestyle of the targeted consumer should be clearly understood and used as direction for the name generation process. As names are generated, it is important to have a method of assessing whether the names meet certain criteria which will make them more effective marketing tools. Because brands are clearly highly valued strategic and financial assets, protecting them from misuse or infringement is an ongoing concern of brand managers. However, we need to be aware that legal outcomes will often vary depending on the geographic jurisdiction and temper of the times; so going to court, even if case law is on your side, may not always be, from the perspective of the brand's asset value, the best strategy. Finding alternative collaborative opportunities for resolving legal differences can provide a big plus for the brand and its business.

The caveat regarding litigation as a last resort strategy for brand managers becomes even more urgent as we enter the global market and are exposed to legal standards in the international community. Global intellectual property rights continue to be subject to each nation's court system, but luxury brands have aided in establishing, through their global presence and prestige and their dogged determination to protect their brands, certain global principles of legal rights; these become the bedrock for brand management strategies.

KEY TERMS

Acquiescence
Associative Projective
   Techniques
Brainstorming
Cease and Desist Letter
Class of Trade
Co-Bbanding
Complementary Positioning
Conglomerate

Consumer Confusion
Costco
Diffusion Brands
Dilution
Diminishment
Exclusive Brand
First Usage
Generification
In Commerce

Infringement
Intellectual Property (IP)
Jury of Executive Opinion
Parody Defense
Secondary Meaning
Tarnishment
Trademark Infringement
Unfair Competition
Unfair Trade

CHAPTER CONVERSATIONS

- How would you tell a friend, who knows nothing about intellectual property rights, what a brand asset is and why it is of value?
- What strategic consumer-centric perspectives do you need to keep in brand-naming?

- How would you, as brand manager, go about establishing the "Secondary Meaning" principle in a case where your brand was the plaintiff?

CHAPTER CHALLENGES

- Louis Vuitton/LVMH v. Haute Diggity Dog
  Facts: A U.S. company designed and distributed to a major big box pet store retailer in the United States a product of dog biscuits named/branded "Chewy Vuitton." LVMH sued, claiming "tarnishment," "dilution," and "customer confusion" as grounds. The defendant countered by claiming the "parody" defense and absence of injury.
  Your Challenge: Write a brief "brief" defending either party. Does the change in product change the legal arguments? As a brand manager, how are your strategies affected?

- North Face v. South Butt
  Facts: North Face managers had an opportunity to withdraw the lawsuit and purchase or manage South Butt's intellectual property. Assume this could be done without publicity.

  Your Challenge: What strategies would you develop to capitalize on the parody argument and turn the negative content into a positive marketing opportunity? Why do you think, given the target consumer, that this approach could be successful?

- Burberry v. Polo Santa Roberta
  Facts: The creative director at Burberry has broad decision-making authority on brand strategies. As brand manager, you are responsible for the business results.
  Your Challenge: Given the "Plaid" case, what are your recommendations to avoid a strategic communications error such as occurred here? Defend your strategy.

ENDNOTES

1. David A. Aaker, *Managing Brand Equity* (New York: The Free Press, 1991), Chap. 2 and 5; see also the importance of the brand associations and the images it conveys to consumers through its name in affecting successful brand extensions in S. M. Broniarczyk and J. W. Alba, "The Importance of the Brand in Brand Extension," *Journal of Marketing Research* (May 1994), and D. A. Aaker and K. L. Keller, "Consumer Evaluations of Brand Extensions," *Journal of Marketing* 54 (January 1990): 28.

2. B. H. Schmidtt and Alex Simonson, *The Strategic Management of Brands, Identity and Image* (New York: The Free Press, 1997); David A. Aaker, *Building Strong Brands* (New York: The Free Press, 1996), p. 17, where the brand name is seen as part of a strategic management undertaking.

3. Brad Van Auken, "Brand Architecture Strategy Guide," January 31, 2014, www.TheBlakeProject.com.

4. For an insightful look at the Dockers success story from a naming and brand perspective, see M. A. Geddy, "Dockers: Creating a Sub-Brand," July 2011, www.StudyMode.com, pp.1–33.

5. See Eric Yorkston and Geeta Menon, "A Sound Idea; Phonetic Effects of Brand Names on Consumer Judgements," *Journal of Consumer Research* 31 (June 2004): 43–51, and K. L. Keller, S. Heckler, and M. J. Houston, "The Effects of Brand Name Suggestiveness on Advertising Recall," *Journal of Marketing* 62 (January 1998): 48–57.

6. For a comprehensive analysis of brand naming as a strategy, see Kim Robertson, "Strategically Desirable Brand Name Characteristics," *Journal of Consumer Marketing* 6, no. 4 (Fall 1989).

7. Christina Passariello, "PPR to Change Name to Kering," *Wall Street Journal*, March 24, 2013, www.wsj.com.

8. V. A. Kari Sara, "Why Did PPR Change Its Name to Kering," April 3, 2013, www.businessoffashion.com.

9. For explorations of this issue, see Dan Horsky and Patrick Swyngedouw, "Does It Pay to Change Your Company's Name: A Stock Market Perspective," *Marketing Science* 6, no. 4 (Autumn 1987): 320–335; Nhut H. Nguyen amd Yubo Liu, "The Valuation Effect of Corporate Name Changes: A 30 Year Perspective: *European Journal of Management* (January 2010); and Saim Kashmiri and Vijay Mahajan, "The Name's the Game: Does Marketing Impact the Value of Corporate Name Changes?," *Journal of Business Research* (July 14, 2014).

10. The classic strategic overview of brand portfolio management can be found in David A. Aaker, *Brand Portfolio Strategy* (New York: The Free Press, 2004); for luxury brands, see J.-N. Kapferer and Vincent Bastien, *The Luxury Strategy*, 2nd ed. (London: Kogan Page, 2012), Chap. 7.

11. Chris Pullig, C. Simmons, and R. Netemeyer, "Brand Dilution: When Do New Brands Hurt Existing Brands?," *Journal of Marketing* 70, no. 2 (2006): 52–66.

12. For an overview of the key concepts and registration processes in brand trademark law, see Greg Genignani, *Basic Principles of Trademark Law*, (Las Vegas: Lionel, Sawyer and Collins, 2004).

13. See Megan Garber, "'Kleenex Is a Registered Trademark' (and Other Desperate Appeals),"September 25, 2014, http://www.theatlantic.com/business/archive/2014/09/kleenex-is-a-registered-trademark-and-other-appeals-to-journalists/380733/.

14. Tiffany & Company v. Costco Wholesale, U.S. District Court, Southern District of New York, No. 13 Civ. 1014 (LTS) (DEF), October 18, 2013; Thomas Holt and Charlene Minx, "*Tiffany & Co. v. Costco Wholesale Corp.*: Avoiding Trademark Genericide," March 18, 2014, http://www.steptoe.com/publications-9440.html.

15. JCK Staff, "Court Doesn't Toss Claim That Tiffany Is Setting," January 20, 2014, www.jckonline.com.

16. McDonnell Boehnen Hulbert and Berghoff LLP, "Tiffany vs. Costco: An Analysis," http://www.pearlhours.com/index.php?tiffany-vs-costco—an-analysis.html.

17. Diane Hensley, "USPA Vindicated in Polo Ralph Lauren Infringement Case," January 30, 2012, www.poloblogs.com.

18. Andrienne Kendrick, "Ralph Lauren Wins Battle Against USPA Over Horseman," March 16, 2013, www.ipwatchdog.com.

19. Laura K. Johnson, "*U.S. Polo Ass'n, Inc. v. PRL USA Holdings, Inc.*, 2013 WL 490796 (2d Cir. Feb. 11, 2013)", June 2013, http://www.finnegan.com/files/upload/Newsletters/Incontestable/2013/June/Incontestable_Jun13_15.html.

20. Ross D. Petty, "Brand Parody Products—Is the Harm Worth the Howl?," *Journal of Consumer Marketing* 26, no. 2 (2009): 64–65.

21. James E. Griffith and Zakia I. Kahn, Law 360, New York, "The Parody Defense Post–Louis Vuitton," June 23, 2011, https://www.foley.com/files/Publication/dd752d57-21d1-4f56-815b-237ecc1ca64c/Presentation/PublicationAttachment/f2aea5d8-055a-48ee-ac09-240eceefb9f9/TheParodyDefensePost-LouisVuitton.pdf.

22. Debra Cassens Weiss, "The North Face Sues the South Butt for Trademark Infringement," December 15, 2009, http://www.abajournal.com/news/article/the_north_face_sues_the_south_butt_for_trademark_infringement.

23. Michael Winter, "North v. South: Big Face Sues Little Butt Over Parody Gear," December 14, 2009, http://content.usatoday.com/communities/ondeadline/post/2009/12/north-v-south-big-face-sues-little-butt-over-parody-gear-/1#.Vxr449QrKUk.

24. Jim Slater, "North Face Settles Lawsuit Against South Butt," *Associated Press*, April 11, 2010.

25. Rich Stim, "What is Trademark Dilution?," August 15, 2014, http://www.nolo.com/legal-encyclopedia/what-trademark-dilution.html; for an interesting take on luxury brands versus mass brands and related strategies, see O. J. Majic and Helena Majic, "Case Study of Gucci vs. Guess—The Failure of Brand Strategies that Rely on Veblen's Conspicuous Consumption," *International Journal of Management Cases*, pp.132–140, Vol, 13:Series 4 (2011).

26. C. H. Stockell and E. M. Hickey, "Are Colors for You? A Primer on Protecting Colors as Marks in the United States," *INTA Bulletin* 64, no. 21 (November 15, 2009), www.inta.org/intabulletin.

27. For a more detailed discussion of color, luxury brands, and trademark protection, see Emilie Winckel, "Hardly a Black-and-White Matter: Analyzing the Validity and Protection of Single-Color Trademarks within the Fashion Industry," *Vanderbilt Law Review* 66, no. 3 (April 22, 2013): 1015–1052.

28. "Christian Louboutin vs. YSL Red Soles Court Case Takes a New Twist," September 5, 2012, http://www.huffingtonpost.com/2012/09/05/christian-louboutin-ysl-red-soles_n_1857992.html.

29. Andrea Allan, "'Soled' Out: Louboutin Is Hot on His Heels," October 3, 2012, http://www.iam-media.com/reports/detail.aspx?g=e4e1713e-8b02-4214-93c3-adffe2640e0a.

30. For a comparable perspective on Italian, French, and U.S. views on color and trademark law, see Antonella Barbieri and Federica De Santis, "Color Trademark Protection in the Fashion Industry," December 5, 2013, http://www.mondaq.com/x/279428/Trademark/Color+Trademark+Protection+in+the+Fashion+Industry.

31. Kit Chellel, "Kraft's Cadbury Wins Ruling in Nestle Suit over Color Purple," October 1, 2012, http://www.bloomberg.com/news/articles/2012-10-01/kraft-s-cadbury-wins-ruling-in-nestle-suit-over-color-purple-2-.

32. For a classic confrontation over the color pink as a brand asset, see Nina Jones, "U.K. Court Rules Victoria's Secret Infringed Thomas Pink's Trademarks," July 31, 2014, www.wwd.com.

33. Arthur Yuan, "Battle of the Crocodile Trademarks," John Marshall Law School, Center for Intellectual Property Law, Chicago, March 3, 2012.

34. Andrew Brown, "Crocodile Tears End Logo Fight," October 31, 2003, http://edition.cnn.com/2003/BUSINESS/10/31/crocodile.logo/.

35. For an excellent overview of key trademark challenges when planning to bring your brand to China, see Kristin Geboers, "Best Practices for Brand Expansion in China," Thomson Reuters, June 2013, http://trademarks.thomsonreuters.com/sites/default/files/rsrc_assets/docs/china_special_report_6.pdf.

Staying On-Brand at Retail in a Consumer-Centric Age

CHAPTER 9

AFTER COMPLETING THIS CHAPTER, YOU WILL BE ABLE TO:

- Discuss the role of brand strategies in dissolving traditional retail models.

- Analyze how retail brands differ in driving relevancy and differentiation.

- Explain how the retail brand experience has become neurologically driven.

> *"Distinct brand names will provide the only worth-while definition of value whether nameplates on stores or on products in stores."*
>
> —Robin Lewis

THE END OF TRADITIONAL RETAILING AND THE ROLE OF BRANDS

In their groundbreaking analysis of retail transformation, Robin Lewis and Michael Dart presented the historical framework of the Four Waves of Retail,[1] as we have discussed in Chapter 1. We have, as of 2000, entered the Fourth Wave.

The **Fourth Wave** (Wave IV) is characterized by an intense focus on differential brand experiences as the driving force at retail. This focus is centered on the consumer, and control of the **retail value chain**, which is all the steps which create value, ranging from how products are made to retail formats that are created and brand promises that are kept. These are central to retail strategies whether the experience is delivered in brick-and-mortar stores, catalogs, online, on mobile devices, or all of these distribution modes together, in what has become known as **omni-channel brand retail**.[2]

We have entered an intensely consumer-centric marketplace as the technology of the smartphone together with the sociology of consumer awareness have forever changed the retail landscape.[3] Retailers, to survive and prosper, must no longer be in a selling mode but in a solving mode. The guiding star must now become what do people tell us they need for a better life and how can we as retailers contribute to that outcome?

This focus on technology, coupled with serving the consumer's needs and wants, introduces the concept of **permission marketing**, which obligates retailers to request and receive from phone owners access to their smartphones and apps before messaging is permitted. Besides the legal limitation to any marketing intrusions, the power of individual consumers as well as consumer communities to grant or withhold permission creates again, as discussed in Chapter 6, a court of public opinion where commercial intrusions are judged and renegade brands sentenced. As we will explore in greater detail in Chapter 11, consumer engagement/nonengagement becomes a metric by which brand behavior in regard to intrusion is measured and with it a shift in power from Madison Avenue to Main Street.

Retail Brand Strategies

The increasing empowerment of the consumer through technology, coupled with the excess in retail space and the overabundance of product supply, have all converged in Wave IV to change the nature of retail strategies. With overabundance and excess inventories, control of the brand and its message becomes paramount. It has been estimated that consumers are now inundated with 3,000 to 10,000 brand messages a day. There is no possibility that we have the neurological capacity to process all of these communications. The role of the brand in this regard is to cut through this communication clutter and reach the targeted consumer with the relevant and differentiated message. However, the determination as to what content is relevant must now be made by the consumer and not by the brand manager. The most successful of these content communications will therefore be personalized as brand managers learn the art of listening. Brands will reflect what has been heard and help serve as a decision-making heuristic enabling consumers to arrive at decisions more efficiently as the brand serves as their instinctive North Star.[4]

Consequently, retailer brands strive to be top-of-mind so your brand and/or store comes first to consumers' minds when they are planning their product purchases and retail destinations. This includes strategies guided by communicating brand images that market the store as a brand as well as the products it offers.

Successful retailers achieve this by being brand focused. This is often expressed with the phrase "**staying on-brand**" or managing the business from the perspective of the brand values and the brand promise, thereby staying "on-course." Staying on-brand has become more than just a guardrail for keeping business from meandering off of tactical operations and daily time and action calendars. It not only infuses the company mission and consumer marketing with a consistent set of corporate values and engagement metrics as we saw in Chapter 6, but it also seeks ways to communicate the unique nature of the store and its promise to deliver a unique experience.[5]

The Store as the Brand

In some instances, the store name and its image are positioned as the brand. In an interesting pivot from Keller's "**Customer-Based Brand Equity**"[6] model, Hartman and Spiro extend the concept to a retail context and explore the central role of retail brand image in informing brand equity and driving consumer decisions.[7]

For this strategy to be effective, the brand promise has to be consumer-centric. There needs to be a clear idea of the loyal core consumer for whom the store is a **destination brand**, that is, one that customers, when planning their shopping for the day, have as top-of-mind to visit, shop, and purchase their brands and products.

An early proponent of the store as the brand was Bloomingdale's, the iconic New York City department store. Store management identified a core cohort of Bloomingdale loyalists whose lifestyle could be used as the basis for in-store experiential marketing. Their profiles included travel abroad, vacation homes, and social activities (charitable giving, support for the arts, etc.). The store could reflect these activities in marketing brands, celebrities, and events (Figure 9.1).

The store became identified for having displays of products from other countries, or designers with elaborate presentations throughout the store. Cocktails and music accompanied the openings, which included

the media and New York City dignitaries, politicians, and fashion leaders.

These events branded the store in the eyes of the trade and the public as unique and entertaining, something that was subsequently captured in the store's tagline and brand promise, *"Like no other store in the world."* The CEO at this time was Marvin Traub, who became identified as the originator of the mantra *"retailing as theatre."*[8] This is one of the earliest expressions of the concept of the experiential brand and forged in the United States the concept of the store as the brand.

figure 9.1
The store as the brand: Featuring fashion by high-profile personalities such as Ivanka Trump made the store the brand.

Another strategy to achieve a unique store identity is built around **private brands**, which are brands developed by and exclusive to the retailers. Let's refer to this as the product as the brand.

The Product as the Brand

During the first three waves of retail (1850–2000), retailers were **distributors**, or resellers. They purchased branded products at what was called **wholesale prices**, or what the brand owner/manufacturer would charge them, and then resell the products to consumers at a **markup**. This markup, sometimes referred to as **margin**, was the selling price needed to cover the retailer's cost and expenses, plus a profit. Both brand owners/manufacturers and brand buyers/retailers usually marked up merchandise between 20 percent and 50 percent. So if Procter and Gamble sold a bar of soap to Walmart for 10 cents, Walmart might resell it for 12 or 15 cents, making a **gross profit** (profit before expenses) of 20 percent to 50 percent. The same markup/margin scenario could be found where a Polo Ralph Lauren might sell Macy's a **men's polo**, those ubiquitous knit tops originally worn by Argentinian polo players (hence the name) that first found commercial success shortly after René Lacoste first wore them in the French Open tennis tournament in 1927, for resale.

As retailers sought both better margins and control over pricing in order to be competitive, they saw an opportunity to develop their own product assortments and control the distribution, pricing, and availability. They often chose not to invest in creating a brand, as this included the brand image, more upscale marketing, and a promise beyond a low price. In this respect, retailers varied in the degree to which they understood and were willing to commit to investing in brand building. Because the initial reasons for the private brand (usually called private label) were to enhance the margins, make more profit, and pay less for the product, branding and the cost associated with it seemed, to many retailers, counterproductive.

The market impact of this introduction of private brands changed the wholesaler/retailer equation. More and more retailers began to develop more and more private label merchandise in both foodstuffs and apparel. One effect which has had major repercussions is that the retailers, who were partners with the wholesalers, have now become their competitors. This is exacerbated by the refusal by retailers to share customer data. The retailer considers the purchaser of a national brand to be the retailer's customer and not the wholesaler's or national brand owner's. This puts the national brand at a brand engagement disadvantage, as it has no direct link to its customer base to deal with problems or opportunities. Conversely, it gives retailers access to sales and consumer preference data from national brand transactions, which opens opportunities to further enhance their own private brand businesses. In addition, shortcomings in store customer service can cast a shadow over the national brand as its products and brands become identified by consumers with the store and its service shortcomings.

Finally, by placing private label product next to, or hanging with, nationally advertised, well-established national brands, the retailer derives the benefit of the halo effect; that is, the store brand (or label) derives the benefit of brand enhancement by association with the more well-known brand (Table 9.1). The retailer derives this benefit without the expense incurred by the national brands from decades of the latter's marketing and advertising investments in those brands.[9]

Eventually, in many of the product categories, private label is perceived by consumers to be in the same league as the more expensive national brand. This is the beginning of the transition of the private label into a private brand.

Confirmation for this transition in perception can be found in surveys where consumers have been shown to perceive store labels as store brands. Add to this that in many assessments regarding comparative quality, at least one source reports that the store brands are seen as equal to many of their national brand competitors and occasionally superior.[10] For instance, in U.S. grocery stores, close to 20 percent of total sales are now private brands.[11]

Table 9.1 Department Store Halo Merchandising Model for Apparel: U.S. Department Stores
Apparel retailers often surround their brands with better known national brands.

Department (Product Source)	Product Description	Fashion Position	Brand Recognition	Pricing
Designer (international name brands)	Only in stores "A" branches*	Directional	Very high	Highest
Bridge/ Contemporary (national brands)	In Stores "A" Or "B" Branches	Trend leader	High	Next highest
Better (mostly national brands)	In all "A," "B," "C"	On-trend	Well known	Midprice
Upper moderate mix of store + (national brand)	In all branches	Basics with a twist	Somewhat known	Lower
Moderate (largely store brands)	In all branches— strong in "B" and "C"	Dependable basics	Known best to store's frequent shoppers	Lowest

*A, B, C designations reflect store size, volume, and range of brands with A = Largest, C = Smallest.

The acceleration of this pattern of the growth of private brands is continuing. One estimate has 50 percent of Walmart's total revenues generated from private brands. For JC Penney, the number is about the same and growing. Some retail research "think tanks" estimate that eventually 80 percent of all apparel products sold in the United States will be private brands.[12]

Controlling One's Destiny at Retail

As we have seen, retailers are aggressively engineering ways to control the value chain and thereby control their destiny at retail. The key link in the chain is the consumer. The strength of this link is dependent on the strength of the brand. As traditional retailers morph into modern wholesale brand builders, traditional wholesalers are following suit by becoming modern retail brand builders. This is built on the

realization that the retailer is not the customer but a conduit to the customer. The retailers, reluctantly, may agree.

The Dilution of Brand Equity

National brand owners (i.e., manufacturers) are faced with the challenge of transitioning from the current distribution strategy of selling to national department stores to opening their own retail stores. The former provide brand exposure and product sales at the expense of eroding brand equity and **product integrity** (how the brand tells its story), especially fashion brands, through being presented as a unified collection rather than as a series of unrelated items. This erosion is the result of department stores' brand management strategy to purchase only the parts of each national brand's seasonal collection that complements their own private brands; thus, the national brand message is lost. However, through their seasonal design and merchandise collections, national fashion brands create and convey a brand identity that is never presented in its entirety in a department store setting.

The Wholesale Brand Management Response

The wholesale owners of national brands are not sitting idly by. Each major brand owner has designed its own single-brand specialty-store development strategy. As noted, major brand owners are opening their own brand stores in order to control their brand identity and the value chain at retail. These formats also provide an opportunity to display the brand merchandise as a brand story. This is something that is often missing in department store merchandising of national brands because the national brands are being bought by the store to complement its own presentations at retail of its private brands.

This fragmentation has an adverse effect on sales and brand equity, both of which can be avoided by controlling the retail environment that comes with owning and opening your own retail stores. Again, the objective is to control the value chain of which the brand experience is a major link.

For example, in 2012 Vans (the footwear and streetwear brand owned by VF Corporation) had over 300 free-standing retail stores and plans to add over 200 more by 2016. Free-standing Wrangler stores (a VF denim brand) have opened as well, and both Vans and Wrangler also distribute to department stores. The overall retail owned-store count for VFC in the first quarter of 2014 was 1,263 wholly owned stores and growing.[13]

VF reported in 2010 that 17 percent of revenues were derived from direct sales to consumers. The CEO had 25 percent of revenues as a 2015 revenue goal from direct selling of brands within the VF portfolio; in 2014 it accounted for 23 percent of revenues, up from 21 percent in 2013.[14]

What becomes apparent is that the very designations "retailer" and "wholesaler" are now obsolete and misleading. Both are brand owners and brand builders!

Owning both the store and the product brand, as with VF and especially for fashion companies, offers the best opportunity to provide a seamless brand experience to the consumer. But what of those companies that are not in fashion and do not have the core capability to create a private brand product collection or retail their own national brands in their own retail outlets? What strategic recourse is available to them?

Creating and optimizing the experiential brand is not confined to fashion retailers. It also appears in retail brands where the service component is central to the brand promise. Forms of service, such as we have seen in our exploration of luxury brands, are naturally suited to the brand experience. This is because they must manage emotional relations between clientele and sales associates and strive for seamless consumer-centricity in the retail experience.

One retail model that based its brand identity on a consumer-centric focus is Best Buy, the world's largest electronics retailer. Here the store branded itself from a service rather than from an event perspective as did Bloomingdale's.

Following the high-relevance/high-differentiation model, Best Buy has forged a brand strategy that transitioned the retailer from one focused on selling products to consumers to one focused on offering solutions for consumers and combines this consumer solutions brand promise with a unique means of delivering it. This combination makes the store the brand and a unique solutions offer, the brand promise.

RETAIL BRAND DIFFERENTIATION AND CONSUMER RELEVANCY

As retail and wholesale businesses dissolve into retail brand businesses, the number of choices available to consumers increases. There are more brands, more competition, and a greater need for relevancy and differentiation. The challenge is to find the balance between maintaining a brand identity and being open to, and capable of, change that builds upon that

Let's take a closer look at Best Buy as a company that for the past decade has been intensely focused on customer-centricity. Best Buy was suffering from marketing myopia. Here are two statements from annual reports that show the company's awareness and recognition of the need for a strategic change from a product/selling culture and brand to a consumer/solution culture and brand: "*Best Buy is being engineered from a product-centered company to one with the capability to provide a trusted perspective . . . in this digital age*" and "*to solve problems for customers.*"[15]

Shortly after these pronouncements in 2008, management purchased the **Geek Squad**, a highly trained cadre of young technicians available 24/7 for installations, repairs, and the most vexing challenge for the ordinary tech consumer—understanding the workings and the capabilities of the technology purchased. The unique graphics on the Volkswagen Beetles that constitute the Geek Squad's repair vehicles (Figure 9.2), as well as their "technicians'" uniforms, was part of the brand repositioning or shifting the brand promise from a selling culture to a solution culture. The vehicles conveyed the brand message that technology could be fun and confirmed, along with other practices that followed, that the company was authentic in its commitment to its brand promise. One statement in the 2010 Annual Report captures this attitude, noting that the company is committed to "*make life fun and easy for consumers.*"

This commitment appears again in the 2014 Annual Report, in the CEO's letter to the stockholders, where he states that the mission

figure 9.2
A Geek Squad service vehicle: A major element in Best Buy's brand.

of the company is to "*enrich and empower people's lives through technology.*" In addition, Hubert Joly makes what might be an unprecedented point for a CEO in a shareholders' letter, that of underscoring the degree of commitment to a consumer-centric strategy by mentioning that the company's Net Promoter Scores were "*up by 30 basis points*"![16]

By redirecting its brand positioning into a consumer-centric company, Best Buy has differentiated itself from its competitors. One of the strategies used to do so was to design a consumer segmentation model that became a platform for executing consumer-centric operational store policies and marketing programs. This took into consideration the fact that there is no such thing as the "average customer" and aligned the brand promise with a more customized and personalized approach to the retail experience. This began by identifying four distinct consumer cohorts as the core consumer base for the brand and included the following

(continued on next page)

personas or cohorts: Buzz, the tech enthusiast; Jill, the suburban soccer mom; Barry, the wealthy professional; and Ray, the family man. There were also smaller subsets. Through surveys and interviews, managers identified the major challenge and/or interest that technology presented to each cohort.[17]

A key to the success of the program was the training given to sales associates. Customer cues were identified that would alert the associates to the type of customer with whom they were dealing. This enabled a sensitive alignment of the solutions-oriented brand promise with the core consumers. Best Buy furthered this strategy by using consumer touch points, through which employees were sensitivity trained to frame and focus on each customer's

purchase objectives. Personnel were picked for their unique capabilities and instructed on how to listen, ask relevant questions, identify the key touch points, and then solve the problem or challenge (meet the "want" or "need") that the customer has conveyed to the sales associate.

With these consumer insights, Best Buy then aligned its store formats so they would be a "fit" for these consumer cohorts. Different in-store merchandising was developed for different markets. For example, in markets with greater visits by female customers who are purchasing for family homes, stores set up "family rooms" as display environments and changed colors and atmosphere to mirror the aesthetic of a home. The relevant marketing messages were adjusted accordingly (Figure 9.3).

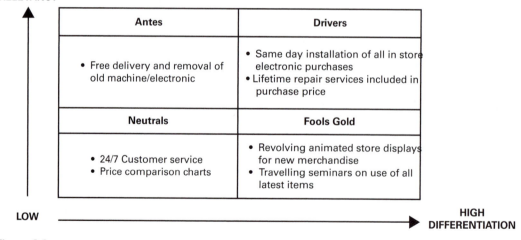

HIGH RELEVANCY

Antes	Drivers
• Free delivery and removal of old machine/electronic	• Same day installation of all in store electronic purchases • Lifetime repair services included in purchase price
Neutrals	**Fools Gold**
• 24/7 Customer service • Price comparison charts	• Revolving animated store displays for new merchandise • Travelling seminars on use of all latest items

LOW → **HIGH DIFFERENTIATION**

figure 9.3
Brand loyalty touch-Point Matrix: Applying the matrix to develop strategies for an electronics retailer.

(continued on next page)

As part of its consumer-centric commitment and the need to differentiate its product mix from that of its competitors in all retail channels of distribution, Best Buy has also entered into the fashion space, much as Apple has with its design sensibility and accessories complements to its electronic products. But contrary to Apple, where the store and the product are part of a unified brand identity, Best Buy and other electronics retailers cannot readily develop a private brand program. They lack the core competency and the technological credibility to compete effectively. The strategy undertaken to compensate is to co-brand with high-profile fashion designers whose names provide cachet and whose design sensibilities can add value to the electronics product offerings.[18]

In the fall of 2014, Best Buy launched designer accessories collections designed by Nanette Lepore, Isaac Mizrahi, and others. This came on the heels of an exclusive launch of similar products under the Kate Spade brand, the latter launch being "*for women who want their devices to express their very personal fashion sensibilities.*"[19]

This strategy of enhancing the store brand by co-branding—in this case joining the store and a product **category** (the general nature of a product) in a joint marketing play such as with well-known fashion designers and presenting specially designed merchandise exclusive to the retailer—is another result of the erosion of traditional lines of retail separation. Thus, electronics stores mimic in their brand offerings brands that in the past were found only in fashion boutiques or upscale department stores. This represents an additional challenge for brand managers who now need to look beyond traditional branding sources to brand strategies that align with fashion trends and consumer-centric lifestyles. Co-brand arrangements generate buzz and store traffic, both of which bring in customers and result in **plus business**, above the usual daily pattern of sales. The shortcoming in the co-brand strategy arises when designer collections are limited editions, available in-store for a limited time and with a limited product assortment. Once the inventory is sold out, so is the buzz. The hope is that the association with the upscale brand experience lingers with consumers so that the store brand becomes permanently associated with the designer brand experience. The empirical research suggests that for luxury brands the congruence between the brands' identities including their hedonic image and personality are key variables; for non-luxury, especially where the positioning of the store brand is on a more functional or utilitarian basis (such as Best Buy), product "fit" or the perception of product similarities tends to drive more successful outcomes.[20]

This is what H&M has so successfully achieved and, as we will see later in this chapter, Target Stores as well. But each of these, Best Buy, H&M, and Target, represent three distinct retail brand models requiring three different approaches to co-branding with designers.

(continued on next page)

Finally, the experiential brand that offers service as its differentiator requires a retail format which offers a feeling of friendliness and intimacy to fulfill its service promise. This is especially so in the electronics space where the challenges of technology usage are still primary challenges for most consumers. Here is this view from Josh Will, a Best Buy vice president in charge of the Best Buy/Connected Store: "*Technology is an amazing place . . . but it is still too hard for customers to use . . . and to understand how it can better your life. It's time that the shopping environment matches that expectation.*"[21]

To achieve this, in 2012 Best Buy launched the aforementioned Connected Store.[22] Smaller in square footage than the traditional Best Buy, it is easier to navigate, see, and shop its various product offerings. The formats are meant to be service, training, and education centers for its customers. For example, at the very center of each location is a Geek Squad Solutions Center. This is another execution of the brand promise and a touch point Driver. To complete this brand identity, trademark, and branding, the name "The Connected Store" would have been a powerful add-on to the brand strategy. However, this hasn't happened and it's unlikely to, because players in the electronics space such as Intel and AT&T already have used this name for concept and service stores. In addition, although there might be some trademark strategies that Best Buy could undertake, there is no indication that it is about to do so.

identity rather than jettisons it for a new one. The guideline for this balancing act is really knowing your consumer and practicing consumer-centricity. This means that what is relevant to the consumer must drive brand strategies rather than brand strategies driving the consumer.

Target's and Walmart's Retail Brand Models

One of the major misconceptions in the comparative analysis of retail competitors is the supposed uniformities of the Walmart and Target brand models. This has resulted in several major brand management errors on the part of Walmart brand strategy teams who misperceived the nature of the Target brand identity as well as their own. It also raises issues of what business Walmart is really in and how this affects its perception of its competitive universe. So let's begin by taking a look at Target's unique brand identity.

Target and The Democratization of Design

As we mentioned in the earlier discussion of Best Buy, the model for the use of designers as co-branding assets and differentiators is Target stores. Their brand identity and the brand narrative which flows from it are based on the concept of The Democratization of Design (TDD), as first discussed in Chapter 3. This brand identity (TDD) is based on the idea that beautiful designs in home goods and fashion, for example, should be and can be made affordable to all. As we shall see, this is a deeply held consumer-centric value proposition within the Target retail culture.

An excellent place to search for these types of brand commitments is in the retailer's annual reports and the CEO's letter to stockholders found at the beginning of each of these reports. Although Target had begun to speak of The Democratization of Design as early as 1999, and has been executing the "democratization" strategy for almost a decade by co-branding with Michael Graves in home goods (2000) and Isaac Mizrahi in fashion (2003), each annual report continues to mention this commitment as the philosophy behind the mission and the tagline *"Expect More, Pay Less."* There is continuity of both content and commitment to this brand identity as exemplified by the 2013 Annual Report in which the commentaries in the "What We Believe In" section speak about *"approachable design," "design for all," "we're dedicated to making good design accessible to all."*[23]

The scope of this commitment is not limited to products alone. In the 2014 Annual Report, in "The Shopping Experience" section, the following expression is found: *"we apply our design philosophy to everything . . . building exteriors . . . mobile apps . . . (technology) tools and systems."*[24]

Brand Differentiation and Consumer Relevancy

A comparison of Target and Walmart, two competitors who see their promise in very different terms, provides important insight into how brands frame and direct business practice. So let's take a look at these two companies that compete in certain category sectors (especially food and home goods) and how they implement their brand promise into an everyday customer experience.

Target's Brand Mission statement: *"Our mission is to make Target the preferred shopping destination by delivering outstanding value, continuous innovation and exceptional guest experience by consistently fulfilling our Expect More, Pay Less, Brand Promise."*[25]

Extended references are made in the Target annual reports to the company's private brands and exclusive brands, as discussed in the preceding chapter, which are those that are not owned by the retailer but that only the retailer can distribute (all of which are listed in the annual report), as examples of how this "mission" is fulfilled: *"The brands are critical to our success, because they are core to our differentiation strategy. . ."*[26]

Consequently, Target's brand image, as perceived by core consumers, is derived from both the store and its private brands as critical elements in the company's business strategy. This is clearly understood as a brand management strategy as reflected again in Target's position on brand image as found in the annual report: *"brand image is a critical element in our business strategy."*[27]

Contrast this with the vision of Walmart's Mike Duke. In response to an inquiry about the briefness of the company's mission statement, Mike Duke, CEO of Walmart, was heard to respond with some irritation saying, *"People are not concerned with their mission statement as they are their prices . . ."* The focus is on Everyday Low Prices (**EDLP**), as shown in Figure 9.4.

Walmart's mission, which appears as a condensed version in its tagline and in all marketing material, is the source of its tagline and the essence of its business: *"Committed to saving people money so they can live better."*[28]

Unlike Target, there is no mention of brands in the Walmart annual report, neither referencing the store as a brand nor its store-owned labels as brands. There also is no mention of either segmentation models as business drivers or the store image/identity as a differentiation strategy, although there is in place within

figure 9.4
Walmart store signage for marketing EDLP: Pricing is not enough to create a competitive advantage.

Walmart's marketing department a very sophisticated brand alignment and consumer segmentation model.[29] In their place are constant references to Walmart's everyday low pricing (EDLP) position, which is meant to convey the idea that the initial pricing on merchandise in the store is the lowest and best value possible day in and day out. For example, here is part of the president's letter from the 2014 Annual Report: *"We invest in price to bring Every Day Low Prices (EDLP). That commitment to price is central to our brand."*[30]

For Walmart, commitment to price is presented as its business strategy and brand promise. But how solid a foundation is this? Is it basically an operational platform for driving commodity products? And is its seminal role in achieving the "price/value" objective of Walmart so strong that it dominates the culture and obscures the possibility of going beyond commodity products, such as fashion, as a retail commitment?

On closer examination, EDLP emerges as an operational tactic derived from logistical efficiencies and Walmart's successful **category management** strategy. The strategy identifies the leading vendor in a product category which is then assigned to manage the business outcomes in that product department. As an example, major vendors such as Procter and Gamble and Levi's are responsible for assisting Walmart in managing the departments within which they are the category product leaders. Walmart's collaborative relationship with these and other vendors along with the store's world-class operations model (supported by **Retail Link**®, Walmart's proprietary category management software) are what help realize those efficiencies.

EDLP, which cannot be trademarked or patented (although the process may be), can be too easily replicated to provide a clear and readily sustainable competitive advantage. It is an Ante, highly relevant to consumers but low in differentiation from competitors. This is why it is not sustainable as a brand strategy; it is inconsistent in its ability to deliver on business objectives.

As evidence of this, witness the weekly changes in the lowest price leadership position on comparable **household basket**, a grouping of the household items most widely purchased for the week and their prices. Independent research firms generate an average weekly price profile of the same forty items/brands purchased each week by consumers from Kroger, Target, Walmart, **Dollar General** (a variety store in competition with Walmart), and others. Here are some of the findings. A 2012 Bloomberg report found that *"Target this month had lower prices than Walmart for the first time since October."*[31] In October 2013 a *Marketing Daily* headline reported, "Dollar General Beats Walmart,"[32] and in 2014, a survey by the Kantar Group, a highly respected price comparison research firm, concluded that Dollar General was lower than Walmart and that *"Dollar General took the crown for a third year in a row."*[33]

In any given week, for any of these grocery and household items, any of the competitors might be number one! This makes it impossible to sustain a definable brand position as *the* low-price leader.

Without this touch point of competitive differentiation, Walmart is left with little more than the old retail adage **location, location, location**. (Often referred to as the first rule for a successful store is where it is located.) There is nothing in its brand identity, image, or mission that can be drawn upon as a possible substitute for EDLP.

A critical aspect of brand management is to properly identify your competitors and the product categories that are most likely to be competitive categories of business. This requires a clear idea of the nature of the category, such as apparel, and of its **classifications**, such as dresses or tops, and whether they are **commodities**, such as white T-shirts, or fashion, such as the latest dress styles. The key question is how the expectations of the store's core customers developed over time, driven and informed by the store's brand marketing and advertising. How do these affect customers' perceptions of style, image, and value in these categories and classifications of business that they associate in their minds with the brand image of the store and which no amount of new advertising is likely to change?[34] It is also imperative that the brand managers, who might be considering a repositioning of the category and its classifications into a new brand offering, understand who their competitors truly are. The temptation to learn from your adversaries must be based on a realistic assessment of who they are. The failure to follow the aforementioned caveats leads to our next exploration of the brand identity crises at retail, an analysis of the failure of Walmart's excursion into what might be called "high" fashion.

Walmart and Fashion Apparel

In 2005, Stephen Quinn, a senior executive brand manager with PepsiCo, and John Fleming, the vice president of marketing with Target, were hired to resuscitate Walmart's ailing apparel business. An attempt to do so in-house, beginning in 2001 with the introduction of a more contemporary looking product and brand called "George," did not gain the kind of loyalty or generate the revenues Walmart had hoped. During this period, Target was clearly the standard and destination for what came to be called **chic, cheap fashion,** or fashion that followed the trends and was affordable to the vast majority of consumers.

Quinn and Fleming had the support of the CEO at that time, H. Lee Scott, who gave public pronouncements that *"what we've got to do is make sure that those customers (who buy food and paper towels) aren't bypassing other departments."*[35] The implication was clear that the other department was apparel. A customer survey of 6,000 Walmart shoppers had confirmed that "fashionable apparel" was a merchandise dimension that was missing from the stores.

The new collection was dubbed "Metro 7," although it is unclear how relevant the name was to current customers since the overwhelming number of Walmart locations were in rural and suburban areas and not in major cities. The notion seemed to be that *Metro* conveyed an image of a cooler, more sophisticated customer and a more fashionable lifestyle.

The merchandise was priced so that complete outfits could be had for under $40. This made it affordable and, from a price perspective, saleable. The styling, however, raised another matter of critical importance. The collection was described by the senior vice president of product development as *"ultra-stylish, trendy, modern, with body-conscious fit."*[36] This provided a flashback to the Metro 7 name and the implicit reason behind its selection. It would reflect and convey the brand promise of an upscale fashion lifestyle often associated with the Seventh Avenue fashion district of New York City.

An immediate red flag was flying, but no one seemed to see it. The description of the style of the clothing spoke to the sensibilities, to say nothing of the body shape, of a much more sophisticated customer than was shopping Walmart for apparel. The key words that were also the barricade to optimizing the new fashion opportunity were *ultra-stylish* and *body-conscious fit*. These terms generally translate into women's sizes 2–6, perhaps sizes 8–10 at the outside. The average U.S. women's size for sportswear, dresses, or jeans is size 14! One might venture to say that many of the Walmart customers, on average, reflect this national size 14 as well. Therefore, from the get-go, the alignment between the brand promise, its merchandise component, and the core potential Walmart consumer was open to question.

The final nail in the proverbial coffin was the marketing and advertising campaign begun by Walmart in September 2005 to launch Metro 7. Target had scooped the entire industry in August, just prior to Walmart's ads and the September New York fashion shows, by taking out ads in the August issue of *New Yorker* magazine. Taking out ads is an understatement. Target bought all of the advertising space (seventeen to eighteen pages), becoming the sole advertiser in the magazine and, in effect, making that issue exclusively its own. It was a first for any brand, at any level of price or fashion, and thereby solidified the heritage of Target's brand promise *"to expect more"* through the democratization of design.

In September 2005, Walmart launched its Metro 7 campaign—eight full pages in *Vogue* magazine, the fashion authority in American media. The campaign was a multimillion-dollar investment and was planned to run for eighteen months to give the new brand and its message time to gain some awareness and consideration from its target audience. However, the target audience was in fact the issue and eventually confirmed as the problem. A look at the *Vogue* subscriber and reader profile made it clear that its customer and Walmart's customer resided in two different lifestyle worlds. By any demographic or lifestyle measure, there was little or no significant correspondence between the two audiences. One would have been hard-pressed to find a subscription in the homes of most Walmart apparel shoppers.

The problem was exacerbated by the presentation at retail. At Walmart, the operations culture places the operation managers, called merchandisers, in charge of floor presentation. Their focus is on bringing the product to the shelf at the lowest possible cost and turning the inventory in the shortest amount of time.

The marketing team in each store does not have the leverage to rework the departments from a marketing perspective. In fashion apparel, romancing, imaging, and presenting the products as lifestyles is a precondition for success. As a consequence, the Metro 7 presentation had signage and some photography but no designated floor environment which set it apart. In addition, no attempt was made to beautify the dressing rooms and to make them proper settings in which to try on the product. Again, driven by operational costs, the dressing rooms where apparel sales are most often made or lost were never upgraded and remained less than the brand image that Metro 7 was attempting to convey.

Fashion merchandise cannot be advertised as hard goods or next to hard goods such as garden equipment. Using **run-of-press (ROP)** ads, which are color flyers inserted into Sunday newspapers, Metro 7 was, at times, presented in less than fashionable company. The final outcome was that production was projected for 1,000 stores with possible distribution to 1,500

Walmarts. The line was never distributed beyond 500 locations. The decade of decline in apparel sales that had begun in 2001 continued through 2011 when Walmart all but abandoned any fashion dimension in its apparel business (Figure 9.5).

One of the strategic issues revolved around whether Target was Walmart's prime competitor in apparel. We think not, especially if we add the word *fashion* to apparel. Walmart's abiding strength is logistics and how that can be fine-tuned to become the most efficient process for cost reduction and, for Walmart, price reduction. One could go so far as to say that Walmart is not really in the retail business but in the logistics business. The company's incredible operational systems provide its competitive advantage over others and constitute its core competency. Its mastery of global logistics has enabled it to drive costs out and prices down and, for the most part, pass this savings on to its customers and thereby fulfill its brand promise. But the very nature of its operations and success obstructs any clear vision of what it takes to drive a fashion business. It isn't about driving costs out and prices down.

The absence of a brand merchandise position within the store as a strategy, and the inordinate focus on price, explains the company's failure to drive fashion apparel. We've seen how this category requires emotional marketing content, brand identity, and alignment with designated consumer niches. As we will see in the following section, this high-margin category, fashion, remains underdeveloped by Walmart's price-driven culture but is being pursued aggressively by many of its true competitors.

This last reference points to the other error that the Walmart brand management team made, given Walmart's culture and brand model: their competitors in apparel were not the same as they were in foodstuffs or hard goods. This misperception was a major strategic blunder. The chart in Figure 9.6 graphically presents those retail brands that are in the same space as Walmart in apparel in terms of price/value but have added some degree of an emotional and experiential dimension to their management of their fashion

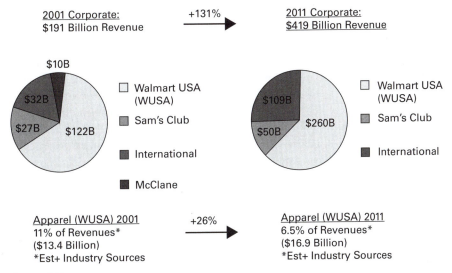

A Decade of Decline: An Overview of Walmart's Apparel Struggle
Distribution of Revenue by Business Units

2001 Corporate:
$191 Billion Revenue

+131%

2011 Corporate:
$419 Billion Revenue

$10B

$32B

$27B $122B

☐ Walmart USA
  (WUSA)

■ Sam's Club

■ International

■ McClane

$109B

$50B $260B

☐ Walmart USA
  (WUSA)

■ Sam's Club

■ International

Apparel (WUSA) 2001
11% of Revenues*
($13.4 Billion)
*Est+ Industry Sources

+26%

Apparel (WUSA) 2011
6.5% of Revenues*
($16.9 Billion)
*Est+ Industry Sources

figure 9.5
Comparative apparel sales as a percentage of overall revenue.

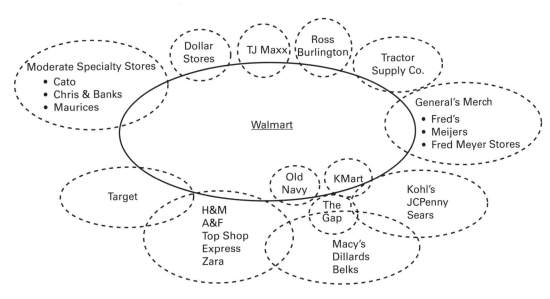

figure 9.6
Walmart's competitive universe: Some key apparel groups/stores.

brands. The chart also indicates those retailer brands that are on the periphery of Walmart's fashion apparel universe and shouldn't be competitive targets against which Walmart positions itself. Target is in that space.

Let's explore some of the retailers against whom Walmart is competitively positioned in apparel to see how they have managed and branded their apparel businesses. What lessons can we draw from them that perhaps Walmart could follow?

Dollar stores have recently been developing their own brand apparel, directly competing for the same customer as Walmart. For example, Dollar General has developed/adopted "**DG®**" as a brand logo as part of both a corporate and product identification brand strategy. Dollar General created DG in order to roll out upscale packaging for store products such as DG Home, Baby, and Health and Body. As an indicator of the degree of its commitment to a brand strategy, Dollar General was able to purchase DG.com from Data General, asset owner of the web address, out-bidding Dolce & Gabbana in its claim for its diffusion line (also DG)!

Given its higher margins, Dollar General wanted to focus on brand apparel and found ways to brand women's sportswear. In order to capture women's attention to sportswear, Dollar General relaunched the Bobbie Brooks brand for women's sportswear with an "I am Bobbie" brand marketing campaign (ironically, Walmart at one time had Bobbie Brooks as an exclusive brand!). In the brand marketing campaign, Dollar General incorporated the aspirational theme of women overcoming personal hardships and professional obstacles as a way to connect women to the brand and to align the brand with key issues concerning the company's female target customers.

In order to connect on a more personal level, Dollar General also used employees as photo-models who tell their story. Here is another opportunity that Walmart, given its nonbranded perspective, fails to leverage. Whereas Dollar General captured employees' stories and tied them to a brand launch, Walmart uses employees in ROP ads without a brand or story theme!

Family Dollar is another dollar store that focused on a brand apparel strategy and is a competitor to Walmart. Beginning in February 2011, Family Dollar began a corporate-wide refocus on apparel. As with Dollar General, Family Dollar was interested in a women's sportswear brand strategy and how it could deliver higher margins and impulse purchases. Consumer research identified an important need that wasn't being served in the company's assortments and an in-store merchandising presentation gap which was hurting sales. Family Dollar discovered that reconfiguring women's sportswear departments to coordinate tops and bottoms and adding a brand identity generated plus sales. Research also discovered that mothers were willing to pay more for quality for their kids even though, given the recession, discretionary income was down. With this new-found information, Family Dollar launched Kidgets®, its own children's wear brand that continues to outperform the revenue and profit plan.

Maurices is a young women's trend-driven apparel and accessories store with moderate pricing; with most of its stores in the Midwest, the company in 2016 was approaching 1,000 retail locations. Maurices is part of the Ascena Retail Group, which includes Lane Bryant (for plus-size fashion apparel), Ann Taylor (for the 30- to 45-year-old misses fashion customer), and other brands; each brand is positioned within the portfolio to appeal to a particular type of consumer. Maurices positioning on apparel is *"Hometown specialty store savvy, fashion conscious girl with a 20 something attitude."* The company's tagline, *"Life's a Fashion Runway,"* reflects clear understanding of who its customers are.[37]

In 2001 Maurices lost brand focus, which required maintaining the balance between being on-trend and offering very affordable prices, and the company had to recalibrate in a way that would bring attention to its apparel and its commitment to fashion. In order to grow and satisfy its customers' needs, Maurices decided to become interactive with its customers on fashion tips and questions they may have. The company created an online presence where consumers could "live chat" with employees and receive "style advice between girlfriends." With these new brand strategies, Maurices was able to make a remarkable recovery. From 2006 to 2011 the company saw record growth in sales. This continues today with robust sales and earnings and with retail growth approaching 1,000 stores.

Part of the brand's new prominence, and lending added equity to the brand, was the serendipitous hiring in 2011 of Christopher Staub, winner for his trendy designs on the *Project Runway* TV program. Having been born and continuing to design in the Minneapolis area (Maurices corporate headquarters), Staub was a natural (the hometown boy makes good!) and a perfect spokesperson and designer for the brand.

In 2011 Maurices was chosen one of the "10 Best Employers in Retail" by *Forbes* magazine and for three consecutive years (2011–2014) was chosen one of the "100 Best Places to Work" by the Minneapolis *Star Tribune*.[38]

Other retail brands have attempted or claim to have a focus on a brand-driven business strategy that is relevant and different but often associate operational changes at the store level with brand enhancement and customer engagement. The Gap Inc., especially the Gap store brand, clearly manifests this confusion with the result of continuing losses of market share. Let's take a look at the source of this misdirection.

Gap Inc.'s 2011 annual report suggests that its distinct brands are its most important assets: "*Our ability to develop and evolve our existing brands is key to our success.*"[39] Gap states that it "*continues to invest*" in its brands and enhances the customer experience through "*significant investments in marketing, enhancement of our on-line shopping sites, international expansion, remodeling of existing stores and continued focus on customer service.*"[40] Yet Gap stores continue to struggle and be subject to closings as the store brand seeks an identity that can serve as the basis of a brand promise.

Analysis of these documents confirms that any commitment to the brand as the business driver is absent. Almost all of these aforementioned changes are operational strategies and tactics and only indirectly point to the role of the brand in business development.

One result is the brand logo debacle and the consumer firestorm, which occurred in 2011 when Gap changed its logo online without ever consulting its customers. To add insult to injury, management attempted to regroup and redeem themselves by immediately holding a contest requesting submissions for a new logo. A week later, never having followed up on these submissions, they re-embraced the original, and the opportunity to engage their customer base with a unique brand experience was lost (Figure 9.7).

figure 9.7
The iconic Gap logo: Management underestimated the degree of emotional attachment to it.

Throughout Gap Inc.'s references to brands and branding, there is not a word about *consumer relevancy*, *competitive differentiation*, or *customer engagement*, which are the key signposts of what constitutes a brand's business objectives and indicates its commitment to the brand experience.

The creation of the unique brand experience, especially when driven by fashion apparel, is what makes Target so unique. The source of this is the company's clear brand identity, which we've described as revolving around the democratization of design. Gap stores are struggling to find that brand identity for themselves, which explains, in part, their difficulties. But the root of the problem is Gap's inability to decide who its customer is, what is relevant to that customer, and how Gap becomes a destination retailer again because it can offer a unique and exciting brand experience.

Although a clear brand identity is a necessary precondition for success, it is not sufficient. As we saw from both the Walmart and Gap examples, there must be a clear consumer-centric relevancy focus and a commensurate execution in delivering the brand experience that the consumer expects. For Target, its clear identity opened up an additional opportunity for co-branding with Neiman Marcus that, however, was not successful as Target lost its consumer-centric focus. Let's take a look at this and explore why this misstep occurred.

THE EMOTIONALLY DRIVEN RETAIL BRAND EXPERIENCE

We witnessed in Chapter 1's discussion of the Build-A-Bear and the American Girl retail brands two of the most successful retail expressions of the brand experience through emotional engagement with the consumer. We alluded at that time to the archetype of the Craftsman and the artisanship of things handmade and self-created.

At the foundation of this is a neurological dimension. We will now examine, in greater detail, what occurs when this dimension, and the archetypes that reside within its dynamic, are not honored by retail consumer-centric brand strategies.

The Brand Experience and The Treasure Hunt

A good part of Target's appeal is its ability to surprise and delight its customers. The unexpected aesthetic of both its store environment and the packaging of its private brands, such as Archer Farms in foodstuffs, found in a so-called discount store, is an unexpected surprise. The same rush comes from the anticipated apparel offerings, which truly combine great price with trend-driven fashion for a highly evolved brand experience. Once the bar has been set high, it cannot come down without repercussions.

This is, in part, because a "treasure-hunt" mentality is what often animates the excitement of discovering these "finds," and that is based deeply in our biology, which we call here the neurologically driven retail brand experience.

Co-branding The Treasure Hunt

The willingness of Target to innovate, especially in apparel, is part of its brand promise reflected in the *"Expect More"* tagline. One such undertaking was its co-branding with the luxury retailer Neiman Marcus for the Christmas selling season in 2012. The retailers developed some fifty various gift ideas all "designed" by world-class designers such as Oscar de la Renta, Marc Jacobs, Jason Wu, Diane von Furstenberg, and others. Prices were from around $20 to $400, and the merchandise carried a dual co-branded, logoed label and similar co-branded hangtags. They each carried the identical product assortments. Both retailers knew that they shared some customers in common, but no one knew how many and if there was a willingness to *cross-shop*, where fresh Neiman's customers would venture into Target and Target customers would find an opportunity to shop at a luxury store. The long-term objective was thought to be that Neiman's would be opening its doors to a younger demographic who, it was hoped, would be prepped to shop Neiman's when they moved up in their careers and their income rose with them. For Target, the cachet of association with a luxury retail icon fit nicely into its democratization of design promise. Perhaps some of the Neiman customers would come over to Target as well. The latter hardly occurred as there was really no incentive to do so. A similar short-fall in Target-generated traffic occurred at Neiman's, although the latter did better in that regard and with the merchandise than did Target. Still, early mark-downs before Christmas were needed at Neiman's to move the merchandise while at Target many units remained unsold in January even though they were offered at 70 percent off the original price!

The blogosphere was buzzing with negative posts almost immediately criticizing the pricing which was easily in line for Neiman's but readily out of line for Target customers.[41] Even though it was "designed" by Marc Jacobs, a scarf at $69.99 at Target has no **price point referent** by which a customer could judge price, value, and styling by comparison to a similar product. This was a fundamental and repeated error as the pricing did not focus on the Target consumers and their expectations of the Target brand.[42]

Further expectations were unfulfilled when the designer names were attached to products in categories with which they were not associated as designers (e.g., Diane von Furstenberg's name on a yoga mat rather than on a dress).[43] This was especially disappointing in the expectations held by consumers regarding the fashion apparel category, where most of the designers involved were best known for apparel. For the Target consumer, the "treasure hunt" never materialized.

The Thrill of the Hunt

The failure of the Target/Neiman's collaboration was a failure in executing a consumer-centric brand management strategy. It failed to create the expected brand experience that consumers are demanding both online and offline. The engagement with the brand has to reach a level of excitement that drives the emotional part of shopping. The following analysis of **Hunter brands**, those which stimulate the Hunter archetype in us, offers some insight into a new and dramatically different customer expectation of the brand experience.

The success of the Gilt Groupe and Rue La La, especially with **flash sales**, those brief online opportunities to snag an incredible designer/luxury product offered for a brief moment at an equally incredible price, can be explained, in part, by their having tapped into the Hunter archetype. This has created a feeding frenzy of brand loyalists who wait, visit, and buy more than they thought they would. The excitement of the chase or the hunt is a deep-seated psychological dynamic, neurologically anchored, which comes into play here and explains the incredible success of two offline retailers, T.J.Maxx and Zara. Although T.J.Maxx, an off-price retailer, and Zara, the originator of the Fast Fashion model, have different business models and different target customers, both have tapped into the hunter mentality of today's consumer. T.J.Maxx finds incredible brands and offers them at heavily reduced prices by making opportunistic buys which are one-offs with limited availability. Therefore, these buys can only be enjoyed by those loyalists who come to the store often enough so they'll be there at the "right" time to snag the deal.[44]

Zara, which we discussed in an earlier chapter, has achieved the same objective as T.J.Maxx. By controlling supply and thereby controlling demand, they stimulate the hunt. Both know their customers well but, as importantly, consistently execute the brand promise.

The depth of the Hunter archetype can be seen in the reaction to the attempted repositioning of JC Penney by the former president of Apple Stores, Ron Johnson, when he became CEO of Penney's. Here's what transpired.

In 2012, Ron Johnson took the helm as CEO of JC Penney, the venerable 100+-year-old department store. With over 1,000 stores and $16 billion in revenues, it was a formidable player, albeit somewhat tired, in the retail space. He announced an ambitious plan to remake the store and offer a new brand experience. He brought with him a successful career at Target Stores and most recently at Apple as the creator of the now legendary Apple retail store, with its Genius Bar and its unique brand experience. With these successes he envisioned the transformation of the JC Penney brand and business.

In Johnson's first public pronouncement, he bemoaned the loss of excitement and relevancy of the department store and the absence of price integrity. The latter was a reference to the deeply entrenched pricing strategy that many would refer to as **artificial inflated pricing**, where inordinately high markups are given to products which are then "discounted" to a more reasonable price and promoted as "on sale." The second part of this strategy was the use of discount coupons, which complemented the markup strategy by listing a series of brands and product categories that could be purchased within a certain time frame with the coupon at a discount. Often, high-fashion brands and product categories were excluded, creating added frustration on the part of consumers who had to read the very finely printed exemptions list on the back of each coupon.

Here is an outline of Johnson's master plan:

1. Create within the current space mini-malls with center walks and interesting boutique-like environments adjacent to the walkways to take the place of current departments.
2. Set up a Town Center in each store with games and food and music, a place to meet and to relax and have fun.
3. Reduce the number of brands carried in order to increase the focus and importance of those that remained. It is estimated that some 300 brands would no longer be available.[45]
4. Institute a **Fair and Square** pricing model, as it was called, which was based on the actual pricing pattern that eventually was the price at which most products sold; the idea was to set this price as the beginning price and to avoid the reductions upon reductions and the incessant promotional marketing that had to accompany each sale. Presetting every other Friday as a sale day would move slow-selling merchandise and avoid coupon mania.
5. Change the logo and icon from JC Penney to JCP set in a square of red, white, and blue, the square being symbolic of the new pricing strategy (Figure 9.8).

Within seventeen months of this announcement, Penney's had lost $5 billion in sales of its $16 billion pre-Johnson revenues, and Ron Johnson resigned. What went wrong?

In addition to a good deal of confused signage and unclear advertising messages, the fundamental problem was threefold.

First, the dream of the transformed environment hadn't occurred, but the absence of sales and coupons had. Therefore, the trade-off between the unfamiliar new pricing policy and

(continued on next page)

figure 9.8
The new JC Penney logo for a modern image (left), compared with the original logo (right).

the familiar old store environment created a real consumer disconnect.

Second, the transformation was radical in a retail culture that was traditional and that tended to be less than enthusiastic in support of these initiatives. Add to this that the consumer base was accustomed to moderate fashion, famous national brands, and a "predictable" discounting shopping experience. This was the brand promise.

Third, the core consumer was never asked about these changes, including the logo and the pricing. No consumer research was undertaken to test reactions to this transformative strategy prior to its being implemented. In the words of Ron Johnson, "*We didn't test at Apple.*"[46]

The culture of Apple and the culture of Penney's probably could not, in the retail world, be farther apart.

Retail pundits including the former CEO of Penney's, Myron Ullman, believed the pricing strategy was the major reason for the failure.[47]

We should add the absence of a truly consumer-centric strategy that failed to factor in the Middle American nature of the Penney's customer base, their inherent traditionalism, and the failure to engage them at the start. After all, it is their store.

A final irony is that Johnson rightfully argued that the modern department store had to make itself as exciting and consumer-centric as the internet. But the emotional engagement which characterizes interaction between brand managers and brand advocates online never occurred and therefore a consumer-centric brand promise was never confirmed.

Finally, we cannot underestimate the hunter mentality that coupons and incessant on-sale days reinforce and validate. As consumers, people are willing to suspend reality and participate in the imaginary "treasure hunt" driven by the excitement of the chase and the belief that they will truly find a bargain. This is neurologically anchored in us and is a clear expression of the Hunter archetype. Both coupons and on-sale days have returned to JC Penney.

SUMMARY

Retailers stay "on-brand" by following some or all of the following brand strategies:

- Brand the store through unique and relevant events.
- Develop private brands not available to competitors.
- Control the brand value chain from product concept to consumer purchase by opening single-brand stores.
- Co-brand with other brands that complement yours and are top-of-mind for your customers.
- Create retail activities that offer emotional experiences.
- Offer a brand promise beyond price.
- Be consumer-centric.
- Honor your archetype.

In Wave IV of retail brand evolution, we discovered that brands became even more central to business planning than they were in Wave III. This is the effect of the explosion in marketing communications which has created more marketing messages than we can absorb. The brand becomes a differentiator, making the messages more likely to be heard by the consumer. However, permission marketing obligates retailers to request and receive from phone owners access to their smartphones and apps before messaging is permitted. The power of consumers to grant or withhold permission by both individuals and consumer communities creates a court of public opinion where commercial intrusions are judged and renegade brands sentenced. Consumer engagement/nonengagement becomes a metric by which brand behavior in regard to intrusion is measured and with it a shift in power from Madison Avenue to Main Street.

Some stores became leaders in creating the store as the brand either through unique events marketing or through equally unique service solutions to consumer challenges such as are generated by the complexities of electronics.

What also has occurred is an elevation of the brand's importance with the launch of private label products that retailers own exclusively and that gradually become perceived by consumers as private brands. This creates a challenge to national brand owners who sell to these stores, for the private brands are presented hanging next to the national brands and, in essence, are competing with them.

The response of the national brand owners is to increase their openings of their own single-brand retail stores with the bigger brands that they own.

Retail brands which seemingly compete against each other need to be more focused on whether this competition is limited to a category of product and/or to a particular type of consumer. We also saw how important it is to correctly identify competitive opportunities in light of the brand promise and operational culture and capabilities. These must all align. Having the financial means to enter a market is not enough as you must be relevant to your core consumers and their expectations.

The retail phenomenon of the Treasure Hunt is driving retail business. The key is to realize how deeply rooted this is in our neurological makeup, which suggests that it has to be factored into our brand engagement strategies. Therefore, it becomes incumbent upon us to discover what deep dynamics exist in consumer psyches waiting to be tapped. Using archetypes can help us pierce this new dimension wherein resides the seeds for creating the successful brand experience. The failure of the JC Penney repositioning should alert us to what adverse effects can occur from a failure to take this approach.

KEY TERMS

Artificial Inflated Pricing
Category
Category Management
Chic, Cheap Fashion
Classification
Commodities
Cross-Shop
Customer-Based Brand Equity
Destination Brand
DG
Distributors
Dollar General

EDLP
Fair and Square
Flash Sales
Fourth Wave
Geek Squad
Gross Profit
Household Basket
Hunter Brands
Location, Location, Location
Markup/Margin
Men's Polo
Omni-Channel Brand Retail

Permission Marketing
Plus Business
Price Point Referent
Private Brand
Product Integrity
Retail Link
Retail Value Chain
Run-of-Press (ROP)
Staying On-Brand
Wholesale Prices

CHAPTER CONVERSATIONS

- What is the advantage and disadvantage in building a consumer brand experience through engaging well-known designers to create collections for your store?

- In what significant ways are Target and Walmart the same, and in what ways do they differ?
- Why is T.J.Maxx successful while the Gap stores are struggling?

CHAPTER CHALLENGES

- "Opening retail single-brand stores is an unnecessary expense that national brand owners should not incur as they have distribution in department stores and can sell on the internet." How would you respond to this assertion?
- You've been given an opportunity to interview for a sales associate position with a chance for rapid advancement at any of the stores referenced in this chapter. Which interview invite would you most likely accept and why?

- You are the brand manager for a retail chain of young men's apparel stores. Your executive vice president of marketing has asked you to replicate the Treasure Hunt models of T.J. Maxx and Zara. He's asked for a report with a strategy. What would you recommend and why?

ENDNOTES

1. Robin Lewis and Michael Dart, *The New Rules of Retail: Competing in the World's Toughest Marketplace* (N.p.: Palgrave Macmillan, 2015).

2. Ibid.

3. Ibid., 39–41.

4. For an overview of the role of the brand in decision making, see Akshay Mishra, "The Importance of Brand Name in Consumer Decision Making," *IRJMSH* 5, no. 2 (2014); for heuristics, see Elke Kurz-Milcke and Gerd Gigerenzer, "Heuristic Decision-Making," *IJRM* (January 2007), and Daniel Kahneman's work which we discuss in greater detail in Chapter 15, *Thinking Fast and Slow* (N.p.: Princeton University Press, 2011).

5. Colin Mitchell, "Selling the Brand Inside," *Harvard Business Review* (January 2002); D. Grewal et al., "The Effect of Store Name, Brand and Price Discounts on Consumer Evaluations and Purchasing Intent," *Journal of Retail* 74, no. 3 (1998): 331–352.

6. See K. L. Keller, "Conceptualizing, Measuring, and Managing Customer-Based Brand Equity," *Journal of Marketing* 57 (1997): 1–22, which he defines as "*the differential effect of brand knowledge on consumer response to the marketing of the brand.*"

7. See K. B. Hartman and R. L. Spiro, "Recapturing Store Image in Customer-Based Store Equity: A Construct Conceptualization," *Journal of Business Research* 58 (2005): 1112–1120.

8. Barbara Thau, "A Farewell to Marvin Traub: The Retail Genius Who Changed How You Shop," *Daily Finance*, July 12, 2012, http://www.dailyfinance.com/2012/07/12/marvin-traub-obit -retrospective-retail-genius-bloomingdales/.

9. For an exploration of the strategies available to national brand owners, see Stephen J. Hock, "How Should National Brands Think About Private Label?," *MIT Sloan Management Review*, Januuary 15, 1996.

10. PLMA, "PLMA Consumer Research Study," *PLMA*, 2013, http://plma.com/2013PLMA_GfK_Study.pdf.

11. Ibid.

12. Ibid.

13. VF Corporation, "VF Reports First Quarter 2014 Results; Raises Full-Year Revenue and Earnings Outlook," *VF*, April 25, 2014, http://www.vfc.com/news/press-releases?nws_id=F7DD0357-01B1-801E -E043-A740E3EA801E.

14. Ibid.

15. Best Buy, "Best Buy Fiscal 2008 Annual Report," 2008, http://media.corporate-ir.net/media_files/IROL /83/83192/08AR/assets/shared/BestBuy_Fiscal08_Annual_Report.pdf.

16. Hunert Joly, Letter, March 28, 2014.

17. Emerson College Press, "Insight into How Consumers Behave—Not Just Who They Are and How They Think—Can Drive Sales," *Emerson College*, March 21, 2011, http://press.emerson.edu/imc/2011/03/21 /insight-into-how-consumers-behave-not-just-who-they-are-and-how-they-think-can-drive-sales/.

18. A. R. Rao and R. W. Ruekert, "Brand Alliances as Signals of Product Quality," *MIT Sloan Management Review* (October 15, 1994): 87–97; C. W. Park, S. Y. Jun, and A. D. Shocker, "Composite Branding Alliance: An Examination of Extensive Feedback Effects," *Journal of Marketing Research* 33, no. 4 (1996):

453–466; E. J. Lanseng and L. E. Olsen, "Evaluations of Brand Alliances: Product Fit and the Moderating Role of Brand Concept Consistency," *Advances in Consumer Research* 35 (2008); see also Hilary Watson and Nathalie Charlton, "How Positioning Strategies Affect Co-branding Outcomes," *Cognet Business & Management* (October 19, 2015): 1–12. For clarity, the concepts "co-branding" and "brand alliances" are often used interchangeably, and we do so as well in this section.

19. Sarah Mahoney, "Best Buy Taps Designers for Exclusive Accessories," *Media Post*, September 24, 2014, http://www.mediapost.com/publications/article/234804/best-buy-taps-designers-for-exclusive -accessories.html.

20. Watson and Charlton, "How Positioning Strategies Affect Co-branding Outcomes."

21. Ibid.

22. Ibid.

23. Target Corporation, "2013 Annual Report," *Target*, 2013, https://corporate.target.com/annual-reports/2013.

24. Target Corporation, "2014 Annual Report," *Target*, 2014, https://corporate.target.com/annual-reports/2014.

25. Target Corporation, "2010 Annual Report," *Target*, 2010, https://corporate.target.com/annual-reports/2010.

26. Ibid.

27. Ibid.

28. Walmart, "2009 Annual Report," *Walmart*, 2009, http://c46b2bcc0db5865f5a76-91c2ff8eba65983a1c33 d367b8503d02.r78.cf2.rackcdn.com/47/2c/b268ed694114acea6e6eeced84e9/2009-annual-report-for -walmart-stores-inc_130221020968947561.pdf.

29. Michael Barbaro, "It's Not Only About Price at Wal-Mart," *New York Times*, March 2, 2007, http://www.nytimes.com/2007/03/02/business/02walmart.html?_r=0.

30. Walmart, "2014 Annual Report," *Walmart*, 2014, http://cdn.corporate.walmart.com/66/e5/9ff9a87445 949173fde56316ac5f/2014-annual-report.pdf.

31. Matt Townsend, "Target Cheaper Than Wal-Mart as Gap Widest in Two Years," *Bloomberg Business*, August 23, 2012, http://www.bloomberg.com/news/articles/2012-08-23/target-cheaper-than-wal -mart-as-gap-widest-in-two-years.

32. Sarah Mahoney, "Dollar General Beats Walmart," *Media Post*, October 27, 2013, http://www.mediapost.com/publications/article/212100/dollar-general-beats-walmart.html.

33. Courtney Reagan, "Dollar General Has the Lowest Prices: Kantar." *CNBC*, October 14, 2014, http://www.cnbc.com/id/102083635.

34. Al Ries, "Why JCP, Walmart and Others Fail at Changing Their Spots," *Advertising Age*, May 14, 2013, http://adage.com/article/al-ries/jcp-walmart-fail-changing-spots/241456/.

35. Pallavi Gogoi, "Wal-Mart Crashes the Fashion Party," *Bloomberg Business*, September 27, 2005, http://www.bloomberg.com/bw/stories/2005-09-27/wal-mart-crashes-the-fashion-party.

36. Michael Barbaro, "Wal-Mart Goes Urban with Clothing Line," *New York Times*, October 7, 2005, http://www.nytimes.com/2005/10/07/business/07walmart.html.

37. "Maurices," *Medford Outlet Center*, 2015, http://www.medfordoutletcenter.com/store/maurices/2563 /2138823354/.

38. Jennifer Hopfinger, "Maurices," *Retail Merchandiser*, 2014, http://www.retail-merchandiser.com /index.php/featured-reports/1817-maurices.

39. GAP Inc., "2011 Annual Report," 2011, digital file. P. 6

40. Ibid.
41. Martha C. White, "Epic Retail Fail: Where Did the Target + Neiman Marcus Collection Go Wrong?," *Time*, January 2, 2013, http://business.time.com/2013/01/02/epic-retail-fail-where-did-the-target-neiman -marcus-collection-go-wrong/.
42. Charlotte Cowles, "Why Neiman Marcus for Target Was Such a Flop," *NY Mag*, January 2, 2013, http://nymag.com/thecut/2013/01/why-neiman-marcus-for-target-was-such-a-flop.html.
43. For a discussion of how consumers process brand congruence and product fit in light of brand extensions, see David A. Aaker and Kevin Lane Keller, "Consumer Evaluations of Brand Extensions," *Journal of Marketing*, 54 (January 1990).
44. Ibid.
45. Brad Tuttle, "The 5 Big Mistakes That Led to Ron Johnson's Ouster at JC Penney," *Time*, April 9, 2013, http://business.time.com/2013/04/09/the-5-big-mistakes-that-led-to-ron-johnsons-ouster-at-jc-penney/; see also Steve Rosa, "Ron Johnson's Attempt to Fix JC Penney's Brand Was Completely Backwards," *Business Insider*, April 15, 2013, http://www.businessinsider.com /why-ron-johnson-failed-at-branding-jcp-2013-4.
46. Tuttle, "The 5 Big Mistakes"; Rosa, "Ron Johnson's Attempt to Fix JC Penney."
47. Tuttle, "The 5 Big Mistakes"; Rosa, "Ron Johnson's Attempt to Fix JC Penney."

Managing the Brand Life Cycle

AFTER COMPLETING THIS CHAPTER, YOU WILL BE ABLE TO:

- Diagnose healthy and unhealthy brands and discuss how the former contributes to business performance.

- Compare luxury and non-luxury brand repositioning/revitalization strategies.

- Discuss strategies for extending brand life by leveraging brand equity.

"A brand is a living entity . . . and it is enriched or undermined cumulatively over time. . ."

—Michael Eisner, Former CEO,
The Walt Disney Company

DIAGNOSING BRAND HEALTH

Over the last few chapters, we've explored the relationship between brands and consumers as one wherein emotionally driven offers generate memorable consumer experiences; these, in turn, provide the basis for the most lasting and intense forms of brand loyalty and significant differences in business performance.

Healthy brands sustain and invigorate these relationships; unhealthy brands do not: *"brand health is linked to current and future value with consumers and differences in competitive position."*[1] Therefore, assessing brand health also requires that we take a long-term view of the impact of management strategies on market outcomes.[2]

This caveat is challenged by the practice of American corporations, which tend to assess the effectiveness of brand managerial strategies from quarter to quarter. But brands are built over time.[3] Evaluating the brand in such brief windows can do irreparable damage to this precious asset.[4] As we shall see in the discussion that follows, luxury brands understand the benefits of a long-term strategy, while mass brands often do not and thereby struggle to maximize their business opportunities or to reposition or revitalize themselves for new ones.

In discussing healthy and unhealthy brands, we should think of the brand as a person interacting with its managers, with its consumers, and with its competitive environment. The managers are responsible for its health. The brand derives its well-being from our role as brand managers and as **diagnosticians** whose job it is to discern the "patient's" symptoms and from the pattern infer the causes of any brand health issues.

Then as "doctors" of prescriptive and preemptive medicine, deal with the cause of the brand's illness or deal with how we might maintain and extend the brand's health.

The Brand as a Person[5]

In the introduction, we asserted that there exists a profound relationship within a brand to its environment, both in terms of consumers and competitors. If we consider the brand as something real, as being a life that grows and responds to its surroundings and then matures, ages, and dies or perhaps simply retires, where does this take us? Can we see emerging problems earlier or recommend better solutions to challenges than with other models of thought? Concretizing the metaphor into a reality will produce better insights by generating problem-solving solutions to brand challenges that get short-circuited when we approach the brand only as a metaphor. This is because the emotional component in treating the brand's challenges is missing if the brand is only an abstraction. If we are to design brand experiences that have high emotional content, we must be highly emotionally involved with the brand. Many of us are already.

Beyond Metaphor: The Brand as a Living Thing

Remember Eisner's quote at the top of the chapter and consider one of the leading pundits on luxury brands, J.-N. Kapferer, who unequivocally states, *"A luxury brand is a real and living person."*[6] Kapferer continues by adding that the brand must come from somewhere and carries with it the unique imprint of its creator, which animates its soul.

As discussed in Chapter 4, using the brand persona to understand and manage a brand provides a dynamic framework for maintaining merchandising and marketing alignment and consistency. The Tommy Bahama Case Study showed how vibrant this can be when recounting the story of how WDA Brand Marketing made a comprehensive marketing presentation to Tommy Bahama for a cologne license for its client, a men's fragrance company. The Tommy Bahama team literally spoke as if "Tommy Bahama" were a real person, explaining the "why" or "why not" in terms of "his" values and lifestyle. This kept the team "on-brand," resulting in a unified decision as to which licensee "got it," which helped ensure the brand's health by protecting the brand's integrity.

Brand Diagnostics

In formulating a healthy brand strategy, we first need to recognize the symptoms that are signs of a brand's poor health. For example, one such "health" problem might be an absence of awareness from key cohorts that the brand's unique value proposition is not reaching the consumer with sufficient clarity or consistency or is not compelling enough in its message to demand attention. In essence, the brand is transparent!

There is a "treatment" for this illness. *Heighten your profile and prominence* in the marketplace (co-branding and cause marketing are some ways to do so). Therefore, your "prescription" or remedy would be to create aspirational messages, PR buzz, and viral marketing, all of which help build top-of-mind awareness and can help to restore the health of the brand. Table 10.1 frames the various challenges that we need to diagnose and treat.

Brand Diagnostic Tools

To effectively serve as our brand's health guardians, we need proper diagnostic tools. If there are problems, what do they look like and how do they differ?

Table 10.1 Building a Healthy Brand: What to Do When Your Brand Is Ill			
Symptoms	**Illness**	**Treatment**	**Prescription**
Declining awareness of brand from key cohorts	Nobody recognizes me. I'm transparent.	Heighten your profile and prominence (co-brand, cause marketing).	Create aspirational messages, PR buzz, virtual marketing for top-of-mind awareness.
Muddled perception of brand's promise	Nobody knows what I am.	Accentuate your core competency.	Stress uniqueness, promote emotional benefits, and tell great product stories.
Sudden loss of acceleration (product launches, etc.)	I can't sustain successes.	Consolidate activities, intensely focus on best practices.	Strengthen corporate values, stress authenticity, leverage any success across the entire enterprise.
Testimonials faltering, consumer complaints increasing	I'm not seen as trustworthy.	Connect emotionally with your customer.	Internalize a customer-centric business model, under-promise and over-deliver.
Comparisons with branded competitors more vocal	I'm not competitive on range of key performance indicators.	Upgrade quality and all deliverables.	Create checklist by benchmarking; perform semiannual customer satisfaction and internal surveys; compare alignments.

With a brand whose product has been marketed and distributed, there are generally two possible points of focus where problems can occur. One is in the marketing and the other is in the selling.

One begins by analyzing how the brand influences the way consumers shop. This includes both a marketing influence and a sales influence and is often graphically represented as a funnel (Figure 10.1). The inverted funnel is meant to represent the movement of many consumers entering as prospects toward an eventual purchasing decision and narrowing to the final few who actually make one. The layers represent different activities that the consumer usually undertakes prior to a purchase (e.g., comparing other, similar brands) but by no means are these to be considered sequential linear steps of an actual decision-making model. In fact, in our next chapter we will introduce a somewhat more sophisticated model that will better serve a wider array of brand management activities. The funnel here should be viewed as a way to organize the key reference points that brand managers need to be focused on to review each activity in the process and to determine what, if anything, needs to be done in terms of brand managing to mitigate possible problems and support the consumer purchase outcome.

To begin, first consider the marketing aspect of the funnel. There are four layers in the funnel for marketing: *awareness, familiarity, opinion,* and *consideration.*

Awareness is the brand's presence and message and what consumers should know of the brand and its identity in the market. For example, in an unaided awareness survey, the brand should be identified, at a minimum, by consumers with its product category. If it has higher top-of-mind brand attributes such as the personality of the brand (is it fun, quirky, traditional, etc.), these should come readily to mind. These may require a more aided or directed type of survey that offers choices to the survey respondent rather than asks an open-ended question.

Familiarity is the next layer in the consumer journey toward a purchase. Here the consumer experiences an increased exposure and comfort level. At this juncture, companies often engage celebrity spokespeople, hoping for an **associative transference** whereby the perceived virtues of the celebrity are, in the mind of the consumer, transferred to the brand and its product (a variation of the halo effect discussed in earlier chapters and related to our country of origin analysis in Chapter 2 and to the concept of contagion[7] discussed in Chapter 5). Later in this chapter, we will

The Marketing/Sales Funnel

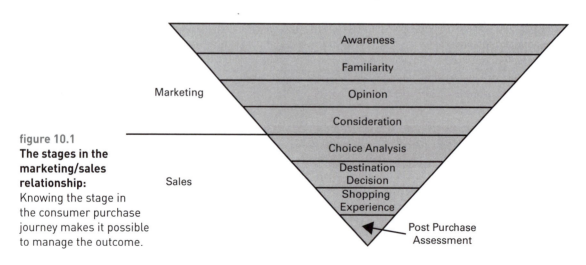

figure 10.1
The stages in the marketing/sales relationship:
Knowing the stage in the consumer purchase journey makes it possible to manage the outcome.

explore the risks and rewards of this tactic as well as the appropriate strategic alignment that needs to be in place for this to work.

The next layer is **Opinion,** or the ranking and rating of the brand and its product as the consumer intensifies the brand focus as your brand is being vetted. Online blogs and consumer reviews as well as friends and family are brought into the assessment process. This is a good point for brand managers to begin to use the Net Promoter System, which we discussed in Chapter 5, to determine the degree to which there are positive as well as any negative attitudes.

Consideration, the act of consumers thinking of your brand and comparing your brand to others in the same competitive category, is most often the sign of decision-making preparation toward a possible purchase. **Points-of-Difference** are explored by contrasting your brand with the nearest competitor brands with similar attributes. **Points-of-Similarity** (sometimes referred to as Points of Parity) occur in the same context as the attributes that the competing brands share in common are also factored into the consideration equation. At this layer, being attuned to the reason for a possible purchase so attractive brand elements can be highlighted or heightened, and marketing messages can be aligned with consumer aspirations, is a key strategy.

The sales portion of the funnel also consists of four layers. These layers are called *choice analysis, destination decision, shopping experience*, and *post-purchase assessment.*

Choice Analysis is the consumer's having come to a decision to purchase. The marketing efforts have paid off, and the consumer is now planning to purchase your brand and product. He or she might be looking at price in terms of special sales as part of the purchase plan to maximize the price/value of the purchase. If your brand is in a market entry mode, offering an incentive to accelerate product turn may be a good way to jump-start a new branded product. Working with a retailer in a cooperative ad or coupon campaign where you plan together and share the costs can be a healthy way to begin both the retail and consumer relationship. The retailer benefits from the constant messaging that generates store traffic and sales, and the consumer benefits through the reassurance, which the messaging reinforces, of the wisdom of the consumer's purchase decision of a new brand.

The next layer, **Destination Decision**, is extremely important because not only must the product be available as promised and advertised, but it must be in the appropriate **channels of distribution**, or retail points of sale, which have been promised in the brand messaging. Second, the retail distributor must have the brand and product on hand and present it on the retail floor in a way that is both accessible and attractive. This must be consistent with the brand image that the brand owner has been marketing to the consumer. The store also needs to be a retailer with a location consistent with the consumer's shopping habits. These market conditions should be part of the initial strategy of aligning the brand, the consumer, and the types and locations of the stores to which you are going to sell the product for distribution.

This is one of the most critical junctures in managing the purchase process, for control over the distribution points may not be fully in the hands of the brand managers. As we discussed in the last chapter, unless you are distributing to your own stores, or you are a **marquee brand** that the store must have because of consumer demand, the advent of major store-owned product brands can leave your brand with less than the best floor space or presentation. Some brands, anticipating this possibility, have trained a staff of field merchandisers whose sole responsibility is to monitor the presentation at retail to ensure that the merchandise gets to the retail floor in a timely manner and is presented in a brand-focused way.

Shopping Experience is the full effect of all of the store's brand touch points impacting the customer. This includes the atmosphere, lighting, and music as well as how easy it is to park, navigate the store aisles and departments, and find checkout clerks and sales associates. For example, one team of retail analysts has concluded that the meteoric rise of Kohl's department store in the 1990s was due to breaking new ground for the department store channel in terms of the shopping experience by restructuring the interior of the stores and having them in the most accessible strip malls and easy-parking locations.[8]

Post-Purchase Assessment is the moment of truth when the consumer evaluates whether her purchase truly met her needs and whether the brand followed through on its promise. This may be the most important layer for determining emotional fulfillment, eventually paving the way for brand engagement and future loyalty. Again, the wide adoption and strategic usage by major corporations worldwide of Net Promoter Systems point to the realization that to maintain a healthy brand, it needs more than an occasional checkup! It requires constant oversight and monitoring.

Applying Diagnostic Tools

Applying a **Purchase Funnel Assessment** (Table 10.2) can help complete this process. It brings the previous Purchase Funnel into play so brand managers might assess at what consumer reference point the problem emerged and how best to remedy it.

Poor awareness is a marketing problem and poor opinion is a sales problem. The marketing problem (poor awareness) can be attributed to having faulty or nonexistent positioning and differentiation strategies. This can result in unclear messaging, wrong media placement, a blurred imaging brand, and/or poor packaging.

As for the sales problem, this can be the result of misalignments between product and its appropriate value proposition. Here the value proposition might be measured by how appropriate the distribution, presentation, pricing, availability, and guarantees/features of the product offering are. Each of these tactics must be assessed as possible fault lines in the strategic landscape. So, for example, a product ad offering a new and exciting product should be coordinated with the points of retail distribution to guarantee the product will be available when the ad is launched.

A final measure of your brand's health is found in a **brand equity review (BER)**. Brand equity is the intangible value of the brand from the point of view of consumers. This is determined through sample surveys of the brand's core consumers and ongoing communication with the **brand's opinion leaders,** such as bloggers and loyalists who are part of the brand community. Questions are asked regarding the brand's imaging, positioning, and value proposition to determine if its original value still resonates.

If your brand fails to meet the benchmarks in the brand equity reviews, a "Back to Roots" strategy may work. This is best when you're retrenching after a failed sales strategy (lost uniqueness, reaching beyond niche, etc.). Or when you think your product can appeal to original customers and/or new ones, because your brand life cycle has not reached its end. It can also work if the brand attributes are extended to a new category which the consumer has indicated is an appropriate fit. However, this needs to be undertaken

Table 10.2 Brand Diagnostics: Purchase Funnel Assessment	
Marketing Dynamics	**Sales Dynamics**
These are a function of having poor or nonexistent positioning and differentiation strategies	These are a function of misalignments between product and its appropriate value proposition
a. Messaging	a. Distribution
b. Media Placement	b. Presentation
c. Imaging/Branding	c. Price Availability
d. Packaging	d. Guarantees/Features

only after a review with target cohorts confirms that the brand aligns with the relevancy of their lifestyle and that its persona is consistent with their own.

Aligning Brand Illnesses with Appropriate Remedies

Some brand managers, in their rush to develop awareness and consideration, make a fatal error—misalignment. A celebrity spokesperson is often chosen for the **associative halo effect**, a strategy that seeks to tie a brand's image to the celebrity's positive persona or stature as a role model for a cohort you wish to reach. This is often part of a repositioning campaign that attempts to alter the brand's perception by a target audience by presenting the brand with a new brand experience or new value proposition. This repositioning, for example, might be focused on moving the brand's positioning and how it is perceived by a younger consumer cohort from a "classic" persona to a "cool" persona.

The case study that follows provides a snapshot of how a brand, in order to be an effective communicator with its target audience, must align naturally with the essence of the brand product. As discussed in Chapter 6, authenticity as the backbone for credibility and for maintaining brand integrity in a consumer-centric market is a critical factor in whether the alignment will be successful.

BRANDSTORMING FAILURE: Tiger Woods and Buick

One such celebrity endorsement agreement was the association of General Motors with Tiger Woods. The fabled professional golfer was signed to a long-term **endorsement contract** to speak and appear in ads on behalf of the Buick brand (Figure 10.2).

figure 10.2
Tiger Woods and Buick: Misalignment of celebrity endorsement can compromise a brand's integrity and lead to revenue losses.

In 1999, the Buick brand was suffering from poor health. One of the oldest, most iconic sub-brands within the General Motors portfolio of brands in the U.S. motorcar industry, it was facing dwindling sales and an equally dwindling pool of core consumers. On various metrics such as market share, sales, and profits, it had not performed as planned. And the demographics of its **core consumer**, that loyal and dependable cohort upon whom the brand managers could project annual business outcomes, was aging.

The median age of Buick owners was 57 and skewed male who was closer to retirement and less likely to continue to purchase a new car every three years. This latter time span was important for achieving economies of scale and hitting profit targets. Brand managers for Buick determined that the other characteristic of their core consumers was that they were avid golfers. Enter Tiger Woods who, at this stage in his career, was breaking golf records with every

(continued on next page)

tournament in which he competed. He was also young (in his 20s), handsome, stylish, and very likeable, great attributes to align with the Buick brand personality and the brand persona.

But here's where things get out of alignment: Buicks were old, ordinary looking (not stylish), and not exactly what you'd call "likeable" (a VW Beetle or a BMW Mini is fun and "likeable" as evidenced by the ad themes and images). It appears that the Buick persona is very different from Tiger Woods's persona and this goes to the heart of whether the association has any authenticity and therefore credibility to it.

To determine authenticity one must begin by asking, "Does the consumer believe that *Tiger Woods* drives a *Buick*?" This is the key question and it's the consumer who will answer it through purchasing or not purchasing the brand. This is the major metric which confirms the brand's *authenticity in this relationship*. Nothing less than the brand integrity is at stake and, with it, its power to generate revenue and build brand loyalty. A major reason for the success of hip-hop brands such as LL Cool J

and the Kangol brand is that the endorsements from music celebrities are perceived as real in that they most often use the product; the performers and the brands are aligned. It's difficult to imagine that Buick is Woods's first choice for his personal use.

Tiger Woods had a 95 percent consumer awareness rating. Although this high awareness is a necessary precondition for driving consideration of the brand, without the proper alignment, it is not a sufficient condition. Consideration requires a closer emotional alignment between the brand and the core consumer's associative perceptions of its values.[9] Without getting past the consideration stage, the purchase path is unlikely to be traversed by the potential customer.

Let's look at sales figures to determine the degree of alignment. Buick's five-year sales profile is shown in Table 10.3. Let's compare it to that of Nike, a brand that Woods also was a celebrity spokesperson for around the same period. If we place the Buick brand and the Nike brand side by side, which did he truly

Table 10.3 Buick Sales Chart: The Need to Measure the Performance of an Endorsement Is Underscored Here as the Numbers Clearly Indicate a Problem

2001	2002	2003	2004	2005*
374	371	259	223	186

*In 2006 Tiger's contract was renewed!

(continued on next page)

endorse? Take a look at these results: Tiger had been "endorsing" Buick since 1999. The table shows the Buick sales figures in thousands of units.

Now compare this with Nike golf equipment/apparel sales. Tiger has been wearing Nike since 1999 and using Nike equipment since 2001. Here are the comparable five-year business outcomes:

- Nike became number two in golf ball sales in five years.
- Nike golf equipment sales moved into the top 5 brands in a fiercely competitive sector.
- Nike golf drove the majority of gross margin improvement for Nike in the last quarter of 2005 and beyond.[10]

Had the Buick brand managers used a pre-audit, such as the brand marketing report card shown in Figure 10.3, this failure to bring the brand back to health might have been avoided. The idea of finding a celebrity golfer was supported by the data, but what was missing was an analysis of the perception of the brand and the appropriate spokesperson. This is a failure of diagnostics which could have been avoided with the proper analysis of the brand's health issue and how best to prescribe an appropriate remedy.

The following is an approach that considers the patient, the malady, and the proper prescription.

There is a senior tour in the professional golf world where the great players 50 years old and over compete against one another. The Buick driver age of 57 is a **median age** for the Buick customer. This means that half are below and half are above 57 years old. There are as many that are younger as there are those who are older than 57. This cohort (baby boomers) was also the numerically largest at the time and far and away the wealthiest. The brand could have been positioned for the entire cohort without the fear of dwindling sales from a dwindling pool. The pool was there and living a more active life longer than their fathers. The half who were younger than 57 (age roughly 45-plus) and who would soon move into the 50-plus age sector was the next wave of potential consumers—and with their most financially productive years ahead of them!

There was a host of mature professional golfers widely recognized and deeply admired, and within their ranks were senior tour golf champions who could have been chosen. They would have looked authentic behind the wheel of a Buick. What we may have seen here are brand managers too stuck on a single demographic and failing to see the variegated market potential of this consumer.

Had the brand managers been systematically using a brand report card as an internal brand audit, they could have stayed "on-brand." The report card would have prompted them to

(continued on next page)

Directions:

- Next to each question, place the numerical value number that best measures your current level of achievement for the marketing activity indicated
- Add up each column, and then add up the total points
- Divide by 10
- Result—Your Marketing Grade Point Average

Grade	A	B	C	D	F
Numerical Value	4	3	2	1	0

1. We know who our customers are, where they are, and what benefits & values they associate with & are looking for from our brand.

2. We know the extent of our brand awareness in our local market.

3. We have developed brand heritage stories, which we systematically tell to consumers in our market.

4. Through our promotional vehicles, consumers get a clear idea and a feel of what our brand stands for.

5. Our brand stays visible to our target market & expands recognition through advertisements events & our website.

6. Our brand is not only advertised properly but is also reaching consumers through press releases and publicity & social media venues.

7. We co-brand with other companies who share our consumer type & brand positioning.

8. We conduct ongoing surveys hosted on our website to learn more about our consumers & their perception of our brand.

9. We consistently brand all our internal & external messages/images.

10. We know our brands market share & that of its competitors.

Totals

Add up the total boxes = Total Points _____

The Business of Branding
Your Marketing Calculator

_____ ÷ _____ = _____

YOUR GRADE

If you averaged a "B+" (3.5 GPA) or higher-
We Congratulate you in advanced for what will be a terrific year...
If not why not give us a call
1-888-771-4WDA
or email us at bill@wdamarketing.com

figure 10.3

Brand marketing calculator: Preemptive "medicine" is essential for brand health; measuring ongoing internal company behavior can catch problems before they fester.

survey targeted and core consumers whose insights could have led to a different strategy.

When we consider any change to the brand's **value proposition**, or what is unique about it that makes it relevant to its core consumer, or a change in its **elements** (identifiable symbols and IP assets by which the brand is readily identifiable), we are entering the realm of repositioning, revitalization, and/or re-branding

(the Three Rs). This differs from a change in strategy or tactics that diagnostics can lead to when they help us to discover the nature of the malady (e.g., is it a marketing problem or a sales problem?). Each of the Three Rs goes beyond changes in strategy, so we will refer to it as "surgery." It is a decision to change some major element of the brand, such as its brand promise, and, depending on the extent of the change, its physiology as well.

BRAND REPOSITIONING, REVITALIZATION, AND RE-BRANDING

Although a more detailed exposition is found in the chart in Table 10.4, a brief outline of the Three Rs is in order. **Re-branding** is the most radical of the Three Rs. Sometimes called "Re-invention," it seeks a new name, new consumers, and often new products and channels of distribution. Repositioning seeks to reach a new audience and avoids changing the brand name and other IP assets because they still resonate with

the new targets. **Revitalization,** sometimes referred to as "Rejuvenation," finds that the brand attributes and values are still sound but the messaging strategy is wanting. New imaging and themes are often introduced and these may find their way into the packaging and labeling as well as the advertising images. All other brand elements and strategies remain the same.

Brand Life Cycles

Over the years, brands experience life cycles that, if the brands are to survive and prosper, require changes in business strategies. This often requires

Table 10.4 The Three Rs: Different Strategies for Managing Brand Health, Depending on the Nature of the Malady and the Business Objective

Types of Treatments: (Brand Management Name)	New Target Consumer	New Brand Name	New Core Products	New Value Proposition	New Brand Promise	New Image	New Retail Distribution
Revitalization	X	X	?	✓	✓	✓	X
Repositioning	✓	X	✓	✓	✓	✓	?
Re-Branding	✓	✓	✓	?	✓	✓	?

• = Prescribed; ✓ = Perhaps Prescribed; X = Not Prescribed

repositioning to a different cohort or, to a lesser extent, a revitalization which retains and often builds upon the prior positioning and seeks to merge heritage with more modern design and/or service sensibility. However, we should be clear that only brands that *"are attached to a single product . . . are subject to Product Lifecycle Management (PLM)"* and that Brand Lifecycle Management (BLM) and PLM do not operate in the same manner. *"A brand is not a product!"*[11]

Products cycle from birth to death quite naturally as do people, yet brands can reach a stage of maturity which need not always lead to decline (Figure 10.4). Again, luxury brands and sound long-term management strategies are required. Let's explore some of these mass and luxury strategies.

Brand Repositioning and Revitalization

Brand repositioning and brand revitalization should be approached strategically. As an example, returning to our discussion in Chapter 1 of Jim Stengel, former global marketing officer for Procter & Gamble (P&G), we can develop some insight as to how he applied the concept of building the Brand Ideal as a revitalization strategy.

Stengel's first brand assignment when he entered P&G was with Jif® peanut butter. The brand had been positioned with a classic CPG (consumer packaged goods) type of strategy. *"More,"* *"bigger,"* *"better value,"* or *"best taste"* was stressed as reflected in its ad campaign slogan *"Taste the Difference."* These are expressions of a features and benefits strategy which we discussed in Chapter 6, "The Brand Promise."

The Jif® business had slowed to a crawl, yet data and research on the brand showed high levels of customer satisfaction. Stengel knew something was missing. As he looked back at the imaging and positioning decisions made previously, he found one factor was most often disregarded—the power of ideals.

At times, we may lose sight of the fact that a brand, through its values, helps define a business culture, which, in turn, can influence people's lives. So if we are, in consumer-centric markets, charged with "delighting" our customers, we need to strive for and realize "amazing" results. To do so, you and the business must stand for something enduring—enter "The Brand Ideal."

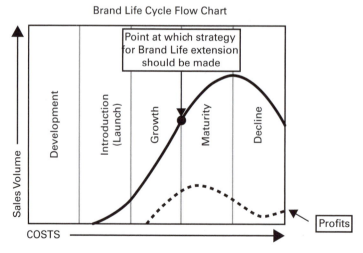

Brand Life Cycle Flow Chart

figure 10.4
Brand life cycle: Brands need not die as products often do; one step is to know where in the cycle the brand is.

Defining a brand ideal as intent to improve people's lives is just the beginning. What divides great business leaders from mediocre ones is the ability to leverage that ideal into successful business outcomes that fulfill consumers' deepest wishes.

Stengel realized that the mind-set of becoming a leader among your competitors by trying to anticipate and manage market conditions is a formula for amateurs: "*It aims too low, locking an enterprise into a business model based on the agenda of the business, NOT of the customer.*"[12]

What was essential in the Jif initiative was to understand the values of the moms who were buying the product for their kids—what were their objectives? Through shop-alongs and in-home visits, Stengel and his team discovered what Jif had to stand for—nutritious and healthy food! Jif's ingredients had to be such and the product had to be positioned as such. The brand team needed to internalize this and communicate to the moms that they were committed to providing a product based on these benefits. This became the brand promise. By this simple insight, the brand became more than peanut butter: "*We were a partner with moms in their young children's development.*"[13] In essence, the repositioning aligned the brand with contributing to children's growth. The financial results confirmed the soundness of the Brand Ideal strategy.

Market share increased by several points (in the category, when fractions were the norm), and both gross margins and revenues proceeded to outstrip plans and market expectations. This market leadership growth continued far beyond year one. The brand had discovered the business it was really in!

All brands run into speed bumps at some point in their existence. Yet what separates the exceptional brands from the mediocre ones is how leadership navigates these challenges. In studying a successful brand revival, a similar strategic and tactical pattern emerges. A chart that reflects these commonalities is found in Table 10.5.

Table 10.5 Successful Brand Revitalization and Repositioning: In Studying Brands Returning to Health, Very Similar Patterns, Tactics, and Strategies Emerge

	Consumer-centric Leadership	Heritage Retail Showcases	Retail Showcases	Brand Building	Cool Imaging	Brand/Product Integrity
Objective	CEO is determined to change and stay true to the brand's DNA	Study mega-trends for strategic as opposed to just tactical insights	Create retail brand showcases to enhance the image	Create new product looks and extensions; "own" a core signature item or classification	Create hip, cool image; aspirational messages (wannabes)	Upgrade and control look, quality, and distribution
Action	Intense market research; asks and listens to consumers	Hire a creative director who embraces the brand's heritage and is a strategic thinker	Open retail showcases, especially in international prime locations	Brand logo transmitted into an icon merchandised into product	Celebrities endorse or wear brand in ads or are photographed with the brand	Renegotiate or recall licenses; upgrade product

BRANDSTORMING SUCCESS: Burberry, Coach, and Lacoste

In order to better understand how brands are revitalized or repositioned, let's take a look at those brands that have been successful and reflect best practices. We've chosen to present well-known brands with deep roots and meaningful heritages. Ironically, the brands with the strongest histories are often those which are both resilient in the face of challenges and inflexible in the face of change. Only those companies that undertake the hiring of new leadership with a clear brand strategy and a broad mandate are likely to succeed in charting a new course.

Burberry was created in 1856 by Thomas Burberry and started off as an "outdoor wear" shop. The discovery only a few years later of a new fabric called "gabardine," woven from a breathable, waterproofed yarn, was to change the course of the company's product and brand history. Some twenty years later, the famous Burberry Trench Coat was designed and became the World War I British Officers Coat of choice. Later in the 1940s and 1950s, this trench coat became a symbol of film noir and of iconic stars such as Humphrey Bogart, Audrey Hepburn, and Peter Sellers, each of whom wore the coat in memorable and now classic motion pictures.

But in 1997 Burberry hit a wall. The brand was hardly stocked at London's Harvey Nichols, and Selfridges and Harrods carried only traditional raincoats. The Burberry Trench Coat was seen as stodgy, old, and tired.

Burberry had to come up with a strategy to regain its place in the market, so in 1998

managers planned to extend and update their product line, hiring Roberto Menichetti as head designer. The plan was to extend the presence of the "*plaid*" as the brand's icon, a strategy that clearly differentiated the brand from its competitors and became synonymous with the modern Burberry.

Continuing its revitalization strategy, in 2000 Burberry contracted with a new ad agency that hired Kate Moss as its spokesperson (Figure 10.5). The objective was to give the brand a new "face," one as iconic as the brand itself. The campaign, and the photo shoot that resulted, was widely acclaimed as groundbreaking for its alignment and seamless integration of modernity with tradition—"*youthful, sophisticated, and fun.*" To continue with its strategy, Burberry hired a new creative director, Christopher Bailey. Bailey represented the new breed of design directors who were no longer merely responsible for the design aesthetic and ads and imaging, but now assumed the role of brand guardian. This encompassed overseeing sourcing, merchandising, and marketing as well as the traditional responsibilities usually associated with the position. To clearly demarcate and lend appropriate authority to the role, Bailey reported directly to the CEO, Rose Marie Bravo.

This resulted in a change in strategic perspective as consumer and cultural values, which contained latent demand, were factored into product development and brand imaging. As an example, Japan had emerged as an excellent Burberry market, which led to the launch of the "Burberry Blue" label. This label appealed to young, Japanese female consumers' penchant

(continued on next page)

figure 10.5
Burberry's revitalization: New design styles and a cooler image in models were two of the strategies; Kate Moss is shown here.

for "baby blue" and "candy pink." Soon after, in 2004, Burberry was voted by women in Japan ages 20 to 69 as the country's most popular brand! Japan became Burberry's largest market.

In the words of Rose Marie Bravo, then CEO:

"There's an admiration [for Burberry] in Asia and America and even Spain . . . They like the British Lifestyle and what they think it stands for whether it's reality or not."[14]

At this point in its "comeback," Burberry decided to extend the brand's presence in affluent but underserved smaller U.S. markets (Columbus, Ohio, etc.), a new and clear complement to its traditional strategy of only "High Street" site selection. The brand was shaking off its "stodginess" in more ways than one. In addition, Angela Ahrendts, who became CEO in 2006, indicated that "ownership" and dominance of the raincoat category should be part of the company's brand positioning: *"The decision was made to focus on our heritage . . . everything we did . . . should start with the ethos of the trench coat."*[15]

This continued to be an effective strategy to maintain the brand's positioning by tapping into its heritage. Finally, Burberry expanded into retail formats in key markets ("High Street" retail locations), creating what Christopher Bailey referred to as *"The Ultimate Brand Environment."* This was coupled with a clear merchandise segmentation model for the brand.

Burberry, continuing the success of its revitalization initiative, reported a double-digit rise in profits and sales for fiscal 2012. The financial successes continued through fiscal 2014 and culminated in a total transformation of the brand value proposition. Added to the brand repositioning was the idea of the "Connected Culture" and *"enduring customer engagement."*[16]

(continued on next page)

The connections were both internal and external and were driven by a total strategic commitment to digital technology, imaging, and communications. Burberry differentiated its brand by embracing the digital world online, in its stores and shops, and in its internal corporate culture and communications. As an example of the latter, the company has an internal platform for open communications called "Burberry Chat" in which all 11,000-plus employees exchange ideas and with whom both the CEO and creative director share new ideas.

This has been achieved without sacrificing the connection to the soul of the brand or its quintessential British roots. As an example, at the London flagship store, backgrounds in its digital displays are designed to convey the classic bad British weather![17] *"We are British, everything we do has to be quintessentially British. The music, the models, everything . . . and that was going to be a huge differentiator, and the outerwear."*[18]

This digital commitment naturally led to reaching the souls of the Millennials, or the next generation of potential consumers, who began to embrace the brand as the brand had embraced their digital way of living. The opportunity to reach this cohort was undertaken as a strategic decision made by Ahrendts and Bailey in early 2007. Here's the reasoning: *"we targeted the millennial customer . . . because that was the customer coming out of these high growth emerging markets . . . Now, everybody is a digital customer. . ."*[19]

The preceding quote is somewhat prophetic. In late 2014 Ahrendts left Burberry to become president of stores for Apple. This is another confirmation of the structural change in the competitive space wherein seemingly unrelated brands compete for the same consumer's share of wallet or what discretionary income is spent on what lifestyle products. Apple is a technology brand which drives fashion through design; Burberry is a fashion brand which drives design through technology.

The brand also announced what might be seen by some as its most radical departure from tradition and the brand's DNA; the company plans to terminate the *"Nova Check"* (iconic plaid pattern), even though it is still a calling card and a status symbol in the highly profitable Asian markets. Why this shift in strategy? The answer given was simply that the brand has *"outgrown it."*

Committed to consumer-centricity, Burberry continues to strive to create an "emotional connection" between the brand and the customer. It has remodeled its customer service into a 24-hour help line that is available in fourteen languages, and it has a live chat option online as well as a Twitter account in which it is responsive to its followers. It is using these strategies and tools to help identify and cater to its very important customers (VICs) all over the world. The company is taking this a step farther by educating its sales assistants in distinguishing the six different categories of Chinese shoppers. There is also a plan to create

(continued on next page)

a similar type of segmentation model for its Brazilian shoppers.

Overall, Burberry has overcome many of the challenges that it faced by revitalization of the brand image and its persona. Some of these involved having its iconic plaid become over-exposed, which now it has downplayed and updated as the brand's calling card. This seemingly radical change has enabled the brand to reduce its dependency on "Burberry Checks," while keeping the brand's image of the "British Lifestyle."

Coach started in 1941 as the seller of handbags and accessories made of high-quality leather, with special dyeing and finishing processes. In 1985, it was bought by Sara Lee, which decided to expand the brand's market presence. Coach was distributed to overseas markets, but by the mid-1990s it began to lose its cachet. Its products were described as "classic and staid" while competitors were offering product and designs that were "hip and trendy." Soon Coach's core consumers were an aging demographic threatening the brand's stability and growth.

In 1996 Lew Frankfort become CEO and brought with him a new merchandising strategy. The question was how to produce timeless, classic pieces which would not be subject to the vagaries of fashion yet appeal to both current and younger consumers and, at the same time, strategize how to go beyond leather and still retain the brand's heritage and cachet. Soon the brand's unique DNA became creating handbags that are built around timeless elegance, while offering consumers lifetime refurbishing and repair service, adding the value of lifetime ownership to each purchase.

However, Coach soon faced another dilemma. Business casual had altered the perception of what type of handbags were appropriate. Brands such as Prada, Kate Spade, and others were seen to be **on-trend**, that is, capturing the fashion direction of the season, while Coach continued to experience an erosion of its core customer base.

At this critical juncture, Frankfort hired Reed Krakoff as creative director and charged him with broad responsibility as the brand guardian. Krakoff loved the brand, and shortly he began to align his sportswear background with the brand's heritage to forge a new sensibility for the brand, albeit one that could now bridge the two seemingly disparate consumer cohorts. He had envisioned "What Business Coach Was Really In!"

Coach was repositioned as "Modern Classics," designing classic products with a modern twist. The company soon introduced fabrics for fashion and enhanced the product merchandise with the brand's icon. Here is how Krakoff envisioned this transformation: "*The . . . brand represents a synthesis of magic and logic . . . a truly aspirational, distinctive American style.*"[20]

(continued on next page)

Coach began to tell brand stories by invoking New York City locales, each of which had a distinct character (e.g., the "Soho" Collection, the "Chelsea" Collection). It also create d its own signature strategy by bringing out new styles each month as opposed to twice a year like other brands. "*We created a lane called 'accessible luxury' and it feels like a super highway.*"[21]

All this was made possible by extensive market research. In its initial repositioning, Coach spent $2.5 million on interviews, focus groups, and the like. It even received updates during holiday season from its stores three times a day and made sure there were no markdowns or sales.

In 2011, Coach launched a collection returning the brand to its roots. It created an entire dual-gender collection that was inspired by its heritage and is now positioned to become the cornerstone of its business. The hope was that the Legacy Collection would not only attract more clientele but also solidify Coach's status as a **lifestyle brand**. Krakoff states that Coach tried to seek and "embrace" the core of what the brand is about as well as modernize it. Everything in the collection was inspired by a preexisting style; Coach continues drawing on the past to ensure its future. In Krakoff's words: "*It's time to reinvest in our past. . .*"[22]

The attempt to revitalize through tapping into the brand's heritage and creating a new product assortment rather than reposition was not sufficiently strategic to overcome the new competitive universe in which Coach now competed. In 2013, the stock price had fallen by 35 percent and sales had flatlined.

As we have discussed in prior chapters, the more modern and "accessible" luxury offerings of Michael Kors, Tory Burch, and Kate Spade had altered the competitive landscape. Coach did not have sufficient equity to counter these competitors, and business continued to spiral downward.

By 2013, Krakoff was gone, and Lew Frankfort had become chairman. A new CEO was appointed, Victor Luis, and soon after a new creative director, Stuart Vevers. Vevers's experience with Mulberry, Bottega Veneta, and other similar brands (competitors to some extent with Coach) prepared him for the new position.

In 2013/2014, the brand undertook a repositioning that included becoming a lifestyle brand by expanding the product assortment to include sportswear and footwear to complement the brand's traditional strength and position in accessories. A much younger vibe and imaging in models served to communicate this shift in the brand's persona. New stores were opened in high-profile markets and the new collections began to receive strong reviews from the fashion media. By 2015, the first signs of a turnaround were in evidence, including a rise in the price and positive recommendations to buy the stock by some Wall Street analysts.[23]

As discussed in our preceding chapter, Lacoste was the brand that "invented" and commercialized for sale the logoed polo shirt in 1928. The shirt was initially worn by René Lacoste, a young, daring, and aggressive player at the French Open in 1927, breaking all the tournament dress rules of that time. Although the

(continued on next page)

BRANDSTORMING SUCCESS: Burberry, Coach, and Lacoste *(continued)*

rules committee was aghast, the shirt was soon in demand and was a commercial success (Figure 10.6).

First positioned as a premium sports brand, the polo has sold millions of units each year. But in 1969 **General Mills**, a multibrand conglomerate with no apparel or fashion brand experience, bought the brand and marketed it as a commodity rather than as a fashion product. Product materials changed from pima cotton to poly/cotton, pearl buttons to plastic ones. But the change that probably affected it the most was the change in quality and distribution. General Mills dropped its price and distributed the product without concern for any boundaries. In 1992, the Lacoste family bought back the brand and pulled it from the market from 1992 to 1996.

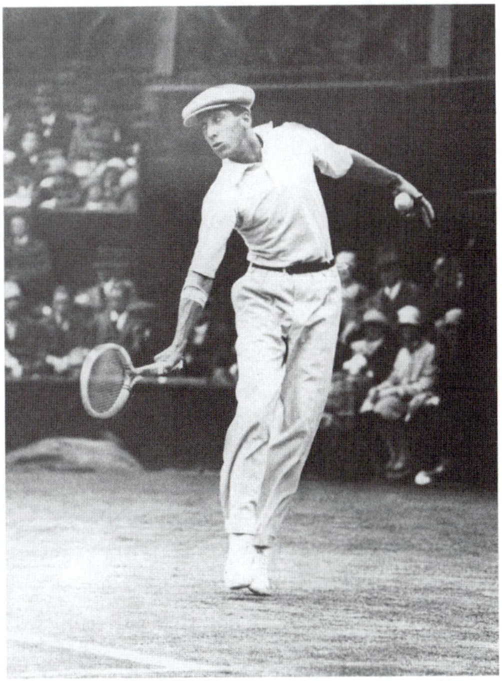

figure 10.6
French tennis champion René Lacoste: René Lacoste in his original polo shirt at the French Open in 1928, breaking the rules of proper dressing for matches; a new fashion category was created which became an iconic style of apparel.

In 2000, Lacoste reentered as a menswear brand and reestablished its premium position. When Robert Siegel (famed for his phenomenal Dockers brand creation and product success) was hired as CEO, he began to reposition the brand for a younger, metrosexual consumer while capitalizing on the "vintage preppy" trend that was emerging in fashion in early 2000. Positioning the brand in price at the top end of the polo spectrum for department store brands, Siegel also changed the specs to conform to the lifestyle and attitude of that target customer by making the silhouette trimmer and the fit closer to the body. Finally, he hired a design director with broad authority to manage the brand identity much like a brand manager would.

In 2004, Lacoste continued to extend its repositioning strategy by launching the "slim fit pique" polo, a refitting of the cut of its "core" item. It added vibrant colors, which merchandised perfectly with low-rise jeans, a current trend at that moment. An enhanced women's product gave an even greater perception of the brand's being "on-trend" and "fashion right." This led to the "tennis-inspired" collection

(continued on next page)

with tongue-in-cheek, visually interesting "tennis player" ads, with its past and present branded as one experience. Siegel believed in the brand's strength because of the brand's heritage. In his words, "*We're not a made up brand.*"[24]

The campaign featured Roger Federer with René Lacoste in fashion magazine ads—the two champions, one from the heritage of the brand and the other representing its new, modern iteration. This communicated to its audience a perfect balance of rebelliousness and athleticism, two prime values for the new generation of customers. Product extensions followed as well as distribution to the company's own refurbished, upscale boutiques with "toney" retail locations. Additional brand marketing strategies included using its website for PR (not for sales) and increasing its product placement strategy for Hollywood and TV.

The results from these strategic changes are impressive. From 2001 to 2009, Lacoste's sales increased from $30 million to over $300 million. Its consumers were now 55 percent male and 45 percent female (globally), reflecting a substantial increase in sales from its women's collections. Its consumer segments became broader in gender, income, and age, helping ensure a more balanced business. Lacoste owned over 1,000 stores worldwide!

In 2012, Lacoste once again began revitalizing itself, with a newly appointed CEO, José-Luis Duran, whose new goal was to "*bring Lacoste into modern day.*"[25]

The plan was to revitalize the brand so that it could meet the needs and wants of a new generation of consumers. Duran hired designer Felipe Oliveira Baptista (who has worked with Nike and Max Mara), who created a collection that he positioned and imaged as "Unconventional Chic." To properly image this ad campaign, Adrien Brody was hired, an actor who is known for being well spoken and cultured and who perfectly conveys the new sensibility and athletic roots of the collection.

This new collection and campaign are intended to convey the brand's commitment to honoring each person's unique identity. And though it may sometimes seem unconventional (as it intends to be), it begins the movement away from the "preppy" or even "sporty" look, to which Brody's sartorial style is distinctly in contrast.

The revitalization, however, was careful to continue to stress the "sporting spirit" of the brand and not relinquish its heritage. Thus, the signing of tennis star John Isner in 2012 to an endorsement contract and continuing as of 2014 to sponsor free tennis clinics in Central Park each summer in New York City help to underscore the commitment to the heritage of René Lacoste.[26]

Re-branding a Company

Re-branding is a change in the identity and character of a brand and/or a company. It usually entails changing the IP elements attached to the brand. At times, this is done to disassociate a brand from an existing negative public perception. For example, when Philip Morris re-branded/ renamed itself Altria, it wished not to be identified corporately with cigarettes and smoking, as that has been falling out of public favor.

Re-branding often involves a change in the target consumer and a commensurate change in the product to align with the new target.

Re-branding a Luxury Brand

Luxury brands are less likely to undergo radical change such as re-branding demands. Their heritage and commitment to continuity of message and image over time, or the concept of timelessness which characterizes the brand promise, would be challenged by such a change. They also tend to be less concerned with reacting to trends or public perceptions. However, the need to re-create an identity arises when a brand becomes tired and its core consumer age may warrant it. What is needed is the leadership of a well-respected creative director and a visionary CEO operating as brand manager who can combine to make such change necessary and successful.

EXTENDING A BRAND'S LIFE BY LEVERAGING BRAND EQUITY

As a brand's life cycle passes maturity, its equity begins to show signs of decline. Reaching the maturity stage in terms of time, which often precedes the decline and demise, does not preordain the decline and demise. It can be arrested by sound brand management and the brand's life line extended. The key areas to manage are differentiation, brand knowledge, and brand image.

The brand must continue to be highly relevant to its core consumer, highly different from its key competitors, and clearly reflected in those terms by the brand image, those "*strong, favorable, unique associations*" that the brand has created in the minds of consumers and distributors.[28] Without points of **retail availability and accessibility**—that is, readily accessible retail locations where the brand can be bought and sufficient inventory and brand displays available and properly presented—no amount of brand equity can compensate for the absence of these retail platforms. This is often overlooked, which is a serious omission, for without retailer buy-in, a key element is absent from the potential success of the brand management strategy.

Relaunching a Tired Brand

Brand managers' first order of business in relaunching a tired brand is to separate product life cycles from brand life cycles. Brand decline is a reversible process while product decline generally is not. Second, the degree of **brand fatigue,** or the extent to which the brand has lost its relevancy and differentiation, needs to be determined. A good starting point would be to undertake research into the degree of remaining stature and strength of the brand using a method such as Young & Rubicam's Brand Asset Valuator (BAV). By generating comparative metrics, BAV offers brand managers insights into the brand's area of remaining strength or weakness and its extent.

Signs of Losing Strength and Stature

A sign of a brand's decline can be seen by monitoring consumer perceptions, changes in distributor relations, and competitive market metrics. A slippage in brand equity, as measured by lower consumer awareness and weaker brand images, is often the first sign. Any sudden slippage in unaided top-of-mind awareness is a serious symptom, potentially more serious than aided

The staid and iconic Yves Saint Laurent brand has been struggling to grow and be profitable within the Kering brand portfolio. Its elegance and customer base were dependable but without great excitement. But the brand had, and continues to have, great cachet, and upon this rock, re-branding finds its most solid foundation.

In 2012, Hedi Slimane took the reins of Yves Saint Laurent as creative director and changed it forever. It is a classic example of a successful re-branding. He tied the brand to the independent rock-and-roll culture and a much younger customer. This included the change in the name from Yves Saint Laurent to "Saint Laurent." This has a friendlier semiotic aesthetic, punchier and less elaborate, yet still reflecting the brand's heritage. It is also more aligned than the original brand name to the values and attitudes of the new core consumer (Figures 10.7 and 10.8). Products changed accordingly. "*Saint Laurent*

offers . . . classic investment pieces that don't go out of style and are competitively priced."[27] The opening of sixteen additional Saint Laurent boutiques also was in keeping with the re-branding effort. More minimalist, trimmer, much like the apparel, the inner design of the shops confirmed the new identity and conveyed the new aesthetic. The brand's new retail interiors were to reflect the brand's new external identity.

To be closer to the culture of the brand's core consumer, Slimane moved the design studio from Paris to Los Angeles. Moving the creative offices from the brand's geographic location synonymous with its heritage (in this instance, Paris) is unheard of for a luxury fashion house but goes to the heart of the extent and completeness of the re-branding strategy. Over the three years, the brand has tripled its sales and profits, a testament to the right way to change an iconic brand's direction.

figure 10.7
The old Yves Saint Laurent name and logo:
A more somber and traditional image is conveyed in this logo and storefront.

figure 10.8
The new updated logo and image:
Brighter, punchier, it speaks to a younger, more contemporary customer.

recall because aided recall levels tend to decline more gradually than unaided. This is because the questions which are asked in an aided recall survey provide the respondent with more information with which to associate an attribute with the brand. This tends to give the brand more stickiness in our memory banks.[29] As we discussed earlier in the chapter, without significant awareness, other aspects such as relevancy to a consumer's aspirations are less likely to materialize.

Changes in consumer perceptions are also important signs. For example, changes in purchase intent or in loyalty levels need to be mined through ongoing consumer research. Discerning **switching patterns**, whereby previously loyal cohorts of customers begin to increasingly switch from your brand to your immediate competitors, is a telltale sign that your brand may be aging.

A second type of sign is in the distributor's plans and priorities vis-à-vis your brand. If you do not have your own single-brand stores and distribute through multibrand retailers such as Macy's, you are in perennial competition with other brands in your product category for retail advertising, floor and shelf space, and budget commitments. Any change in patterns, such as smaller orders, lack of or reduction in cooperative ad support, and less than primary floor space allocation and presentation at retail, are signs that the brand has become less important to the store. This may be a function of a shifting of priorities to the store's private brand, the emergence of a strong new competitor, or a change in trends that calls for a different brand in the category. If it is none of these, the brand is aging.

Finally, brand managers need to keep a steady finger on the pulse of the market and several key performance measures. Declines in unit sales, market share, or profit levels suggest that the brand's health may be at issue. Attempted remedies such as lower prices or product extensions may be tried, but if they do not change these market outcomes, the problem may be in differentiation.

The remedy, however, must not be worse than the illness. Several years ago, St. John Knits, a premium brand and market leader in its category sold in Neiman Marcus and other upscale retailers, suffered several years of erosion of these market performance measures. It assumed that the brand needed to appeal to a younger, more contemporary cohort and a repositioning was undertaken.

The brand's core customer had always been a very elegant, upscale, sophisticated, and older woman (median age in her 50s) whose brand loyalty was legion. Without consulting her, the company contracted the actress Angelina Jolie as the new symbol and spokesperson of the brand. She appeared in its advertising and made personal appearances on behalf of the brand. She even had input on the brand's design direction. Ad images became less than elegant. Then, fit patterns were altered to align with the smaller-figured new target consumer. The **size specs** on the garments, those calculations that must align with the prototypical figures of the core consumer, were no longer the traditional fit (which was more accommodating for an older clientele) and became quite contemporary. Complaints mounted and the brand managers had to retract and reverse their strategy. But much damage had been done, and the brand today has not regained its prior market leadership position. We see here a misalignment similar to the one we discussed earlier in our Buick example.

Remedial Strategies

What needed to be done in the preceding situation was to determine the cause of the malady. Once again, improper diagnostic methods exasperated a set of symptoms which could have been remedied had they not been seen as causes of the brand's poor health. In retrospect, managers discovered that the issue was one of relevant differentiation as the brand had gotten into a rut and had not updated its unique approach to a more classic woman's sense of style.

Resurrecting a Dormant Brand

The three critical questions that brand managers need to answer prior to attempting to resurrect a **dormant brand**, or one that has not been in the market for several years, are as follows:

- Can the brand regain its former glory? (Brand Knowledge)
- Can it be made to stand out and be unique? (Differentiation)
- Does the company resurrecting the brand have the leadership, creative capabilities, and financial capacity to get the customer's attention?

Luxury versus Non-Luxury Brands

The quest for so-called Sleeping Beauty brands is built on the notion that nostalgia resides in the minds and hearts of both luxury and non-luxury consumers. We long for a past of mostly imagined better times and therefore seek the symbols of bygone eras represented by brands and their artifacts.[30] These artifacts include all aspects of intellectual property (IP) that can be found, including logos, ads, labels, hangtags, and packaging that capture the spirit of the brand.

Searching archives for **signature products**, that is, those products that represented the unique soul of the brand and its timeless image, also should be done.

BRANDSTORMING FAILURE: Halston

Roy Halston Frowick was an American designer often described as the first "Superstar" American designer. He began in 1957 and was most famous for his design of the pillbox hat for Jackie Kennedy, for introducing Ultrasuede, and for his dresses that even today, at a less than designer price (Halston Heritage) are available for sale at moderate to better price points. At its pinnacle, the brand had its own boutique in Bergdorf Goodman. For over twenty-five years after Halston's death in 1989, the brand never regained its designer standing, distribution, or luxury pricing. It went through no less than five different owners, including a period in 2010 when the actress Sarah Jessica Parker was president and chief creative officer. All attempted to resurrect the dormant brand and none succeeded. The overriding explanation was poor management. In each instance, the brand managers made the fundamental mistakes that cannot be made with a luxury brand:

- Each of the owners, who acted as the brand managers, sought volume first as the basis for a return on their investment.
- They sought to realize the return quickly, before the brand could be resuscitated.
- They all licensed the brand into multiple categories, further diluting its equity.
- There was never leadership that had authority to guide the business and who saw themselves as the brand guardian.

In the words of Harvey Weinstein, once a part owner, "*If you are going to go luxury or high end, you have to be patient.*"[31] Commenting on the absence of leadership, the *New York Times* reported in a 2011 article that "*Halston's Brain Trust was more like a many headed hydra.*"[32] By 2015, Halston ownership had again undergone a change and the positioning as a luxury brand abandoned. It now can be found in its own better-to-premium-priced boutiques.

Let's compare this with a French brand in the luxury space, Moynat.

Moynat was founded in Paris in 1849 as an artisan shop of exquisitely designed and crafted baggage and trunks, a rival to Louis Vuitton. In 2010, the business closed and the brand and its IP assets were purchased by LVMH and Bernard Arnault, the CEO.

Arnault undertook no surveys to confirm the brand equity. He has made sure that there is very little media publicity (there is no advertising) as the brand managers are charged to develop small collections for very limited distribution. There is no business plan, and Arnault has in conversation mentioned *"15 years"* as the timeline for LVMH to recoup its investment. More specifically he has charged the brand managers in resurrecting the brand to *"see if you can make people dream again."*[33]

There also must be no surprises in terms of hidden IP ownership. Ownership should be firmly established and validated through trademark search. Then the communication effort which integrates the previous search for the brand's symbols must show a clarity in its identity as reflected in the consistency of the imaging and messaging in the artifacts. If possible, find the heritage. It is here where dormant luxury brands have an advantage over non-luxury brands as the latter need to construct a brand narrative while the former already possess one.

SUMMARY

Considering the brand to be a person opens up a path for an emotional relationship between the brand manager and the brand. This creates a greater degree of sensitivity to the role of brand guardian which all good brand managers must play. It also enables us to manage the brand's health by being watchful of symptoms which may be signs of the brand losing its business effectiveness. By aligning symptoms and illnesses with treatments and prescriptions, we bring a time-proven process to brand management, building a

healthy brand. Part of this skill set is to have the right diagnostic tools. Using a Purchase Funnel allows us to isolate the points at which problems can occur. Healthy brands show a resiliency to challenges and a deeper degree of linkage to their loyal customers. This adds to their value and to the strength of their competitive position. American brands tend to evaluate their performance by quarters, which doesn't consider the long-term growth trajectory that brands need for performance success. Mass brands suffer more from this time frame problem, while luxury brands tend to avoid it as their managers take the long view of both development and performance.

By delineating marketing from sales problems, we saw that when we make this distinction, we can more readily align the appropriate remedy with the illness that it has been designed to cure.

We also looked at strategies to keep brands fit. These include repositioning, rejuvenation, and re-branding, each of which helps to meet a different set of marketing and image issues and move the brand to firmer ground. By examining how both luxury and premium brands are subject to these Three Rs, we avoid bunching them all together and treating them as if they are the same, a mistake often made as they are different remedies for different maladies. Rushing headlong into celebrity endorsements is a risky repositioning campaign strategy as it not only requires a relevant outreach to a new customer base but also needs to stay relevant to the existing one or risk alienating some or losing both cohorts as customers.

Exploring the challenges of relaunching a tired or weakened brand and resurrecting one that been deceased requires following the ground rules for leveraging Brand Equity. For example, determining the degree of residual saliency in the brand from the perspective of its target consumer is essential to success. In this regard, luxury brands need to undertake a strategy which is different from that of non-luxury brands; for example, luxury requires time and patience for a successful relaunch.

KEY TERMS

Associative Halo Effect
Associative Transference
Awareness
Brand Equity Review (BER)
Brand Fatigue
Brand's Opinion Leaders
Channels of Distribution
Choice Analysis
Consideration
Core Consumer
Destination Decision
Diagnostician

Dormant Brand
Elements
Endorsement Contract
Familiarity
General Mills
Lifestyle Brand
Marquee Brand
Median Age
On-Trend
Opinion
Points-of-Difference
Points-of-Similarity

Post-Purchase Assessment
Purchase Funnel Assessment
Re-branding
Retail Availability and
  Accessibility
Revitalization
Shopping Experience
Signature Products
Size Specs
Switching Patterns
Value Proposition

CHAPTER CONVERSATIONS

- In what ways is envisioning the brand as a person helpful to brand managers?
- How would you determine whether to reposition or rejuvenate a brand?

- How do luxury and non-luxury strategies differ in resurrecting a deceased brand?

CHAPTER CHALLENGES

- As brand manager for Nike footwear, you've been asked to recommend a celebrity sports star for endorsement of a new product. What steps would you take to help ensure the success of your recommendation?

- You are the president of a company whose sales manager wants to fire most of her sales team for failing to meet their sales goals. What would you advise her to do?

- You're a brand manager for a premium brand apparel company. The marketing director has learned that a deceased luxury brand is available and wants you to recommend to the CFO that he fund a budget for its acquisition. How would you respond to this idea?

ENDNOTES

1. J. D. Berg, J. M Matthews, and C. M. O'Hare, "Measuring Brand Health to Improve Top Line Growth," *Sloan Management Review* 49, no. 1 (Fall 2007): 60.

2. See K. L. Keller and D. R. Lehmann, "Assessing Long-Term Brand Potential," *Journal of Brand Management* 17 (2009): 6–17 where they posit the need to maximize long-term brand persistence and growth.

3. For an empirical/longitudinal study of brand health, contribution to company market goals, and a typology for assessing brand health in this context, see A. Mirzaei et al., "A Behavioural Brand Evaluation Typology to Measure Brand Performance over Time," *International Journal of Business and Management* 10, no. 10 (2015), also in *Journal of Brand Management* 22 (May 2015).

4. Ibid., 27.

5. See Susan Fournier, "Consumers and Their Brands: Developing Relationship Theory in Consumer Research," *Journal of Consumer Research* 24 (March 1998); and Jennifer L. Aaker, "Dimensions of Brand Personality," *Journal of Marketing Research* 34 (August 1997): 347–356.

6. Jean-Noel Kapferer and Vincent Bastien, *The Luxury Strategy: Break the Rules of Marketing to Build Luxury Brands* (Philadelphia, PA: Kogan Page, 2012).

7. See George E. Newman and Ravi Dhar, "Authenticity Is Contagious: Brand Essence and the Original Source of Production," *Journal of Marketing* 51 (June 2014).

8. Robin Lewis and Michael Dart, *The New Rules of Retail: Competing in the World's Toughest Marketplace*, 2nd ed. (New York, NY: Palgrave Macmillan, 2014).

9. For an extensive analysis of this dynamic, see A. Dwivedi, R. E. McDonald, and L. W. Johnson, "The Impact of a Celebrity Endorser's Credibility on Consumer Self Brand Connection and Brand Evaluation," *Journal of Brand Management* 21 (November 2014): 559–578.

10. Nike, "Nike Inc.—'10-Q' for 1/6/06," *SEC Info*, January 6, 2006, http://www.secinfo.com/d9xWk.vc.htm.

11. Jean-Noel Kapferer, *The New Strategic Brand Management: Advanced Insights and Strategic Thinking* (N.p.: Kogan Page, 2012), 215.

12. Jim Stengel, "The Case for the Brand Ideal," *Strategy+Business*, May 14, 2012, http://www.strategy -business.com/article/00113?pg=all.

13. Ibid.

14. Laura Barton and Nils Pratley, "The Two Faces of Burberry," *The Guardian*, April 14, 2004, http://www.theguardian.com/lifeandstyle/2004/apr/15/fashion.shopping.

15. Angela Ahrendts, "Burberry's CEO on Turning an Aging British Icon into a Global Luxury Brand," *Harvard Business Review*, January 2013, https://hbr.org/2013/01/burberrys-ceo-on-turning-an-aging -british-icon-into-a-global-luxury-brand.

16. Ibid.

17. Ibid.

18. Ibid.

19. Ibid.

20. "Coach and BeautyBank Sign Exclusive Fragrance Development Agreement; Coach Enters the Beauty World in Its US Retail Stores," *Business Wire*, September 22, 2006, http://www.businesswire.com/news /home/20060922005077/en/Coach-BeautyBank-Sign-Exclusive-Fragrance-Development-Agreement# .VS7oF9zF-So.

21. Meredith Derby, "Coach Still on a Roll: As Profits Leap 60 Percent, Big Expansion Ahead." *Women's Wear Daily*, October 27, 2004.

22. Christina Binkley, "Coach Comes Around to Reclaim Its Iconic Look," *The Wall Street Journal*, July 13, 2012, http://www.wsj.com/articles/SB10001424052702303644004577521072256706462.

23. "Coach: Investor Sentiment Turning Positive," *Seeking Alpha*, March 2, 2015, http://seekingalpha.com /article/2964326-coach-investor-sentiment-turning-positive.

24. Greg Lindsay, "Lacoste's New Look," *CNN Money*, March 24, 2006, http://money.cnn.com/magazines /business2/business2_archive/2006/04/01/8372798/.

25. Keith Levy, "The Crocodile Rocks—Lacoste Evolved," *Forbes*, June 1, 2012, http://www.forbes.com/sites /keithlevy/2012/06/01/the-crocodile-rocks-lacoste-evolved/.

26. Lisa Lockwood, "Lacoste Sponsoring Tennis Clinic in Central Park," *Women's Wear Daily*, August 14, 2014, http://wwd.com/fashion-news/fashion-scoops/warming-up-7838544/.

27. Robin Mellery-Pratt, "The Secret of Saint Laurent's Success," *Business of Fashion*, March 5, 2015, http://www.businessoffashion.com/articles/intelligence/the-secret-of-saint-laurents-success -saint-laurent-hedi-slimane.

28. Ibid.

29. For more on awareness and recall, see David A. Aaker, *Building Strong Brands* (New York, NY: The Free Press, 1996).

30. Rebecca May Johnson, "'Sleeping Beauty' Brands: Myth or Magic Formula?," *Business of Fashion*, December 11, 2014, http://www.businessoffashion.com/articles/intelligence/sleeping-beauty-brands -myth-magic-formula.

31. Ibid.

32. Laura M. Holson, "The Men (and Women) Who Would Be Halston," *New York Times*, September 2, 2011, http://www.nytimes.com/2011/09/04/fashion/the-men-and-women-who-would-be-halston.html?_r=0.

33. Ibid.

Consumer Brand Engagement

CHAPTER 11

AFTER COMPLETING THIS CHAPTER, YOU WILL BE ABLE TO:

- Establish the connection between consumer engagement, brand communities and brand loyalty.

- Compare and contrast Engagement and Satisfaction and how each impacts research and business decisions.

- Assess the role of Engagement in driving community brand value creation and brand loyalty.

"The most successful brands connect with customers far beyond the level of a single transaction. . ."

—Gensler Survey, March 2013

THE CONSUMER ENGAGEMENT/BRAND LOYALTY CONNECTION

The focus in this chapter on the concept of Engagement, referenced in earlier chapters, will now lead us into a much deeper analysis of this key strategic variable and the completion of Part III. We will argue that it should be the primary consumer objective and business metric by which the successful management of the brand is measured.[1] Its central importance is in its role as the bridge between the "healthy brand," the brand loyalist, and the emotional connection that sustains and maximizes the relationship they enjoy. It also offers us a much more insightful and effective approach to understanding the customer than the concept of "satisfaction," so often used in sample surveys and which we will suggest should be replaced as a measure of loyalty and a predictor of behavior. *"Customer satisfaction surveys are unreliable indicators of intention to purchase or the likelihood of repeat business."*[2] The two concepts termed *engagement* and *satisfaction* are, at times and mistakenly, used interchangeably. This is often the result of misreading the idea of what "market orientation," discussed in Chapter 1, means.[3] We'll take a deeper dive into this later in this chapter.

If the ultimate objective is to develop consumer engagement strategies, the ultimate goal of consumer engagement is customer loyalty. The link between the two, therefore, becomes a critical element in developing a brand management strategy. As we will see, high and sustainable levels of brand loyalty correlate positively with high and sustainable levels of corporate performance and similarly with brand equity, brand value, and the brand's life cycle.

What Is Customer Loyalty?

In Chapter 5, we discussed the various consumer behaviors that define and confirm consumer loyalty. Let's revisit this so we have the associative elements that align with brand engagement. This will enable us to determine which types of engagement actions we need to design and manage so that each aspect of loyalty is aligned with a specific management action and is ministered to in a way that honors the relationship's commitment between loyal consumers and the brand.[4]

Here is the checklist of loyalty elements:

- Consistently and frequently shops the brand over time
- Is willing to purchase brand products at full price
- Rebuys and dedicates a larger share of wallet to the brand
- Resists marketing offers from competing brands by not switching
- Forgives the brand for its mistakes
- Touts the brand's virtues when asked
- Recommends the brand to family, friends, and colleagues

Loyalty Levels

An effective alignment between engagement elements and loyalty best begins with referencing a brand loyalty pyramid (Figure 11.1). This enables us to see the differing degrees of loyalty and the attitudes which differentiate each tier. This is important in creating an engagement strategy. Brand managers need to know where the best opportunity lies and what different engagement modes are likely or unlikely to be effective. By aligning the different modes of engagement with varying degrees of loyalty that those tiers represent, managers get a more consumer-centric snapshot of what's needed to help maximize each opportunity.

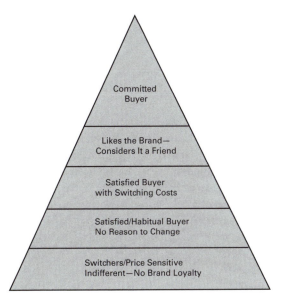

figure 11.1
Aaker's classic brand loyalty pyramid: A good visual segmentation model depicting various degrees of loyalty culminating in the Committed Buyer at the apex of the pyramid.[5]

Loyalty Behaviors

Each type of loyalist represents a type of shopping behavior framed by distinct attitudes toward the brand. At the base level of the pyramid are those who have no loyalty to brands and who are driven by price incentives or other "deals" such as buy one, get one free.

Next are the consumers who are satisfied but not committed. They would switch if there was a benefit that they derived from the brand that was no longer available—for example, if the brand experienced a price increase.

The next level is satisfied buyers who feel that the benefits of switching are not worth the costs. These "costs" may be the inconvenience of finding an outlet nearby (often this applies to banks and their branches) or where fit or usage is involved (this often applies to apparel brands where the fit has been confirmed as right for the purchaser).

In the fourth level we begin to see an emotional basis for the brand loyalty. The consumer, although she may have some rational reasons for her assessment born of utilities such as quality, actually "*likes the brand . . . a friend.*" This emotional engagement scores higher as the loyalty motivator than the rational assessment, showing up with greater frequency/intensity in survey research. This latter emotional quotient is a precondition for the engagement dynamic to take hold because, as we will see in the next section, successful engagement is driven by feelings.

Finally, at the last level, or the apex, are the committed loyalists, sometimes referred to as advocates or **brand ambassadors**. This is because their loyalty is pronounced and their unsolicited promotion of the brand to friends, family, and colleagues is unparalleled.

The pyramid can be considered on a continuum. Each step is a potential stage in moving consumers toward the apex, which brand managers seek to do through their engagement strategies. To effectively do so, the brand managers will need to know which stage various cohorts are at regarding their evolution toward the apex. This will enable managers to offer customized engagement incentives that, given that engagement is built upon trust and intimacy, necessitate a more personalized offer. This offer confirms that the brand is interested in a meaningful and relevant relationship with that consumer. "*What brands need now is a reliable measurement method which will enable them to identify exactly what stage they occupy on the brand loyalty continuum.*"[6]

It is essential during this interaction with consumers that the 80/20 rule (discussed in Chapter 5) continues to be kept front and center. To refresh our memory, the rule substantiates a **statistical tendency**, meaning the numerical ratios will vary with variations in the circumstances that surround the event or element being measured, that 80 percent of our business outcomes are effected by 20 percent of our customers.

The immediate implication is that engagement and loyalty follow that same statistical tendency: 80 percent of our engagement will come from 20 percent of our most loyal customers. It becomes incumbent upon us as brand managers to first identify that 20 percent cohort and then to personalize a special custom message and offer for them. Next, we need to identify and nurture the next potential cohort whose values predispose them to embrace the brand. This cohort can then replace members of the 20 percent group as its members, for a variety of reasons, leave the brand. An underlying message here is that the rule suggests that we need not engage all of the consumers with whom we may interface in our daily business dealings but only those who show that their values align with the brand's values. These are the best candidates for sustainable engagement and long-term brand loyalty. In addition, a word of caution. The 80/20 rule is a statistical tendency. Consequently, we should not cease our efforts to engage just because we have "reached" our 20 percent "threshold" or feel that we have fallen short of our performance goals if we find our ratios at 85/15 or 90/10. We may even experience 70/30 or 75/25 and, although these are less likely to occur, they are by no means outside the realm of probability.

What Is Brand Engagement?

Brand engagement is a love affair. It is, at its highest level, an emotional involvement with a degree of intensity found in those who are in love. It is a decision made to share one's life with another. Continuing our position from the preceding chapter, think of engagement here as between two people who plan to marry or be together for a lifetime. It is a serious commitment with responsibilities on both sides, with the brand making a substantial contribution to the relationship. In the words of the leading authority Susan Fournier, in her groundbreaking article in the *Journal of Consumer Research*, "*thinking about the brand not as a passive object of marketing transactions but as an active, contributing member of the relationship dyad is a matter more deserving of note.*"[7]

Implied in the exchange of symbols, meanings, and emotional rewards is a contract, which we discussed in Chapter 6. Jean-Noel Kapferer, like Fournier, also speaks about the brand contract with the consumer and how they are emotionally bound together by promises, expectations, and experiences.[8]

When we take this perspective, it also provides a frame of reference, a deeper understanding of what we as brand managers need to do to sustain and optimize the relationship. This is a function of the reality that, given our emotional commitment to aid the relationship as part of our responsibility, we too have emotional "skin in the game."

The Emotional Connection

Consumers choose brands that align with their values and their self-image.[9] This is why the brand persona that carries the brand's value proposition into the world must be clear and must align with the prototypical core consumer's persona.[10] The nature of this alignment decision is based on what Daniel Kahneman has labeled **fast thinking**, or consumer decision making based more on emotional beliefs and values than on reasoned calculations.[11]

Research confirms that the degree to which this division is present in human decision making is thought to be 70 percent emotional, or based upon feelings, and 30 percent reasoning, or based upon calculations. These percentages represent both overall decision making and/or certain types of decisions where both emotion- or reason-based decision making comes into play.[12] The percentage of contribution from each process will vary depending on the nature of the decision that must be made, but the connective tissue in personal relations is driven more by emotions and feelings.

Invariably, relationships are anchored in the deepest recesses of our neurological and psychological being. We are bound together in our relationship with the brand we love, and the brand with us, through our common genealogy based on mutually compatible archetypes.

The Brand Management Challenge

The challenge for brand managers comes from two places: first, the extremely personal nature of the connection and the need to discover who the loyalists may be and the cohort with which they are associated, and, second, how to nurture a relationship with the cohort once it is discovered. Returning for a moment to the 80/20 rule, knowing the 20 percent of your customer base that contributes to 80 percent of your business outcomes enables you to begin at a point that has been shown to have some measure of loyal customers within the 20 percent. The fact that you have substantiated that a steady cadre of customers exists strongly suggests that there also exists some degree of loyalty among them. The major question is whether there are degrees of differential loyalty, or subgroups, within this cohort, and how you would segment these subgroups based on their patterns of behavior toward the brand.

This necessitates discerning the archetypical basis for the behavior that is being manifested by the cohort and its subgroups. A key question that should be asked (and answered) is, is there a single archetypal identity in the cohort or are there complementary ones, each compatible with the other, but still requiring different modes of nurturing in order to maintain their emotional connection and relationship with the brand?

However, people do not give up their private selves so readily, which makes connecting with cohorts and gathering information a delicate management process. This becomes even more of a challenge with luxury brands and their clientele whose desire for privacy may be even greater than that of the non-luxury consumer and whose willingness to connect is less than forthcoming. "*Connecting with customers on an individual basis is often the missing piece in the engagement puzzle . . . only a few leading brands have mastered these human connections.*"[13]

To accomplish this, brand managers must first be aware of the signs of consumer behavior that presage the interest consumers have in a relationship with the brand. Once again returning to the human dimension of an engaged couple, maintaining honesty and trust are central to the well-being of the relationship. And when consumers are displaying the need for the brand to champion such values, the need is often preceded by cues that have to be identified and interpreted by the brand manager. These are likely to be subtle at times, as the consumer may be testing the integrity of the brand's values such as honesty. However, if the consumer's desire for the relationship is deep, these cues will coalesce into a discernible pattern: "*there are notable patterns in consumer behavior that signal readiness to engage in a relationship with brands.*"[14]

Managers, to effectively discern this relationship dynamic, need to begin to think much like analysts working in strategic intelligence. In this capacity, they will be gathering consumer communications, translating them into data that are imbuing raw content with meaning and significance, and arriving at reasonable conclusions from the pattern of the communications content. Such content analysis can take place both offline and online. Offline, one example we have already discussed is the Net Promoter System and how that measures consumer loyalty. Although we will deal with social media in a subsequent chapter, we should mention that content analysis online also has its methods of pattern gathering and ways of assessing the nature of the brand/consumer relationship.

In this regard, one of the distinctions drawn between types of engagement is between active and passive participants and how they differ behaviorally. **Active engagement** can manifest itself in such behavior as writing blogs and postings, sharing such postings or blogs, and participating on YouTube productions and points to high degrees of brand loyalty. Non-active or **passive engagement** would be those who read the various content and offered likes and click-throughs, but take no active part in creating content. Their passive engagement will be shown to correlate with lesser degrees of loyalty than the active participants. A final segmentation model will have these two types, active at the beginning, or top, and passive at the bottom, or end, of a brand engagement continuum (or a pyramid, whichever model is used) with gradations in between.

This is the type of model that needs to be integrated with the pyramid model discussed earlier. First steps would be to decide on the model that can best accommodate each source of data (pyramids, funnels, concentric circles, or others). Then unify the concepts in the model so there is one language and eventually, when outcomes are measured, one set of metrics that can readily and reliably measure those outcomes.

At some point, these two data sources, online and offline, need to be fully integrated so that brand managers may have **one version of the truth**—that is, one viewpoint that does away with conflicting or competing data and arrives at a single management strategy.

Finally, a tracking system, such as an engagement funnel or elliptical overlays (Figures 11.2 and 11.3), needs to be created. The system needs to integrate both the **purchase journey** (the path taken by a consumer from awareness to buying), and the **loyalty journey** (the path taken by a customer from reengaging the brand to the highest level of brand engagement, which is acting as an ambassador for the brand).

We prefer the elliptical model in Figure 11.3 as it more realistically portrays the purchasing and the loyalty paths in a complex and omni-channel world and how purchasing and loyalty intersect as well as influence each other. For example, consumer indecision is

graphically displayed through the **analysis/paralysis** (referring to the tendency of consumers to defer a decision when they have too much information) elliptical space on the chart and suggests how it can temporarily derail the consumer's journey to a purchase. It also gives brand managers a route to follow to loyalty to see stages in the evolution and perhaps influence or accelerate an outcome.

The model is therefore more dynamic than the funnel (see Figure 11.2) because the funnel doesn't graphically convey movement or how the stages interact with each other. The model also appears to suggest that the engagement with the product or the brand occurs by steps from top to bottom in a linear progression. The empirical evidence shows that the consumer pathway to engagement is much more circuitous than this, but the funnel's graphic design doesn't reflect that empirical reality.

Forrester Research, a market leader in consumer-centric marketing research, has concluded that the funnel is obsolete. In a recent report on the subject, the opening section is entitled "The Marketing Funnel's Linear Approach Is Outdated" and contains the following observation: *"The marketing funnel fails to represent the far more complex landscape that 21st century consumers and marketers have to face."*[15]

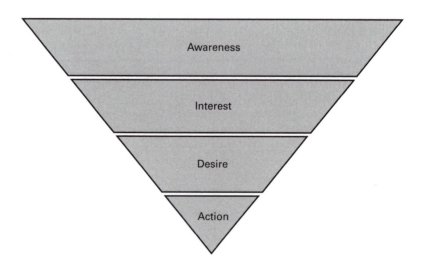

figure 11.2
Purchase funnel: A basic one-dimensional visual which depicts the stages consumers go through to reach a purchase.

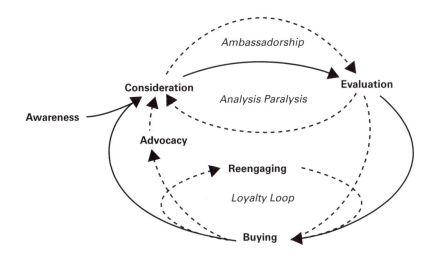

Figure 11.3
Customer engagement life cycle model: A more complex model which captures the purchase journey and shows that it is not linear; brand managers are apprised of the dynamic process.

Figure labels: Ambassadorship, Consideration, Evaluation, Awareness, Analysis Paralysis, Advocacy, Reengaging, Loyalty Loop, Buying

Although we agree with the overall assessment, perhaps "obsolete" is a bit strong. It is incumbent upon us as brand managers to be cautious in discarding a vehicle (the purchase funnel) that has served us well for some fifty years. Although we agree that its linear approach (given the web and consumer-centricity) makes it less relevant as a tool for tracking and managing consumer behavior, we've suggested in the prior chapter how it might be put to good use. In addition, as we seek to integrate online and offline brand management and brand marketing strategies, we should consider holistic solutions that may call upon models from both online and offline platforms.

CONSUMER SATISFACTION AND CUSTOMER ENGAGEMENT

A consumer can be satisfied with a shopping experience but only a customer can be engaged with a brand. This somewhat simplistic distinction suggests a clear difference between a **transactional brand experience** (one that is purely based on a commercial exchange between a buyer and a seller) and a **value-driven brand engagement** (one that can be characterized as an emotional exchange between a customer and a brand). With these also come differing degrees of emotional commitment which require distinct brand management strategies.

Consumer Satisfaction Management

The shift to a consumer-centric marketplace brought with it an increase in customer service and consumer loyalty programs. It is important that we do not confuse the latter with customer loyalty. Consumer loyalty programs such as frequent flier miles or special discounts at restaurants and retailers are based on distributing functional or utility benefits as rewards (some say bribes!) for one's frequent and continuing patronage. However, the data suggest that satisfied customers defect from the brand (that is, switch to others) only slightly less compared to those whose satisfaction rating is "less satisfied" or "moderately satisfied." In one banking study, 6 percent of "extremely satisfied" customers closed their accounts compared to the 5.8 percent of "less satisfied" customers who closed theirs. This suggests there is no appreciable difference between the two levels of satisfaction in terms of consumer behavior. The implication is that satisfaction as a loyalty metric does not align with or drive loyalty.[16]

Therefore, switching brands is always a lingering threat when brand managers embrace satisfaction metrics as the central focus of a brand management strategy that seeks to optimize loyalty. This strategy is doomed to failure because to forestall consumer switching, the management strategy must continually increase the rewards in the hope that the largess will result in higher indices of loyalty. Unfortunately, this occurs so infrequently that avoiding the inconvenience of switching brands seems more to be the motive for consumers remaining a "customer" than any emotionally anchored loyalty commitment.

With these reward programs came satisfaction surveys that attempted to chart and measure their effectiveness. But "effectiveness" for what purpose and for what business objective? What were we (and what are they) measuring? How does the nature of satisfaction and the nature of certain business goals coalesce into a meaningful strategy?

Satisfaction versus Engagement

The satisfactory shopping experience can be a **one-off**, a transaction that occurs once and is never repeated again. It may be driven by the convenience of the shopping location, an immediate need or want met by a vendor, or a purchase with such a low level of emotional investment in the event that an evaluation of "satisfied" is all that can be mustered.

For engagement, it is the opposite dynamic at work. As we've discussed, it necessitates a deep emotional connection that characterizes a meaningful brand experience and evolves into a relationship and customer loyalty. In addition, because engagement is anchored in relationship building and relationship building occurs over time, the outcome is more aligned with business timelines than are satisfaction surveys which are anchored in consumers' past behavior. Past consumer behavior, when based on utility rewards that are at the foundation of satisfaction surveys, have little or no reliable predictive value as to how the consumer respondent may behave in the future.

Business strategies and their policy decisions seek long-term company stability and growth. But satisfaction metrics are set up to measure short-term responses to immediate experiences. Again, no meaningful emotional content is being measured and no long-term data are sought. Additionally, the nature of the rewards is such that they do not encourage the development of any emotional commitment. All you need to do to "earn" the reward is be patient, organized, and persistent in which brand you use. The absence of a relationship with the brand is why there is no significant correlation with long-term positive business outcomes that loyalty engenders. Loyalty is not being measured and, therefore, cannot be effectively managed.

Let's compare the two psychological dynamics (Table 11.1). This chart points to how brand loyalty, by forging deeper relationships between brand managers and customers, is more likely to result in long-term and better business outcomes. This business outcome occurs, in part, because engagement leads to longer and deeper relationships between brands and a broader swath of customers, which avoids the added cost of finding new customers and not retaining existing ones for very long. If we were to look at just one metric (we'll examine others later in the chapter), the so-called **Rule of Five**, we can see the monetary

Table 11.1 Comparative Consumer Dynamics: Brand Satisfaction Versus Engagement Which Alerts Managers to the Signs of How They Differ

	FACULTY IN PLAY	COMMITMENT	BRAND LOYALTY	BRAND ADVOCACY
SATISFACTION	THINKING	DISCRETIONARY	UNDEPENDABLE	PASSIVE
ENGAGEMENT	FEELINGS	OBLIGATORY	DEPENDABLE	ACTIVE

benefit of engagement and retention. It takes five times the investment to win a new customer than it does to retain an existing one. In addition, loyal customers contribute to a brand and company four to six times the value in **monetized benefits** by contributing to higher margins, greater revenue, larger share of more markets, and bigger stock valuations than those that have low customer retention levels and high customer **churn** (a measure of the customer turnover rates relative to customer retention rates). Loyal customers do so by buying more, more often, and often at full price. To say nothing of the role they play as ambassadors and advocates in converting friends and families to the brand and possibly to brand engagement as well. We can assume that, at some point in time, higher rates of loyalty follow within this friends and family relationship group. This is because, in a certain sense, the same type of emotional relationship exists between brands and loyalists and is being tapped into in the same manner as one would experience with friends and family.

The distinction between satisfaction and engagement, therefore, is not simply a matter of semantics. This is true in spite of the fact that the terms are too often used interchangeably. This creates both analytic and strategic problems for brand managers who must apply results from surveys and formulate policies based upon real and not imagined brand loyalists.

Consequently, keeping these concepts clear and separate will enable brand managers to respond with the appropriate brand strategies.

Satisfaction Surveys

As we stated at the start of this chapter, the two concepts, engagement and satisfaction, are at times and mistakenly used interchangeably. Again, this is often the result of misreading the idea of what "market orientation" discussed in Chapter 1 means.[17] If read as "customer-led," it tends to be reactive and short term in perspective and engenders business strategies that are primarily concerned with "satisfying" short-term customer-expressed needs. This is in comparison to being "market-led" and understanding customer latent needs as well as market conditions and thus is more long-term and proactive in its market orientation.

Satisfaction surveys are designed to discover problems, not measure satisfaction. When they are used in this manner, they can yield useful insights. When their usage is thought by the research or brand managers to be more ambitious, the survey results may border on generating misleading information.

Consumer satisfaction surveys are snapshots in a moment of time based upon what may very well be a passing disposition. In addition, the responses are often, given the questionnaire design, forced into choices which attempt to capture and measure gradations of differences or reasons framed by the design. Most satisfaction surveys are designed to use what is known as a **Likert Scale**, which is a means of measuring answers to survey questions by offering different degrees of choice to the respondents. As an example, Table 11.2 shows a questionnaire design using a Likert Scale.

There are two issues. First, can you place an equally weighted quantitative number on a qualitative opinion? And second, is the distance between the choices presented in the Likert Scale really equal in weighted value? For example, choice 3, which appears from the wording to be equidistant in value from choices 2 and 4, can easily be interpreted to be negative rather than neutral by reading the language to mean "indifferent" or "detached" or "not caring." This seems to move the needle more toward the negative than the positive or the neutral.

Table 11.2 Likert Scale: Displaying How Researchers Seek to Quantify Qualitative Responses

Strongly Disagree	Disagree	Undecided	Agree	Strongly Agree
1	2	3	4	5

This interpretation fits with our previous insight into the human tendency to be critical as opposed to complimentary. Then there is the overriding issue of the calculation method.

The respondent circles the number that supposedly corresponds to his or her degree of satisfaction or dissatisfaction. The numbers are added up from under each choice and the sum is divided by the number of respondents who participated in the survey. In our example in Table 11.2, the satisfaction winners are those with the score that corresponds to the satisfaction ranking. One effect is that the method of calculating doesn't factor in and therefore fails to capture the emotional intensity of the consumer's responses. Once again we are not measuring one of the key dynamics influencing behavior—the degree of emotions attached to the opinion. Similarly, for satisfaction assessments on social media, "like" parallels "satisfied," a sign which is a positive affirmation that has little or no emotional resonance in it. It can be linked neither to a propensity to purchase nor to any future degree of loyalty to the brand.

Finally, this type of survey cannot be the basis for determining loyalty for it lacks the test of **longitudinal reliability**, or the ongoing confirmation over time of the research findings. As we have indicated, satisfaction surveys are a snapshot in time and an attempt to quantify a perception that is held in a moment of time. Research outcomes, to be considered significant, need to be replicable over time. Without the engagement anchor, there is no way to use such research findings and to build a strategic business case with any long-term objectives.

In conclusion, if it is long-term strategies that brand managers need in order to plan, monitor, and manage their business responsibilities, then satisfaction surveys should not be the methodology of choice. If a quick snapshot is desired to discern possible problems that the brand may be experiencing, consider these types of surveys as adequate early warning systems.

CASE STUDY
J.D. Power and Associates

Let's look at a leading user of satisfaction surveys, J.D. Power and Associates, as a way of pointing out the uses and limitations of satisfaction surveys. J.D. Power is a global consumer research company that has been in business for over fifty years. The firm focuses on satisfaction surveys for several business sectors (health, hospitality, etc.) but its prominence rests on its work with the automotive industry (Figure 11.4).

The J.D. Power and Associates surveys seek to assess the degree of consumers' satisfaction regarding their experience with recently leased or purchased automobiles. In the surveys, framed around automotive brands, researchers attempt to ascertain the degree of satisfaction with the quality of the car and the driving experience. Although researchers merge these two metrics, they are distinct elements. This is the first of several issues in the measurement of satisfaction.[18] What is it that we are measuring? Quality assessments are objective and quantifiable; experiential assessments are subjective and qualitative. The former can be measured by the extent of the repairs, for example, that are needed. The latter raises questions of comfort and status and other such values that are emotional in nature. Blending the two into one score is tantamount to combining a baseball player's batting average with a metric that measures how much he contributes to leadership in the locker room and then dividing by two for an imaginary "holistic batting average."

figure 11.4
J.D. Power and Associates Satisfaction Seal:
The issue of whether it is a research company
or an advertising agency depends on the
client's use of the seal.

J.D. Power performs two types of survey
inquiries: one a ninety-day quality assessment,
and the other a quality review after three years
of ownership of the vehicle. The automotive
companies want to be able to claim that their
quality is superior to that of their competitors.
Therefore, they undertake the satisfaction
surveys less to better their quality and more
to advertise that they are superior in certain
prescribed ways (e.g., number one in initial
quality). They then license the results from J.D.
Power (if they are to any degree positive) which
permits the clients to use the J.D. Power logo
in their advertising as a type of **Good Housekeeping Seal of Approval**. This seal of approval

was developed by *Good Housekeeping* magazine in conjunction with its independent testing
lab set up to evaluate products for the home
and for the homemaker. The seal of approval
was enormously influential in part because
of the stature of the magazine but more so
because the grant of the seal from the research
facility was independent of the influence of the
magazine. The results were clearly the objective conclusion of a valid research process.

Can the same be said about J.D. Power, which
solicits companies, after performing research
regarding their product? It then sells them a
program which includes the research results
and the temporary use of the widely recognized J.D. Power logo and seal. The company
has positioned and marketed itself as an
objective and independent research company
and experts in consumer satisfaction surveys.
Here are some of the issues that brand managers should be aware of, especially if they are
approached by this or any satisfaction survey
research house and solicited for a research
program.

We never hear of the degree of dissatisfaction,
only the degree of satisfaction. This differs from
Consumer Reports and should not be equated
with it. *Consumer Reports* does not permit
commercial usage of its findings which might
compromise either the research method or the
perception of the findings. *Consumer Reports*
performs independent research—not satisfaction surveys—and in this regard it is more like
Good Housekeeping.

For J.D. Power, the problem of conflict of
interest therefore lingers. In addition, there
are methodological issues stemming from the
size of the samples used in its research, the

(continued on next page)

questionnaire design, and the very nature of satisfaction assessments and measurements. Let's begin with satisfaction assessments and measurements.

Satisfaction assessments play to our tendency as human beings to be more likely to find fault than to administer praise.[19] Research studies point to what is called the **Negativity Heuristic**, a tendency to be instinctively more negative than positive, which reduces the positive to less of an affirmation of quality or value but more to a residue of what remains after the negative calculus is derived. Satisfaction surveys do not encourage positive responses, and that may skew the resulting research findings. Next is the issue of the size of the sample used in the research.

J.D. Power researchers claim that they question a minimum of 100 owners for each subject matter inquiry that they are undertaking. This may be research regarding "initial quality" or "overall comfort" or other such elements. One hundred is a very small sample if the objective is to have the conclusions from the research projected as a reflection of the total population of owners of the brand, model, year, and the element under satisfaction review. **Sample size**, or how many respondents are required to be representative of the population (or the "pool"); the **margin of error** (a statistical variability concept not to be confused with a mistake) planned for in the research design, or how close the sample is to capturing the characteristics of the population studied; and **confidence levels**, or how often can we be confident that the margin of error will fall within a given range (usually 90 to 95 percent), which is a measure of how much variance in the outcome we are willing to tolerate—all are matters that are not made public and could, depending on the answers to the preceding questions, change the reliability of the survey and/or the validity of the conclusions. In general, the smaller your sample size, the higher your margins of error and the lower the confidence levels. If the methodology is uncertain or less than robust (e.g., too small a sample) and the conclusions drawn are presented as indicative or merely suggestive, then it has some merit. If it is more than suggestive, it is incumbent on the research organization, in the interest of clarity if nothing else, to qualify the results. As brand manager, these are some of the concerns you should have and questions you should be asking.

Customer Engagement Management

We saw in the preceding section that satisfaction surveys do not engage customers but reflect their opinions in a moment of time. Because these opinions are based on past behavior, they can't tell us what the future behavior of the consumer is likely to be. Customer engagement management seeks to do just the opposite. It seeks to predict future customer loyalty behavior based on engagement analytics. The key to understanding this behavioral outcome is first to determine how to create engagement and how engagement drives loyalty.

Internal Brand Management

Successful external brand management depends on first achieving successful internal brand management: *"Powerful brands are built from the inside out."*[20]

This requires that brand managers align the cultural values found in the everyday operations of the company with a **culture of brand engagement**, one that clarifies the company's brand values and encourages its employees to embrace the vision of the brand. The other side of this engagement equation is not only that the employees have access to and a clear understanding of the brand vision but also that they are emotionally bound to it: *"The goal of internal branding is to make sure the employees know the brand vision and critically, that they actually care."*[21]

The brand vision is often articulated by the CEO and/or founder of the brand. This is often the case when the brand is at a pivotal juncture in its business and wants to be certain that the employees truly care and engage with the brand's vision. There are three such pivotal moments and strategies that, staying with our health metaphor from Chapter 10, we have labeled Preemptive, Preventive, and Prescriptive. Here are some examples:

- Preemptive: Zappos's CEO Tony Hsieh offers $2,000 to any new hire who leaves within the first week of employment, feeling the job is not right for her. This "preempts," or helps to weed out early, non-caring employees (Figure 11.5).

- Preventive: P&G's CEO A. G. Lafley announces "The Customer is Boss" as the new consumer-centric brand vision. He orders all hires, promotions, raises, and retentions of employees to be based on new metrics that measure how well this vision is implemented within the company. By tying engagement to professional advancement, he will "prevent" those who have not internalized the brand vision from advancing in the company.

- Prescriptive: In 2008, Starbuck's CEO, Howard Schultz, found the brand experience was wanting. He shut down over 7,000 stores for a day-long, company-wide retraining session. He made it clear that the "prescription" for customers engaging the brand went beyond coffee, it went to the coffeehouse experience. This would be the "prescribed" remedy for resuscitating the brand.

At the heart of engagement is the degree of relevance that the engaged employee feels.[22] The concept of relevance here operates on two levels. First, the employee needs to be shown how his activity contributes to the business outcome; that is, how is his

figure 11.5
Zappos CEO Tony Hsieh: "Delivering Happiness" is the business Zappos is really in!

work relevant to a bigger picture of which he must be made privy. Transparency breeds trust and there can be no engagement without trust. Second, the engagement must feel relevant to what is important to the employee and must align with where she is in her own personal development. The most basic and fundamental of these is that the employee feels safe in the work environment—safe to innovate, safe to take chances, safe to make mistakes.

Here we can invoke Maslow's Hierarchy of Needs and the idea of Peak Experiences. His pyramid, re-created in Figure 11.6, points to the basic need that the employees must first feel—safety, or trust (Maslow's Tier II, Safety and Security)—before the path to engagement, and dependable employment, can be pursued. This is a precondition for ascending

the pyramid to higher experiences and deeper levels of relevant engagement, to say nothing of the foundation, or the first tier, Physiological Needs, which implies a decent wage and working conditions.

At the very root of the "caring" that David Aaker references as "critical" in the quote earlier in this chapter is that people want to be engaged. Jim Hauden describes this as follows.[23]

People want to:

- *make a difference*
- *be part of something big*
- *feel a sense of belonging*
- *go on a meaningful journey*[24]

Taken together, these needs are a definition of the human need for engagement.

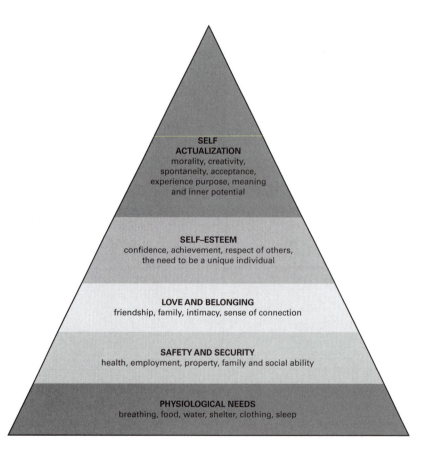

figure 11.6
Maslow's Hierarchy of Needs: The gradual ascendency toward reaching our human purpose is depicted here; we also can use this as a benchmark to assess how brands are doing in terms of social responsibility.

SELF ACTUALIZATION
morality, creativity, spontaneity, acceptance, experience purpose, meaning and inner potential

SELF–ESTEEM
confidence, achievement, respect of others, the need to be a unique individual

LOVE AND BELONGING
friendship, family, intimacy, sense of connection

SAFETY AND SECURITY
health, employment, property, family and social ability

PHYSIOLOGICAL NEEDS
breathing, food, water, shelter, clothing, sleep

External Brand Engagement

Brands are value systems that flourish from consumer engagement. They grow by becoming part of customers' lifestyles and their habits of living. Whether it's going to a Starbuck's or seeking out the latest Apple technology, consumers are acting out their self-designed engagement roles. Driven by brand values, brands both gain from and give to these customers a degree of personal signification through engagement. "*A person's favorite brands tend to align with his or her personal values, especially when that brand or company has successfully articulated what it believes.*"[25]

Monitoring external brand engagement requires the development of research programs to survey the brand's customer base. These should be ongoing activities and be budgeted for at the start of the fiscal year as with any other essential operation within the company.

Developing a customer database, which we have discussed in prior chapters, reemerges here as a fundamental management tactic. Here the database should be structured and tiers of customer differences should be built around an engagement metric. At a minimum, the measurement should be tied to depths of emotional connectedness and the frequency with which the customer interfaces with the brand in an engagement mode.

The values and objectives that we've just annunciated for internal engagement should guide the external engagement outreach as well. The need for signification, the social impulse to belong as reflected in the Love and Belonging third tier in Maslow's Hierarchy of Needs, and the desire to be part of something bigger than yourself and to make a difference, should all be sources for building metrics that enable brand managers to know if they are interfacing with engaged brand supporters and the degree of their emotional connection to the brand.

A consumer engagement strategy should also include supporting and encouraging brand communities. This not only generates brand value between the managers and communities but includes an even more authentic source of value through the co-creation of brand value from "*among community participants,*"[26] also referred to as "*the process of collective value creation within brand communities.*"[27] The value that these communities engender goes beyond the generation of consumer loyalty as the engagement creates a sense of belonging, often a special place for the member from the association and new social roles such as mentor or storyteller for the group which provides deep emotional fulfillment beyond any monetary measure.[28] To be proactive guardians of these social benefits, brand managers should be consistently evaluating their contact and communications with consumers and communities. Here is how one might go about doing so.

A Report Card, such as the "Connecting with the Consumer" example in Figure 11.7, should be periodically reviewed through an internal brand engagement audit team to self-grade the efforts of brand management in reaching out to and nurturing relationships with brand loyalists and brand communities.

ENGAGEMENT, BRAND LOYALTY, AND BUSINESS GROWTH

Robert Passikoff, president and founder of Brand Keys, which we first spoke of in Chapter 7, has done significant work in developing the metrics, methodologies, and business performance indices to measure the correlations between brand engagement, brand loyalty, and business growth. His definition of brand engagement is one that ties engagement to a higher brand vision based on an emotional ideal: "*it's the point where consumers see the brand as better meeting their ideal in the category where the brand competes.*"[29]

He then adds that engagement based upon this emotional connection correlates very highly with sales and profitability, something that's very significant and that we will explore in our final section of this chapter.[30]

Directions:

- Next to each question, place the numerical value number that best measures your current level of achievement for the marketing activity indicated
- Add up each column, and then add up the total points
- Divide by 10
- Result—Your Marketing Grade Point Average!

Connecting with the Consumer
Your Marketing Calculator

$$\frac{\quad\quad\quad}{\quad} \div \quad = \quad$$

YOUR GRADE

If you averaged a "B+" (3.5 GPA) or higher- We Congratulate you in advance for what will be a terrific year....

	Grade A	B	C	D	F
	Numerical Value 4	3	2	1	0
1. We have an excellent consumer database which we systematically mine.					
2. We know who our best consumers are and what they spend each year.					
3. We communicate with our consumers in personalized ways consistent with their values.					
4. We communicate with our best customers with periodic "Thank You's".					
5. We make sure our brand's image, message, & ads are consistent with our consumers' vision of it.					
6. To be aware of changing consumer attitudes, we monitor this with formal & informal surveys					
7. We know who our consumers see as our competition and use this in our business strategy.					
8. We know customers' place of residence by zip code & where and/or how they prefer to shop.					
9. We know their shopping habits/ patterns and why they buy our brand/product.					
10. We ask consumers if they recommend our brand to friends, family, and colleagues.					
Totals					

Add up the total boxes = Total Points _____

figure 11.7

"Connecting with the Consumer" report card: Just as we sought to measure our brand marketing acumen, this report card offers metrics for our consumer relationships.

Customer Types, Brand Values, and Engagement

We've seen that true engagement is emotionally grounded. Therefore, if we are to understand this dynamic, we need to create an engagement model based on a typology anchored on variations in emotions. Next, we'll need to align these emotional types with their corresponding value sets. Different levels of emotion tend to correspond to different clusters or sets of values.

Engagement Segmentation Models

Several segmentation models have been suggested by leading research companies that have much in common—Gensler Research and Gallup, the latter famous for the Gallup Poll, the first consumer survey. Gensler is a relative newcomer that has conducted a highly consumer-centric research design with a strong emotional quotient. They both mine for emotional brand connections and the degrees of those connections, and they frame the segments into four cohorts as shown in Table 11.3.

Brand Values and Brand Loyalty

The questions asked by both research firms have a high degree of emotional content as evidenced by the values-driven character of the questions regarding the brands and the consumer's relationship with them. The values alignment between brands and their customers is essential to both methodologies. In Gensler's section on Alignment, commenting on its survey results, the opening sentence reads: "*87 percent say they choose brands that match their values.*"[31] Complementing this statistic in the Gensler study is its counterpart that 71 percent avoid those brands whose value systems do not align with theirs.

This corresponds to Gallup's values approach. In its standard eleven-question survey of engagement, no less than eight of the questions are value-oriented and set in the context of emotional language. Here are several examples:[32]

- "*Brand X always delivers on what they promise.*"
- "*If a problem with Brand X arises, I can always count on Brand X to reach a fair and satisfactory resolution.*"
- "*I can't imagine a world without Brand X.*"

The overall conclusion from Gallup's research is that high-emotion consumers voice values such as love, honesty, and integrity as motivating their brand choices while low-emotion consumers skew toward practical utilities. As we have discussed in prior chapters, those who stress the "features and benefits" approach to brand communications and engagement are not reaching the souls of their customers. Although this focus on practicalities can generate sales, it is not sufficient to generate loyalty.

Table 11.3 Gensler and Gallup Segmentation Models: Here We Can See Two Different Languages Which Seek to Measure the Same Consumer Emotional Dynamics	
GENSLER	**GALLUP**
High Emotional Connection	Fully Engaged (Attached)
Mid-High Emotional Connection	Engaged (Beginning Attachment)
Low-Mid Emotional Connection	Disengaged (Neutral)
Low Emotional Connection	Actively Disengaged (Dislike)

Engagement Metrics and Business Growth

The metrics that are most often cited and used when discussing consumer loyalty behavior are the following satisfaction metrics: *repeat purchases, frequent store/brand visits, category brand preference* (as measured by percentage of wallet or percentage of wardrobe, for example, of a brand category), and *robust referrals* to friends, family, and colleagues. Again, these are measures of behavioral satisfaction and are useful starting points. However, without emotional engagement, they do not correlate consistently over time with loyalty and cannot be seen as long-term drivers of business growth.

Correlating Engagement with Business Growth

Let's return to the Hyundai example we discussed in an earlier chapter and look at this as a brand engagement strategy and the business outcomes.

If you recall the facts, during the 2009 financial crisis, Hyundai made an unprecedented offer. If you lost your job and had purchased or leased a Hyundai, the company would take it back and refund the full amount of what you paid. Hyundai management would ensure there would be no negative impact on your credit rating. The brand message was one of "caring" and "identifying with" customers' *feelings.* This was a statement of brand values aligning with the deepest of values that most consumers were feeling—a sense of uncertainty which created great anxiety.

Hyundai expressed the Maternal/Caring archetype which reached the emotions of its customers.

Less than 3 percent of the cars were actually returned. The resulting business growth metrics were impressive: an increase in consumer "consideration" of the brand to nearly 60 percent, a market share jump to 4.3 percent, and a sales increase of 27 percent. This happened while the sector was experiencing a 22 percent decline! One loyalty measurement service (Brand Keys) determined that the effects were long-term as indicated in the increase in the loyalty index from 295th place to 24th. Fast forwarding to 2010, Hyundai experienced a 24 percent sales increase and by 2012, record sales of 8.9 percent over 2011.

In a similar engagement study conducted over a two-year period by the Gallup organization in the restaurant space, **customer engagement ratios** were calculated that quantified engagement profile results from the Gallup questionnaire we discussed earlier. It then compared these with lower engaged customers who dined at competitors. The restaurant group with the highly engaged customers saw its sales increase by 30 percent over the two-year period while the competitors saw a decline of 2 percent.[33]

As these examples show, engagement can correlate with **business metrics**, those key measurable objectives without which businesses cannot grow and sustain themselves. These include market share growth, increased revenues, or higher profits. Without some or any of these, the value of the concept can be called into question. The Coca-Cola case that follows provides even more evidence that engagement works!

Each year since 2011, the Coca-Cola Company has collaborated with a high-profile luxury brand fashion designer for a limited edition redesign of the Diet Coke can and bottle for European distribution. In 2011 it was Karl Lagerfeld, in 2012 Jean Paul Gaultier, and in 2013 Marc Jacobs (Figure 11.8). This is a classic example of how mass and luxury find common ground similar to what we've discussed in other chapters regarding luxury designers creating capsule collections for mass retailers. In these examples, the objective is to enjoy the merchandise. But the consumer also is motivated as much by owning the iconic bottle enhanced with the designer's name or signature as with consuming the contents. This is where the brand's iconic image comes into play as the items purchased become **collectibles**, valued more for their brand attributes and associations than for their practical use.

Enter the next "collectibles" strategy from Coca-Cola called "Share a Coke." In the summer of 2014 (after a successful test in Australia in 2011 where consumption among young consumers increased by 7 percent), Coca-Cola launched a customer engagement campaign in the United States that provides a full complement of the elements that unite the emotional brand experience, brand engagement, and measurable business outcomes.

Coke managers identified the 250 most popular first names for teens and Millennials in the United States. It then had these names placed on individual bottles and cans of Coke (Figure 11.9). In addition, kiosks were set up in selected markets across the country where bottles could be purchased from vending machines and the bottles printed by the machine from a list of over 100,000 names.[34] Other bottles had terms such as "Family," "Friends," and other similar references. A major social media campaign plus traditional media placements (i.e., billboards) supported the program. The messaging of sharing was consistent with Coke's archetypes of the Innocent and the Family. This was part of the brand narrative and the brand's classic message

figure 11.8
Karl Lagerfeld and Coca-Cola: The co-branding and mixing of luxury and mass brands are in evidence in this special edition of Coca-Cola cans, designed by Karl Lagerfeld.

(continued on next page)

figure 11.9
Share a Coke Campaign: This enormously successful "personalization" campaign underscores the brand's real business, which is "everyday happiness" through simple human interactions.

of having a Coke with family and friends as simple, everyday, shared experiences. The personalization clearly plays to the target cohort of teens and Millennials who engage each other by sharing photos, videos, and "selfies" as a matter of course. Some of the evidence of engagement included over 500,000 photos on Instagram of the bottle and person including one of a dog named Crystal, whose owner was able to secure a bottle with the dog's name on it.[35] Bids on the bottles on eBay ranged from $2.99 to $5.24, with one going for $80.00.[36]

The interactive social media sites generated some significant numbers as Coke lovers browsed photo galleries and searched for stores near them that carried the program. As of September 2014, here were some of the online statistics:[37]

- Facebook likes: 88.9 million
- Twitter followers: 2.6 million
- Instagram followers: 318,231

After a decade of declining Coca-Cola sales, the campaign led to more than a 2.5 percent increase in sales in a market where a fraction of a percent is worth significant amounts of revenue and market share. Such an increase in one selling season is rare.

In conclusion, by examining both the social media numbers and the sales percentage increase, these outcomes confirm that the brand message aligned with and engaged the values of the core consumer. This helps to explain the success of the campaign and provides sound lessons for what constitutes a successful brand engagement program.

SUMMARY

The prime objective of this chapter is to understand what drives brand loyalty and how engagement is aligned with that objective. Loyalty is the objective because business growth is the goal and high degrees of loyalty correlate with high degrees of business growth.

Brand engagement is driven more by feelings than by reasoning. It is the natural outgrowth of the idea of the brand as an experience and how emotional benefits, rather than utilitarian benefits, are driving customer fulfillment and loyalty. This is reflected in brand communities and how the members through their interaction with each other co-create brand value and high levels of brand loyalty.

To effectively manage brand loyalty requires building loyalty segmentation models and designing them to capture varying motives for and degrees of brand loyalty. Therefore, there is no "average" loyalist. We also need to draw a distinction between loyalty programs and those consumers who are loyal to the rewards versus loyal consumers who are loyal to the brand.

The satisfaction metric differs from the engagement metric. Satisfaction may be a starting point in understanding how well the brand is serving the customer, but satisfied customers are not necessarily loyal customers because they have little or no emotional connection with the brand. This is in part because satisfaction surveys are a call for an opinion regarding a single moment in time and are an assessment based upon past behavior. Past behavior does not necessarily portend future behavior. Engagement happens over time and is anchored by the tendency of highly committed and emotionally connected customers to be in a love relationship with the brand. The two concepts engagement and satisfaction are, at times and mistakenly, used interchangeably. This is often the result of misreading the idea of what market orientation means. If read as customer-led, it tends to be reactive and short-term in perspective and engenders business strategies that are primarily concerned with satisfying short-term customers' expressed needs; this is in comparison to being market-led and understanding customers' latent needs and market dynamics and thus is more long-term and proactive in its market orientation. Consumer satisfaction surveys often, given the questionnaire design, force choices which attempt to capture and measure gradations of differences or reasons framed by the design. As such they change the nature of the answers. Survey methods can also affect the reliability of data from surveys and attention needs to be paid to sample size, margins of error, and confidence levels, and brand managers should be aware of the significance of these variables.

Customer engagement starts with employee engagement. The company culture must align with the brand's values and give employees a sense of the importance of their contribution to the brand, for the employees are the most natural brand advocates. For brand communities, engagement also creates a sense of belonging, which offers more than a monetary calculus of value and naturally leads to brand loyalty.

Finally, for engagement to be useful as a brand management tool it must correlate with business growth. Examples from automotive, restaurant, and soft-drink industries support the conclusion that engagement does drive business growth.

KEY TERMS

Active Engagement
Analysis/Paralysis
Brand Ambassador
Business Metrics
Churn
Collectibles
Confidence Levels
Culture of Brand Engagement
Customer Engagement Ratios
Fast Thinking

Good Housekeeping Seal of
   Approval
Likert Scale
Longitudinal Reliability
Loyalty Journey
Margin of Error
Monetized Benefits
Negativity Heuristic
One Version of the Truth
One-off

Passive Engagement
Purchase Journey
Rule of Five
Sample Size
Statistical Tendency
Transactional Brand Experience
Value-Driven Brand
   Engagement

CHAPTER CONVERSATIONS

- How would you describe brand loyalty to some-one who knows nothing about it?
- Is satisfaction a useful metric for brand management? Why or why not?

- What is the purpose of identifying customers' values?

CHAPTER CHALLENGES

- The human resources department of a consumer products company wants to do a satisfaction survey of its employees and asks you—as a corporate brand manager—to weigh in on the design and objectives. How would you approach this request and what would you recommend?
- A luxury automobile marketing department wishes to reward loyalists. It wants to identify who they are, where they are, and what the rewards should be consistent with the brand's identity and image. You are the brand manager for the brand. What would you recommend as the best approach for achieving its objectives? What brand "guardrails" would you advise it follow?

- The board of directors of a U.S. soft-drink company, who are not brand savvy, would like you, as the brand manager, to make a presentation explaining how the company can increase and sustain business growth using the Coca-Cola brand as the North Star for guidance. Given the background of the board, what would your presentation strategy be and how would you respond to their request that, in your business growth strategy, you should be guided by Coca-Cola?

ENDNOTES

1. R. E. Goldsmith and E. B. Goldsmith, "Brand Personality and Brand Engagement," *American Journal of Management* 12 no. 1 (2012): 13.

2. S. F. Slater and J. C. Narver, "Customer-Led and Market Oriented: Let's Not Confuse the Two," *Strategic Management Journal* 19 (1998): 1002.

3. This discussion follows the path we developed in Chapter 1 (see the section "Avoiding Marketing Myopia") and draws upon J. C. Narver and S. F. Slater's significant insights first presented in "The Effect of a Market Orientation on Business Profitability," *Journal of Marketing* 54 (October 1990): 20–35.

4. David A. Aaker, *Building Strong Brands* (New York: The Free Press: 1996), Chapter 10.

5. Ibid.

6. "How Adequate Are Brand Loyalty Models?," *Emotional Logic*, May 10, 2012, http://emotional-logic.co.uk/loyaltymodels.

7. Susan Fournier, "Consumers and Their Brands: Developing Relationship Theory in Consumer Research," *Journal of Consumer Research* 24 (March 1998); see also Kevin Lane Keller, *Strategic Brand Management: Building, Measuring, and Managing Brand Equity*, 4th ed. (N.p.: Prentice Hall, n.d.).

8. Jean-Noel Kapferer, *The New Strategic Brand Management: Advanced Insights and Strategic Thinking*, 5th ed. (Philadelphia, PA: Kogan Page, 2012).

9. Lucia Malär et al., "Emotional Brand Attachment and Brand Personality: The Relative Importance of the Actual and the Ideal Self," *Journal of Marketing* 75, no. 4 (2011): 35–52; see also Goldsmith and Goldsmith, "Brand Personality and Brand Engagement."

10. See, for example, Goldsmith and Goldsmith's study (note 1) of the North Face apparel brand where the salient concepts with which consumers' identified and which were sources of intense engagement were those which they personally valued and with which they identified themselves and the brand's persona.

11. Daniel Kahneman, *Thinking Fast and Slow* (N.p.: Princeton University Press, n.d.).

12. Kahneman, *Thinking Fast and Slow*; see also "2013 Brand Engagement Survey," *Gensler*, 2013, http://www.gensler.com/uploads/document/354/file/2013_Brand_Engagement_Survey_10_21_2013.pdf.

13. Ibid.

14. Ibid.

15. Corinne Munchbach, "Embed the Customer Life Cycle across Marketing." *Forrester*, January 22, 2013, http://www.catapultecommerce.com/uploads/Embed%20The%20Customer%20Life%20Cycle%20Across%20Marketing.pdf.

16. People Metrics, "Customer Engagement vs. Customer Satisfaction: Which Should You Follow?," *People Metrics*, September 30, 2010, http://www.peoplemetrics.com/blog/customer-engagement-vs-customer-satisfaction-which-should-you-follow; see also Thomas O. Jones and W. Earl Sasser Jr., "Why Satisfied Customers Defect," *Harvard Business Review*, November 1995, https://hbr.org/1995/11/why-satisfied-customers-defect.

17. See note 3.

18. David Lazarus, "What's Behind Customer Satisfaction Awards? J.D. Power 'Cozy' with 'Winners,'" *The Elsmar Cove*, July 25, 2005, http://elsmar.com/Forums/showthread.php?t=12856.

19. Ibid.

20. David Aaker, *Aaker on Branding: 20 Principles That Drive Success* (New York, NY: Morgan James Publishing, 2014); see also Rajendra K. Srivastava and Gregory M. Thomas, "Managing Brand Performance: Aligning Positioning, Execution and Experience," *Journal of Brand Management* 17 (2010).
21. Aaker, *Aaker on Branding*.
22. Jim Haudan, *The Art of Engagement: Bridging the Gap Between People and Possibilities* (New York, NY: McGraw-Hill, 2008).
23. Ibid.
24. Ibid.
25. Ibid.
26. R. J. Brodie et al., "Consumer Engagement in a Virtual Brand Community: An Exploratory Analysis," *Journal of Business Research* 66, no. 1 (January 2013): 105.
27. Hope Jensen Schau, Albert M. Muñiz Jr,, and Eric J. Arnould, "How Brand Community Practices Create Value," *Journal of Marketing* 73, no. 5 (September 2009): 30.
28. Susan Fournier and Lara Lee, "Getting Brand Communities Right," *Harvard Business Review* (April 2009).
29. Robert Passikoff, "Defining 'Brand Engagement,'" *Forbes*, June 17, 2013, http://www.forbes.com/sites/robertpassikoff/2013/06/17/defining-brand-engagement/.
30. Ibid.
31. Ibid.
32. Susan Sorenson and Amy Adkins, "Why Customer Engagement Matters So Much Now," *Gallup*, July 22, 2014, http://www.gallup.com/businessjournal/172637/why-customer-engagement-matters.aspx; see also Theo Muller, "Loyal Customers Don't Quit . . . Satisfied Customers Do," *MM Research*, January 2010, http://mm-research.com/uploads/files/article_customer_engagement_jan10.pdf.
33. Ibid.
34. Kristina Monllos, "Brand of the Day: How 'Share a Coke' Went Beyond Ingenious Packaging to Boost Sales," *Ad Week*, September 29, 2014, http://www.adweek.com/news/advertising-branding/brand-day-how-share-coke-went-beyond-ingenious-packaging-boost-sales-160444.
35. Mike Esterl, "'Share a Coke' Credited with a Pop in Sales," *Wall Street Journal*, September 25, 2014, http://www.wsj.com/articles/share-a-coke-credited-with-a-pop-in-sales-1411661519.
36. Ibid.
37. Ibid.

Mass Brand Management in a Digital World

AFTER COMPLETING THIS CHAPTER, YOU WILL BE ABLE TO:

- Discuss strategies for aligning offline and online brand metrics.

- Determine strategies for managing online brand engagement, co-creation, and brand communities.

- Assess the challenges of tracking online ads, offline sales, and engagement.

"Not everything of value can be measured, and not everything that is measured is of value."

—Albert Einstein

ALIGNING OFFLINE AND ONLINE BRAND METRICS

In Chapter 11, we discussed the importance of engagement as both a strategy and a metric leading to customer loyalty. In this chapter, we will take a look at how this concept translates into the digital online space and how it joins with relevance and co-creation to guide digital brand management and create brand value.[1] Given that *"brand value co-creation is enacted through brand engagement platforms..."*[2] can engagement provide a bridge over which online and offline managers can innovate together and develop a unified strategy for brand building? Is relevance the key to successful engagement that helps lead the way to brand loyalty? These are the major questions we'll address.

A Single Version of the Truth

With the ascendency of social media and its platforms for communications and business development, brand managers are faced with the challenge of aligning offline and online strategies, each of which has varying methods of measuring business success. The overarching business goal is not only to align but eventually to integrate offline and online brand management strategies and objectives. Achieving this will aid in the more efficient use of resources such as time, budgets, and personnel, and lead to the development of a seamless offline/online organization with more impactful business outcomes.[3] We refer to this integration as **a single version of the truth**, one set of metrics to measure the **return on investment (ROI)**, or the measure of the return (monetary and otherwise) from the investment of company resources in pursuit of its business objectives.

Aligning Offline and Online Business Objectives

The pursuit of a single unified strategy begins with the fact that both offline and online managers seek to manage the same outcomes although, at times, with varying strategies. For example, brand awareness is a metric and a business objective that crosses both offline and online spheres but has different yet similar instruments for realizing the awareness objective. An example of this would be pop-up ads that are found online and pop-up stores that are found offline. **Pop-up ads** seek to create brand awareness by surprise appearances, often on high-traffic sites. They convey a brief brand message and then disappear. **Pop-up stores** are stores located in high-traffic neighborhoods that are meant to generate awareness by serendipitous discovery. There is a sense of urgency from consumers to visit these locations because they are open only for a short time. A few questions arise regarding the objective of these pop-up vehicles. Is it primarily for marketing purposes, such as the introduction of a new product or brand, or is it for sales? Or is it to introduce the brand into a new geography or a new social media platform? Are they to be planned and budgeted from the marketing department or from the sales department?

An integrated offline and online organization would plan these two operational venues together, as one strategy, with one set of objectives and metrics to measure success. At this juncture, for some companies, this doesn't exist so we don't know for sure which is returning the highest ROI. Even if the integration existed, questions such as the meaning and measure of **traffic** (the number of visitors offline in the stores and online in the social media platform) would have to be determined beforehand. Even the question of what constitutes a "visitor" needs to be defined, for a visitor has, at this juncture, very different meanings and impact offline versus online. A visitor offline may meander around the shop for some time absorbing brand messages and asking questions about the products and prices. A visitor online may click on for a few moments and hardly engage or absorb any part of the brand message. If we were measuring the return from each venue, in what way can we count their "visitor" presence as equal?

Some differences between offline and online are a function of the variations intrinsic to the digital space when compared with the nondigital platforms. These are likely to present greater challenges in the effort to integrate the two. For example, digital platforms such as news feeds tend to be more dynamic than non-digital platforms such as newspaper editorials. This makes comparative analysis more difficult because of the rapid changes in digital feeds. Others are the result of differing views as to what the priorities of brand management might be. For some time, online managers were more concerned with generating sales than with building brands and developing brand loyalty. Building brands requires a sequential process over time of building awareness, conveying the brand identity through telling brand narratives, and then managing the online brand image through listening to consumer conversations and responding accordingly. Early efforts often generated only short-term growth because of the absence of building loyalty to the brand. As an example, in the early days of internet marketing, brand awareness was not thought to be of great importance.[4] The good news is that traditional

offline concepts are now often used by online managers and can be of use in framing a dialogue between offline and online managers. This assumes that both understand the concepts in the same way—that is, with similar meanings.

The chart in Table 12.1 gives us a starting point to see how the two brand management venues, offline and online, can find alignment and common ground over a **consumer's purchase journey**, those steps culminating in a purchase.

To align the comparatives, the chart should be read from left to right. As an example, brand awareness offline is discerned from ads, friends' recommendations, and the like. Brand awareness online is through keywords, search engine optimization (SEO) models, influencers, and the like. At some future point, a single language will be needed to fully unify and integrate the two approaches. To provide a common foundation for this, brand managers should continue to ask and remind each other, "What business are we really in?" This will help provide a common foundation and reinforce internal branding and cultural values. Brand archetypes should also be revisited for they will generate a common emotional context that will help ensure managerial engagement and keep relevant the changes that will be necessary for the integration to successfully take hold.

Table 12.1 The Consumer Purchase Journey: Seeking Common Ground—Comparative Metrics Offline/Online	
Offline	Online
Brand Recall (Brand Awareness) (friends, family, ads, etc.)	Brand Search (Brand Awareness) (keywords, SEO results, social media influencers)
Preference (short list of preferences)	Navigation (direct to sites)
Consideration (rank order of preferences)	Average Time Spent on Sites (compare with competitors)
Purchase Intent (store/department/catalog repeat "visits")	Repeat Landing Page Visits (time spent and purchase outcomes)

Relevancy, Engagement, and Loyalty

The advent of the digital space has obligated brand managers to be even more focused online than offline, strategizing the relationship and linking relevancy, engagement, and brand loyalty. This greater focus is the result of social media being **content driven**, or intensely immersed in social messaging, information, and images that are important to consumers because it touches their emotions and personal values. This results in what has been called *"freely created brand meaning..."*or the co-creation of the brand identity through its interaction with online content creators.[5] Relevant messaging and information gathering as part of the consumer purchasing journey both increase awareness[6] and drive engagement, or those actions taken by consumers in investing time and effort with the brand which, over time, can engender brand loyalty. To follow this connection, we first need to define relevancy. Relevancy, as discussed in Chapter 3, is about how the brand aligns with core customers' emotions, personal values, and lifestyle priorities. A classic example of this returns us to the Harley-Davidson brand and the community that the brand has engendered. On its site is a Harley owners page, aptly labeled HOG (Harley Owners Group). HOG is not only an acronym for the community of owners but also an insider, self-deprecating reference to the robust size of their motorcycles vis-à-vis the smaller competitors.

Owners are encouraged to post photos and itineraries of trips taken on their Harleys, including places to ride and to stay where motorcycles are a welcome part of the local culture. This relevancy of the content reinforces the sense of community and drives the engagement and brand loyalty as reflected in repeat purchases of the brand over time. As we discussed in Chapter 11, it has also fostered something deeper and more meaningful, referred to by one scholar as "The Brotherhood of Riders" to describe the sense of community and the depth of brand equity.[7]

The impact of this can be seen in the very survival of the brand and company when in 1983 it was on the verge of bankruptcy. Then from 1985 to 2005, a total transformation of the brand and the business was engineered, in part by engendering and encouraging, without being intrusive, the online brand community, resulting in accelerated membership from a myriad of global markets. Brand managers created the platform for the community plus social events and relevant information for the bikers' lifestyle and then turned the content and internal communications over to the bike owners. By 2005, Harley-Davidson was ranked as one of the top 50 global businesses and brands with revenues in excess of $7 billion annually. This repositioning of the brand has been described by the same scholar as *"community-centric positioning"* wherein *"a motorcycle manufacturer ... understood bikers on their own terms."*[8]

The HOG community worldwide now numbers over a million owners strong! This is brand building at its best, built upon engagement and community (Figure 12.1).

Much brand building misses the mark because it focuses on the product offer and fails to focus on the hearts of its customers. Again, this approach too often assumes the "Rational Man" model of decision making discussed in earlier chapters that tends in its marketing outreach and communications to emphasize utilitarian promises and practical outcomes from the purchase decision. This is often less effective because *"it does not engage customers ... especially when the offering is ... detached from their lifestyle. This is especially true for digital strategies that hope to activate a community."*[9]

David Aaker speaks about connecting the brand to a "sweet spot," his metaphor for a place within consumers' hearts and lives. What really moves them, and how can you create a "shared-interest" program that establishes a relationship between the brand and the consumer by offering something of consequential content beyond the product?[10] As an example, he points to Pampers and its Pampers Village online site. Here the content offered contains all aspects of what mothers and male household caregivers are likely to need to know in child-rearing challenges

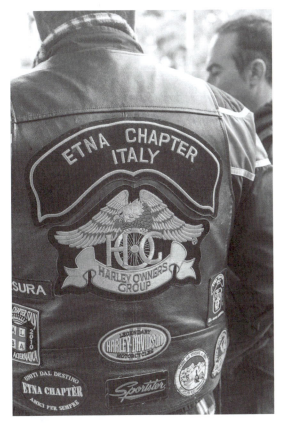

figure 12.1
HOG Italian member's vest: The Harley Davidson brand is truly international, as seen from its brotherhood of riders/HOG community owners.

and opportunities. There is also an online community where mothers-to-be and current moms can exchange information and insights and ask questions of each other, sharing their own experiences.[11] Much like our discussion of Jim Stengel and the Brand Ideal in our earlier chapters, the "village" ties the brand back to something bigger than itself: "*The program demonstrates that Pampers understands mothers and works to establish a relationship between the brand and the mother that will potentially continue throughout the mother's Pampers-buying life.*"[12]

The eventual goal of such a program is to engage consumers emotionally so, at the consideration stage in the purchasing journey, the brand is in the **consideration set**, meaning it is among other similar brands in the product category under purchase consideration or review.

The consumer will also need to make a decision regarding a product category and subcategory (e.g., beer/light beer) and whether a brand fits the category (has credibility in the product space) prior to being a contender for the consideration set.[13]

Consequently, driving relevancy also requires that the brand manager has tied the brand's identity to the category in which it competes (e.g., beer/light beer) and has so framed the alignment between the brand and the category or subcategory that there is little or no room for competitors.

Creating the relevant "sweet spot" helps drive the association between the brand, the product, and the category and/or subcategory. It does so by resonating with core consumers and breaking out of the communication clutter that advertising and marketing messaging in the digital age have made even more pervasive than in the traditional communications space. Again, the content and the cause need to be relevant to the lifestyle and values of the core customer. It is best when they are organically connected to the brand and the brand promise. This enables brand credibility to be established and consumer notions of disingenuous brand self-interest to be minimized. These last achievements will help set the stage for brand loyalty to emerge. Without these, the loyalty quotient will be diminished and brand loyalty less likely to occur.

Customer loyalty is measured by more than just significant purchases over time. Profit levels are driven by other variables such as **customer retention** (the savings from having long-term customers and not having to invest in finding new ones), and **advocacy** (the extent to which the customer refers others to your brand), and, of course, consistent purchases over time. These are three ways to drive business development and should be viewed as the triad of the concept. Thus, a definition of loyalty needs to go beyond sales to fully capture its value and for brand managers to see the scope of its strategic importance. Here's one we feel does this: "*Customer loyalty is the degree to which customers experience positive feelings for and engage in positive behaviors toward a company/brand.*"[14] The next steps are to develop the touch points that are unique to the digital and social media brand experience. This follows the same path that we took in an earlier chapter where we introduced the loyalty matrix. The key for the brand manager is to properly identify the drivers, those relevant values and experiences that are likely to engage customers and build loyalty, as well as the antes, those values and experiences that are givens if a brand is to even begin to compete in the competitive game. To refresh our memories, antes should not be promoted as brand offers because the consumer expects them to be within the brand's promise and the company's competencies. Promoting any of those antes can not only waste resources but perhaps even more importantly create a credibility gap between the brand and the customer. The question may arise as to why the brand continues to "sell" what the customer has already "bought," for the consumer may well assume the brand should have the service or capability attribute to be a fully effective player in the digital space.

It is also important to realize that the model outlined in Figure 12.2 is dynamic; that is, the boxes are not sealed off from the competitive environment. Depending on competitive challenges, trends, and innovations, changes can occur in both the touch points and the quadrant they occupy. A driver can become so commonplace that it falls in to the antes box and therefore suddenly warrants little brand promotion. As an example, "user-friendly platforms" were, in the early stages of social media development, drivers, but now, given the expectations of consumers, they have become antes. This should alert brand managers to the need to diligently and systematically review the status of all touch points and to confirm that they continue to be drivers of brand loyalty.

Ongoing, strategically preplanned consumer surveys, and the monitoring of key social media sites and conversations, will provide the insight and answers to this needed confirmation.

Building an Integrated Marketing Strategy

In the ongoing quest to maximize loyalty, building an **omni-channel communications** platform that includes a seamless integration of brick-and-mortar stores, direct mail catalogs, websites, and a mobile apps strategy has become a consumer expectation and a means of creating relevant platforms for consumer engagement. For the **Millennials**, that cohort of 18- to 34-year-old consumers, this omni-channel platform is fast approaching the status of an ante as mobile apps are the driving communications force behind this new business platform. Omni-channel apps are this cohort's communications technology of choice. Brand managers who are available as problem solvers and attentive listeners are in a position to capitalize on building brand loyalty among these and other cohorts who are, through mobile apps, some of the most highly engaged customers. When we combine these two, apps and listeners, we achieve a very strong combination which translates into a compelling brand promise. One example of this is Best Buy and how it has built an integrated system of customer service and omni-channel communications.

Integrating Communication Platforms

Best Buy has systematically offered more and more mobile applications with relevant information and customized, real-time opportunities on services and brand communities. In addition, when it seamlessly integrates offline and online venues, it stands the best chance of engaging and eventually winning the loyalty of the consumer.

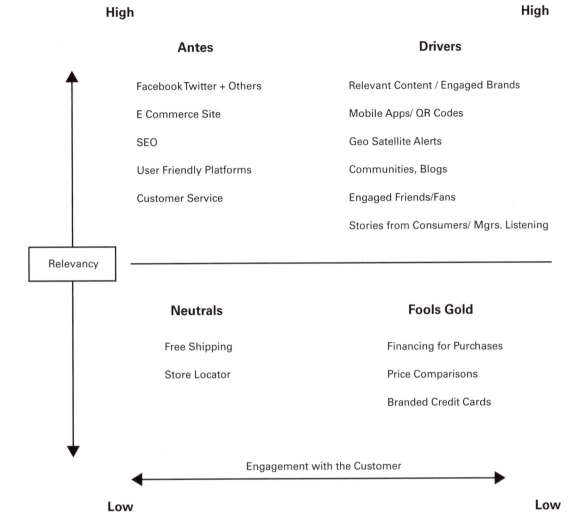

High   **High**

Antes

Facebook Twitter + Others

E Commerce Site

SEO

User Friendly Platforms

Customer Service

Drivers

Relevant Content / Engaged Brands

Mobile Apps/ QR Codes

Geo Satellite Alerts

Communities, Blogs

Engaged Friends/Fans

Stories from Consumers/ Mgrs. Listening

Relevancy

Neutrals

Free Shipping

Store Locator

Fools Gold

Financing for Purchases

Price Comparisons

Branded Credit Cards

Engagement with the Customer

Low   **Low**

Digital Brand Touch points

figure 12.2
Digital brand loyalty touch points: Just as we applied the brand loyalty matrix offline, here is how it could be useful online.

One example of a successful integration is Best Buy's omni-channel/360° brand experience through its "Connected World" mobile marketing initiative. Here are some of the ways in which the company aligns itself with customer lifestyles: Consumers can scan in-store item QR codes for product reviews/specs so that they can obtain and keep the information in their phones while shopping. Best Buy also has mobile apps for which it has created brand names as a means of intensifying consumer focus and differentiating its platform from those of competitors.

For instance, Best Buy has created what it calls a "Twelpforce"® on Twitter. This is a combination of "Twitter" and Best Buy's "Help Force." Customers can easily ask questions or register concerns through tweets and have them answered by an agent. Best Buy has over 600 employees connected to this mobile app to respond 24/7 to any questions. This relates back to its "Connected World" initiative, a broader example of what we see as essential internal and external brand marketing in the digital age.

Employees voluntarily join the Twelpforce and go through a training program that is focused on keeping them "on-brand." In introducing a Twelpforce online training video, a slide asks several orientation questions of the trainees, which it then answers. One of the questions is: "Why are we doing this/What is our objective?" The answer that comes on the next slide is "Because the customer owns the brand"![15]

The program was launched with a major television ad campaign explaining the service to the public. This is a good example of the integration of both offline and online strategies for brand loyalty development. It has been estimated that the annual ROI of the program is considerable. In the words of the Best Buy brand manager for the program, "*Factoring in call deflections and sales influence, our online community engagements provide around $5 million benefit to the organization.*"[16]

Therefore, as the digital and physical worlds interface, brand marketers will continue to search for ways to align and integrate these two venues. To sum up the key questions that need to be answered:

- How do we align offline brand marketing metrics and online brand marketing metrics so we compare the effectiveness of each with the same measurement tools in terms of ROI?
- How does brand building occur online and does it differ from offline brand building strategies?
- What impact does brand marketing online have on online and offline sales?
- How do we measure brand advocacy and loyalty in the digital world?

The need to have a clear understanding of these issues, and a brand management vision and strategy in place to manage them, is underscored by the online concept of social shopping. **Social Shopping** refers to how individuals interact online with each other and how they interface with brands. More often than not, the interactions are not primarily for purchasing products or services but for an exchange of thoughts and information. In an instant, customers can mine information about products from other shoppers (comparisons, reviews, etc.). Ratings and reviews can be exchanged in real time, impacting a buyer's decisions. Mobile devices have allowed word-of-mouth to become an instant decision-making fulcrum. Customers can now "share" with their friends on social sites like Facebook, Twitter, YouTube, Pinterest, Instagram, opinion leader's blogs, and other platforms, their brand experience in words, pictures, and videos (Figure 12.3). This is the foundation for online brand building which requires 24/7 brand management oversight.

An example of what needs to be done but was not effectively carried out is reflected in the headline "United Breaks Guitars!" The headline points to the power of social media to transform an accident into a serious public relations challenge for a brand and a company.

In this incident, due to carelessness in baggage handling, an expensive guitar was broken. United Airlines refused to take responsibility. The owner of the guitar wrote a song and music video about the occurrence and posted it on YouTube. The video

went viral with content that was severely critical of United for failing to respond to the serious damage resulting from the inappropriate handling of the instrument. After the video went viral, United's stock price plunged 10 percent, resulting in a loss of $180 million in market capitalization! The brand image of the company suffered as well because it was seen as unreliable and unresponsive to customer complaints.

This was a public relations nightmare for United. Since the video was posted on social media, it meant that the content could not be managed or controlled by United's brand managers. As one observer commented, *"Consumers will talk and with the power of social media, their voices are louder than ever before."*[17]

United's culture and its brand promise were not as aligned with social media as they should have been, and the delays and denials created a thunderstorm of protest. It also raises the question whether the company's tagline "Fly the Friendly Skies" is truly a brand promise or merely an advertising slogan. Here is where archetype anchorage and a brand persona might have helped avoid this failure to align with consumer values by serving as a North Star and providing a clear direction for resolving the dispute.

When management finally responded by making a donation to the Thelonious Monk Institute of Jazz, they reacted way too late. Within the first four days of the video being posted, it had 1.5 million views. As of this writing, it has over 4 million views. Social media gives the online community a megaphone to spread their opinions. This viral voice can either build or tarnish a brand image, to say nothing of the adverse effect on ridership for United, something that cannot be measured but is most likely to have occurred.

Identifying and Engaging Influencers

Voicing opinions has taken on an even larger role in affecting brand images through the advent of opinion leaders known as influencers. Opinion leaders, or **influencers**, are those who have a large following on their social media sites and who engage their followers by providing content and conversations about companies and brands. These influencers can be a key tool in the word-of-mouth channel of marketing if they can be made into **brand advocates**—influencers who talk about, recommend, and spread the word

This is an example of the link between social media funnels influencers and a traditional sales funnel, and how brand building can result in sales. In 2010, the Ford Motor Company was able to find a clear ROI and linkage to purchases in a **buzz marketing** campaign where the objective was to generate viral conversation about a brand. Here it was undertaken for the launch in the United States of Ford's new Fiesta car model (Figure 12.4).

Ford identified 100 social media influencers (aka brand advocates) and gave each a car to drive. They were sent on a "mission" that was videotaped, shared, and placed on YouTube; 6.5 million views later, it generated 50,000 information requests leading to 10,000 cars sold in showrooms within the first six days the cars were on the market! Ford's brand strategy included having these savvy influencers explain their experience through the videos posted on YouTube and Facebook and the rest is history.

The Fiesta Movement campaign was wildly successful after the Fiesta video went viral. One reason it was so successful was that rather than Ford telling consumers why the Fiesta is good, it let consumers' peers do the reviewing and then provided the venue (the web) and the platform (YouTube) for disseminating the message. In addition, consumers had more trust in the reviewers because these influencers were also potential purchasers and, as part of the targeted cohort, constituted a brand community. This added to the positive perception of the Ford brand image and the resulting brand engagement.[20]

Another of the main reasons this tactic was so successful is because Ford also integrated offline with online communications. The traditional automobile showroom was used as an online visitor's offline showroom to see the actual models, adding a tactile, "touch and feel" dimension to the virtual brand experience.

The communities represented by these influencers suggest another more powerful perspective on brand building: "*The value of a brand is linked to the relationship it fosters.*"[21] A shared experience that feels like friendship and community is both highly relevant and highly engaging and is a driver of brand loyalty.

This revisits the fundamental shift that brand management needs to embrace as we discussed in Chapter 11, a shift from a purely transaction-based interaction with consumers to a brand experience that feels like friendship. This emotional brand/consumer relationship highly correlates with brand loyalty. Brand building begins here and sales are likely to follow.

figure 12.4
Launching the Ford Fiesta: Using an integrated offline/online strategy made all the difference.

about a brand through engaging their followers. In our case study of the launch of the Ford Fiesta, we'll take a closer look at the role of Influencers in the successful outcome of this campaign.

The pivotal role of Influencers in connecting targeted consumers with brand management strategies has led to the emergence of a number of third-party companies such as Ninja Metrics and Speakr that specialize in connecting companies to relevant influencers. These companies follow the conversations that the advocate has about your brand and creates a projected ROI from the advocate's **reach** (or the number of targeted consumers who have seen an ad) as well as the quality of the followers relevant to the brand. These sites can go into specific detail as to which conversations actually lead to sales, thereby providing the brand manager with a direct measure of the value of these connections.[18] Here brand building is taking place and brand managers continue to be the brand guardians by monitoring and measuring brand-rich online brand mentions. The objective is to listen, learn, and respond; the goal is to add to brand equity by engaging those Influencers and consumers who can champion the brand. Taking this one step farther, several platforms have emerged such as Tap Influence that launched "TapFusion" which works with brand managers to identify the appropriate influencers, vet them, and recruit and monitor their contribution to designated business outcomes.[19]

SOCIAL MEDIA BRAND ENGAGEMENT

One of the responsibilities of the brand manager in managing social media brand engagement in this regard is to analyze and evaluate the strength or weakness of the influencer and his or her followers. Here are three key variables that are the basic monitoring elements that need to be assessed.

Media Platforms and Conversations

Brand managers should be focused on both the platform and the content that provides the emotional context within which brand engagement takes place. Therefore, inappropriate content is a more obvious issue requiring management evaluation, while the proper alignment between platform, images, and messages posted by influencers and others are equally important and at times more difficult to evaluate given the added complexity of discerning the fit between what we might call "site" and "sound."

Monitoring Brand Equity Variables

The monitoring of these variables is essential if managers are going to determine the credibility and the capability of the influencer and followers (Table 12.2). To begin, the sentiments by **social media types** (e.g., passive versus active engagers) is an important aspect of the degree of engagement with the brand. It is essential to ascertain not only the numbers but the quality of fans and advocates based on an assessment of how consistent and how long their allegiance to the brand has been in evidence. To confirm the degrees of consistency and allegiance to the brand, managers will need to recruit a sample of the cohort and design a sample survey with questions that can capture degrees of loyalty. This can be administered online using a cost-effective research platform such as Survey Monkey. Finally, the brand manager is concerned with the churn, or the ratio and rate of loss

Table 12.2 Variables Impacting Brand Equity: Online Metrics Need to Be as Robust as Offline Metrics		
Reputation of Brand	**Churn**	**Loyalty**
Sentiments by social media type	Rate of dropouts over time	Quality of fans and advocates

of followers relative to the replacement of those who disengaged from the influencer's blog or website. This latter metric will give you a sense of the stability of the following and the dependability vis-à-vis the numbers of followers that the leader is likely to deliver at any given time.

Brand Building and Brand Narratives

Brand building also requires evaluating brand personality attributes, including those suggested by its engaged customers, which aids in building equity in the brand. To effectively manage this, a crucial shift had to occur from brand managers focused on "storytelling" to brand managers focused on consumer centric "story listening" and then rebuilding brand narratives. This provides brand managers with the opportunity to create new personality dimensions within the brand personas by tweaking existing brand attributes in response to significant and relevant consumer insights. The challenge is to do so while retaining the essence of the brand's DNA. Here again, reaching back to the brand archetype will provide a guideline for maintaining the brand's most enduring values and its timeless identity.

SOCIAL MEDIA: ALIGNING VISITOR DATA WITH SALES FUNNELS

This dynamic relationship between consumers and their brands requires 24/7 monitoring of social media sites and being responsive with various engagement strategies. These strategies must be aligned with different types of visitors, participants and the various reasons for their visit, content, and conversation.

Using **Social Media Funnels** (Figure 12.5) enables managers to manage different types of visits by directing visitors to solutions that align with the purpose for which they engaged the brand, which is an important step in continuing.

The use of a social media funnel enables brand managers to achieve two of the key objectives of brand management in the social media space:

- Aggregates activity from a variety of social media platforms for mining insights and delivers the right content to the right cohort at the right time
- Unites the traditional sales and marketing funnel with social media, enabling evaluation of

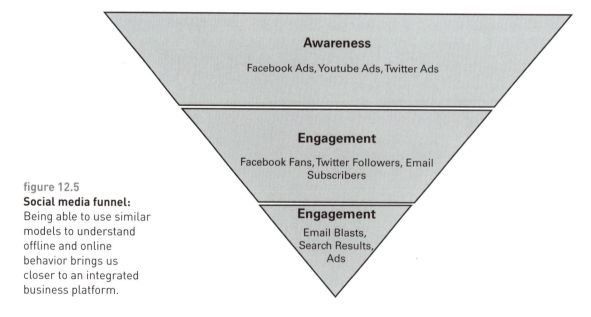

figure 12.5
Social media funnel:
Being able to use similar models to understand offline and online behavior brings us closer to an integrated business platform.

Awareness
Facebook Ads, Youtube Ads, Twitter Ads

Engagement
Facebook Fans, Twitter Followers, Email Subscribers

Engagement
Email Blasts, Search Results, Ads

where impact is coming from, where problems exist, and where opportunities appear that can be managed

One challenge in this brand management scenario is to properly identify the advocates who are influencers. This returns us to the concept of engagement. Table 12.3 shows a chart that outlines the stages, from involvement to influence, of brand advocates and how to track and measure their degree of engagement.

Tracking Influencers

The key to successful tracking is to monitor the stages by tracking the point the potential influencer has arrived at. At the point of transformation to Influencer, the brand manager should engage the individual as a form of initiation and congratulations. This personal contact is an essential part of the engagement process, keeping it real and the relationship meaningful (Table 12.4).

Staying On-Brand

Throughout these processes, brand managers must find a balance between succumbing to public opinion and engaging core consumers who present meaningful values that correspond to the brand promise. The other alternatives—that is, do nothing, or do everything that's communicated—are not sound

strategies. The former will lead to online communities seeing the brand as insensitive and nonresponsive, breaching the emotional engagement that brand advocates expect in a true engagement relationship. If the do-everything strategy is pursued, the brand will be a **chameleon brand**, changing with every change in the social media space and thereby losing its identity and with it its integrity and customer relevancy.

TRACKING ONLINE ADS, OFFLINE SALES, AND BRAND ENGAGEMENT

Traditional online metrics such as click-through rates, impressions, and conversions seemed sufficient until it became apparent that long-term objectives such as brand building and brand engagement required a different set of metrics. "*Nielsen research has shown that virtually no relationship exists between clicks, brand metrics or offline sales.*"[22] However, this is not to say that online ads do not have a meaningful impact on offline sales. The evidence suggests they do, but to what extent is unclear. This sets the stage for the development of a new model for integrating offline, traditional marketing metrics with online web-based counterparts so we can measure to what degree they do so.

Table 12.3 Managing Social Media Visitors: Because Visitors to Social Media Venues Come with Various Objectives in Mind, Managers Need to Identify Differences and Engage Accordingly

Types of Visitors	Prospects	Customers	Media	Influencers	Unknowns
Brand Marketing Objective	Move to marketing sales funnel	Provide service	Position brand image	Equip and encourage	Determine profile
Strategies for Engagement	Manage brand Engage in conversation	Engage in conversation Collect feedback	Manage brand Engage in conversation	Fuel word of mouth Collect feedback	Provide product info Engage in conversation

Table 12.4 Tracking Engagement of Brand Influencers in Social Media: Consistent Tracking Is Needed to Provide the Appropriate Responses

	Involvement	Interaction	Intimacy	Influence
What to Track	Site visits Time spent Pages viewed Keyword searched Navigation paths Site log-ins	Contributions to blogs Number of reviews, comments, etc. Posts Uploading photos Catalog requests	Track sentiment on third-party sites Internal customer contributions Opinions in customer service calls	Net Promoter Score Product ratings Brand affinity Content sent to friends Posts on high-profile blogs
Why to Track	Measure actual presence of passive engager	Encourage beginning of active engager	Measure brand affinity, sentiments, and feelings	Recognize advocacy of brand to friends and family Honor beginning of loyalty
How to Track	Web analytics	E-commerce and social media platforms	Brand mentions monitoring Customer service calls Surveys	Brand mentions monitoring Customer service calls Surveys

The Impact of Online Marketing on Offline Sales

A starting point is the use of traditional consumer purchase panels online and asking classic brand awareness and recognition questions such as:

- "Do you recall seeing a product X ad online?"
- "Have you heard of brand Y?"
- "With which brand do you associate the following message . . .?"
- "Will you purchase brand Y in the future?"
- "What is your opinion of . . .?"

These questions are classic recall and awareness questions, used by offline ad agencies to validate the ROI of ad campaigns. They are usually administered through standing consumer panels that can be administered offline (in person, by mail, or via telephone), through social media platforms capable of research, by tapping into online communities who wish to participate, or to consumer panels permanently available to the brand manager such as those created and managed by P&G for ongoing consumer research purposes. The positive news is that these are now being used more and more frequently by online researchers, setting the stage for the integration of offline and online metrics that we have been urging and discussing.

Thus, the ultimate challenge of finding a common language, methods, and measurements for integrating online and offline brand management plans is being addressed. Nielsen, for example, is building an integrative brand marketing platform applying the same metrics to online brand assessment that have characterized traditional media measurement and is leading to a unified assessment model called **brand effect**. This will eventually result in tying online brand ads, intent to purchase, and behavior, or actual product purchases, into one unified measurement platform. Companies that embrace the solution will have an enterprise-wide dashboard of the most common and relevant brand management metrics. The conclusion is that well-executed online advertising can drive brand metrics—and sales.

The Effect of "Clicks" and "Likes"

The controversy over the degree to which online Facebook ads drive offline sales of high-profile brands reached a tipping point in 2012. "*The crux of advertisers doubts centers on whether Facebook ads actually sell goods* and if they can be measured in a way that can be compared to other forms of advertising."[23] This does not include click-ons which can be tracked to a direct online purchase. Monetizing "likes" is difficult. "Thumbs-up" (Figure 12.6) may increase on a page that is "liked" but in testing the engagement metric, "...*the number of people engaging with the brand stayed the same.*"[24] With word-of-mouth as the number one driver of new sales, brand managers have been pushing to have Facebook let them know what consumers are saying about their brands. Citing privacy issues, Facebook has resisted doing so, but truth be known, Facebook didn't have the measurement metrics to evaluate ad impact. In addition, Facebook managers were following a classic account list strategy which has been a core brand value, that of privacy and the overriding importance of the customer experience.

Sharing customer lists would infringe upon these values and give away an asset that Facebook has invested much time and money to design and develop. Perhaps more important is the possibility that advertisers, if they knew the actual names and addresses of those "likes" and "clicks," could directly contact those consumers and bypass Facebook pages. Facebook's value as a marketing platform, therefore, is in **social ads**, where brands get their fans to be viral advocates

figure 12.6
The Facebook "like" button: What began as a hopeful metric of customer preference has become less so when further research disclosed that "likes" led to neither sales nor loyalty.

for the brand among their friends and "*brands are willing to pay to extend the reach of those endorsements.*"[25]

Now, a new tracking system is being developed and tested. Here are the key elements and how developers envision the system working. A headcount by industry sector and geographic region of how many have seen the ad will be provided to the brand. This is then compared to how many encountered the offline ad in print, radio, or TV in the same sector/region. By comparing ads online/offline to sales and sales lifts, a common metric is emerging and with it measurable ROIs.

Control group tests also are being run. One region's sales with a demographic profile similar to that of the Facebook cohort that has viewed the same ad serves as a control group mirroring the brand's demographics gleaned from Facebook's customer views. Comparable outcomes and costs can then be evaluated, in essence comparing apples to apples.

The challenge to this metric is that it requires a company like General Motors (GM), for instance, to coordinate both its online and offline ad and marketing programs (which it eventually will do but at this writing has no set operational platform in effect for doing so). It must also control for weather factors and economic inhibitors such as gas prices and political factors (demonstrations, social unrest, etc.) that might keep potential offline buyers from going to GM showrooms. In addition, the nature of showroom auto sales wherein commissions are often tied to who initiates the transaction on the showroom floor leads to difficulties in determining "influence" on the purchase outcome since salespeople seek to take credit for the transaction. Online ad watchers have no such limitations.

One way that social media sites are helping link "likes" to sales is through programs such as Nordstrom's **Like2Buy**. Nordstrom's customers can "like" a photo on Instagram, "click," and be taken to the site to buy the product. Similarly, going beyond this and with little doubt that this will be embraced by more and more social media sites, Twitter has teamed with Shopify and offers its retail merchants access to Twitter's consumer base through Twitter's Buy Button and its tweets, pictures, and platform. What members "like" can now be shared in a more dynamic way as viral opinions can find their way into sales transactions. Another site that engages the "likes" and "clicks" issue is Pinterest. Pinterest combines social media and e-commerce in one package. On Pinterest, the user clicks on a product that she sees and goes directly to a site on which she can then make a purchase. This helps clear up some of the ambiguity as to whether "likes" are driving sales because although the original purpose of Pinterest was to browse themed photos of interest, if a user clicks on the link to the picture's website, she is most likely doing so to make a purchase. However, a **bounce back**, such as a notification to the brand posted confirming the purchase, would be helpful in confirming this but is not as yet part of the system. The social part of Pinterest is that users can see what their friends and other people have posted on their accounts and then make a purchase when they find something that they like as well. A large part of Pinterest revolves around fashion and accessories. Marketers can follow trends as well on Pinterest to help them market their brands more efficiently. This like-click-buy model is swiftly becoming the norm as sites that began as purely social morph into commercial selling platforms and brands have established from these social exchanges high levels of

awareness. This is especially the case when the target group is high profile and the opportunity to sell is apparent from their lifestyles such as Millennials. One such example is Snapchat, the very popular mobile, video messaging site. With its strong Millennial following and its fashion vibe, it is in the process in 2016 of adding a "Buy Button" to its "Sweet" platform.[26]

In spite of these transformations, "likes" and "clicks" still appear as challenges for brand managers who seek metrics other than sales to measure the ROI of social media. The "likes" and "clicks" controversy has resulted in a set of formulas called the **Value of a Like (VOAL)** formula that was created to put a numerical value on the interaction and worth of a company's social media efforts. The system takes various metrics involved with "likes" and "clicks" to analyze the value of the interactions that consumers have with a company's social media. This is also important in terms of the overall brand image of the social media site because a site sets the tone for how consumers perceive a company. Getting hard numbers rather than abstract assumptions as to how a company's social media is performing, therefore, is vital in maintaining brand equity. If a company's social media metrics are falling short, then the brand identity isn't being effectively conveyed to the consumer.[27]

When all is said and done, General Motors could advertise on Facebook for no charge! Here is a possible strategy for brand managers whose budgets are limited. GM has over 8 million followers on the site and what needs to be done is "*to create something compelling enough to go viral without a major media spend . . ..*"[28]

Social Media Platforms and Offline Sales Metrics

Although it has since returned, GM made a bold decision in 2012 to stop advertising on Facebook. GM decided to still keep interacting with consumers through its Facebook page but not to run paid advertising. Some may think that this was a questionable decision, because social media is a relatively low-cost way to attract sales. However, national advertisers had three persistent objections to continuing paid ad campaigns, which Facebook found difficult to overcome.

Facebook ads, when they are working, work on a pay-per-click system which lowers the cost-per-sale. But following which clicks led to sales is one issue that companies face when trying to calculate their cost-per-sale. If a sale is not counted as a sale due to Facebook, even though it is, it can skew the cost-per-sale. Another issue in the metrics is that the "like" is devaluing. On average, Facebook users "like" 3.5 pages per day. "*In a world where liking is as common as blinking, a like no longer signals that a consumer loves your brand.*"[29]

The third issue is that companies adopt a one-size-fits-all strategy when advertising on Facebook. This means that the messages that companies pay for that are blasted all over our newsfeeds are becoming less effective because they are not aligned with target audiences. One glaring example is when the University of Phoenix advertised to a Facebook fan that it offers teaching certifications even though the author clearly expressed on his Facebook profile that he works in advertising.[30]

As discussed, one of the issues GM faced was that it could not connect a direct line between visits on Facebook, Twitter, and other social media to actual sales. This continues to be the fundamental online challenge and Facebook along with other social media platforms continues to develop programs in response.

The most recent undertaking by Facebook in an attempt to answer the GM objection is found in its Grapevine program.[31] Grapevine is a marketing program developed by Facebook that collects public sentiment through different posts on Facebook. Television programs watched or movies favored are recorded as Facebook monitors and categorizes those posts and then sells selected companies the data to formulate ad content strategies that will help them tailor their Facebook ads to targeted consumer cohorts. By aggregating individual posts and creating algorithms that capture an identifiable pattern of wants or needs, client ads can be designed to meet the specific complaints and feelings that fans on the site have expressed as concerns. For example, a shampoo company can get insight into what consumers feel about frizzy hair and then tailor its ads to address these sentiments and how its shampoo alleviates the consumer concern.

There are several caveats, however, that continue to be followed by Facebook which to some extent circumscribe the data and limit its **granularity**, or whether it is sufficiently detailed to be useful to the advertiser in making business decisions. First, none of your data will be available to competitors nor will competitors' data be shared with you. Having these data would help to differentiate the ads from those of one's competitors. Second, insights are aggregated so no individual names or user-specific data will be made available. Third, the methodology is proprietary and cannot be tested by the advertiser. However, actual product users are identified and their feelings are cataloged, which provides the kind of psychographic insight that can be of great value in tailoring ads to targeted audiences. Finally, this program is available only to the largest Facebook advertisers and should be viewed as a step forward in the measurement challenge. To date, some advertisers have lauded this approach while others maintain a watchful eye.[32]

Tracking Brand Engagement

Tracking engagement metrics has shifted focus from assessments of consumer value leading to a purchase decision to what one observer has called "*engagement with the heart.*"[33] This parallels our earlier discussion of the shift from "features and benefits" as drivers to emotional experiences as the key drivers in forging consumer loyalty and alerts us to pricing questions and metrics that align with this change so we are measuring what is meaningful and not simply measuring what is measurable.

Tracking Methods

There are many different applications that help in monitoring and tracking different social media activities and engagement. Facebook offers insight into

CASE STUDY
Instagram versus Twitter

So-called brand engagement metric battles are being waged all over the internet. Facebook's Instagram versus Twitter's Vine and Instagram versus Twitter are two of the most enduring and high-profile competitive face-offs. This is a function of the ongoing media coverage and stock market profile of these brands, both of which, given their size and phenomenal growth, are headline news. In addition, their vast consumer followings make every measured consumer behavior of any consequence a matter for media headlines.

The ramifications from a business and monetary perspective are what drive this level of attention because changes in metrics can result in billions of dollars in plus revenues and profits. However, there is another dimension that generates this buzz which is the race to discover the ultimate metric or metrics that capture and measure meaningful consumer behavior and result in a clear differentiation of one social media site over another.

The confrontation between Instagram and Twitter is part of this competitive scenario. In one market, the two sites seek to be in the top rankings on Socialbakers, a UK tracking firm which charts the top 25 most engaging online social media brands. The key metrics here are the degree of performance as measured by the *"sum of re-tweets, replies and favourites features, such as those on Twitter"* and a December 2014 report from Socialbakers, which indicated that *"brands gain nearly 50 times more engagement on Instagram than Twitter."*[38] The sites were compared in part because of their comparable user size which at that time was around 300 million users each. Thus, although the fifty times "reach" in terms of engagement that Instagram is generating over Twitter is impressive, it does not tell the entire story. The two platforms have different value propositions. Twitter's value is to instantly broadcast breaking news and messages in real time throughout the world. Instagram's value proposition is to engage imaginations by displaying pictorial imagery. Additionally, the interface by which users engage the sites is very different and affects entry counts to each site. Therefore, the sites should be chosen based on what we discussed earlier; that is, brand managers should determine the best sites on whether they best serve the business objectives and not simply on how large the reach numbers may be.

As an example, in a subsequent marketing campaign, Instagram was used by a major TV channel whose business objective was to increase awareness. After the campaign, managers were able to conclude some significant lifts in measured outcomes, including higher ad recall, identifying the station with the ad, and consideration to watch. All these areas increased considerably.

page activities on Facebook. Third-party applications for other forms of media such as Twitter exist to help companies keep track on the performance of the account. Various applications create comprehensive analyses of social media use through widely used platforms such as Google. Google Analytics is useful in this regard for brand management because it helps keep track of engagement with possible customers who move from site to site and who, for example, return. Tracking viral messaging, for instance, is a method widely used by all social media platforms. However, the question that remains is whether the linkage between the messaging and the consumer behavior the brand manager wishes to achieve is being realized.[34]

Tracking Metrics

As we move closer and closer to the integration of offline and online metrics, we see important steps being made in the use of a common metrics language. Brand recall, reach, and purchase intent are three such metrics that have crossed over and serve both domains.

The most important question a company needs to ask when tracking is, "*what metrics are important for aiding in reaching specific goals?*"[35] There are many different metrics to track, but only certain ones meet the test, which is, "*does the method help your decision-making?*"[36]

Here are four major categories of metrics that can be tracked and the type of goal that aligns with each:

- **Consumption metrics** deal with how many people "*viewed, downloaded, or listened to this piece of content.*"
- **Sharing metrics** deal with "*how resonant is this content, and how often is it shared with others.*"
- **Lead-gen metrics** ask "*how often does content consumption result in a lead?*"
- **Sales metrics** ask "*did we actually make any money from this content?*"[37]

SUMMARY

The concept of a single version of the truth underscored the need to integrate offline and online brand marketing metrics for more effective and efficient management of the brand. Some of the challenges were from differing concepts and meanings in the metrics and measurements that are used to weigh the ROI of programs that cross both venues. Online platforms are focused more and more on engagement as both a metric and a business objective. It joins

consumer relevancy to forge an axis which, like the loyalty matrix discussed in earlier chapters, needs to be optimized to successfully build the brand and the business.

The role of Influencers in social media, and the social nature of online shopping, introduced an even more intense focus on the power of the social communities that Influencers sometimes develop and often lead. Harnessing, without controlling, these social groups is a responsibility of brand managers. Failure to do so can create public relation debacles, such as befell United Airlines, but perhaps more importantly it forfeits an opportunity to unleash a potent brand marketing force from which all can benefit. Harnessing social groups and not trying to control them results in what has been called "*freely created brand meaning*" or the co-creation of the brand identity through its interaction with online content creators. This applies to online brand communities as well, as we saw in the Harley-Davidson Brotherhood of Riders strategy. Integrating the offline and online worlds continues to be a goal that companies such as Nielsen are fast making into a reality. Use of funnels from traditional marketing, and aligning this with a brand engagement model, offers an excellent opportunity to realize this business objective.

The issue of whether online ads drive offline sales, and how we can measure this, continues to be a key business challenge and opportunity. Facebook is making strides to stay true to its brand promise of customer privacy while creating metrics that enable advertisers to see, to some degree, who is engaging their ads. Facebook does not offer what other social media sites such as Pinterest and Instagram have implemented which enable people to directly "click on" the images that are posted by the brand, sending the engager directly to the brand's shopping site to make a possible purchase as more and more social media sites are adding "Buy Buttons." In this regard, an ongoing competitive battle continues to loom between Twitter and Instagram as to which site can best deliver and show the measurements for successful consumer engagement with brands on its site.

A Single Version of the Truth
Advocacy
Bounce Back
Brand Advocates
Brand Effect
Buzz Marketing
Chameleon Brand
Consideration Set
Consumer's Purchase Journey
Consumption Metrics
Content Driven

Customer Retention
Granularity
Influencers
Lead-Gen Metrics
Like2Buy
Millennials
Omni-Channel
   Communications
Pop-Up Ads
Pop-Up Stores
Reach

Return on Investment (ROI)
Sales Metrics
Sharing Metrics
Social Ads
Social Media Funnels
Social Media Types
Social Shopping
Traffic
Value of a Like (VOAL)

CHAPTER CONVERSATIONS

- Why was the Ford Fiesta campaign so successful?
- What are the biggest challenges in monitoring brand equity online?

- Are "clicks" and "likes" still relevant metrics for brand management today? If so, in what way? If not, why?

CHAPTER CHALLENGES

- Your online marketing department in a fashion apparel company is resisting the idea of integrating the online and offline brand management initiatives. As the brand manager, what arguments would you make to convince them otherwise?
- You are the chief marketing officer in your company. To effectively manage conversation online, what suggestions would you make to the head of social media? How might you ensure his compliance?

- A controversy is brewing as to whether Twitter or Instagram should be the primary platform for a personal technology product company's social media advertising campaign. As brand manager you've been asked by the CFO, prior to her allocating funds for the campaign, which is the best choice. How would you present this?

ENDNOTES

1. V. Ramaswamy and K. Ozcan, "Brand Value Co-Creation in a Digitalized World: An Integrative Framework and Research Implications," *International Journal of Research in Marketing* 32 no. 1 (July 2015): 2.

2. Ibid.

3. William Roy, "Why You Should Integrate Online and Offline Marketing," *Immerge Technologies*, October 13, 2015, https://www.immergetech.com/blog/detail/why-you-should-integrate-online-and-offline-marketing.

4. For an exploration of this, see Katie Burke, "What Your Traditional Marketing Education Didn't Teach You About Marketing Today," HubSpot Blogs, May 13, 2013, Blog.Hubspot.com/marketing.

5. Christoph Burmann, "A Call for User-Generated Branding," editorial, *Journal of Brand Management* 18 (2010): 1–4.

6. Kevin Lane Keller, "Building Strong Brands in a Modern Marketing Communication Environment," *Journal of Marketing Communications* 15, no. 2 (2009): 139–152.

7. Susan Fournier and Lara Lee, "Getting Brand Communities Right," *Harvard Business Review* (April 2009).

8. Ibid., 3.

9. David Aaker, *Aaker on Branding: 20 Principles That Drive Success* (New York, NY: Morgan James Publishing, 2014).

10. Ibid.

11. Ibid.

12. Ibid.

13. David Aaker, *Brand Relevance: Making Competitors Irrelevant* (San Francisco, CA: John Wiley & Sons, 2011).

14. Bob Hayes, "What Is Customer Loyalty? Part 2: A Customer Loyalty Measurement Framework," *Business Broadway*, January 30, 2013, http://businessoverbroadway.com/customer-loyalty-measurement-framework.

15. Corey Padveen, "Social Media Case Study: Best Buy," *t2*, May 2, 2013, http://t2marketinginternational.com/social-media-case-study-best-buy/.

16. Gina Debogovich, "Best Buy Case Study: Social CRM Connects Customers and Drives $5M Benefit," *Lithium*, 2012, https://www.lithium.com/pdfs/casestudies/Lithium-Best-Buy-Case-Study.pdf.

17. Ravi Sawhney, "Broken Guitar Has United Plaing the Blues to the Tune of $180 Million," *Fast Company*, http://www.fastcompany.com/1320152/broken-guitar-has-united-playing-blues-tune-180-million.

18. Nicole Fallon, "Turning Social Influencers into Brand Advocates," *Business News Daily*, October 13, 2014, http://www.businessnewsdaily.com/7277-social-influencers-for-brands.html.

19. See Erin Smith, "TapInfluence Launches TapFusion," *TapInfluence*, September 18, 2015, https://www.tapinfluence.com/tapinfluence-launches-tapfusion-the-worlds-first-influencer-marketing-automation-platform/.

20. Jeff Bullas, "The 7 Secrets to Ford's Social Media Marketing Success," *jeffbullas.com*, http://www.jeffbullas.com/2010/02/18/the-7-secrets-to-fords-social-media-marketing-success/.

21. Matthew Egol, Mary Beth McEuen, and Emily Falk, "The Social Life of Brands," *Strategy+Business*, 2012.

22. Nielsen, "Beyond Clicks and Impressions: Examining the Relationship Between Online Advertising and Brand Building," *Nielsen*, October 21, 2012, https://www.facebook-studio.com/fbassets/resource/32/Nielsen-BrandEffectandCTRWhitePaper.pdf.

23. Shayndi Raice, "Inside Facebook's Push to Woo Big Advertisers," *Wall Street Journal*, August 15, 2012, http://www.wsj.com/articles/SB10000872396390444246904577575351814047494.

24. Ibid.

25. Cotton Delo, "Big Spenders Push Ad Line, but Facebook Holds Ground," *Ad Age*, May 28, 2012, http://adage.com/article/digital/big-spenders-push-ad-line-facebook-holds-ground/235007/.

26. "Photography," February 11, 2016, www.digitaltrends.com.

27. Dan Zarrella, "How to Calculate the Value of a Like," *Harvard Business Review*, November 26, 2012, https://hbr.org/2012/11/how-to-calculate-the-value-of.

28. Jim Edwards, "Facebook's Worst Nightmare: After GM, Here's How the Other Dominoes Could Fall," *Business Insider*, May 15, 2012, http://www.businessinsider.com/facebooks-worst -nightmare-with-gm-pulling-its-ads-heres-how-the-other-dominoes-may-fall-2012-5.

29. Ben Kunz, "Why GM and Others Fail with Facebook Ads," *Bloomberg Business*, May 22, 2012, http://www.bloomberg.com/bw/articles/2012-05-22/why-gm-and-others-fail-with-facebook-ads.

30. Ibid.

31. Garett Sloane, "Facebook Lets High-Rolling Brands See What Users Really Think in This Elite Program," *AdWeek*, November 21, 2014, http://www.adweek.com/news/technology/facebook-lets-high -rolling-brands-see-what-users-really-think-elite-program-161589.

32. Ibid.

33. Kevan Lee, "Which Stats Matter: The Definitive Guide to Tracking Social Media Metrics," *Buffer Social* (blog), April 30, 2014, https://blog.bufferapp.com/definitive-guide-social-media-metrics-stats.

34. Melissa O'Conner, "10 Top Social Media Monitoring and Analytics Tools," *Tweak Your Biz*, March 6, 2013, http://tweakyourbiz.com/marketing/2013/03/06/10-top-social-media-monitoring-analytics-tools/.

35. For a clear and concise summary of options, see Angela Hausman, "The ROI of Social Media: How Do You Measure Up?," May 15, 2013,www.hausmanmarketingletter.com.

36. Kaltrina Bylykbashi, "Instagram Shows High Levels of Brand Engagement in Comparison to Twitter," *Marketing Week*, December 17, 2014, https://www.marketingweek.com/2014/12/17/instagram-shows-high -levels-of-brand-engagement-in-comparison-to-twitter/.

37. Ibid.

38. Ibid.

Luxury Brand Management in a Digital World

AFTER COMPLETING THIS CHAPTER,
YOU WILL BE ABLE TO:

- Describe the digital challenge to luxury's exclusivity and accessibility.

- Explain how luxury brands integrate digital and offline stores.

- Assess the digital strategies of luxury managers for staying on-brand.

". . . a luxury brand can be as exclusive . . . on the internet as it is on the street."

—Frederico Marchetti, CEO, YOOX

THE DIGITAL CHALLENGE TO LUXURY

In earlier chapters, we explored the two pillars of luxury, exclusivity and accessibility, that when properly managed together, help maintain the appeal of luxury brands. These two elements join to create a perceived value, driven by the rarity of the luxury experience. In a certain sense, luxury brands are kept hidden in that they are available, but not easily accessible. Their brand guardians understand that their value is, in part, the mystery that surrounds them. They are readily seen and not easily acquired. They emerge, and are maintained, as high-value experiences. This is partly due to the social stratification in societies that create differences in rank that affect both the purchasing power and ownership appreciation of luxury brands.[1]

Enter the digital internet world which is characterized by transparency, accessibility, and the democratization of information and communication. How can luxury maintain its mystery and its exclusivity in such an open place if it is thrown among the many premium, masstige, and mass brands that abound on the web?[2]

Managing the Digital Challenge

The emergence of digital retail and social media has been accelerated by the introduction of mobile devices, the Millennial generation, and omni-channel integration. Luxury brands cannot afford to remain on the sidelines as this digital revolution continues to grow and become the dominant mode of both social media interaction and retail transactions. The key to successful entry can be found in the idea that luxury brands must, in the digital space, stay true to the luxury experience; that is, for luxury brands, *"the internet and digital world are not sales tools, but unique communication and customer service tools."*[3] The next generation of consumers will begin to develop their interest and taste for the luxury experience only if the brands begin to offer that online. The challenge becomes to retain the current cohorts of core consumers and brand loyalists while reaching out to these next-generation consumers whose purchasing dynamics may differ.[4]

Because the Millennial generation will be the next generation of potential loyalists, luxury brand managers need to begin strategizing in light of this cohort's shopping habits and emotional proclivities. Millennials expect to shop and interact across all electronic platforms. This requires the integration of mobile, web, and physical stores as part of the brand's commitment to omni-channel retailing and communications. This is the case even if web sales are offered with limited inventory, availability, and merchandise assortment or only a future possibility. This places additional challenges before luxury managers since all these venues need to provide a **seamless brand experience**. Regardless of where the brand is accessed by the consumer, the same experience must unfold.

But what experience is really taking place in the "high-touch" luxury boutique? It is a willingness to be part of a performance, as an actor in a play. Luxury retail, when it fulfills its promise, is great theater and is an extension of the luxury dream.

Luxury's Digital Advantage

Luxury brands have flourished through what J.-N. Kapferer has described as offering a world of dreams.[5] Luxury offers a vision, an experience beyond the everyday. This is, in part, its "allure." Luxury brands luxuriate in a way that, upon reflection, reminds us that they share much with the arts. There is a magical dream-like atmosphere surrounding things luxury, much like film or the theater.[6] As with the arts, to emotionally embrace these luxury experiences, one has to be a willing participant in what Samuel Taylor Coleridge, the nineteenth-century English poet, described as *"the willing suspension of disbelief. . ."*—a willingness to transcend physical realities for the exhilaration of the emotional reality that the arts provide.

Luxury brands provide both stage and script for this. The retail brand experience, whereby we are indulged beyond our expectations, coupled with the brand narratives and a heritage steeped in a romantic history, is what consumers are asked to believe is real. And, for a moment in time, when we consider the possibility or make the decision to purchase, the dream is real, a type of virtual reality. The extent of how deeply this reality is anchored in us is confirmed, in part, by the phenomenal growth of the sector over the last two decades.[7] Consequently, luxury consumers have been preparing for the digital age, for its presence, much like the theater and poetry, is a virtual reality where dreams are made. Therefore, contrary to what might be considered conventional wisdom, luxury brands are well suited for operating in the digital world as the digital world is a virtual reality.

The immediate challenge for the luxury brand is to replicate the effect of the retail luxury experience in the virtual luxury space. The error would be to attempt to replicate the physicality of the offline experience which is neither needed nor available for the luxury experience to be transmitted in the online space. This calls for a further examination into what is being transmitted, or what business the luxury boutique is really in. To answer this requires recalling the multidimensional experience that "high-touch" luxury service delivers.

The memories of the "high-touch" experience may well be, for many luxury consumers, more important than the products. This is, in part, a function of our neurological dynamics that make meaningful and emotional experiences more memorable with the passage of time. Although we will delve into this in greater detail in Chapter 15, suffice it to say that the **experiencing self** (what we experience) and the **remembering self** (what we retain and around which we choose to fashion a story) are different. The more memorable experience drives and enhances our recollection of it. Therefore, this becomes fertile ground

for luxury brands to create highly emotional experiences and to deliver them in the online space.

Luxury brands are well suited to create these experiences through their brand narratives which can function as virtual online dreams. They are likely to find great success in reaching the emotional milieu of online participants, for the luxury brand heritage imbues their narratives with a mark of authenticity that resonates with consumers, especially Millennials. This is a function of the fact that, contrary to other categories of brands, luxury brands are anchored in an authentic heritage and history. They play readily into our wish to be in a purer place, which social media, because it is a virtual reality almost without limitations, can conjure for us.

Managing Luxury Gossip

There is no turning away, or turning back, for luxury brands in terms of their digital engagement. They are already a major factor in content, conversations, and communities that have forged a virtual reality online.

The good and bad news is that luxury brands are, disproportionate to their numbers, one of the most widely discussed brand categories in the digital space.[8] Given this inordinate degree of interest, without brand management surveillance, luxury brands run the risk of intended and unintended misinformation regarding the brand as well as unanswered streams of critical chatter that can be damaging to the brand's image. The exposure of the brand to the greater possibility that the chatter will be negative is a function of the openness of social media to all who wish to participate and the universal tendency of humans to be more prone to gossip than to all other forms of conversational exchange![9]

This exposure to gossip is exacerbated by the advent of mobile phones. Gossip, even prior to mobile phone usage, was confirmed by several studies to be 65 percent or more of the content of conversations. Mobile phones accentuate and enhance the tendency toward gossip. As one writer has put it, *"mobile phones are the new garden fence,"* a metaphor for the setting where conversations are often held by next-door neighbors in suburbia.[10] Gossip by its nature tends to be critical. This alone behooves luxury brands to enter the digital conversation because the integration of mobile with other digital omni-channel platforms provides an even wider field over which such conversation can be transmitted.

The Merger of Bricks and Clicks

As part of the integration driven by omni-channel communications, the notion of **bricks and clicks**, or the seamless alignment of physical and virtual retail platforms, has come into our vocabulary.

We are seeing the blurring of internet and brick-and-mortar shopping as more and more e-commerce brands are also building stores to enhance the personal shopping experience. One might say that the future and the past of retailing are merging into a new digitally driven business model in which luxury is participating. As consumers experience this reversal (brick and mortar mimicking the web), it makes the web a more acceptable luxury venue for the luxury consumer since all retail and social media become differentiated more by what the brand conveys than where it is experienced or through which channel the experience is delivered. "*It is one of the ironies of our time that a digital medium, the internet, is making the in-person shopping experience a more human one.*"[11] More and more often, online retailers are opening traditional brick-and-mortar stores on high streets, because it provides opportunity to present products and services in an interactive way. "*Many people like to shop in bricks and mortar locations. There is the possibility of theatre and human interaction there—these things shouldn't be underestimated.*"[12] The distinction between brick-and-mortar and e-retailers will likely continue to diminish, for as brick-and-mortar stores have embraced the internet today more and more, e-retailers are creating pop-up shops and traditional stores for complementing an online presence.[13] This again reflects what one expert has famously called **emotional branding**, or the understanding that the contacts and communications that resonate most deeply with us are those personal, authentic, everyday interactions by which our common humanity is confirmed.[14]

The Dissolution of the Digital Divide

As omni-channel communications grow in usage, this also has accelerated the need for a seamless retail and social communication platform and the resurgence of the physical retail space by online brands. Online retailers such as TOMS and Warby Parker, to name two, have recently opened retail brick-and-mortar stores to showcase their brands and provide another platform for forging a brand-consumer connection.[15] In the offline brand world, the reverse has occurred. Luxury brands such as Burberry and Louis Vuitton have created digital spaces with virtual realities within physical retail locations that are marvels of virtual reality.[16]

The future of luxury stores will be best served when they fully embrace the technological and integrative nature of omni-channel retailing. However, they must do so without violating the luxury expectation of their core consumers that the experience will continue to be nonintrusive.

This will be a challenge. Here are some dramatic changes that luxury managers will have to consider implementing:

- Shoppers will use their cell phones to compare brands and prices and to buy. High Street stores will need to become connected, with free Wi-Fi services, to help shoppers connect with and compare brands. Staff will need to roam the store with mobile point-of-sale technology. This will mean the end to checking out in front of a cash register.
- High Street stores will need to compete to become a destination. As larger retailers move out of town or online, the High Street will be populated with boutique "experience" stores, coffee shops, and restaurants.
- As High Street retail space shrinks, **click and collect**, or concluding the monetary transaction

at points of sale, will become more popular, as retailers want to use their floor space more efficiently and cut overheads. This will challenge the nonintrusive luxury.

- The lessening of the High Street's stature requires flexibility in retail formats. Retailers with a physical store presence will need to adapt formats regionally and locally to cater to consumers' changing shopping patterns. Luxury brands will need to adapt to this.
- It will become vital for luxury brands to continue to add value to the shopping experience in order to remain relevant in a multichannel world. Retailers will need to turn shops into brand destinations that offer a highly immersive and interactive shopping experience. Retailers need to ensure that they offer multiple fulfilment options. Retailers can no longer run their physical stores and online operations as separate functions. Consumers will expect a fully integrated service from retailers with the ability to order online and pick up in store or order in store for home delivery.
- Mobile will be the channel that links all parts of a retailer's multichannel operation. This also will prove to be a challenge to luxury as it increases visibility and accessibility and diminishes exclusivity and the magic of the rarity of the luxury experience.[17]

Aligning Digital and Physical Retail

The best of both virtual and physical experiences will be those that touch the archetypes nestled in our psychology, because the **brand experience** (the idea that the experience a luxury brand provides is a product unto itself) is best retained when it is seared into our very beings through an emotional archetypal experience. This is the overriding reason why the luxury brand managers must stay true in the social media space to the brand's DNA, its core values and brand promise. The power of the brand's authenticity to forge deep emotional relationships with new consumers will be realized through honoring its integrity.

Having a social media presence is not only for defensive purposes but also for connecting with the next generation of potential brand loyalists. The latter objective still needs to be guided by the values and strategies that have made luxury brands successful in the offline space. Here are three guidelines that successful luxury brands that are online display:[18]

1. Do not compromise the brand's core values, such as inaccessibility. Maintaining a discrete distance still matters by offering, if at all, only a very limited assortment of product.
2. Create communities of like-minded brand advocates who can share brand experiences and provide a point of access for new brand visitors to become acquainted with the brand's DNA and its promise.
3. Preserve exclusivity online by limiting accessibility to websites to current customers.

All of the above strategies, for example, are embraced by Hermès, which seeks both to appeal to the next generation and to maintain its positioning and image. Consequently, it does not sell online any of its most desired items such as the Birken or Kelly handbags or other parts of its best-selling collections. Its website indicates that it wishes consumers to enter into the world of Hermès by experiencing its heritage, artisan craftsmanship, and the museum which captures and conveys the creative culture of the brand. Even on its Silk Knots mobile app, the objective is informative—the best and various ways to tie a Hermès scarf!

Educating the next generation also sets up an inducement, as their incomes rise, to experience the exclusivity of the brand in a brick-and-mortar retail setting. These are the types of strategies that one observer has called for in order "*to infuse the luxury brand with a greater sense of allure.*"[19]

This integration of the digital and physical spaces in the luxury arena was only a matter of time and is the natural outgrowth and inescapable evolution of the craftsman and the magician who, like alchemists, conjure innovations and experiences that capture our

In 2013, Angela Ahrendts left her position as CEO of Burberry and joined Apple as head of retail. Her departure from Burberry and her hiring at Apple is both symbolic and indicative of the merging of luxury, fashion, and technology into what might be called the new social retail. In this new milieu, traditional definitions, distinctions, and boundaries between "clicks and bricks," or between social shopping and product shopping, no longer apply. As an expression of this, a report in 2015 placed Apple as the "most favored 'luxury' brand in China to give for gift giving." This has led to the assessment by many that Apple is a technology company driven by design, while Burberry is a design company driven by technology. In light of this, Arendt's move to Apple makes perfect sense.

This union has made Burberry a relevant and aspirational brand for the current and the next generation of consumers. It's also earned Burberry the distinction of being the most popular luxury brand online.[21]

As Angela Ahrendt stated just prior to her departure from Burberry for Apple, "Burberry has delivered a strong first half, reflecting our continued investment in innovative design, digital marketing and retail strategies."[22]

Burberry invested heavily in a savvy digital portfolio, masterminded by Ahrendts, as the key to the heritage brand's strong growth. With many of Burberry's customers shopping online, Ahrendts set out to produce a digital platform that combined social media and enterprise software to form an innovative one-stop shop. The move helped revamp the iconic British brand's image while appealing to younger consumers and extending Burberry's global reach.

A key to the success of the strategy can be found in the flagship store in London (Figure 13.1). Here we find the seamless integrations of online and offline digital experiences. The classic building has been refitted with technology woven into the new interior. Massive

Figure 13.1
The Burberry flagship store: The interior of the flagship store in London has been "refitted" into a digital brand marketing and sales experience.

(continued on next page)

video screens provide ongoing runway fashion shows. Other screens are interactive whereby a customer considering a purchase will set off the **RFID chip**, a radio frequency chip coded with specific instructions to activate a video or audio receptor attached to the garment that generates a series of images on a nearby screen. The images show that customer how the product may be worn and what accessories or other garments coordinates with it. Other kiosks enable consumers to touch and explore new happenings and events consistent with the Burberry image and lifestyle. Included in this is the ability, as with online, to pre-order pieces directly from the runway before they are shipped to the store (as we discussed in Chapter 2, the collection is now also available for purchase directly from streaming videos of Burberry's runway shows each season!). There is also the possibility of **customization** (the expectation that products can be given by the purchaser personalized details and customized to his or her desires). Both of these offer Burberry's customers a unique brand experience as a digitally driven expression of a new form of "high touch" luxury service that is paramount for the luxury experience.[23] In the words of Ahrendts, "*Walking through the doors is just like walking into the website. It is Burberry World Live.*"[24]

imaginations and our dreams.[20] Here is luxury's strong suit. Like priceless works of art, luxury brands do so by creating timeless masterpieces presented in retail gallery-like settings, virtual or physical, that resonate in every language and culture because they touch the global archetypes in our universal human psyche. Later in this chapter, we will visit an entirely new retail luxury concept where the total integration of art and commerce is seamlessly fulfilled.

MANAGING DIGITAL LUXURY

Luxury brand managers will need to determine who are the true digital brand advocates and lasting brand loyalists. Part of this challenge will be to develop ongoing methodologies to discern, from blogs and other postings of content and opinion, who are the true opinion leaders (Figure 13.2).

Influencer marketing programs for luxury brands will not aim to develop loose perk-based engagement mechanics. They will seek to generate authentic recommendations and advocacy that will expand the brand's values within its identified target audience and territory.[25]

For example, Nordstrom has on payroll an influential blogger with a substantial following. The blogger is flown to Nordstrom headquarters in Seattle, Washington, to review product lines before they go into production. One question is, how objective can these people be if they are on payroll?

Monitoring Influencers and Honoring Loyalists

Differentiated by the various luxury segments, brands will need to determine the spheres of influence and degrees of separation between influencer and the target customer. Followers of Influencers should be organized into segmentation models tiered by the degree of online engagement with the brand so one can measure the continuing or declining involvement with brand narratives and other brand content.

figure 13.2
Chiara Ferragni, an Italian blogger, at a Calvin Klein event: Independent entrepreneurs have emerged as major brand influencers with followings; brands are embracing them rather than seeing them as a problem.

This will also provide a means of maintaining a running assessment of the strength or weakness of the Influencers.

Aligning Digital Content, Consumers, and Communities

Building such programs in a luxury world will require going through the following main stages:[26]

1. Clearly define objectives and the related target audience. Specific programs could focus on brand advocates, socially active communities in specific territories associated with the brand (e.g., travel for Louis Vuitton, horse riding for Hermès), or important stakeholders, such as employees.

2. Identify, recruit, and select program members who are committed to the brand and can best propose the brand's content and values.

3. Design exclusive content that will generate authentic engagement and endorsement by program members.

4. Measure, optimize, and iterate. Brand managers should avoid content that can be seen as campaigning for the brand; it is about building long-term and personal relationships.

Going Beyond the Merchandise

"Whether you are Ralph Lauren or Tommy Hilfiger or a luxury brand like Louis Vuitton or Hermès, your brand really has to go beyond the merchandise that you offer."[27] Going beyond the merchandise includes meeting the growing expectations of luxury shoppers in the digital space. Although at this writing, it accounts for only a little over 5 percent of luxury purchases, online retail is growing six times faster than brick-and-mortar retail sales.[28] In addition, a study by McKinsey and Company in 2013 found that over 75 percent of luxury shoppers own and some 40 percent use mobile devises to pre-shop online prior to offline purchases.[29] Thus, the so-called digital divide is fast closing and the luxury brand manager is challenged to stay on-brand and transfer those brand attributes to the digital space.

Staying On-Brand

The very principles that guide luxury, such as impeccable quality and timeless design, should animate the brands' social media content and platforms. In addition, style and content must be on-brand. In this regard, aligning the right social media platform with your content should be consistent with the brand image as it is understood in the offline market.

For luxury brands to be successful in this regard (engaging the right consumers and distinguishing themselves in the digital space from mass brands), they have to be able to answer three key questions:

1. What are the core competencies of each of the major social media platforms?
2. What content is appropriate for each customer segment for staying on-brand?
3. Which brand elements are appropriate for which social media platform?

Brand Image, Identity, and Social Media

Aligning the brand image and brand identity with that of the appropriate social media site is an important part of online brand management. The content of brand communications takes on differing looks and efficacies depending on how well the business objectives align with the site. For example, Twitter can be used for sales transactions with its recently introduced sales button, but how well does this align with luxury that wishes to tell a deeper story either pictorially or through narratives? Twitter's limitation of 140 characters doesn't align with this. For Chanel, which does not sell online except for fragrances and jewelry, the pictorial narrative is central to its image building. However, conveying the brand identity through a brand narrative requires a different platform. This is better conveyed by the decision its brand managers made to post an incredible YouTube video of a Chanel craftsman at creative work, which is a masterpiece in communications!

Luxury shoppers are accustomed to a unique and immersive experience when it comes to digital destinations and online content, and they expect that it will correspond to their experience in physical store locations. Currently, with some major exceptions, there is a disconnect between a luxury brand's online and in-store experiences. Opportunities are being missed by not gathering customer data and driving awareness from store visits to ensure a more integrative and seamless experience.[30]

Integrating Physical and Virtual Retail

A major exception to the issue of achieving integrative platforms is Louis Vuitton (LV). LV management understands that luxury is something all people want to experience, even if it may be beyond their immediate financial reach. They also understand that their target audience still buys print and loves print magazines. So they designed an app combined with magazine ads that integrated digital and physical into a single campaign. By integrating offline and online, they were able to achieve a greater audience reach as well as appeal to both the current core customer and the next generation. What was most impressive is that there was a completely seamless opportunity to purchase the luxury items advertised in the fashion magazines (although from a limited inventory) directly from the app. In a time where so many luxury brands insist that the customer go into the store, LV is clearly targeting the next generation in terms of how they shop. But it does so without alienating the habits of the current core consumer of the brand. This explains why LV consistently ranks highest in its effective embracing of the digital space.[31]

Luxury Shopping as Digital Theater

A sense of retail theater continues to animate many of the best luxury brands in their physical retail spaces. Whether it's Burberry replicating London's infamous weather by having it as the background for digital ads or LV's imaginative elevator within the LV Townhouse shop, located in Selfridges Department Store in London, the brand experience is paramount (Figure 13.3).

At the Townhouse shop, a state-of-the-art brand experience begins with a circular elevator surrounded with a helix-like transparent wraparound displaying all the LV products from each of the collections (men's, accessories, women's, etc.) that riders see as they ascend three floors to the top. It is meant to be a transformative brand experience. As one customer was overheard saying, "*for a moment, you forget where you are.*"

figure 13.3

Shoppers waiting to enter a Louis Vuitton store: In spite of a robust online presence, the brand controls accessibility by selling most product in its own boutiques.

The idea of personal service also undergoes a transformation in LV's Townhouse strategy. Personalization of product offerings via technology adds to the traditional "high touch" luxury service expectation, an additional digital dimension through LV's digital **atelier** (an atelier is an artisan's shop where innovation in product development is the norm). While in the Townhouse, customers have an opportunity, through the digital kiosks, to enjoy a personalized experience with touch screen technology that allows them to design their own bespoke bags.[32] By using the reference to an "atelier" as an associative attribute of the brand, LV stays on-brand by invoking its heritage of craftsmanship and then sharing that with its loyalists who now can participate in the brand's heritage by creating their own unique brand experience.

LUXURY RELATIONSHIPS IN THE DIGITAL SPACE

Relationship building online offers an opportunity not only for luxury brands to connect with their current and future customers but also to play to their strong suit, building relationships with luxury consumers. Luxury brands such as Chanel, LV, and many others have built their businesses by building a following of loyalists who, through word-of-mouth, conveyed the brand's superior craftsmanship and innovative artistry. With the advent of luxury conglomerates such as LVMH and Richemont (the Swiss luxury conglomerate which has Cartier and other such brands in its portfolio), the brand message, and with it the personalization of the relationship, was challenged by expansion as these conglomerates sought to leverage, for corporate growth, the equity in the brands they had acquired. To offset this loss of intimacy, single-brand luxury boutiques were developed which returned intimacy to the luxury experience. They were transformed to where the entire retail experience was designed to replicate the personal touch of the original brand persona.

The extension of this approach required an endless building of high-profile boutiques, which has its limitations in terms of costs and locations. More importantly, the mobility of today's luxury customer coupled with their digital savvy had made the old models less efficient. Consequently, a new customer relationship model based on internet culture and technology is fast becoming a business necessity.[33]

Building Luxury Relationships

Luxury brands have grown by building relationships through traditional networks of high net worth individuals. This was achieved through the development and management of a client base, known as **clienteling**, wherein sales associates have in-depth profiles of their customers and reach out in a personalized manner informing them of events, special new collections, or private sales, and continues today as a key practice in successful in-store luxury retail. In this regard, both Brooks Brothers and Mitchells, referenced in earlier chapters, come to mind. This current in-store clienteling provides a sound basis for online engagements as these skill sets and the culture that supports them are transferable from offline to online venues. The challenge is to create strategies that achieve scale for volume without compromising the luxury brands' core values. Here are some guidelines:

- Communication content, including tone and language, needs to be presented with discretion. This requires review by those with a facility in English, if that is the first language of the brand, and a deep immersion in the brand's DNA.

- Personal privacy, including names and contact information, must be maintained. Monitoring sites for leaks or breaches in security becomes an essential part of brand management and should not be thought of as a technical issue.

- An omni-channel platform must be operational so that wherever the luxury consumer is in the world, and whatever means he or she chooses to interface with the brand, they are known everywhere in the brand organization as the same customer—with all of their personal particulars and product preferences known as well.

Social Media and Emotional Branding

Brand managers in the luxury space have ample opportunities to forge emotional relationships with clients by adhering to what is on-brand and avoiding what is not on-brand. Some specifics include the admonition of one luxury brand commentator, "*Luxury brands don't flood feeds*,"[34] an allusion to flooding web feeds with excessive content.

As an example of being on-brand, Hermès's Instagram account only allows you a peek inside a little orange box with the teaser tagline "*Peek inside the orange box*," thereby holding on to a degree of exclusivity and mystery by not displaying the entire brand offering.

Another admonition is "*Remain Aspirational!*" In other words, engagement cannot feel fully approachable and imagery is best kept aspirational and suggestive rather than concrete.

Finally, the service component for which so much of the luxury brand experience is sought after and what differentiates it from wannabe brands is a core responsibility of brand management. It must be designed to replicate the emotional effect of the physical in-store experience. This can be done, in part, by colors, professional photography, messaging that is elegant rather than brusque, and a service component that is as personalized as possible without being intrusive. YOOX, the highly successful Italian online luxury retail platform, achieved sales volume in 2013 of over $600 million in revenue by shipping 3 million orders to luxury shoppers in over 100 countries! It insists on having the primary focus of its sixty photographers on the image of the brand and not the product of the brand and to capture this in every photo. It can boast of its client list that it includes the likes of Moncler, Roberto Cavalli, Giorgio Armani, and an initially reluctant Brunello Cucinelli.[35]

This success of YOOX and the future of luxury online has not been lost on Richemont. In 2015, YOOX was purchased by Richemont and linked to its other luxury online retail format Net-A-Porter, an equally successful venture.

"High Touch" Digital Clienteling

Irrespective of the industry or the retail venue, luxury brands continue to abide by the four major pillars which support successful brand marketing:[36]

1. The Brand Experience: As we explored in an earlier chapter, Ritz-Carlton is one of the leaders in the hospitality space and in digital media undertaking. It quickly became the most exclusive private residence in the Caribbean on the heels of its experiential transmedia campaign. Since the experience a luxury brand provides is a product unto itself, the brand must devote as much quality to the experience as to the product it sells.

2. Exclusivity: Digital marketing offers the most elegant opportunity to control and enhance a brand's exclusivity with prestige technology. From the St. Regis E-Butler app to Chanel's interactive Gamified Culture microsite, high-tech marketing makes luxury brands appear cutting edge, giving them an experimental dimension and creating a vibrant counterpoint to their usually classic image. This creative contrast broadens their appeal without

compromising the brand values for cutting edge. It sits well with luxury brands' associative archetype, Innovation.

3. Engagement: When it comes to luxury brands, engagement is synonymous with a brand story, and storybook sells! Tiffany & Co. reported a 20 percent uptick in sales after the public and press alike lauded the company's "What Makes Love True" microsite and "Engagement Ring Finder" mobile app. These two digital marketing elements are classic examples of how success can follow when a brand weaves a narrative that the consumer knows or feels is authentic because it corresponds to the brand's archetype. In this instance, the archetype is the Lover, which underscores and provides the foundation for Tiffany's powerful brand story about realizing true love.

4. Emotional Branding: Without the deliberate, appropriate application of one key emotion among its customers, long-term luxury brand success cannot exist. Consumers are loyal to Burberry because they want to feel "authentic" and "timeless." They stay at the Ritz-Carlton to feel "august." They buy Tom Ford to feel "triumphant." They frequent Tiffany's to feel "love." Luxury brands must embrace the fact that their primary products are actually manifestations of deeply rooted archetypes and that their physical products are mere mediums through which consumers experience their own complementariness to those brand archetypes. Therefore, a luxury brand must determine its emotional value first, and construct its physical and digital manifestations to express and extract that specific emotion. The associative attributes which constitute the brand's persona, coupled with its DNA which is anchored in the brand's archetype, is where the emotional identity resides.

LUXURY TRAVELERS AND THE DIGITAL EXPERIENCE

As luxury consumers seek less conspicuous consumption and more substantial experiences, tourism has taken on new retail dimensions. Vacations become more than just getaways. Multigenerational luxury cruises have emerged for families that are so time pressed that they rarely have time together can now, on board, emotionally reconnect.[37] They are part of the new need for personal fulfillment that has come to characterize many of the traditional luxury loyalists. Here, digital communication plays a key role both in terms of planning and in terms of enjoying the actual experience.

"Retail tourism is potentially one of the big growth areas for luxury." The participants of The Luxury Traveler Technology Survey, a representative group of global luxury travelers, reported that the most important online activity to them while in transit to or staying at a hotel (for business or vacation) was reviewing information on local area activities (59 percent). In fact, the survey revealed that guests spend an average of 18.3 minutes a day in their rooms researching online the destination that they are in.

To meet this demand, every hotel and resort on The Four Seasons website features custom information related to the sights, sounds, and tastes indigenous to the region or locale where the hotel is located. In addition, The Four Seasons recently enhanced its Facebook presence with new tools and a refreshed design to provide visitors with compelling content such as exclusive promotions for dining, spa, and other services, and interactive touch points like a contest on Flickr for the best travel photo. Between its corporate and individual hotel presence, containing nearly ninety local pages, fans of The Four Seasons total nearly 225,000—and growing daily.

For Twitter, a luxury following is also growing. With annual increases of the wealthy active up 350 percent in 2010 over 2009, the tool's ability to provide consumers real-time access to luxury brand information is making it a core digital media tool. For example, The Four Seasons leveraged Twitter for its winter spa campaign, providing unprecedented access to spa experts globally on #FSspa. Twitter chats enable luxury consumers to obtain inside information about what clothes may be needed or the extent of the spa's services. This is how The Four Seasons has tailored its social media presence to align its brand with different content designed for differing consumer needs and seeded with content appropriate to what the site does best. So, for instance, in the Twitter example, the nature of the site is best for current chats and real-time exchange of information.

Curated Brand Experiences

The Four Seasons also develops highly curated content for the site, again offering sights and sounds of properties and available local experiences, further enhancing the brand connection with the core consumer. Statistics on video views are continuously increasing, with video views in 2012 totaling over 280,000—30 percent higher compared to the previous year.[38]

The power of digital virtual imaging and messaging in the social media space provides an ever-growing opportunity for luxury brands to connect with consumers without violating the rules of luxury marketing. This is one outcome of the shift that we've noted earlier from the conspicuous consumption of luxury goods to a yearning for a deeper luxury experience.[39] Luxury consumers are opting for authentic and creative experiences, such as being part of the next generation of artisans by actually participating in the process of their creativity through hotel-sponsored contributions to product design. Other such undertakings include adventure trips that are educational excursions or hiking safaris to exotic locales or immersion in the cultures of faraway places and tying these back to selected social media sites frequented by the brand's core consumers.

Another example of the luxury brand hotel experience driven by digital communications is Ritz-Carlton's "Epic Bucket List Experience." The Ritz-Carlton, Laguna Niguel in Dana Point, California, is the ultimate hideaway and getaway for luxury travelers. Situated on a bluff overlooking the Pacific Ocean, it offers guests the opportunity to *explore the environment above and below the sea with expert naturalists on eco-adventures organized by the hotel.* This offers the luxury consumer more than just the luxury hotel experience. In addition, the "bucket list" is consistent with the hotel's core loyalists who, on average, are older in age and life stage and who perhaps missed adventures while building home, family, and business and now have time to experience them.

Throughout the year, the hotel aggregates possible experiences and communicates them through weekly online posts. The campaign uses both Facebook and Twitter (#BucketList and #RCMemories), and encourages its guests to follow and suggest bucket list ideas, making the program interactive and increasing brand engagement.

The brand manager, in speaking of the program, is clear that the experiences offered must be truly memorable and on-brand as authenticity is a key to a successful brand engagement and a meaningful customer emotional experience. Here is how the hotel brand manager framed the brand promise: *"Creating memories for life is what we at The Ritz-Carlton do every day. We create a personalized experience—an emotional connection with our guests. Our ladies and gentlemen (aka guests) are driven by those connections they make."*[40]

Hospitality, Travel, and the Global Brand

In a virtual shopping community, through the use of social media, consumers are not only comparing products and prices but sustaining their own relationships and building brands. Immersed in the rapidly changing digital age, the retail, hospitality, and tourism industries have been forced to understand and respond to their transformed customers, because their profits depend on it. Recent research by Bazaarvoice, an internet marketing company, supports this with data that indicate that cell phone shoppers who review customer content in the form of product reviews are 133 percent more likely to make a purchase.[41]

The financial stakes in the hospitality (aka hotels and resorts) and retail travel space are high enough that they drive the kinds of strategies that the preceding data suggest need to be implemented. Revenues from travel retail, which also includes sales on airplanes, rose 9.4 percent in 2012 to $76.6 billion, according to a market study by Generation Research. According to the study, that number is projected to double by 2020. **Travel retail**, an expression that defines retail outlets located within travel environments such as airports, has evolved into **traveler retail** which is using any retail outlet to harness growth by international travelers. Brands have started to realize that travelers do not shop only in airports. They shop everywhere, especially on the High Street luxury retail brick-and-mortar locations. One brand focused on this market is Duty Free Shoppers (DFS; Figure 13.4).

DFS is engaged in the type of strategic planning and communication referred to as point of origin marketing:

> *"We talk about customer touch points, so we try to be in contact with the customer when they are thinking about the journey. We do that through alliances with travel magazines, websites or blogs, and travel booking organizations. The travel agent might post them a programmer which includes visiting a DFS store and, on the plane, there might be something telling them about DFS and so on. We are regularly in contact up to the moment when they arrive in our store, where they shop and we register them into our loyalty program. Then we can stay in contact with them after they leave and go back and maybe ready for them for their next trip."*[42]

The company is also increasingly targeting travelers with stores placed beyond traditional travel

figure 13.4
**A Duty Free Shoppers
store in San Francisco
International Airport:**
Retailers continue to
look for meaningful
brick-and-mortar
locales where the brand
intersects with their core
consumers' lifestyles.

corridors with recently rebranded T Galleria locations in city centers. "*The downtown model stemmed from the idea that when you were in the town, even when you were flying off you had little time at the airport but a lot of time in town.*"[43]

According to The Affluence Collaborative, a research powerhouse that dives deep into the habits of high-income consumers, the affluent seek out companies and brands that can simplify and improve their lives. In the travel sector, this translates into increased expectations around personalization cutting across all touch points, including digital media platforms, as luxury travelers research, purchase, engage in, and reflect upon their travel experiences.

The Luxury Traveler Technology Survey, commissioned by The Four Seasons and made up of a representative group of global luxury travelers, set out to uncover how consumers want technology to blend seamlessly into their experience, and how those preferences have changed in recent years. Here are some key finds that confirm much of what we see in non-hospitality retail as the expectations of luxury consumers:

- **Customization:** 34 percent expect that products and services should be customized to their needs and desires.
- **True Distinctiveness**: 32 percent expect that the company should be an innovator, successfully rewriting the rules in its category.
- **Constant Exceeding of Expectations**: 32 percent expect surprise and delight; many extend that to once-in-a-lifetime experiences, and 25 percent expect to learn from the products and services they buy.

What becomes clear is that luxury and a luxury internet presence on social media are centerpieces of luxury hotel strategies and that hotels and hospitality brands such as spas and resorts are following the general trend of luxury retail into entirely new dimensions where the lines between technology and retail and physical and virtual reality are dissolving into a world of infinite possibilities (Figure 13.5).

The ultimate manifestation of this can be found in Starwood Corporation's (The Luxury Collection, St. Regis, and W Hotels) StarLab. Opened in 2015,

figure 13.5
The Four Seasons Hotel in Moscow: The Four Seasons hospitality brand engages in the same level of uniform service no matter the global market.

StarLab is a corporate think tank in New York City occupying 46,000 square feet in the Garment Center! It is not a hotel but a digital center displaying user (hotel guest) generated content, Twitter comments from hotel guests around the world (a digital chandelier offers a live ticker of guests' tweets), and five digital displays with guests' current Instagram photos. "Huddle spaces" and flexible workstations provide opportunities for cross-functional integration of brand managers, omni-channel communications managers, and hotel design. Michael Tiedy, vice president of global brand design and innovation for Starwood, sums it up this way: *"We have reached a tipping point where it is more important than ever for our teams to think differently about our business: from the unique design of our hotels to . . . programming that brings our brands to life and the leading edge technology that enables us to deliver personalized service around the world."*[44]

SUMMARY

Managing the luxury brand in a digital world is a challenge, but luxury can meet, and is meeting, the challenge. Initially, it appears that luxury, with its aristocratic, exclusive, and inaccessible culture, is at odds with the web, with its democratic, inclusive, and transparent culture. However, on closer look, the bridge over which luxury crosses into digital is virtual reality and the psychology of participating in a life of dreams. Here, luxury is experienced as it has forged emotional ties with its clientele by creating virtual realities in terms of their aspirations and of fulfilling those aspirations with brand experiences which conjure a world of timeless dreams.

Even if luxury wished to remain on the digital sidelines, it could not because it is already a major topic of online content and conversation. Better to try to manage what already is rather than risk distortions of the brand's image. This alone would be good reason to get on board.

The other dynamic that is driving all brands to the web is the demand for a seamless consumer experience called omni-channel communications—the integration of web, phone, and physical retail platforms. Luxury has embraced this and has looked at this as more of a culture play, bringing this rarified world of luxury to the many but doing it in very discreet and on-brand ways. The strategy to achieve this is often unique communications and selective customer

The creation of Zivarly®, a new approach for luxury retail, has found its way into one of China's most exquisite and avant-garde retailers called Upper Luxury. The concept is to curate from different luxury brands and artists who are also artisans, one merchandised statement and present it in a retail setting where the design elements of the products become artistic and fashionable complements to one another. The clients who view the collections can either enjoy the aesthetics, as one would in a gallery, or purchase the particular presentation (say, handbag, hat, and gloves) and be perfectly attired.

The concept is based on a philosophy of living. The sensibilities driving this new creative force can be summed up as follows:

- A global outreach by the luxury entrepreneur to artisans who share an Eastern cultural sensibility about a spiritual lifestyle
- The search for artists and artisans whose creativity is a passion for life and a quest for personal identity through their work
- Artists who offer a unique integrity in what they create, as their art precedes the product as a seed precedes a flower and its bloom
- A curator-designer approach to both product development and merchandise presentation where "collecting" the artisans' art and "consuming" the resulting products become one and the same
- Products and presentations are unique, adding "*modern heirlooms*" to the luxury consumer's purchase drivers

In accessories, the result at retail is nothing less than revolutionary. The brand positions itself as a statement accessory brand which brings wearable and useable art from and into people's daily lives. The brand is showcased with traditional luxury brands! The price of entry for each brand is not how popular it is but how it complements other works of art. The presentation is in a museum-like setting, in specially lighted minimalist formats. Brands, previously seen purely as competitors and housed in separate shops, fixtures, or cases, are now integrated in lifestyle presentations—hats with scarves and handbags, for example. Cross-merchandising the brands recognizes the reality of how consumers shop and dress, mixing brands for their own unique lifestyle identity. Complementary colors, textures, and prints—the design elements—unify the presentation.

Zivarly is a luxury brand born in China and finding its unique opportunity there as well. Its founder approached the general merchandise manager at Upper Luxury (Figure 13.6) to combine European luxury classic brands with the modern/artistic designs of Zivarly®. This "mix-match" would be a win for both. The merchandise teams from Luxury and Zivarly met and determined the merchandise/mix strategy. This was followed by each company's visual merchandising teams meeting to design the "gallery" presentation at retail (Figure 13.7).

The process began in early 2014, and six months later the results were impressive. Foot traffic and on-floor **hang-time** (time consumers spend on the retail floor) were up for these consumers, as was their positive feedback. And the traditional metric, sales, followed accordingly.

(continued on next page)

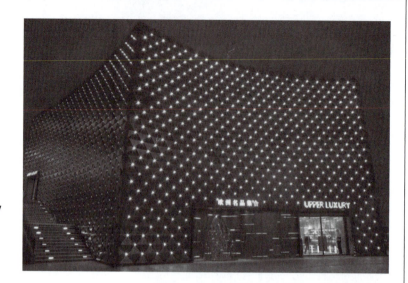

figure 13.6
Exterior of Upper Luxury in Beijing, China: A more dramatic and modern luxury image verging on architectural art.

We have here an example of restoring art and theater to the luxury experience and recapturing the dream of artisanship and beauty without losing the business opportunities that this approach presents.

The Zivarly brand now enters its next stage, seeking placement in art exhibitions and museum shops. It can be found in China's most famous modern art museum, Today Art Museum, similar to the Museum of Modern Art (MOMA) in New York City.

The artistry is aligned with technology. Given the brand's value proposition, an appropriate technology platform is one that offers articles plus photos. Sohu.com rather than Twitter is used so that words and photos can be posted together to fully express the brand's identity and its DNA. A recent article posted on Sohu (which can be accessed through its website, mobile phone, and Sohu APP) generated over 300,000 clicks.

figure 13.7
An example of a lifestyle Zivarly display: Merchandising becomes more about curating, thereby creating a new luxury artisanship.

Zivarly was asked to make a presentation in May 2015 to Lane Crawford, the Neiman Marcus of Asia, where it may find its place as a new luxury brand among the others while offering Lane Crawford a new concept in curated luxury.

service initiatives as we've described in our discussions of Louis Vuitton, Burberry, and others. This is not to say that luxury does not sell products online, it does, but often from limited inventory and as often to limited audiences of brand loyalists. The success of platforms such as YOOX and the demand to shop via smart phone is changing the receptivity of luxury brands selling online.

More and more, luxury is becoming experiential theater creating curated opportunities to enjoy events as well as products. This is clearly evident in the hospitality space where luxury hotels are strongly committed to delivering images and messages via social media to deliver aspirational brand experiences to their loyalists.

Finally, the merger of artisanship, art, and theater may portend luxury's future as these are all ingredients which have played, often separately, to luxury's successful past. It may be the source for its most promising future.

KEY TERMS

Atelier
Brand Experience
Bricks and Clicks
Click and Collect
Clienteling

Constant Exceeding of
   Expectation
Customization
Emotional Branding
Experiencing Self
Hang-Time

Remembering Self
RFID Chip
Seamless Brand Experience
Travel Retail
Traveler Retail
True Distinctiveness

CHAPTER CONVERSATIONS

- How would you describe the similarities in "virtual reality" between the luxury and digital spaces?
- What rules would you recommend for ensuring that a luxury brand stays on-brand in social media?

- Why do you think the luxury hotel industry is well suited for curated brand experiences for its clientele?

CHAPTER CHALLENGES

- You are a brand manager in a luxury conglomerate. Your CEO wants to take one of its famous old and successful brands to a luxury retail site for sales. The founder/designer of the brand is resisting. What would you do?
- The vice president of global retail at your luxury company wants to build additional boutiques to expand the business of its fast-growing contemporary luxury brand. You are its brand manager. What would you recommend and why?
- A tired luxury accessories brand in need of regeneration has been given to you and, as the brand manager, you've been asked to prepare a strategy for its resurrection. What steps would you take to bring the brand back? Why do you believe your strategy will work?

ENDNOTES

1. Jean-Noel Kapferer and Vincent Bastien, *The Luxury Strategy: Break the Rules of Marketing to Build Luxury Brands* (N.p.: Kogan Page Ltd., 2012), 17.

2. For why the platform is right for luxury, see David Dubois, "The 'Social Media New Deal' for Luxury Brands," *Insead Knowledge*, October 21, 2014.

3. Kapferer and Bastien, *The Luxury Strategy*, 161.

4. K. L. Keller, "Managing the Growth Tradeoff: Challenges and Opportunities in Luxury Branding," *Journal of Brand Management* 16 (March–May 2009): 293; see also Uche Okonkwo, "Sustaining the Luxury Brand on the Internet," *Journal of Brand Management* 16 (March–May 2009): 302–310.

5. Kapferer and Bastien, *The Luxury Strategy*, 158–163.

6. Uche Okonkwo, "The Luxury Brand Management Challenge," Editorial, *Journal of Brand Management* 16 (2009): 288.

7. Libby Banks, "Defining Luxury for a Modern Era," *New York Times*, March 26, 2015, http://www.nytimes .com/2015/03/27/fashion/in-craftsmanship-defining-luxury-for-a-modern-era.html?_r=0.

8. David Dubois, "Why Social Media Is Luxury's Best Friend," *Insead* November 6, 2013, http://knowledge.insead.edu/strategy/why-social-media-is-luxurys-best-friend-2951.

9. Joseph Grenny, "Stop Enabling Gossip on Your Team," *Harvard Business Review*, January 9, 2015, https://hbr.org/2015/01/stop-enabling-gossip-on-your-team.

10. Kate Fox, "Mobile Gossip," *Social Issues Research Centre*, 2001, http://www.sirc.org/publik/gossip.shtml.

11. Lindsay Baker, "Online Retailers Move into Bricks and Mortar Stores," *BBC News*, November 6, 2013, http://www.bbc.com/news/business-24728406.

12. Ibid.

13. Jesse Weltevreden, "The Digital Challenge for the High Street: Insights from Europe," *Hogeschool Van Amsterdam*, November 2014, http://www.hva.nl/carem/publicaties/content/publicaties-algemeen /the-digital-challenge-for-the-high-street-inisghts-from-europe.html.

14. For a wonderful and insightful vignette describing a French market in these terms, see Marc Gobe, *Emotional Branding: The New Paradigm for Connecting Brands to People* (New York, NY: Allworth Press, 2009), 244.

15. Baker, "Online Retailers Move into Bricks and Mortar Stores."

16. Lauren Said-Moorhouse, "Inside Louis Vuitton's Townhouse: Wooing Luxury Shoppers in the Digital Age," January 5, 2015, http://www.cnn.com/2013/11/18/business/inside-louis-vuittons-townhouse/; V. A. Kansara, "Burberry Remains Digital Luxury Leader," *Business of Fashion*, October 9, 2014, www.business offashion.com; "Luxury Retailers Go Omnichannel," January 27, 2015, www.thrivingmalls.com.

17. "UK Online Retail Report: Mobile and Web Driving Changes to High Street," *Digital Strategy Consulting*, April 21, 2011, http://www.digitalstrategyconsulting.com/intelligence/2011/04/uk_online_retail_report _mobile.php; Said-Moorehouse, "Inside Louis Vuitton's Townhouse."

18. "UK Online Retail Report."

19. Nigel Cooper, "Targeting High-End Consumers—How Luxury Brands Can Make the Most of Social," *Qube*, October 31, 2014, http://qubemedia.net/social-media-and-luxury-travel/targeting-high-end -consumers-how-luxury-brands-can-make-the-most-of-social/.

20. "Leading Luxury Brands Merging Digital and Physical Spheres through Innovation," *The Future of Luxury*, April 15, 2015, http://www.thefutureofluxury.co.uk/retail-store-design/.

21. Doug Grinspan, "7 Luxury Brands That Have Digital Media Wired," *Media Post*, July 9, 2014, http://www.mediapost.com/publications/article/229637/7-luxury-brands-that-have-digital-media-wired.html.

22. Roger Scoble, "Digital Luxe: Social Media Strategies for Luxury Brands," *Pursuitist*, November 14, 2014, http://pursuitist.com/digital-luxe-social-media-strategies-luxury-brands/.

23. Molly, "Luxury Retailers Go Omnichannel," *Thriving Malls*, January 27, 2015, http://thrivingmalls.com/2015/01/27/luxury-retailers-go-omnichannel/.

24. Ibid.

25. Minter Dial, "Why Relationship Marketing Is the New Model for Luxury Brands," *Social Media Today*, April 28, 2014, http://www.socialmediatoday.com/content/why-relationship-marketing-new-model-luxury-brands.

26. Ibid.

27. Ibid.

28. Linda Dauriz, Ambrogio Michette, Nicola Sandri, and Andrea Zocchi, "Digital Luxury Experience: Keeping Up with Changing Customers," *McKinsey and Company*, April 2014, http://www.mckinseyonmarketingandsales.com/digital-luxury-experience-keeping-up-with-changing-customers.

29. Brittany Mills, "High-Touch vs. High Luxury," *Mobiquity*, http://www.mobiquityinc.com/high-touch-high-luxury.

30. Ibid.

31. Ibid.

32. Ibid.

33. Hilary F., *Hourly Nerd* (blog), comment posted 2014, https://hourlynerd.com/ask-a-pro/view-answers/9d17f6d5/what-are-some-best-practices-for-a-luxury-goods-social-media-strategy/.

34. Duke Greenhill, "4 Pillars of Digital Marketing for Luxury Brands," *Mashable*, November 29, 2011, http://mashable.com/2011/11/29/luxury-marketing-digital/.

35. Four Seasons, "The Luxury Consumer in the New Digital World: Then and Now," *Four Seasons*, 2012, http://www.fourseasons.com/content/dam/fourseasons/web/pdfs/landing_page_pdfs/2012_TRD_Report_final.pdf.

36. Nancy Buckley, "Ritz-Carlton Laguna Niguel Helps Consumers Check Off Bucket List Items," *Luxury Daily*, January 22, 2015, http://www.luxurydaily.com/ritz-carlton-laguna-niguel-checks-off-bucket-list-items-in-2015/.

37. Marc Gobe, *Emotional Branding*, 288.

38. "How Can Downtowns and Main Streets Reinvent Themselves in the Digital Age?," *Small City Branding Around the World*, December 15, 2014, http://citybranding.typepad.com/city-branding/2014/12/how-can-downtowns-and-main-streets-reinvent-themselves-in-the-digital-age.html.

40. Robin Mellery-Pratt, "Tapping Travellers Beyond Traditional Corridors," *Business of Fashion*, July 9, 2014, http://www.businessoffashion.com/articles/intelligence/as-sector-shifts-travel-retail-taps-travellers-beyond-traditional-corridors-global-blue-dfs-group.

41. Ibid.

42. Ibid.

43. Nancy Buckley, "Starwood Seeks Multichannel Environment to Foster Creativity," *Luxury Daily*, February 26, 2015, http://www.luxurydaily.com/satrwood-seeks-multichannel-environment-to-foster-creativity/.

44. Ibid.

CHAPTER 14

Global Brand Management

AFTER COMPLETING THIS CHAPTER, YOU WILL BE ABLE TO:

- Identify the fallacies in the belief in a global consumer.

- Explain the influence of national cultures on global brand strategies.

- Discuss the role of language and semiotics in global brand marketing.

THE FALLACY OF A GLOBAL CONSUMER

Luxury and Mass brands had found their way into international markets many decades before the advent of the internet and the emergence of the Free Trade movement. However, by the early 1980s, a new global economic landscape emerged from the confluence of **free trade agreements**, which significantly lowered or did away with trade barriers such as tariffs and prohibitive duties on the exchange of goods between nations, and the emergence of the internet.

As free trade eliminated commercial barriers, free internet eliminated communications barriers. Thomas Friedman, in his groundbreaking book *The World Is Flat*, extended this development by adding to his analysis fiber optics, which accelerated electronic communications and further eroded national boundaries, seemingly leading to the arrival of the Global Market with a Global Consumer. He concluded that, through the confluence of these three phenomena— free trade, fiber optics, and the internet—we were entering a new era which he called "The Flat World," implying that the traditional barriers to unobstructed commerce and communications were quickly disappearing and with them a new global economy and global consumer were emerging.[1]

In this flat world, national boundaries would no longer result in consumers whose consumption values were derived from national brands and tied to national brand loyalties. Although a nation's brands would still exist, they would become less relevant to daily economic life. This new global marketplace would eventually bring forth a consumer whose consumption mind-set was global and not national and whose brand loyalties followed suit. This homogenization of consumer dispositions would take hold with different degrees of intensity in every country but the transformation in kind would be uniformly global.[2]

Homogenization and the Rational Consumer Model

The homogenization of national consumption dispositions resulting in a global consumer was based upon the rational consumer model which we discussed in Chapter 5. If you recall, we discussed the idea of "utilities" in consumer decision making. This is based upon the widely embraced economic theories of Jeremy Bentham, the nineteenth-century English philosopher who popularized **utilitarianism**.[3] This doctrine held that human beings are motivated to pursue pleasure and to avoid pain. They engage in rational calculations to determine courses of action including consumption calculations that will maximize the former and minimize the latter. Following this line of reasoning, businesses merely need to perform similar calculations to arrive at the highest **net utility** (or the remainder when the pain utility is subtracted from the pleasure utility) and thereby determine which products or services offer the greatest pleasure and bring those to market.

Product-centric Branding

This utility theory of consumer behavior found implicit support in a controversial piece in the *Harvard Business Review* in 1983 by Theodore Levitt entitled, *"The Globalization of Markets."*[4] In it, Levitt argued that the global economy would gradually lead to a global consumer and this would provide companies a global distribution network with a distinct economic advantage. Uniform global demand would result in achieving economies of scale (as we saw in Chapter 7) wherein manufacturing large numbers of standardized products would drive production costs down. Leveraging of uniform advertising and marketing would accompany this and result in a revenue and profit boom because there would be no need to customize products for individual national or regional cultural tastes, and no incurring of the costs associated with variances in the production process. These benefits would also find their way into brand marketing, as the homogenization of the consumer's tastes and preferences would mean a single image campaign for each product across the globe. Although not spelled out by Levitt, the final implicit benefit was that brand equity and brand valuations would continuously rise with the rise in consumer consumption, leading to portfolios of mega-brands in terms of their strength and market value.

Consumer-centric Branding

The fallacy inherent in the argument is that it was a model not only driven by the "rational man" model but based more on FMCG products (described in Chapter 3). It assumed the objective of global business would continue to achieve economies of scale as consumers would be limited in choice to those big brands that controlled most production and distribution. As such, its focus was operational and the assessment made from the perspective of the management of the organization and not the consumer.[5] It also underestimated the enduring influence of national cultures on consumer behavior, something we will discuss throughout this chapter. As we have argued in prior chapters, this production-driven model gave way in the 1990s to the emergence of consumer-centric brand strategies that attempted to meet the growing ascendency of the consumer given the shift in supply and demand. More importantly, the rise of luxury brands and middle- and upper-middle-class consumers in global markets added an additional purchasing dynamic to one basically focused on necessity (commodities) to create one now focused as intently on aspirations (luxury and fashion) as competitors for global consumers' share of wallet. Finally, the internet further shifted the balance of power from product and production to consumers and aspirational consumption. This shift also affected a pivot from viewing global brand value creation from the perspective of managers to that of consumers. Studies such as those by Steenkamp and others empirically confirmed the role of global consumers in defining brand value. In this aforementioned study, there were strong correlations between global consumers' perceptions of global brands as being of higher quality because they were global, especially in comparison to local brands in the same product category.[6]

This positive shift in the perception of the role of the consumer in creating brand value was underscored by a more deleterious shift and awareness in consumer behavior—the reality of the scope and extent of commerce in counterfeit goods.

Counterfeiting

An unintended consequence of this shift to aspirational consumption is the accelerated pace of global **counterfeiting**, or the illegal copying of logos, designs, and/or products and presenting them for sale as authentic. It is estimated to be across all business sectors in excess of $600 billion to $1.6 trillion a year.[7] The problem exists on both the mass and luxury levels, but the impact is more intense for luxury products where the desire for social status through *owning and displaying* are part of the associative attributes of luxury brands and what imparts significant levels of value to the purchase.

Counterfeiting is exacerbated by the global marketplace and the borderless internet which provides no single legal authority to enforce or try cases and, in both instances, makes it more difficult to police the transgressions and bring the perpetrators to justice (Figure 14.1).

The internet adds to the challenge of a borderless market. Portals which provide B2B services to retailers who hope to use the portals' reach and stature to attract consumers are now facing lawsuits from brand owners. Although some have argued that counterfeiting may be seen as a positive in that it shows demand and sets up the purchaser for the real thing once the reality of poor quality and questionable design trumps low price, the overwhelming number of brand owners see it as a threat and respond accordingly.[8] Here are some of the major arguments pro and con:[9]

Pro	Con
Indicates high demand	Tarnishes value to full-price owners
Free advertising	Undermines brand image/IP value
Forces brand to innovate	Luxury brands innovate naturally
Gateway to real product purchase	Diverts revenue from the brand
No evidence of cannibalization	Misses the brand experience value

On this last bullet point, this quote from an LVMH brand manager, Pierre Gode, aptly sums up luxury's main concerns: "*We have invested so much money to enhance and protect our brands* and our brand experience [bold added] *that it is impossible to accept . . . someone who has no understanding of this . . . and destroy that value.*"[10]

Luxury brand managers have been exceedingly aggressive in this latter regard; Kering, the luxury brand conglomerate that owns Gucci, Saint Laurent, and others had sued Alibaba, the massive Chinese internet portal, twice in the last two years (most recently in May 2015) alleging failure to monitor and being complicit in the sale of counterfeit products bearing Kering brand names. LVMH has been similarly vigilant, having won a case against eBay for failing to screen and provide protections similar to those demanded by Kering.[11]

The stakes in this confrontation are high; luxury brands sue based on estimated loss of sales revenue, royalty revenues from licensing fees that would be paid by the counterfeiter if it proceeded legally, and for some monetary restitution for the dilution of brand equity. For luxury brands, the last factor can exceed the first two in estimated loss of value as the argument is put forth that the perception of uniqueness and rarity is compromised, which is assumed to have longer and more insidious adverse effects on the brand's stature.

figure 14.1
Chinese counterfeit watches: The desire to own even fake displays of luxury points to its all-pervasive cross-border appeal.

Mass brands, especially in the pharmaceutical sector, undertake similar defenses of their patents against counterfeiters. Here their countermeasures are often as intense as those of the luxury brands for patent law protection of their drugs from generic competitors is usually limited to a finite window, often no more than fifteen years. Free from competitive pricing pressures, pharma brands charge high premium prices for the period under which they are protected by their patents. This opens the door to counterfeiters who dramatically underprice their products in the global marketplace.

However, the more compelling conversation is why and what type of consumer participates in this and to what extent are there cultural differences driven by national identity and cultural values?

Although we cannot explore all of these dynamics in depth, suffice it to say that cultural values, social standing, and the degree to which consumers are risk averse all come into play in the knowing purchase (also known as "non-deceptive" consuming) of counterfeit products.[12] Studies of consumers who buy counterfeit products show different degrees and styles of acceptance of the practice. So, for example, a study of Indonesian consumers found a more accepting and widespread pattern as there are less cultural or social stigmas attached to the practice when compared with Singaporean and Chinese consumers. For the former, where the social norms regarding obeying the law are quite strong, the practice is frowned upon (although still practiced) while for Chinese consumers, losing face by purchasing counterfeits is somewhat of a deterrent on the mainland offset by the deep desire for social status that even displays of luxury copies conveys.[13] This latter disposition often results in an increase in counterfeit purchasing when traveling abroad.[14] In a study on U.S. counterfeit purchasers, the degree of risk aversion was found to be a prime determinant.[15]

Brand owners are countering by engaging technology in an attempt to monitor and inform retailers, web portals, and consumers alike of counterfeits. The use of unique QR codes embedded in hang-tags and electronically aligned with web-based verification platforms are now being tested. However, the willingness to use them still will require that honesty trump acquisitiveness in consumer desires and motivation. What might you recommend to stem the counterfeiting tide? Or are you of the mind that it is a positive rather than a negative?

Global Brand Management Strategies

Variations in strategies for going global are driven by the opportunities they offer in terms of early entry into emerging markets, balancing currency fluctuations and diversifying risk, offsetting slowdowns in domestic markets, lowering costs for marketing through uniformity in communications, having a mark of prestige and brand stature for business development, and having access to worldwide innovative developments. Economies of scale are also a major consideration but vary with the character and category of the product or service that is offered.

Luxury Brands

If we look at luxury brands in light of the above strategies, prestige rather than economies of scale is a key factor in maintaining the perception of a marquee brand with all that this implies. Included in this is the status for the consumer by association, a more cosmopolitan stance which adds value to its pricing model, and a sense of its timeless staying power in its ability to resist economic calamities. The other factors mentioned also are, in various degrees, operative as strategic imperatives.

Non-luxury Brands

In the non-luxury space, issues of prestige, status, and a cosmopolitan image are not the operative drivers but the other variables that are in play, including economies of scale, are often the primary determinants in global expansion. In fact, as global household product brands forge market entry strategies, local tastes and cultural habits are often more part of a consumer-centric view of the opportunities than with luxury products. This is a function of the reality that those who are in the lower social and economic strata are less exposed to new lifestyle alternatives and are often most tied to local and regional patterns of consumption. Conversely, luxury and even premium brand consumers have often been exposed through associates, lifestyle, and travel to the various global lifestyle values which transcend their own culture and country.

Standardization versus Adaptation

This raises the ongoing issue of standardization versus adaptation for global brands in foreign markets. By **standardization**, we mean that the strategy which characterizes the go-to-market brand identity and strategies in terms of the classic four Ps of marketing (product, price, place, promotion) remain largely unchanged. For **adaptation**, the converse is the case with some or all of the Ps undergoing some degree of adjustment or transformation to accommodate the foreign market and its internal local markets. Several generalizations should guide us in coming down on one side or the other. First, it is not an either-or proposition, but a matter of scale or degree based on markets. Second, in general, luxury brands adapt less than do mass brands with the latter especially in food products where deep-rooted cultural habits are obstacles to standardization. For example, Oreo cookies, struggling in China, discovered that one of the keys was that Chinese consumers preferred, besides a slightly less sweet taste, wafers over cookies. The solution? Chocolate-covered wafers, and a huge turnaround resulted![16] Interestingly, although packing and pricing changed (three of the four Ps), the one P that didn't was "promotion" as the iconic twisting of the Oreo cookies into two sections to enjoy the inner cream filling and the dunking of the outer cookies (now wafers) into milk was considered so iconic to the brand's associative brand identity that these images were retained. This tableside practice has no counterpart in China and yet the brand managers made a decision that captured something universal—the sharing of family-time experiences through food or snacks in a kitchen that families around the world enjoy, an archetypal connection that paid big dividends!

Similarly, luxury brands have made certain adaptations such as Montcler in India where it has enjoyed strong success. India is a multitude of subcultures and languages. Different regions and states have different habits and even cultural personalities (Punjabi customers are more flamboyant than the Gujarati consumers who tend to be more reserved, for example).[17] In the fourteen states where Montcler has boutiques, each boutique gets unique product packaging and communication copy in the local dialect, adapting the "promotion" part of the four Ps to local market realities without compromising the brand identity; all

other variables in the four Ps remain the same.

Another challenging situation where standardization and adaptation were in dynamic tension with each other was the Best Buy brand experience in China. Best Buy entered the China market in 2006 with its standardized U.S. business model—high-profile brands, good service, and premium prices all of which constituted its brand identity. At the same time, it bought the Five Star appliance business, a moderately priced Chinese appliance retailer and infused it with the Best Buy name and business model. By 2011, the strategy wasn't working as the Best Buy brand was relatively unknown in China and local competitors were well established with strong followings, lower prices, and a retail culture wherein Chinese consumers were accustomed to bargaining on price, something not part of the Best Buy model.[18] In 2012 it shifted its focus back to Five Star retail units and closed its nine Best Buy branded stores, hoping to make its pricing more competitive and its promotional position through the familiar local brand more attractive to the Chinese consumer. However, the competition and a growing shift to online purchases with warehouse pickups doomed the shift in strategy. By December 2014, Best Buy announced the sale of its Five Star chain and its exit from China.[19] One observer has noted that "*its model that emphasizes customer service never really caught on in price sensitive China. . .*"[20] The failure to make this adaptation may have doomed Best Buy's market entry from the start.

GLOBAL VERSUS INTERNATIONAL BRAND MANAGEMENT

Companies that have made a commitment to global brand distribution differ from those that are brands that sell internationally or are multinational companies. This is more than a semantic distinction. International brands operate under a different business model which offers certain advantages but more often, disadvantages, if they wish to be serious competitors in the foreign markets where they are marketing the brand.

In general, global brands set up corporations and organizations in the markets in which they wish to distribute, including hiring (and, if needed, training) local professionals on the global company's culture and brand values. They operate in different countries but view the world as a single country.[21]

Viewing the world as a single country can provide a competitive advantage. This is especially the case when there are products that are amenable to standardization. Then, economies of scale, coupled with communicating a consistent marketing message and global brand image, can be more readily realized.

International sellers sell from their home organization to the foreign market. This has the benefit of low initial investment and the absence of having to build an organizational infrastructure in the country where the brand is being distributed. Often, licensing arrangements or local distributors are contracted and may provide offices, warehousing, and other facilities, offering the international seller a relatively low cost of entry. Also, should it decide to shut down operations, cost is less a factor in the decision than if it had developed a full-fledged organization and operations in the market country.

Glocal Brand Management

Truly global brands have the same name in every market and, in many instances, a similar image and positioning. A brand such as Gillette comes to mind with its easy to convey and readily translatable brand promise, "*the best a man can get.*" In this instance, the change occurs in packaging and translations.

This positioning has resulted in, and helps to maintain, a global share of over 70 percent in the safety razor market for Gillette without having to change product specs. This also may be a function of the fact that food, taste, and cultural consumption patterns are less in play with a shaving instrument than with food or drink. Thus, Coca-Cola, clearly a global brand, undertakes a **glocal brand management strategy**.

This strategy seeks to strike a balance between local and national cultural habits and tastes and the brand's global persona. So for a cola drink company, it adjusts the taste of its cola drinks to align with local tastes while adhering to its universally understood archetype of innocence and fun in its marketing messages.[22]

Accommodation to Local Needs

Besides taste, global brands, in order to accommodate local needs, often make adjustments in pricing or size of packaging. For example, in India, P&G, after prelaunch market tests were very positive for its shampoo, found that sales simply did not materialize commensurate with the research findings and strong preference scores from Indian women consumers. Follow-up research through **in-depth interviews** (where researchers met one-on-one with prototypical target customers) discovered that the size of the package led to a price that made the purchase unaffordable for many low-income Indian women. The brand managers had priced the product competitively, but the size of the bottle meant a higher price per ounce than what was affordable locally. By reducing the size from five-ounce packaging to one ounce, even though it increased the cost per ounce, the Indian consumers could afford the product they so clearly liked in prelaunch tests. Additionally, the purchasing habits and patterns for these goods by low-income Indian cohorts was such that they frequently shopped close to use of the product from local vendors and not from big box retailers. This led not only to a change in packaging but also to a change in distribution strategies (the "placement" variable in the four Ps) by P&G and confirmed that the smaller package was of benefit to both the end-user and the distributor. Distributors who were most often small shopkeepers had limited space and ran cash businesses. Consumers who had limited cash purchased as close to use and need as possible. The smaller packaging was a win-win for both.

A very similar local market challenge was met in Mexico and Indonesia, where low-income consumers wished to purchase the brand but limited income and buying close to need made them willing to pay more per ounce to enjoy the "value" of the global brand. Here again, P&G brand managers met local needs without altering the ingredients and without sacrificing the brand identity or its product quality.[23]

The brand management lesson here is that the idea of what constitutes value in foreign markets (and for that matter, in all markets) is seldom a function of price, or price alone. Local economic patterns need to inform global economic strategies if the global enterprise is to find a foothold in the local market. This insight should alert all brand managers that when they distribute in foreign markets, cultural and social realities need to be front and center prior to, and as guidelines for, formulating global brand strategies.

The Role of Cultural Brand Ambassadors

A strategy to help smooth the transition from global perceptions of marketing strategies to incorporating local values is the use of cultural brand ambassadors. A **cultural brand ambassador** is a well-known celebrity who is seen by the consumers in the country as synonymous with the brand. The objective is to tap into the associative attribute halo that we discussed in Chapter 10.

The internet and the global exchange of movies, books, and theater has created a broad field of celebrities who have differing ranks and stature in different cultures. The ambassador for the foreign brand may be from the market entry country or may be so well known that he or she has a global presence that transcends national borders.

The leading figures in this regard often are not who we think they may be. For example, in China, with its frenzied love of basketball, Kobe Bryant, the star for the Los Angeles Lakers, ranks number one on a list of movie stars, rock musicians, and the like. Before recruiting ambassadors, research needs to be undertaken to determine who the leading stars are, how they are perceived in terms of the values they represent, and how this aligns with the brand persona, all of which is likely to differ from market to market.[24]

Another example of an unlikely celebrity whose stature continues to exceed her presence is Audrey Hepburn, the iconic U.S. movie star who became famous for her role in *Breakfast at Tiffany's* where she introduced the so-called little black dress that became a woman's must-have fashion basic. Although she passed away in 1993, she continues to hold an absolutely unique status position in China, where "*she has a massive iconic appeal for elegance and sophistication.*"[25] Therefore, the fact that she is no longer with us should not deter brand managers from searching for strategies that tap into her image or search for and confirm who might be the heir apparent to this unique position that Hepburn holds (Figure 14.2).

Often, a brand ambassador is a well-known celebrity from the country who can both advise the brand managers on courses of actions and smooth the market entry of the brand. Whether this is a soccer player in the UK or a Bollywood star in India, the purpose and the process are fundamentally the same. The associative characteristics of the celebrity and the

figure 14.2
Audrey Hepburn: Glamour and elegance are personified in Audrey Hepburn, among others who appeal across national cultures because they touch universal archetypes.

global brand need to be aligned. The brand ambassador needs to be immersed in the brand values and personality so that she or he is not just a figurehead but transitions into the role of an authentic spokesperson for the brand.

One such example is the use by L'Oréal in China of its most famous actress Fan Bing Bing (Figure 14.3). In 2015 she once again made the Forbes list of the 100 most influential Chinese stars and has served as brand ambassador for the likes of Louis Vuitton, Chopard, Cartier, Mercedes-Benz, and others.[26] It has been estimated that keyword searches in her name on Taobao,

figure 14.3
The celebrated Chinese movie star Fan Bing Bing: Another iconic image who transcends borders as she serves as spokesperson for many global brands.

the Chinese e-commerce site, generated close to $75 million in revenue for sellers on the site.[27]

Finally, brand managers need to look beyond the home country for home stars. Again in China, soap operas are very popular and many of the most popular are broadcast from Korea. Major endorsement deals have been made with the Korean stars of those shows to endorse products in China.

The caveat in all of these examples is the cost and management challenges such as contracts, logistics, event planning, and advertising production that add time and costs to operationalizing the endorsement strategy. If you are a company of modest means, there are alternatives. In the following case study is an example of a strategy that approaches celebrity endorsement from a different strategic angle which, if executed correctly, can be very impactful and certainly less costly.

Global Brand Communication Management

The management of brand communications differs somewhat between luxury and non-luxury brands. Luxury brands are more likely to retain their country of origin identity, in name for sure and in logo and packaging most often as well. This is a function of their drive to remain exclusive and rare, which requires the protection of their identity no matter where it may appear in the global marketplace. In addition, part of the value of the brand is its name and the experiential high that consumers around the globe feel when they partake of it. This effect is differentially experienced by consumers when they travel from their home and engage the home-based brand in a foreign country. Brand meaning changes with the environment in which one finds oneself, and this raises questions regarding communication consistency: *"despite perceived standardized global brand platforms, consumers develop divergent brand meanings abroad."*[31] Retaining the outer trappings of the inner brand, or the so-called **consistency rule**, had been thought to be one of the sacred principles of global marketing:

BRANDSTORMING SUCCESS: Bonnie Jean

It is possible to create a strategy wherein the celebrity does not directly endorse the brand but can serve by his or her popularity as a virtual endorsee. One such example was a strategy devised by WDA Brand Marketing in its market entry undertaking for the American brand, Bonnie Jean.

Bonnie Jean is a young girls' dress brand that has strong distribution in all of America's major department stores. Its strategy, which as of this writing is in the process of being implemented, is to tie together the positioning of the brand in the United States as one that serves the interests of modesty and appropriateness in young girls' attire and connects this back to the idea of encouraging esteem and self-respect in young girls. This combination of modesty and empowerment is an emerging Chinese mothers' dream for their daughters and seemed to fit in 2014/2015 with President Xi Jinping's China Dream of a fulfilling life and the lifting of the **one-child policy**. This policy, for many years, limited Chinese families to one child as a population control device and imposed heavy fines for failing to adhere. Failure to do so by Communist party members could result in expulsion and loss of privileges and even livelihood. The other 95 percent of the population struggled with this policy because having sons in China was culturally seen as more positive than having daughters. This often led to unwanted terminations of pregnancies when it was known that the forthcoming child was female. If she survived, and even if she was healthy, she was often put up for adoption or suffered the horror of abandonment, neither of which was likely to occur with male babies.

The lifting of the ban, and a general sense of a new respect for women, seemed good timing for the positioning strategy. As one Chinese female writer commented, a new era was opening in China in which the brand manager for Bonnie Jean thought the Bonnie Jean brand could play a part.[28]

The basis for this is in the complementary positioning of the brand and the Chinese consumer. Here is how Helen Wang, an expert on China's middle class framed this: "*The Chinese concept of femininity is very different from that of American. In China, feminine is more about 'sweet and soft' rather than 'smart and strong.'*"[29]

Contrary to Wang's too-broad generalization of America's concept of femininity, the former is precisely the positioning for young girls of the Bonnie Jean brand in the American market and why, in part, it has carved a successful niche for itself. "Sweet and soft" imaging, and dresses that capture this design direction, is reflected in the product's aesthetic sensibility and continues to be the brand's unique value proposition.

Therefore, this offered the opportunity to bring the brand persona, and the messages, to China. The challenge would be to confirm whether the linguistic perspectives of the cultural meanings of "sweet and soft" and "modesty" were a cross-cultural archetype that readily migrated between the two consumer cohorts so that they were, in effect, interchangeable.

The popularity of President Obama in China, and a stroke of luck, combined to place him

(continued on next page)

and his daughters in the center of the strategy—a front-page photo of him in *US News and World Report*, a leading U.S. magazine, with his youngest daughter in a Bonnie Jean dress (Figure 14.4)! A brand narrative was written around this serendipitous event and reproductions of the photo went into the **brand book** which outlined the marketing, entry strategy, targeted consumers, and prototypical products from the brand. The purpose of the book was to present a single unified brand view to factory owners, researchers, and distributors who might be hired. This would help ensure they

all stayed "on-brand" and could also offer their views on whether the strategy was aligned with the China market. It was quickly learned that the Obama connection was confirmed by all as a winning strategy. The team had to move quickly since President Obama's term would expire in one and a half years and with it the halo glow effect and the hoped-for associative strategy that could capitalize on it. Also this was a way to tie the halo effect into a program of educational scholarship from Bonnie Jean to young Chinese girls. This was part of meeting the China Dream of a better life for young Chinese girls, something that Helen Wang strongly advocated in the above referenced article.[30]

In conclusion, tapping into a virtual endorsement requires adhering to the following steps and project management planning:

figure 14.4
President Obama with daughter Sasha in a Bonnie Jean dress: This photo provided an opportunity to capitalize on the president's popularity in China for market entry as part of an indirect endorsement of the brand.

- Undertake consumer research in the market being entered to determine the leading popular celebrities; be sure the popularity index aligns with your target customer.
- Determine whether the favorability rating is on the ascendency or is at least stable.
- Be sure your distribution team knows how to leverage the celebrity in their presentations to retailers; travel with them to presentations with an interpreter, if needed, to confirm this.
- Confirm that the values represented by the celebrity can cross cultural borders without losing their meaning; research is needed.
- Be sure that you have the rights or that there are no encumbrances to using names and photographs, both of which are best when they are **public domain** (no ownership of IP rights that others can claim that would restrict your usage).

"Thou Shalt Not Alter" the visual, verbal, auditory and tactile brand identity across geographies.[32] Although we have discussed some ways in which luxury abides by and deviates from this injunction, this mantra tends to be less adhered to by mass brands which, as we will see later in this chapter, make adjustments to regions and cultures which at times lead to a change in the brand identity symbols such as names and logos; what does remain constant, and therefore continues to abide by the consistency rule, are the brand positioning, value offer, and operational execution.[33]

Those brands which provide solutions to aspirations of mobility such as automobiles, luxury hotels, and airlines are in a stronger position to retain as much of the IP brand identifiers as possible. The reason is that these types of brands can trade on the consumer perception that the brands are "international" in scope and retaining their national identities is part of what well-traveled clients expect.[34]

The so-called international brands, especially luxury brands, that represent the stereotypical association with a country's claim to excellence or specialization (Made in Germany for engineering, Made in Italy for fashion, etc.) *"opens up the global market since the stereotype invoked is a collective symbol breaking national bounds."*[35]

Therefore, L'Oréal and BMW, for example, stay with their name, logo, and identity (one as a French company and the other as a German engineering company) because those associations resonate globally and are part of the reason global consumers purchase the products—to purchase the brand and to enjoy the benefits of the association with the virtual symbolic experience.

Non-luxury is more sales-driven rather than image-driven and seeks anchorage in the local markets that can sustain its sales and revenue efforts. This often means purchasing local brands whose names are well known and not expending great amounts of money and energy in building awareness and consideration of its own brand. Issues of logistics, distribution, and learning the cultural patterns to properly price and position the offering often are more important than

the brand and its elements. As we saw earlier in the chapter, this was the strategy of Best Buy in purchasing Five Star in the China market and using this brand and business model in place of Best Buy, and it has been used by Walmart in India and in other foreign markets.

Integrating National and Global Marketing

Successful global brands seek a way to retain their brand promise across national borders and markets by finding a language that works in both venues. Again, the key is to tap into those universal, compelling human needs. *"The rise of a global culture does not mean that consumers share the same tastes or values . . . people in different nations participate in a shared conversation upon shared symbols. One of the key symbols in that conversation is the global brand."*[36]

Positioning may differ from country to country in light of culture and competition, but the quest is still to find the universals. For example, P&G in its purchase of Pantene Pro V shampoo thought it had a winner and positioned it as a luxury brand in France and America. The results were disappointing. Taking the brand to Taiwan changed everything. In Taiwan, shiny hair is seen as a sign of health.[37] Using the tagline "Hair so Healthy it Shines" resonated with Taiwanese values and the product was a huge success. Taking this globally, tests were run in other countries using this positioning. It was not merely a local cultural dynamic in play; shiny and clean went together in over seventy countries where the product was launched and where it continues to generate impressive results.

This provides us with a view that the process of market entry isn't simply from global to national. Countries, such as in the Taiwan example, may act as a springboard market for global distribution rather than the notion that all of the insights for market penetration come from global headquarters; they do not. For instance, Maybelline, the New York–based global cosmetic brand, found its niche in Japan when it developed a wet-look lipstick that made the mouths of

Japanese women, which tend to be small, more glamorous looking.[38] This became a fashion statement and successfully found its way into other national markets such as New York.

Integrating Global, Regional, and Local Product Strategies

Global brands often find that national cultures, in terms of cultural patterns, food, or fashion, are unique in their sense of taste or style and their offering cannot migrate to other markets with any degree of success. One example is Burberry's enormously successful "candy pink and baby blue" design direction within its Burberry Blue sub-brand collection. The latter continues to be a big hit in Japan but has not been brought to other markets. Why? The penchant of young Japanese women, especially single women, for these colors is a cultural dynamic whose roots are clearly Japanese and seem unlikely to find fertile ground and gain traction in other countries and cultures. Burberry set up a special product development team and marketing approach to serve them for not only was the unique collection doing well, but the Burberry brand has Japan as its strongest Asian market. This is one of the few examples of luxury product adaptation where the product component in the four Ps is subject to local market tastes. Having the global brand serve a niche in an extremely profitable market again shows part of the difference between luxury and non-luxury brands. Economies of scale are not at issue but **brand affinity** is. The emotional closeness that consumers feel for a brand is at issue and this strategy serves to reinforce that luxury business objective.

Regionalization also complements global brand strategies. L'Oréal in China, for example, considers China a set of regional markets because the size of the country and the differing ethnicities and climates have created different skin types and skin care needs. No less than four separate formulas of the same skin care product are available in four different regions of the country, but they all bear the L'Oréal brand and imaging. Yet, a mass consumer product company is likely

to take a different approach. P&G in Europe changes the names of its Tide, Whisper, and Clairol brands (all mega-brands in the U.S.) to Ariel, Allways, and Wella.[39] This is not undertaken just for the sake of change. P&G, which spends more on research as a percentage of revenue than any competing FMCG company (such as Nestlé), determined that the American-grounded brand names would not fly in Europe.

This phenomenon applies to product content as well as to brand names as global brands seek to adjust formulas to meet regional and local tastes. The largest fast-food chain in China, and with a presence throughout the world, is KFC (formerly Kentucky Fried Chicken), a brand within the portfolio of restaurants owned by the Yum! corporation, an American company. The selection in the Chinese stores in no way reflects the brand's offerings in the United States and, for that matter, KFC varies its menus to accommodate local and regional tastes and cultural eating habits.

Table 14.1 shows a globalization matrix. It presents the various strategies that brand managers have available to them in deciding how best to approach the variety of markets.

Finally, brand managers in charge of global brands use videos and/or brand books to keep the essence of the brand's identity consistent from market to market. Although McDonald's accommodates local tastes in food and pricing, worldwide advertising managers are instructed to maintain the image of the brand and its promise. This would include its brand persona and its personality. This directive is to ensure that these are aligned with, and represented in, local brand communications and that all ads show people in everyday life situations doing what people do, especially families having fun at McDonald's. Here the P in promotion is kept as a global constant. Images of food and drink are peripheral to the messaging, for McDonald's is not about the food. This is the ultimate type of strategy that integrates global, regional, and local messaging and maintains the objective of reflecting local styles and cultural patterns while achieving the goal of staying on-brand. McDonald's knows the business it is really in.

Table 14.1 Luxury versus Mass Globalization Strategies: A General Guide to Standardization versus Adaptation

	Luxury	Mass
Brand IP Assets	Maintain brand elements	Change if local/regional demand
Product Content	May adjust for major market	Will alter for each market as Needed

THE POWER OF NATIONAL CULTURES AND VALUES

Peter Drucker, the management guru, was quoted as saying in regard to the overarching influence of corporate cultures on strategic policy making and execution, *"Culture eats strategy for breakfast."* The implication is that the values and unwritten norms and mores that structure behavior in a company are stronger in influence than strategies in driving business outcomes. Therefore, if strategies are to be successful, they need to embrace the cultural values in a way that complements rather than confronts these frames of reference, for these structure our patterns of behavior.

The same can be said for a nation's culture. Brand managers need to familiarize themselves with history, anthropology, and the sociology of the country in which they are to do business. The immediate questions that arise are, what is culture and where can we best find it? We suggest that language is a dynamic repository of much of a nation's culture, its history, and its social values and that brand managers need to begin here.

Language as a System of Values

Culture is shared meaning through symbols called language and meaning is synonymous with values or life's priorities. All of these are ingredients in our belief systems which frame our views of reality and are presented to us, and to each other, through language.

Without language, values would get obscured in the unstructured flow of thoughts. However, with language, we are circumscribed and influenced in our behavior including our patterns of consumption in terms of what practices are both relevant and acceptable to our culture and its values. This can go so far as to define what a "family" meal is, which first requires a definition of *family*. This in turn will impact on the content and clarity of brand messaging in both headlines and taglines and often in brand names as well. As an example, the chain of fast-food Italian restaurants, Olive Garden, has as its brand promise *"When you're here, you're Family."* Allowing for the poetic license of "family" being suddenly created from a restaurant experience, the first order of business for global brand managers is to define *family* for each culture in which the brand will be marketed. For example, family structure can be nuclear (the parents and immediate children) or extended (including uncles, aunts, and grandparents) and clan- and kin-driven (clusters of people with whom you are unlikely to interact but are linked to by blood). More importantly, these are permanent institutionalized ways of living and relating—not merely descriptions, but prescriptions or value systems. Therefore, they become words laden with emotional content whose meaning, and therefore acceptance, will vary with the appropriateness of the context in which the content appears. Table 14.2 shows some of the possible variations in types of families.

Failure to include through images and/or language some reference to these relevant elements would result in a description somewhat less than that

Table 14.2 Variations in the Meaning of "Family" by Cultures: Failing to Adapt Messaging to Obvious Differences in Social Norms Challenges Both Luxury and Mass Brands

Type of Social Culture	Description of Family Elements	Example
Individualist	Parents + Children	United States
Collective	Above + Grandparents, Godparents, Aunts, Uncles	China
Communal	Above + Others in Villages	Clan/Tribal

of a family and challenge the consistency of the brand message. What becomes evident through the preceding exercise is that brand managers need to undertake research to establish cross-cultural confirmation of meaning. Focus groups and in-depth interviews are two approaches that can generate insights into these comparable meanings.

The importance of this cannot be underestimated as the marketing landscape is littered with translation errors that either derailed entry strategies or caused a reworking of the brand communication at a loss of time and revenue. The launch of the Chevrolet Nova model into the South American market is almost legendary in this regard as the car, after great success in the United States, was a dismal seller in South America. Translating Nova as "No Go" in Spanish should have been a "No" brainer, but it wasn't and finally was seen as a major source of the market entry failure. A similar shortfall temporarily derailed the repositioning of Pepsi in China when its tagline and brand promise, "*The Choice for a New Generation*," stumbled into a translation that came out as "the drink that brings your ancestors back"—not a good idea as a brand promise and certainly not for a culture that deeply honors age and the departed. Similar issues arose when the tagline was translated into German and Thai.

The Brand as a Universal Language

For many years the United Nations has toyed with, and recommended, the adoption of a global language called Esperanto; nothing has ever come of it. This would make communications and commerce flow more expeditiously as words and symbols would take on common meanings and be universally understood. Enter global brands that, in effect, have become a global language insofar as consumers worldwide have learned the meanings of the symbols and images of brands and act upon them.[40] This is probably even more pronounced with luxury brands, where symbolic messaging tends to be most consistent and more emotionally compelling.

The Role of Storytelling in Global Brand Building

Brand narratives have become more than just stories introducing websites; they are global connectors between brands and consumers. In the words of Christopher Bailey, CEO and creative director of Burberry, "*I think storytelling is important globally, but in China it stops things from being mere product and starts to give it life. Everything has a story—your clothes, buildings, videos, music. I think it's important for people to go along with this journey, otherwise it becomes a faceless product.*"[41]

Storytelling seeks to engage with the customer to gain, as Angela Ahrendts once remarked, "*mind share*" that one day may turn into "*market share*." To do so, the content and context need to be culturally anchored. As an example, the iconic Johnnie Walker alcohol spirits brand has had as its tagline and brand promise "*Keep Walking.*" The context in which this content is placed in ads and marketing material includes backdrops symbolizing forward movement and progress. This has had the effect of broadening the meaning to encourage people to follow their dreams, to keep moving forward, and to progress in their self-development. This has also been confirmed as a universal motivation and has been localized across 120 countries through over 100 quotations either from, or relevant to, the cultures by stories in each of those countries. This strategy is best served by finding relevant quotations such as Johnnie Walker uses in China from Lao Tse, the Chinese sage and philosopher, "*A journey of a thousand miles begins with a single step*"[42] and running those in the country from which they originated. Again, global brands tend to find ways to maintain their brand IP elements while changing the communication that makes it relevant to the culture without changing the brand promise or its meaning.

Much like myths as Joseph Campbell, the author of *The Power of Myth*, saw them, brand stories work when they capture truths reflecting what resides within each of us in the deepest recesses of our psyches and souls.[43] Stories mirror how we are wired as human beings. We are more prone to remember and absorb myths than mathematics as "*studies show that we are wired to remember stories more than data, facts and figures.*"[44] In addition, further research into our brain patterns shows a remarkable consistency in reaction to the same content whether it be in virtual or physical reality. "*The human brain does not distinguish reading or hearing a story and experiencing it in real life. In both cases, the same neurological regions are activated.*"[45]

This neurological dynamic must be embraced by brand managers for it impacts both brand communications and consumer decision making. By understanding how we function biologically, we can only excuse our failure to develop brand narratives and images that resonate by admitting that we do not know our customers and/or that we do not know how to create a clear, consistent, and compelling brand story.

THE ROLE OF ARCHETYPES IN GLOBAL COMMUNICATIONS

Earlier in the chapter, we suggested that global brands are operative substitutes for the absence of a global language. The symbolisms, imagery, and translated messaging combine to form a communications cluster that transcends the limitations of cultural differences that consumers bring to the market. This clustering is at its best when it is anchored by natural archetypes which give the messages an authenticity and timelessness that no artificial construct can match. Therefore, "*the primary rationale for incorporating the archetype paradigm into global brand marketing . . . is grounded in the premise that associating archetypes with product brands serves to provide symbolic meaning with which consumers can construct identities across cultural boundaries.*"[46]

Archetypes, Branding, and the Collective Unconscious

Archetypes, as discussed in Chapter 1, are generalizations about human roles and actions by which we frame and give meaning to our experiences. They are universal, preconscious images or ideas and are deeply rooted in what it means to be human. Thus, every culture has the idea of Father, Mother, Hero, Lover, and the like. Carl Gustav Jung, the Swiss psychiatrist who developed this insight, called this psychological dimension the **collective unconscious**, which suggests that archetypes exist in every culture and every human being and are present before birth and psychological consciousness.[47] By providing the insight that humans have a universal consciousness, Jung set the stage for exploring the global macro-determinants in human decision making, which we introduced in Chapter 4 and will explore in great detail in Chapter 15. It also provides us with a glimpse as to how we can be universal in our shared processes yet be distinctive in our value systems; thus, for example, in the discussion of semiotics that follows, we see the influence of cultural codes and the distinctive ways in which cultures define archetypal values and expected behavior.

The existence of archetypes helps explain the ability of brands to communicate their values across cultures and peoples. They are the symbolic language that transcends the limitations of the lettered language, and they communicate by reaching us where our emotional selves reside.

We often find this communication taking place in what is called **semiotics**, or brands, conveying their meaning through signs, symbols, and coded communications. Here are examples as to how this works and when it doesn't.

Semiotics: Brands, Symbols, and Signs

Semiotics is the study of signs and symbols and how they convey meaning. As we have seen in our discussion of the word *family*, and how languages don't always translate their original meaning accurately, symbols and their associations become of critical importance in brand management, often substituting in place of language that doesn't cross the cultural divide.

Returning for a moment to the Chinese market, semiotics becomes especially important in terms of brand naming. There are three dimensions to the process: creating a name from Chinese characters, creating it in **pinyin** (Mandarin in romanized letters), and finally having the pinyin phonetically sound like the brand name. Both brand marketing in building awareness and trademark registrations are best served when all three are registered and are achieved. If you recall from Chapter 8, the legal challenge that Hermès faces in China is the result of failing to register the Hermès brand phonetically.

For example, the Bonnie Jean brand name was registered in China in English and in Chinese characters. But managers couldn't transliterate the brand promise message of modesty and appropriate dressing into the Chinese characters, so the semiotic cues they wished to promote lost some of their meaning. The good news was that in pinyin, Bonnie Jean was spelled *Bang Ni Qun Zi*, which phonetically was very close in pronunciation to Bonnie Jean! It suggested that if TV commercials were run which ended with a voiceover it could transmit the brand name.

A different problem faced McDonald's in China. The name came out in pinyin as *Maidanglao*, close but no cigar. Especially problematic is that although the word *mai* means wheat or barley, seemingly referencing the hamburger bun, there is no culinary cultural context in China for conveying "hamburger" which would help clarify the meaning! Here is where symbolic semiotics comes to play a major role. The McDonald's arches are found everywhere in China and their red and gold colors are important symbols and positive associations with prosperity and good luck in Chinese culture. Thus, by a stroke of good fortune, this may more than make up for the word meaning issue.

A similar challenge faced Carrefour, France's largest and most successful supermarket chain. As always, and especially in China, names must be easy to remember and, to the Chinese consumer, be meaningful. *Carrefour* in French was chosen for France because it meant "crossroads," suggesting the convenience of finding a Carrefour at most important junctions in the country. This of course had no relevancy or meaning for the Chinese consumer. The name managers settled on did not phonetically sound like *Carrefour* but, perhaps more importantly, the Chinese characters meant "family, happiness, and luck," all extremely important values in China and with which the brand is now semiotically associated.

SUMMARY

The idea of a global consumer came about from the intersection of the internet, free trade agreements, and the rise of significant numbers of middle- and upper-middle-class consumers in all major markets. The marketing and transformation of international brands into global brands, plus international travel and digital communications, added to this global consumer viewpoint and the sense that the transformation and gradual erasing of the influence of national cultures as determinants of national consumption patterns was just a matter of time. This would result in standardized products and services being distributed to all markets around the world with little customization and in significant benefits from economies of scale. However, these results did not, and have not, materialized as the deeply embedded value systems of

BRANDSTORMING SUCCESS: Shanghai Tang

Shanghai Tang is a Chinese retail brand launched in Hong Kong in 1997 by David Tang, a Chinese national and entrepreneur, offering apparel and homewares with a Chinese sensibility. It began with Tang's vision to recapture the romance of Shanghai in the 1930s when it was dubbed "The Paris of the East" and to establish the brand as China's first luxury brand (Figure 14.5).

A gala opening in 1998 in New York on Madison Avenue established the glamor and elegance of the concept, but the brand identity could not get past the product as it was either too expensive or a one-time purchase for collectors of Chinese artifacts and traditionally styled apparel such as the classic long dresses with mandarin collars called *cheongsams*. It closed and reopened later after being purchased by Richemont, the Swiss luxury conglomerate, which positioned the brand as the "*Global curator of modern Chinese aesthetics.*"[48] The challenge was to make the brand truly global, to make the product truly wearable, and perhaps most importantly, to make the consumer truly international so a balanced consumer base not overly dependent on the West and the United States could be counted on to support the brand. This latter objective would prove to be a significant challenge since the brand had been directed toward Westerners and there had emerged a quiet resentment by Chinese consumers that the brand pandered to U.S. and Western consumers and a criticism that the brand had not been true to its origins in China. Therefore, the identity with a national culture provided a unique brand identity and positioning opportunity (which it always had). This made

figure 14.5
An elegant Shanghai Tang evening dress: Since its purchase by the luxury conglomerate Richemont, the brand has found the proper balance between its Chinese cultural roots and its modern fashion sensibility.

its value proposition always interesting and a source of potential strength but required a pivoting by brand management to embrace the very consumer who would be most proud and receptive to the home-grown luxury brand. This had to be achieved while continuing to honor its American clientele and building the brand image internationally as a true global brand.

(continued on next page)

BRANDSTORMING SUCCESS: Shanghai Tang

"*It is no secret that Shanghai Tang has dedicated itself in the past decade to courting the Chinese market.*"[49] Following are some of the strategic shifts that have been undertaken to reposition the brand for these geographic and consumer markets.

- Reestablishing China as the brand's geographic headquarters and the China market as central to the brand's growth along with opening the Cathay Mansion flagship store in Shanghai, the city where the brand was born. The very name captures the romance inherent in the poetic and literary reference word for China—*Cathay*—combined with the French metaphor for a luxury design house—*Mansion*—if pronounced as a French word.
- Opening over thirty stores in China in addition to the over fifty worldwide.
- Hiring an international team of designers and a creative director, a Chinese national educated in a famous London fashion school.

- Creating design contests and scholarships focused on Chinese designers.
- Capturing the nuances of Chinese history and culture in each collection while staying attuned to fashion sensibilities.
- Opening a B2C web platform in 2010 that caters to a truly international clientele.

Through these initiatives, mainland Chinese represent some 20 percent of the business with U.S. consumers representing some 18 percent. Overall, China contributes 51 percent to revenues while Westerners contribute 49 percent, thus reaching the balance brand management was after. Selling wholesale to luxury department stores in Europe and in other markets, plus launching its licensed fragrance line, has completed the implementation of the strategy. The patience and deep pockets of Richemont, the brand's corporate owner, helped smooth the way.

---

national cultures and social systems continue to retain their saliency for consumers worldwide.

This has led to the need for brand managers to pivot in these global strategies and accommodate the local cultural systems and attitudes of their consumers and align brand strategies and communications with these cultural realities without compromising the identity and DNA of their brands. When entering foreign markets, the challenge for global brands and companies is to find the balance between standardization and adaptation. Luxury brands seem to be in a stronger position to do so as their brand identities are anchored in meaningful narratives and archetypes that have been embraced by the consumer. This is a function of the distinction between mass brands/

FMCG brands, which tend to communicate features and benefits as the essence of their brand communications and product/service offers, and luxury brands, which offer more vibrant emotional experiences.

The advent of cross-border trade and communications and the global accessibility of the web have not only catapulted luxury brands to the center of consumer aspirational interest but also led to a global market in counterfeits. Some have argued that counterfeit products are not necessarily a bad thing for brands although the majority of brand managers continue to believe that counterfeiting is a negative. Although there are differences in how acceptable such copies are to different types of consumers, some national cultures have value systems which encourage this type of indulgence while others discourage it. The alignment of global and local dynamics is often referred to as glocal brand management and is, at times, supported by recruiting cultural brand ambassadors to promote the brand through the associative halo effect. These are often high-profile celebrities, and brand managers need to be watchful that the perception of their personas aligns with that of the brand and that the ambassadors continue to be popular in the markets with which they have been aligned.

It is also possible to tap into famous public figures at less cost and risk. But their time in the spotlight may be limited and their saliency for the consumer cohort targeted needs to be confirmed.

The strength of national cultures also finds its way into national languages as a challenge to global brand communications. Ideally, as the notion of a global consumer of standardized product/service offers is attractive since it offers economies of scale and efficiency in operations, the same concept attracts brand managers when they approach global brand marketing communications. One brand imaging for the world would be ideal but fails to consider the realities of how language and culture intercept and recast any global strategy. The conventional brand management wisdom that brand identity should be consistent across cultures and geographies is challenged by the aforementioned realities. Besides the errors in translation which can upend market entry campaigns because the translations of the brand message fail, culture and language play a significant role in brand naming. In China, for example, where language forms are more complex, sound, sight, and symbol all play a role in communications. Enter semiotics, or the understanding of how best to communicate through signs, symbols, and cultural cues. These work best for global brand managers when anchored by archetypes built on the neurological foundation of the collective unconscious. Then, by discerning the signs and symbols that resonate with the local targeted consumers and identifying the universal archetype at their foundations, brand managers are able to align local and global dynamics into a glocal brand communications strategy.

The case study of Shanghai Tang points to the challenges of honoring national identities and scoping out a global strategy that incorporates the strength of the uniqueness of those identities for the brand with a global outreach that gives the brand and the business global appeal and a more substantial audience for growth.

KEY TERMS

Adaptation
Brand Affinity
Brand Book
Collective Unconscious
Consistency Rule
Counterfeiting

Cultural Brand Ambassador
Free Trade Agreements
Glocal Brand Management
    Strategy
In-Depth Interviews
Net Utility

One-Child Policy
Pinyin
Public Domain
Semiotics
Standardization
Utilitarianism

CHAPTER CONVERSATIONS

- What is the significance of the rational consumer model for brand management?
- What strategies do you think work best when global brands are entering local markets? Why?
- Is brand marketing communications a challenge in all countries? Why or why not?

CHAPTER CHALLENGES

- The regional managers for a global mass market conglomerate want to use local dialects in their ad campaigns. What strategic advice would you, as global manager, give them? How would you frame your strategy to include the way a global brand becomes a global language and bridges differences in national cultural values?
- You are the global brand manager for a luxury apparel company. How would you explain the nature, and the practical applications, of the archetype concept to a group of American business investors who are thinking of investing in your business?
- You are the brand manager for an American casual sportswear company that has no unique product or service offer. You have a significant business in the United States and your CEO has asked for a China entry strategy. What would be the first steps that you would advise be taken?

ENDNOTES

1. Thomas L. Friedman, *The World Is Flat: A Brief History of the Twenty-First Century* (New York, NY: Farrar, Straus and Giroux, 2005).
2. G. Ger and R. W. Belk, "I'd Like to Buy the World a Coke: Consumptionscapes of the Less Affluent World," *Journal of Consumer Policy* 19, no. 3 (1996): 292.
3. Jeremy Bentham, *An Introduction to the Principles of Morals and Legislation* (Mineola, NY: Dover Publications, 2007).
4. Theodore Levitt, "The Globalization of Markets," *Harvard Business Review*, May 1983, https://hbr.org/1983/05/the-globalization-of-markets.
5. D. B. Holt et al., "How Global Brands Compete," *Harvard Business Review*, September 2004.
6. R. Steenkamp et al., "How Perceived Brand Globalness Creates Brand Value," *Journal of International Business Studies* 34, no. 1 (2003); see also Maria Merino and Silvia Gonzalez, "Global or Local? Consumers' Perception of Global Brands in Latin America," in *LA—Latin American Advances in Consumer Research*, Vol. 2, eds. Claudia R. Acevedo, Jose Mauro C. Hernandez, and Tina M. Lowrey (Duluth, MN : Association for Consumer Research, 2008), 16–21, and Z. Ismail et al., "Factors Affecting Consumer Preference of International Brands over Local Brands," International Conference on Social Science and Humanity (2012).

7. "Counterfeit.com," *Economist*, August 1, 2015, http://www.economist.com/news/business/21660111 -makers-expensive-bags-clothes-and-watches-are-fighting-fakery-courts-battle.

8. Colleen Jordan Orscheln, "Bad News Birkens: Counterfeit in Luxury Brands," *John Marshall Review of Intellectual Property Law* 249 (2015).

9. For an insightful analysis and research on the issue, see the work of Renée Gosline from MIT.

10. Quoted in "Renée Richardson Gosline: Fakes Can Be Good for the Luxury Industry," by Jonna Dagliden, LS:N/Global.com, March 22, 2010.

11. Nate Raymond, "Alibaba Sued in U.S. by Luxury Brands over Counterfeit Goods," *Reuters*, May 8, 2015, http://www.reuters.com/article/us-alibaba-lawsuit-fake-idUSKBN0O02E120150518.

12. G. Pendergast and L. H. Chuen, "Understanding Consumer Demand for Non-Deceptive Pirated Brands," *Journal of Marketing Practice* 20, no. 7 (2002): 405.

13. For a qualitative empirical study, see Liang Jiang and Veronica Cova, "Love for Luxury: A Preference for Counterfeits; A Qualitative Study in Counterfeit Luxury Consumption in China," *International Journal of Marketing Studies* 4, no. 6 (November 2, 2012).

14. For an empirical study on Chinese consumer patterns, see A. P Cui, T. A. Wajda, and M. F. Walsh, "Luxury Brands in Emerging Markets: A Case Study of China," *Advances in International Marketing* 25 (2015): 287–305.

15. K. Wilcox et al., "Why Do Consumers Buy Counterfeit Luxury Brands?," *Journal of Marketing Research* 46, no. 2 (April 2009): 247–259.

16. See Geoffdasilva, "Oreos in China: Example of Product Adaptation Strategy in Global Marketing," YouTube, 2013.

17. Agata Seidel, "In India, Luxury Brands Need Localized Strategies," *Business of Fashion* (2014).

18. See "Best Buy Shuts China Stores to Expand Five Star Retail Brand," *Bloomberg News*, February 22, 2011, www.bloomberg.com/news/articles.

19. Doug Yound, "Best Buy Bows from China with Five Star Sale," *Seeking Alpha*, December 5, 2014, http://seekingalpha.co/article2734725.

20. Ibid.

21. Warren J. Keegan and Mark C. Green, *Global Marketing*, 7th ed. (Upper Saddle River, NJ: Prentice Hall, 2013).

22. Ibid.

23. "Fighting for the Next Billion Shoppers," *Economist*, June 30, 2012, http://www.economist.com/node /21557815.

24. Anita Chang Beattie, "China's Favorite Foreign Celebs: From Audrey Hepburn to Nicolas Cage," *Ad Age*, April 2, 2013, http://adage.com/article/global-news/favorite-celebrities-china-kobe-nicolas-cage/240652/.

25. Ibid.

26. Jing Daily, "Fan Bingbing Tops Forbes' Chinese Star Power List," *The Business of Luxury and Culture in China*, May 6, 2014, http://jingdaily.com/fan-bingbing-tops-forbes-chinese-star-power-list/.

27. Ibid.

28. Helen H. Wang, "Why Barbie Stumbled in China and How She Could Re-invent Herself," *Forbes*, October 24, 2012, http://www.forbes.com/sites/helenwang/2012/10/24/why-barbie-stumbled-in -china-and-how-she-could-re-invent-herself/.

29. Ibid.

30. Ibid.

31. A. Bengstsson et al., "How Global Brands Travel with Consumers: An Examination of the Relationship Between Brand Consistency and Meaning Across National Boundaries," *International Marketing Research* 27, no. 5: 519–540.

32. See John Roberts and Julien Cayla, "Global Branding," in *The SAGE Handbook of International Marketing* (Thousand Oaks, CA: Sage Publications, 2008), 350.

33. David Reibstein, "House of Brands vs. Branded House," *Global Agenda* 3 (January 2005): 175–177.

34. Jean-Noel Kapferer, *The New Strategic Brand Management: Advanced Insights and Strategic Thinking*, 5th ed. (London, UK: Kogan Page, 2012).

35. Ibid.

36. D. B. Holt et al., "How Global Brands Compete," *Harvard Business Review*, September 2004, 16.

37. David Aaker and Erich Joachimsthaler, "The Lure of Global Branding," *Harvard Business Review*, December 1999, https://hbr.org/1999/11/the-lure-of-global-branding.

38. Ibid.

39. Ibid.

40. D. B. Holt et al., "How Global Brands Compete."

41. Divia Harilela, "Storytelling Key to Burberry's China Strategy, Says Christopher Bailey," *Business of Fashion*, April 26, 2014, http://www.businessoffashion.com/articles/global-currents/storytelling-key -burberrys-china-strategy.

42. Chris Bolman, "How Top Brands Localize Global Marketing Campaigns," *Percolate* (blog), October 27, 2014, https://blog.percolate.com/2014/10/how-top-brands-localize-global-marketing-campaigns/.

43. Joseph Campbell, *The Power of Myth* (New York, NY: Anchor Books, 2000).

44. Jennifer Aaker, "Harnessing the Power of Stories," *Lean In*, 2012, http://leanin.org/education/harnessing -the-power-of-stories/.

45. Brianne Carlon Rush, "Science of Storytelling: Why and How to Use It in Your Marketing," *The Guardian*, August 28, 2014, http://www.theguardian.com/media-network/media-network-blog/2014/aug/28 /science-storytelling-digital-marketing.

46. Shu-Pei Tsai, "Investigating Archetype-Icon Transformation in Brand Marketing," *Journal of Marketing Intelligence and Planning* 24, no. 6 (2006): 648.

47. C. G. Jung, *The Archetypes and the Collective Unconscious: Collected Works of C. G. Jung*, Vol. 9, Part 1, translated by R. F. C. Hull (Princeton, NJ: Princeton University Press, 1980).

48. Divia Harilela, "Shaping Shanghai Tang," *Business of Fashion*, September 1, 2013, http://www.business offashion.com/articles/people/shanghai-tang-raphael-le-masne-de-chermont.

49. Ibid.

Insights and Trends in Brand Management Research

AFTER COMPLETING THIS CHAPTER,

YOU WILL BE ABLE TO:

- Discuss the links between neuropsychology, behavioral economics, cultural anthropology, and consumer decision making.

- Explain the connection between archetypes, Systems I and II, and cultural codes.

- Evaluate the contributions to brand management by research findings.

KEY SYSTEMS IN CONSUMER DECISION MAKING

Scholars such as Bernd Schmitt from Columbia, Kevin Lane Keller from Dartmouth, and others have called for more interdisciplinary research in understanding consumer-based brand equity and consumer behavior.[1] One expression of this interdisciplinary perspective can be found in Ming Hsu's insightful review, *Neural Basis of Brand Equity*,[2] which presents an integrative approach to *"how insights from cognitive and behavioral neurosciences are helping to organize and interpret the relationship between consumers and brands."*[3] This chapter presents some of the possible avenues for further exploration of this relationship in terms of neuropsychology, behavioral economics, and cultural values and how they relate to more comprehensive brand management objectives.

As introduced in Chapter 4, research in neuropsychology, behavioral economics, and cultural anthropology can be viewed as attempts to forge a deeper understanding of the foundations of human decision making and thereby lay a more scientific foundation for brand management.

Linking the Three Systems to Consumer Decision Making

All of these systems of thought, to some degree, tap into biology. Neuropsychology combines the fields of biology and behavioral economics. Behavioral economics joins psychology and biology, while biology has also found its way into at least one cultural anthropologist's approach as well—Clotaire Rapaille's **cultural codes**. These cultural codes study the impact of national value systems, all of which to some degree differ, on our emotions, the symbolic modes of communicating those values called "cultural imprints," and the role of our neural systems in providing receptacles for storing these "cultural imprints."

Taken together these three systems of thought provide us with a common perspective that seeks to understand how our biology influences our decisions.[4] *"It seeks to comprehend how the neural circuits in the brain allow us to perceive the world around us . . ."*[5] from perception to memory to recall to the role that emotions and culture play in our thinking processes. This includes the process by which brand loyalty is developed. As such, it enters into the realm of consumer behavior and brand management.

Neuropsychology

One of neuropsychology's interests is how this decision-making process interfaces with brand marketing and communications, especially the process by which purchase preferences (consumer decision making) are made in response to marketing stimuli.[6] For example, the three systems of thought also allow us to explore later in this chapter consideration sets, or how we process marketing stimuli and decide which brands to "store" in our neural systems for future purchase consideration (Figure 15.1). Questions such as the above, that could not be readily answered, now have a basis in the science of the mind that offers the possibility of greater insights into how we function. For example, *"insight into the principles of memory storage and retrieval it has established so far can help us identify laws in branding."*[7]

Our approach in this chapter is to explore the implications for brand management of a selected group of studies from the three aforementioned systems of thought. We include and integrate into our analysis the understanding that the discipline of neurobiology complements classic and current psychological understanding and the anthropology of cultural values which taken together are the macro-determinants of consumer decision making. A graphic model representing this integration is shown in Figure 15.2.

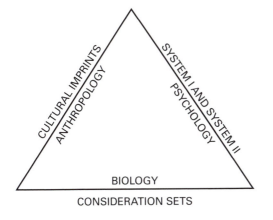

CONSIDERATION SETS

figure 15.1
Key systems in consumer decision making:
Understanding the relationship between these three decision-making approaches opens new possibilities for understanding and managing brands.

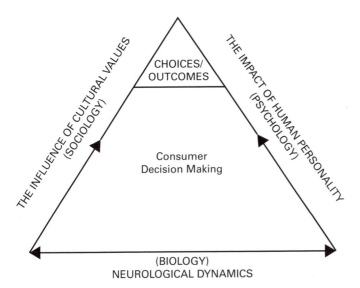

figure 15.2
Macro-determinants in consumer decision making: On a broader platform, we can also look at these approaches as systems of thought with broader cultural and societal sources and impacts.

Behavioral Economics

Much of the escalation of the discipline of Behavioral Economics to a position of central importance in behavioral psychology is a result of the work of Daniel Kahneman and Amos Tversky. In less than a decade, Kahneman's groundbreaking work, *"Thinking Fast and Slow,"* has become a classic and the go-to work for research findings that provide clinical studies and empirical findings detailing the neuropsychological basis for decision making.[8] As a Nobel Prize–winning psychologist, Kahneman has been interested

in understanding how economic stimuli and offerings are processed by human beings and how our models of understanding (e.g., "The Rational Man") give way to more complex and emotionally driven scenarios.[9] His landmark framework, System I and System II thinking (Figure 15.3), is the outcome and will serve to explain much of what we discuss in the chapter.[10]

System I thinking can be discerned when we behave seemingly without needing to reflect before taking action. Something as simple as deciding, as the light turns red, whether to cross the street is a

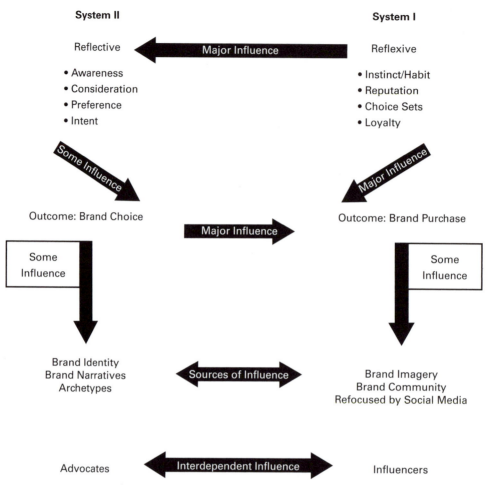

figure 15.3
How we make brand choices: The overwhelming importance of nonreflective thought processes is underscored by this understanding of decision making.

classic example of System I thinking in operation. There is no paced pattern of weighing alternatives and degrees of risk/reward and then reaching a conclusion that results in action. Here is the description in Kahneman's words: "*The operations of System I are fast, effortless, associative, and often emotionally charged; they are also governed by habits, so they are difficult either to modify or control.*"[11] The immediate concept

that comes to mind would be "instinct" recast by Kahneman as the concept of Heuristics as discussed in Chapter 2. Two keywords in the description that we will revisit are "associative" and "emotion" as these play back into our discussion in prior chapters of the relationship between these concepts and the triggers that brands bring to the decision-making process to influence consumer behavior.

System II thinking, Kahneman tells us, is conscious, filled with effort, deliberate, and analytical. This is not to say that the Systems operate in two separate spheres of reality; they interplay. For example, when we make a System I decision which requires a tactical or operational mode of implementation, a Systems II deliberation as to how best to do so kicks in. Nonetheless, the greater majority of our decisions are driven wholly, or in part, by System I thinking. The best indicator as to which system is operating is the difference in the degree of effort or effortlessness.[12]

Although powerful in its simplicity, Kahneman's model has been criticized as much too simple; the brain is more complex and engages in activities beyond instinct and reasoning, such as empathy, for example. Nonetheless, it provides us with a strong operative framework for understanding the limits of utilitarian content in marketing communications and, with other thought systems discussed in this chapter, offers us one part of what could be seen as a powerful, holistic, fresh approach to understanding consumer decision making.

A key question that Kahneman raises is, "What brings thoughts to mind?" The immediate answer for the brand manager is the power of brand associations stored in our long-term memory bank.[13] From this perspective, we can argue that the role of brand managers is to develop those pieces of brand information filled with meanings that are salient because they are emotionally laden in part through images and relevant to the consumer receiving them. These "networks of associations" with the brand are "*interconnected by neural links of varying strengths.*"[14]

As an example of this concept in action, let's return to the Coke and Pepsi taste test comparison discussed in Chapter 7. Now, let's look at it from a neurologically based perspective (Figure 15.4).

If you recall, the participants in the taste tests were not informed as to which brands they were consuming. When asked for their preference, the groups tended to find the drinks tastes of equal merit, implying that there was an equal propensity to purchase. When informed of the brands that they had been taste testing and asked their preference, some three-quarters said they preferred Coke.

This taste test was rerun in 2003 by neuroscientists S. McClure and Read Montague who brought functional **MRI imaging** (photographic images of areas

figure 15.4
Coke versus Pepsi: The taste test competition was more about preconceptions already stored in our memory than about taste per se.

of the human brain that, when under external stimuli such as marketing messages, display their suggested influence on different facets of human behavior) into the clinical study.[15] The results confirmed the original insight but added neurological confirmation to the outcome. After the initial taste test, participants were told they were drinking Coke and were retested. Seventy-five percent changed their assessment as to which they preferred and functional MRI imaging recorded neural activity in a System I area. The neural activity was in a section of the brain where emotions and affect drive behavior (in the prefrontal cortex) which became highly active on the imaging screen.[16]

The study suggests that different brain responses were in play and that the second opinion was driven by information stored in the participants' long-term memory triggered by reference to the brand. When a decision had to be made, the questions asked evoked a response at the moment of decision making. This further suggests that one of the major objectives of brand management is to determine the triggers of an instinctive (System I) brand loyalty commitment leading to a consistent brand preference.

What is apparent from these results is that the brand associations had been emotionally stored in the neural storage system, *"and that functional preferences (such as taste) can be overridden by brand preferences retrieved by long term memory at the moment of choice."*[17] The operative question which emerges from this is, what creates this kind of preference? Or again, in Kahneman's words, what brings thoughts to mind?

Cultural Anthropology

The preceding question is difficult to answer, and the determination of neural activity does not erase the fact that an individual's values and the degree of personal commitment are also influenced by cultural upbringing and how this is processed by individual personalities. We raise this point at this juncture to caution against any research finding that suggests a single variable and/or a deterministic explanation of human behavior—that is, one that removes differences in cultural upbringing and personalities as

contributing to consumer decision making. As we proceed in the chapter, the deep-seated influence of cultures will become even more evident and take its place next to the first two systems that we have just discussed.

The Emotional Basis of Choice

Antonio Damasio, the world-famous neuroscientist, has been quoted as saying, *"we are not thinking machines that feel, we are feeling machines that think."* This returns us to System I and to the dynamics of emotional choice in brand preferences. In determining the dynamics that affect choice, we first need to explore what is known as the **consideration set model**. This is based on the principle that in decision making and brand choice, consumers do not choose from all available brands of which they are aware, but from a selective set which are stored in the long-term memory bank and which are called into play when evocative stimuli trigger their **neural chemistry**. In addition, we will need to distinguish between brands that are already in our neural system and those that try to enter it for the first time (a distinction which we will examine later in the chapter) as the latter follow a different entry path and call for a different brand management strategy.

Part of the dynamic at work by the neural system is limiting both entrance into our neural systems and having a plethora of brand choices at decision-making time. Not every brand can enter, and primary brand status in the consideration set is a function of a survival mechanism which enables the avoidance of systems overload. It has been estimated that there are thousands of brands and tens of thousands of brand messages that seek permission to enter our mind-set. The sheer necessity to avoid systems overload keeps most brands at bay. This factor points us back to the classic concept of top-of-mind, or the ready recall of a brand when the category is presented, as one of the objectives that brand managers want to optimize. We also are aware that the process by which all of these functions are occurring is largely taking place in our subconscious (System I) and although System II may be called upon, especially when the purchase is a more complex one such as a luxury purchase, we nonetheless make sound decisions. That is, the decision is emotional and those brands that are called into the consideration set have been emotionally prequalified. Thus, the traditional recall methods and measures of awareness fit nicely into this neurological framework, for spontaneous awareness correlates positively with emotional commitment. *"The brands that come to mind spontaneously, also happen to be our favorite brands."*[18]

This initiation into the neural brand set is preceded by a subconscious saliency or relevancy assessment; that is, does the brand serve my most important values and things of personal importance to me? Here again is where the influence of cultural values and personal preference play both a primary and a supporting role. From marketing messaging that we experience, **choice cues,** those visual signs, symbols, images, and auditory and olfactory stimuli that represent the brand promise to the consumer and which drive action, come into play. These combine to generate the awareness and, if frequent, compelling, and emotionally charged, gain entrance into our memory banks.

Choice Cues and Emotional Communications

The choice cues that are emotionally based have been shown to have measurably better business outcomes than those that are more rationally written and staged. An omnibus study of eighteen high-profile UK brands by the prestigious and independent International Practitioners Association sought to measure the emotional content of brand ads and correlate them with concrete and traditional business outcomes that are fundamental to a company's longevity and success.[19] These outcomes included the following:

- Increase in market share
- Reduction in price sensitivity
- Savings in customer acquisition
- Increase in profits
- Increase in degree of loyalty

Ads were pretested by the traditional ad metrics including **degree of persuasion** (a measure of how the ad content and image were persuasive as to their purpose), **brand alignment** (how the ad content aligned with the brand's values), and **key message confirmation** (how well the primary message of the ad registered with the ad readers). The metrics were rational recall and remember measures, or fundamentally aligned with System II thinking. The results of the ads that had these rational (System II) contents correlated less positively with business outcomes than did those ads which were clearly emotional in content and context.

A similar result occurred in a famous ad developed for Cadbury (Figure 15.5). Pretested for validity and alignment with company objectives by Millward Brown, the internationally established brand management and research agency, the ads did poorly on brand awareness and brand appeal metrics for the female audience that was being targeted. Similar pretests were run for men and the results suggested only an average performance score for the male cohort that was being targeted. Although Millward Brown indicated the outcomes on other variables were stronger, these scores often would be sufficiently low to lead to a reworking of the ad content or a rethinking of the entire campaign.[20] The metrics cited are **key performance indicators**, critical benchmarks by which ad success is measured. That is, without a positive confirmation that the ad was likely to deliver on these metrics, the ad would be unlikely to result in reaching its business objectives (which again, could be any or all of the five preceding bulleted factors). The ad was run as tested and the results far exceeded expectations. The ad content was a breakthrough concept for it was entirely off-center for the usually staid UK Cadbury brand. It featured a gorilla playing drums in a band and was truly funny. The ad ran and the business outcomes confirmed that an emotional connection had been made with the targeted core consumer cohort. Post-testing showed very positive brand perception indicators, followed by millions of views on YouTube, a sales increase over the norm and the sales

figure 15.5
The Cadbury gorilla: Pretesting suggesting that the ad, given its nontraditional theme and imagery for a classic brand, would fail proved to be incorrect.

projections for the period being measured, and an overall ROI three times the average in the product category. Again, using System I metrics and content, the ad scored a stronger performance assessment by both qualitative and quantitative measures.

Relevancy therefore is not merely what is important to the individual but what is emotionally charged as well. This could include funny, sensual, patriotic, and other such emotional content. Studies also confirm that emotionally experienced phenomena are better remembered than irrelevant or neutral events. Finally, the evidence also suggests that these types of emotional experiences trigger dopamine in the cells and neural systems which provide a feeling of pleasure.

One argument which supports the consistent prominence of luxury brands is that they are a source of high pleasure so that not only is the possession of them stimulating to the neural system but the thought and anticipation of the experience of having such possessions triggers the exact same cellular response.[21] As pointed out in Chapter 14, the human brain makes no distinction between actual and virtual realities and our dreams are a form of virtual reality. Powerful brands create reward signals which are welcomed into the neural system if they are properly framed, managed, and align with our dreams.

Managing Choice Cues

Relevance involves the process of organizing brands into categories and subcategories.[22] It is a distinctively human activity found in every culture and society. We seek to organize related data or impressions into generalizations whereby, by condensing the similarities, we make the information easier to process and retain. Humans also seek to find a prototype or a representation that characterizes the category. For example, if the category in question is luxury hotels, the prototype might be the Ritz-Carlton. Besides categories, we also organize information such as the above into subcategories. Using the luxury hotel example, a boutique luxury subcategory may be established, such as the Ritz-Carlton Boutique Hotels, which becomes a consumer reference point when personal relevancy is at hand (i.e., the consumer is formulating a choice decision regarding a small or boutique luxury hotel). If there is no leading example which can serve as a prototype, the ideal category as understood by the consumer may be conjured and an assessment made as to whether the brand choices fit the category. This is determined by whether the brand has the appropriate attributes.

BEHAVIORAL ECONOMICS

The importance of these psychological dynamics is such that it has become a central strategic frame for positioning by relevancy. Developing the right choice cues that will trigger recollection of the brand as either the leader in the category, or at least one of the leaders, is key to being in the final consideration set when decisions are made as to which brand to choose. This is, in part, due to the human tendency to want to simplify and then hold constant the perception of the category to which a brand belongs. Once established, the identification of a brand with a category is very difficult to change. Research studies, for example, have shown that reversing the attributes of products often is not enough to change the consumer's mental association, if the initial perception is that the brand belongs in an earlier associated category.

Brand Attributes as Choice Drivers

The importance of brand attributes associated with a brand is such that this is required for activation of the brand. Cues from the marketing environment including those that are culturally relevant, if well developed and delivered, will help to trigger the associative memory of the brand.

This process is even more attribute driven than brand name driven when dealing with higher stakes purchases (such as a vacation home in a foreign country). Here is where System II analysis plays a key role in the decision-making process. Assessments of government regulations, tax laws, politics, and history may all be called in to aid in the determination of which country is best suited for the purchase. In this example, countries serve as brand names and enter the process after the associative attributes are identified

and ranked as important. Then the search for other brands (countries) and the consideration set process follows the System I decision-making path.

The implications for brand management become evident when you consider that, although the two decision paths follow later in the process the same type of path, the cues that are sent to the consumer will differ in content and context. For example, the marketing communications for purchasing the home may focus on important attributes such as the enjoyment of a garden or pool or privacy that a home can offer. Photos providing context may be added to this so that the imagery reinforces the text. Where the purchase is less reflective and more reflexive, such as with the purchase of a cereal or candy bar, the brand plays a more commanding role in the preference outcome. In either case, there is a screening process where trade-offs often are made. The time when trade-off does not occur is when the consumer is seeking a particular attribute and refuses to compensate or trade-off if that attribute is not present. For example, a lease on a luxury car may be sought but given the winter driving conditions under which it must operate, it must have all-wheel drive. Therefore, even if the overage on the mileage is reduced to make the lease more palatable, this situation is referred to as a "non-compensatory decision" because no trade-off is possible for this brand to enter into the consideration set. In the final analysis, the test of relevancy still pertains. The more complex the purchasing situation, the more the brand managers need to sort out the essential determinants of value. Thus, even in a new product category or sub-category, *"The challenge for the brand manager . . . is to position around one or more clearly defined dimensions with a bar set as unambiguously as possible."*[23]

Heuristics, System I, and Consideration Sets

It is precisely in matters such as the preceding commodity purchase of candy that heuristics come into play as System I shortcuts to decision making. Heuristics are models, or shortcuts, that we have in our memory as to how past events played out in the decision making. However, the reality is that consumers are not drawing on their experience but on the memories that they have retained and archived about that experience.[24] Here again is where the cues aligned with associative attributes become important for brand managers. What is retained and then confirmed by associative choice cues can drive the decision outcome. Asking customers an unaided recall question as to which brands they believe can deliver on the attributes they have embraced can help remove those brands from the consideration set that do not make the cut. Here is where the brands that display a high degree of saliency are confirmed as having the right to remain in the consideration set. Those brands that cannot be recalled without being aided are unlikely to be candidates in the decision outcome.[25]

Framing, Anchoring, and Narratives

To be effective, brand managers need to factor into the associative attributes that can drive brand choice. They need marketing communications that reflect and embrace framing, anchoring, and narratives.

Framing (affecting the outcome of a decision by how information is presented), **anchoring** (judging the quantitative value of something by reference to a number occupying the same time and space as the object or situation being assessed), and **narratives** (stories that afford us a sense of control by linking events and painting pictures of cause and effect that seldom mirror the reality) are placed together here as they are the major heuristics that impact consumer perceptions. Therefore, they should be fully understood and embraced by brand managers as they affect the process by which consumers make decisions.

Framing can take the form of how a price is presented or how attributes are presented to consumers in marketing communications. There is abundant research which confirms this and serves to further the System I dominance over most consumer decisions.

Participants in surveys, when asked to choose between two hamburgers, one presented as being 90 percent fat free and the other as having 10 percent fat, consistently chose the former over the latter although the utility value of both offerings is exactly the same. The "frame" creates the perception of value rather than any objective measure. What may be operating here is our society's abhorrence toward any mention of the word *fat* unless it is qualified (for example, with the word *free*). Failed attempts to convince people that some degree of fat is needed for a healthy diet also are probably in play here. Framing, therefore, must also take into consideration the cultural and sociological influences that currently command attention in the society in which the category is being presented. This includes social media communities which have been found to exert powerful influences on members as they serve as a source of validation for choices and confirmation that the individual is accepted by the community. One ramification of this community blessing is that the recipient feels legitimized in sharing, blogging, and otherwise broadcasting the brand, and the decision to purchase, to others.[26]

In another study, wine drinkers were offered a taste of a wine from a North Dakota winery named Noah Winery; an identical glass of the same wine was offered as a California wine. Not only was the latter voted as tasting better but the participants who said so also indicated that their food tasted better and they spent more time after dinner at the restaurant table. Equally important, when the participants were asked if their behavior was any different from experiment one to experiment two, they answered it was not. As reported by Aaker, "*None believed the wine label influenced them in any way.*"[27]

These examples add the dimension of perception to both the System I and System II processes and suggest that frames can impact feelings and emotional assessments, adding to or subtracting from the reality of the situation. Here, we may also be witnessing the pressure to conform from one's peer group or the need to believe that we are above such a System I effect.

Another heuristic that needs to be understood is anchoring. Here, the implications can be quite insidious or relatively harmless. In an experiment with a group of sentencing judges, the former may be the case. Each was asked to roll dice (which were fixed at numbers nine for one group and three for another) and record the number. Shortly after, each group was then asked to render a jail time sentence to a convicted defendant wherein the judges had some statutory latitude as to the extent of the sentence. Those who rolled a three tended to give lower sentences closer to this number while those who rolled a nine tended to give longer sentences closer to the higher number, both for the same offense.

In a less insidious example, another research study placing a higher priced product with an upscale companion product that hadn't been selling resulted in the latter product experiencing a sales increase. This anchoring heuristic, in this case the anchoring heuristic determining value, only became apparent when there was a comparison against which to benchmark it. The heuristic altered the perception of value of the new upscale product which, if it stood alone, would have seemed too expensive.

Finally, the narratives. They go so far as to include recasting our story after we have changed our minds to reset both the public perception and the self-image that we labored to create so that it now aligns with this new understanding. From his research studies, Kahneman concludes that *"most people after they change their minds, reconstruct their past opinion."*[28]

What is the neuropsychological basis for the impulse toward creating narratives? We are wired to make sense of our surroundings, and storytelling gives us an opportunity to cast that net. It is also driven by the archetypal dimensions of our inner beings that long for confirmation and alignment with the world around us. Storytelling, like Greek mythology, is all outer stories of inner realities. Brand managers need to be in touch with how these are framed and anchored and how the archetypes can bring a broader purpose to our Systems thinking.

Neural Branding through Storytelling

The way in which our neurological system processes stories places storytelling at the center of the neuropsychology of branding. Studies of brain waves, and the firing of synapses when under frequent and repetitive external stimuli, show a remarkable excitability and strengthening in signaling when transmitting emotional and relevant stimuli. *"The degree to which brand information is of personal relevance to us strongly influences the degree to which this information is stored in long-term memory and the ease with which it can be retrieved from it."*[29]

Because we are storytellers and construct stories of our experiences and then selectively place them into memory, the brand story we embrace (or one that we construct) can become vividly real and laden with emotional content and vibrant imaging context. This increases the neural receptivity and recall of the brand when the appropriate brand choice cues are presented to us.

An example of a brand story comes from the voice-over for Ralph Lauren's 2014 ad campaign during PBS's airing of *Downton Abbey*: outside an English manor house, a woman, elegantly dressed in an evening gown, descends a curved stone staircase toward an awaiting limousine: *"I create a world beyond fashion. I want to conjure a feeling of romance and vintage glamour. This is how fashion becomes timeless and tradition becomes forever."*

Both content and context unite to create the emotional feelings of timeless elegance and a certain accessible and relevant aristocratic lifestyle. For the Ralph Lauren brand, these are essential values and, when called into play to affect a brand choice decision, become choice cues which stimulate the memory cells to place the brand into the consideration set. When the marketing messages continue with "repeated specificity," they increase the probability of winning the battle of what has been called **cortical representation,** or those brands that, because they are most salient among competing brands stored in memory, win the battle to be called out of memory and are most influential in affecting consumer choices.[30] The story being told here also works because it is anchored by the Ruler archetype. *"The Ruler archetype is not just about wealth or power. Rulers are about being models for* *ideal behavior in the society. Thus propriety and taste are of the utmost importance.*"[31]

Ralph himself is known to ask at photo shoots, "*What is the narrative that we want to tell?*" And the answer that the Ruler archetype guides us to recite is, How can we learn the social graces of "Old Money" without having been born into it?[32] That is the business Ralph Lauren is really in!

Archetypes as Brand Narratives

Stories make us human. Great stories make it possible for us to feel that we can do great things. This power can be seen in certain transformative archetypal stories that changed the way consumers viewed certain brands and product categories.

The archetypal stories must transform the category but can do so only if they re-create the perception of the brand and challenge the dominance of the category by the market leaders who occupy it. This requires that the associative elements that link the brand to the category be reset in a way that is felt to be consistent with the brand's relevance, consistency, and emotional richness of the choice cues. Finally, they are more likely to support a change in consumer perceptions of the brand/category relationship when the archetype being used to affect the transformation is deeply rooted in the legitimate and defining values of the culture. Therefore, a change in one factor is not enough—a holistic strategy is needed for success.

Two archetypal stories that were so powerful, in part because they were rooted in timeless, cross-cultural aspirations and whose foundations are in our neural systems, are those of Nike and Apple. Both brands came to be associated by consumers with the category and subcategories which they later came to dominate.

Again, as we have discussed, the categories and subcategories are what brand managers need to affect for they are the settings in which the brand will be seen as appropriately placed (or not) by consumers. Changing a category reference point is extremely difficult because this is how human beings organize the world around them and then, through habit, close the category to further definitions or brand entry.

When Nike began its *Just Do It* campaign in the 1980s, sneakers were a relatively unglamorous commodity. The campaign went against the convention that a sneaker could be something more than a good running shoe. That is, it could be a symbol of every man's and every woman's dream of reaching higher in his or her physical and athletic accomplishments. Nike then extended the reconstruction of the subcategory by designing sneakers that were sport specific and aligning them with equally iconic athletes. From here, the sneaker entered the realm of footwear and fashion, another subcategory breakthrough. This is the overall business that Nike wanted to be in, and it asked the everyday person to join it.

As discussed in earlier chapters, a similar situation pertained to Apple in its 1986 breakthrough that directly challenged IBM and its dominance in the computer culture and the category. The idea that every man and every woman could control his or her own destiny by having his or her own personal computer flew in the face of the dominance of the category that was characterized by large, stand-alone mainframe machines through which IBM defined the category. Apple brought a new sensibility to the category with the Apple personal laptop and then with the subcategory as well with the i series of lifestyle, elegantly designed electronic components that enhanced modern living. Both these brands became iconic by first being the very opposite, by being irreverent. They tapped into the Rebel archetype that is deeply ingrained in our cultural psyches from our historical origins as revolutionaries against authority to our ongoing political values of free speech and the constitutional protection of minorities and outliers. Both brands continue to dominate the categories and subcategories in which they do business, in part because they reinvented the categories and then maintained best practices so they could continue to dominate the categories and the subcategories. Both brands are innovation cultures. If one looks below

BRANDSTORMING SUCCESS: Archetypes and Ice Cream

The objective of all good market research is to determine not merely what consumers like but why they like it and what triggers their purchase decision. One such undertaking was a research study prompted by the pending launch of a frozen dairy product much like ice cream. The research sought to determine what made ice cream different from other grocery snacks, what are the psychological drivers behind the purchase, and how would this provide insights for a brand identity and image campaign that would be salient and resonate with the targeted cohort.[35] The platform for the research was focus groups, a survey technique for deeper explorations of targeted consumers' feelings regarding products and brands. The various snacks were broken up by how consumers generally viewed their relationships. Crackers and cookies might go together, nuts and granola bars, pretzels and chips, and ice cream–related snacks such as ice cream, sherbet, and the like. Through the questioning by the focus group leader, the ice cream "stash" or the "ideal" of ice cream began to take on a specific identity. Phrases such as "*cool and creamy*" and "*satisfies a craving*" began to emerge and to differentiate the category from the other snack foods. Words like *indulgent*, *satisfying*, even *luxurious*, emerged, further illuminating the emotional response that the category engendered. The focus group process then turned to the probing of the group's collective unconscious. If you recall, this is the subconscious reservoir in Jungian psychology that harbors the universal archetypes that characterize our longings and create the

basis for many of our expectations in human relations. A deck of archetype cards was presented and the focus group participants were asked to associate the card images (Mother, Mystic, Rebel, Caretaker, and others) with the various clusters of grocery products. The new ice cream product was introduced and archetype cards were drawn which the participants placed with the new product. Similarly, cards were placed next to the ideal. The respondents' choices of the archetype cards for the two ice cream products were very much the same with Mystic, Lover, and Healer cards coming up as descriptors. The other product categories aligned with very different archetypes (such as Companion) and failed to bring the deeper emotional content that ice cream generated, which was confirmed by the cards. "*Consistently . . . women described the power of ice cream to comfort, restore and heal them, from everyday challenges. . ..*"[36] Tapping in to the collective unconscious brought out emotional values that did not appear from ordinary exchanges with the focus group leader. The idea of ice cream being the ultimate comforting food, with a kind of mystical power to please, led to the campaign theme for the new product: "*The mystical power of ice cream.*" It also gave the client a sense that it had tapped into something that gave greater veracity and permanency to its marketing campaign because the campaign was based upon enduring emotions and not upon the superficial features of the ice cream itself. Ice cream, when properly positioned and imaged, suddenly took on a relevancy all its own.

the surface of business cultures dedicated to innovation, you will find residing there the archetype of the Rebel, for what is innovation but constant rebellion against the status quo?

Accompanying these category dominations were narratives regarding the brand. These were accomplished with items such as interviews with Phil Knight and Steve Jobs, web and traditional marketing, and the transformation of the retail experience into an experiential brand narrative redefining the category as to what a retail environment should feel like.

The Brand Ideal as an Archetype

We have seen in this chapter, and others, that deeply held values generate positive neural responses through System I, "Fast Thinking." This transfers into associative elements linking positive sentiments and feelings to brands and their archetypes that consumers identify as aligned with the values and the things people care about.

The concept of the Brand Ideal fits readily into this perspective. Brands that reach higher in terms of social responsibility have been studied to ascertain the degree of loyalty and profitability that they are able to generate and sustain.[33] Jim Stengel, the former chief marketing officer of P&G whom we visited in earlier chapters, has been a leading advocate of the idea that "doing good and doing well" are not in conflict. In fact, he, in conjunction with Millward Brown, has taken it a step farther. In a study of fifty companies, Stengel and Millward Brown's neuroscience division tested consumers' associative responses to fifty brands and people's personal ideals such as aiding the environment, being positive, and living a life that includes giving back to the community. The testing method aligned with System I reflexive thinking, which suggests that the brands already occupied space in the respondents' neural systems and the research cues triggered the associated brand/ideal connections.

The fifty brands that grew the fastest from 2000 to 2010 correlated highly with these aforementioned types of ideals and with solid business achievements, growing on average three times faster than other brands in their competitive space. The testing did not use functional MRI imaging but the feel-good dimension that resulted from the associative cues led researchers to suggest the impact again of dopamine and the feel-good feelings that high ideals stimulate in our neural systems. "*One of the important insights that came from this . . . is proof that associations with ideals have a strong relationship with consumer preference, consideration, and choice.*"[34] In addition, in reviewing the brands with which each ideal could be associated, there are clear archetypal identities which played out in their marketing communications and brand imaging.

KEY DYNAMICS IN CONSUMER DECISIONS

Successful brands have the most influence over consumer choice when they display relevance, **coherence** (the need for brands to be both specific in the brand message and more frequent, but spaced over time, and across as many touch points), and a **richness** (which refers to how active the neural connectors are in generating impulses in the synapses in the brain) in content and context. These constitute the basis of the three principles of neuropsychological branding. Although some of what we explore in this concluding section has been touched upon in previous sections of this chapter, the complexity of neuropsychology and the three principles which will inform much of a brand manager's responsibilities suggests that a review of concepts are in order and now follow. In addition, the principles which at times are referenced as "laws" because they show "a law-like regularity" should not be thought of as invariant as the laws of nature.[37] However, they have, we should note, a history of consistent confirmation by brand managers who tend to recognize and follow these principles which may now benefit from a more scientific confirmation of their truth value by being even more widely embraced.

Brands as Networks of Neural Associations

The neurological approach that we have been exploring in this chapter requires that we make a slight alteration in our understanding of what a brand is. Traditional definitions speak about brand loyalty or attitudinal dimensions that consumers have about brands that lead to various types of behavior. This is all well and good. We'd like to complement this definition by thinking of the brand "*as a set of associations—ideas, memories and feelings in the mind of an individual.*"[38]

This does not do away with existing definitions that can be seen as complements to the neural definition, much as quantum physics did not erase the principles of Newtonian physics but merely added a new dimension of understanding to those principles. The very notion of branding as a creative and communication idea also changes somewhat to accommodate this neural dimension. For example, we have seen, and will explore in more detail, the notion that to win the battle for awareness, "*brands must create as many* synaptic connections [those active depositories of the brain's chemical signals] *between choice criteria and the brand name within their own association network.*"[39] The role of brand managers is now seen as creating the associations between the brand name and its semiotic symbols "*with those pieces of information, meaning, emotions, images and intentions that are of key importance in the decision making process of customers. . . ,*" increasing the likelihood that the brand will be chosen.[40]

Again we must add that the cultural influence and personal psychology that constitute each consumer's perspective need to be factored in here; so a nation's prevailing values and an individual's personal dynamic continue to play key roles in understanding consumer decision making. Therefore, the design of either cultural or psychological segmentation models will aid in defining the relevant semiotic symbols which will help inform the aforementioned associations by giving them granularity and a richer, more relevant cultural context.

Cortical Representation of Brands

The battle for cortical representation is driven by System I. It is the neurological equivalent of creating awareness outside of one's mental world. The key is finding those choice cues from the marketing stimuli that activate the associations in the brain and fire the relevant synapses releasing the awareness at the point of choosing the brand among and over its competitors. Those brands that are most salient win the battle to be called out of memory and are most influential in affecting consumer choices. So in the consideration set for a running shoe, Nike, Reebok, and New Balance may all be called forward, but the brand that has generated the strongest choice cues will be top-of-mind.

We Choose What We Recall

Although building brand awareness is the first order of business, creating high levels of saliency (relevancy) drives, from the standpoint of neural activity, availability. Again thinking in terms of System I, we choose what we are most likely to recall. And we recall what is most available in terms of its heightened associations with brand cues buttressed by associations of values with which the brand is identified by the consumer (Figure 15.6).

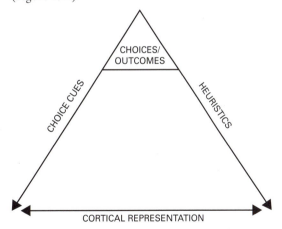

figure 15.6
Key dynamics in consumer decision making:
A graphic representation of the elements called into play at the moment of choice decision making.

Principles of Neuropsychological Branding

Drawing upon the upcoming discussions, the Three Laws of Neuropsychological Branding can now be stated as concise principles. The brand will be chosen when the three are in effect as follows:

- Distinctive relevance drives brand choice.
- Coherence in messaging across time and space drives brand choice.
- Richer interactive environments drive brand choice.

Relevancy, Coherence, and Richness

The three principles of branding have as postulates, or preconditions, these three concepts; relevancy, coherence, and richness. The principles can only become operative when these postulates are in effect.

Relevancy, again often used interchangeably with saliency, is built upon brand managers creating emotionally charged experiences with customers. The greater the relevancy, the greater the probability that the brand will be stored in our long-term memory and enter our neural system from which it can be retrieved. A key here is to be meaningfully or "distinctively relevant." These are also driven by the category and the occasion, each of which may have unique choice cues.[41]

Coherence refers to the need for brands to be both specific in the brand message (the choice cues) and more frequent, but spaced over time, and across as many touch points as possible. The more likely these stimuli are taken together, the more likely they can result in the firing of the memory where the brand is stored. Frequency of the firings also strengthens the neural associations and gives these brands an edge up on competing brands on being retrieved at the moment of choice.

Richness refers to how active the neural connectors are in generating impulses in the synapses in the brain. This is a function of how many connections there are with the brand which is a function of how wide and active the environmental stimuli are.

Therefore, the more types of interactive media called into play that can arouse cellular activity, the more complex and richer will be the synaptic network. For example, working with a product such as Build-A-Bear or American Girl can generate deeper and more active neural connections rather than simply purchasing the product off the shelf.

Archetypes and Semiotics

We have seen in the preceding sections that human memory works by associations with choice cues. We also have seen that System I decision making is far and away the source for most purchasing decisions, especially those dealing with everyday commodities. In this regard, colors and symbols and other such semiotic signs serve as System I shortcuts to decision making, and archetypes can keep semiotic symbols on-brand by offering a consistent reference point and suggested appropriate symbolism.

As an example, in 2009, PepsiCo, owner of the Tropicana orange juice brand, decided to undertake a revitalization of the brand's packaging. The company saw this as an updating or modernization and replaced the image of a fresh orange with a straw in it with a glass of orange juice.

The archetype of orange juice is a Caretaker who provides health and well-being, and fresh oranges rather than frozen are a plus. This imagery is what the old packaging conveyed. It was on-brand because it was "on-archetype." The new packaging conveyed the wrong visual signal. This was confirmed by a sudden fall in sales. What does a glass of orange juice convey? A glass of orange juice! Managers took away the association and thereby took the choice cue out of play. A reversal of the packaging to the old symbolism followed, but not before millions in sales were lost.

Cultural Archetypes, Codes, and Choice Cues

Returning to Clotaire Rapaille's unique research approach and successful application of his findings for companies such as Jeep, P&G, Nextel, and many others, often in various cultures around the world, we see in his company's name *Archetypal Discoveries* his vision of the human psyche and the role of brand managers in discovering the Archetype! This provides the insight into the emotional cues that are the energizers that form the imprint and inform the neurotransmitters in the brain. As Kahneman speaks of the dominance of System I thinking or the limbic section of the brain, the relevancy of a leading role played by another part, the **reptilian** (the subconscious where one finds our deepest survival instincts), finds one of its strongest advocates in C. C. Rapaille and his concepts of cultural archetypes and culture code theory of human decision making.[42]

Now we can begin to sketch in more detail the link between the three systems of thought, neuropsychology, behavioral economics, and cultural anthropology. Beginning with a classic three-part model of the brain (limbic, cortex, and reptilian), these find their correspondence in Kahneman's System I (limbic, or the unconscious) and System II (the cortex, or the conscious). The reptilian is not a focal point in Kahneman's system, but it finds its strongest representation in Rapaille's cultural codes theory.

Neuro-Cultural Imprints

Rapaille postulates that we place experiences into this subconscious depository at a very early age. The deeper the emotional experience the child undergoes, the deeper the forging of a permanent commitment to the culture's values and to the initial archetypal experience. He calls this "*imprinting.*"

These are commonly archetypal notions of what constitutes an experience with Mother or Rebel or Magician and so on and these are embedded in the neural systems of our reptilian brains by our cultures. Although they share in the archetypal categories of the universal collective unconscious, cultures differ to some degree in their definitions and priorities, or their cultural codes. Job number one of global brand managers now becomes to identify these cultural

archetypes and their corresponding cultural codes and align marketing messages (cultural choice cues) and management strategies to correspond to them.[43]

The Reptilian Brain and System I

From the perspective of global brand management, these experiences are clearly where System I thinking originates and Rapaille's culture codes, or deeply held instinctive feelings that are highly influenced by cultural value systems which become embedded in neural systems, act as heuristics "instinctively" driving consumer decision making.

The criticism often leveled against this approach is that it fails to factor in free will and the ability of an individual's personality development to override early childhood learning. This is not to say that Rapaille does not recognize the individual—he does. In Rapaille's words, "*You have your unique script, what I call personal script; then you have the cultural archetype; then you have the biological scheme.*"

But for Rapaille, because the cultural archetype is rooted (imprinted) in our neurological biology (the reptilian brain), it, in his words, "*always wins*"! One can argue that this is overstated and borders on **biological determinism**, or the error of explaining all human behavior as being driven solely or overwhelmingly by our biology.

In addition, there is a tendency in his reasoning, when determining the cultural codes, to overgeneralize what it means to be "French" or "American," two cultures whose cultural value systems are much more complex than being reducible to one or two characteristics (so, for example, he describes Americans as being "impulsive" and the French as being overly "rational").

That being said, Rapaille's approach with its strong cultural dimension works well in understanding the power of culture in global brand management, as discussed in Chapter 14. Therefore, it should be studied and understood in this dynamic brand management context.

A brand that reflects many of this chapter's principles in its mission and operations is the company Method and its brand of household and personal cleaning and care products. Started from the back of a car by two California friends, the premise was that cleaning products could be made both safe and effective. In fifteen years, the company has begun to challenge the market leaders with its scrappy, irreverent "we can fix the world" attitude that has taken consumers and the market by storm. This includes design awards for bottles of hand soap; a 75,000-square-foot roof garden growing pesticide-free foods on top of a newly opened 150,000-square-foot environmentally sustainable soap factory in Chicago; and the latest—green, biodegradable bottles to be made from ocean debris as part of an ambitious recycling effort to rid the oceans of plastic waste. The green initiatives are managed by a "Greenskeeper." Method's website boasts that the company has consumers covered by offering products that are environmentally sound and safe to use in over sixty product categories and is the only company of its kind "*protecting*" consumers from "*Cradle to Grave*"[44] (Figure 15.7).

The company has also recently reincorporated as a **public benefit corporation**, obligating Method to balance profits with both environmental and social responsibilities. This formally adds to its corporate responsibility of having been a B corporation, which added stakeholder interests into its corporate governance procedures by such requirements as higher standards of operational and financial transparency. There is no mention of this on its labels

figure 15.7
The Method brand's ecofriendly factory: Going beyond products to the brand's emotional connection with its core consumers is the hallmark of the brand, which has engendered a neurologically driven body of loyalists.

(continued on next page)

save that products are natural and packaging is biodegradable. The founders do not tout any of this on packaging or through press releases. They do no green marketing but prefer to speak with their customers online and share their vision. One such community is "People Against Dirty," open to anyone who believes in greater transparency in the labeling of household cleaning products. With this word-of-mouth approach comes a high degree of authenticity and much customer love.

The list of causes engaged by the brand and its managers is endless, as is the adoration and emotional engagement of its loyalists. Here is a sample of the consumer emotional

engagement and the neurologically driven and anchored loyalty that the brand engenders: *"On the first encounter with the brand . . . what caught my attentions immediately was mint dish soap . . . now, I'm a mint fanatic . . . plus the gorgeous . . . packaging didn't hurt things one bit and that was the beginning of my, should I say, Lust affair with Method."*[45] Shortly after making this comment, the same loyalist launched his blog, Methodlust.com, with the explanation that *"I'm a Method addict! I love the stuff!"* Surely dopamine at work!

Clearly, the business Method is in has little to do with soap. How would you describe it? Here's a hint: the archetype is both Rebel and Caregiver.

SUMMARY

The convergence of research in neuropsychology, cultural anthropology, and behavioral economics has produced fresh insights into the foundations of human decision making. For brand managers, these should be studied and, when appropriate, find their way into brand management strategies.

Neuropsychology provides a scientific basis for understanding the relationship between brands and their psychological impact on human behavior. As such, it offers added insights into what we might understand intuitively by using more rigorous methods of research but which need to be complemented by cultural and behavioral findings and influences and neural activities in response to brand cues and marketing stimuli.

Its original academic source is behavioral economics, which studies the effect of micro-economic stimuli on human behavior and how this relates to the human brain and the manner in which it makes decisions. This latter process has been labeled System I and System II thinking. The former describes

more impulsive, nonreflective processes where the brain makes judgments based upon memory called heuristics which are shortcuts by which a decision is reached. Often these are incomplete, requiring System II, the more reflective and logical process of decision making. However, most consumer decisions are based on the more emotional System I, which also is subject to distortion regarding objectivity due to such perceptual influences as framing, anchoring, and our need to spin narratives reconstructing reality into neat patterns of storylines.

Another aspect of human thinking affecting brand management is our tendency to generalize and then through habit maintain the generalized or summary view that we've created. We do this, for example, by creating product categories and deciding which belong in them. The importance of managing categories, and not just products, is part of what brand managers have learned based on how people organize thoughts and how they generalize their experiences.

Storytelling, or brand narratives, are often driven by deep-seated archetypes, those universal ideal types of human behavior which taken together make us part of the human community. The stories both mirror and make us human by reflecting the deepest desires, longings, and expectations that we have. Brands often align with these expectations by having as their promise an archetype that mirrors our own. These archetypes help brand managers stay "on-brand." This often results in brands and advocates together in a highly emotional relationship that can be seen in how the neural systems in our brains process and store brands and then retrieve them for consideration at the point of a purchase decision. Well-managed brands create the right choice cues that stimulate neural associations and enable the brand to be placed into a consideration set which is the stage just prior to the decision. Studies also indicate that choice cues are culturally rooted and that cultural values need to be factored into consumer decision-making assessments and strategies; it is also apparent that individual personalities can overcome deeply rooted imprints creating additional challenges for managing brands. Each of the three schools of thought contributes insights for brand management:

neuropsychology shows the limits that our neural systems have to retain brand messages and calls for getting into the memory of core consumers early and often; behavioral economics confirms the emotional basis for decision making and suggests the limitations in ultrarational messaging; and cultural anthropology alerts us to the pervasive influence of cultural values on human decision making and makes us more sensitive to the need for nuances in global communications.

More and more, successful brands have values which transcend self-interest. Consumers are migrating toward these in greater numbers as both realize that there is no contradiction between "doing good and doing well" in business.

The Three Laws of Neuropsychological Branding can be summed up by advising brand managers to be highly relevant, specific, frequent, and consistent in messaging, and experientially rich in interactions between the brand, cultural values, and the emotionally engaged consumer. The Method company, and the Method brand, by following these laws, has carved out a successful and sustainable business.

KEY TERMS

Anchoring	Cultural Codes	Neural Chemistry
Biological Determinism	Degree of Persuasion	Public Benefit Corporation
Brand Alignment	Framing	Reptilian
Choice Cues	Key Message Confirmation	Richness
Coherence	Key Performance Indicators	Synaptic Connections
Consideration Set Model	MRI Imaging	System I
Cortical Representation	Narratives	System II

CHAPTER CONVERSATIONS

- Why is neurobiology a useful addition to brand management? Could you manage your brand without it? Explain your position.

- Is it possible to resist the effects of framing and anchoring on decision making?
- How might archetypes be used in consumer research?

CHAPTER CHALLENGES

- You are the brand manager for a commodity brand of paper towels. Your marketing manager wants to trade up to a more upscale category of products and commit serious ad dollars to effect the change. What would be your advice and why?
- The CFO of the company where you manage a portfolio of brands has decided that it would be more economical to change the packaging to a single corporate name with a product reference distinguishing each product as a brand. She's asked for your opinion—what would you recommend, and why?
- You are the marketing manager. Prepare a training video script as a voice-over to explain to your sales team how the brand ideal can lead to more sales than transactional selling. What images would be in the video and what would the major points be?

ENDNOTES

1. B. Schmitt, "The Consumer Psychology of Brands," *Journal of Consumer Psychology* 22 (2012); K. L. Keller, *Strategic Brand Management*, 4th ed. (Upper Saddle River, NJ: Prentice Hall, 2103), 538; see also H. Plassmann et al., "Toward an Interdisciplinary Understanding of Consumer Decision-Making," *Journal of Consumer Psychology* 20 (2012): 3.

2. Ming Hsu, "Customer Based Brand Equity: Insights from Consumer Neuroscience," Haas School of Business, University of California, Berkeley (2014), http//:faculty.haas.berkeley.edu.

3. Ibid.

4. Hilke Plassmann, "Branding the Brain: A Critical Review and Outlook," *Journal of Consumer Psychology* (2012): 18–36.

5. Tjaco H. Walvis, "Three Laws of Branding: Neuroscientific Foundations of Effective Brand Building," *Journal of Brand Management* (2008): 176.

6. For an analysis from a communication perspective, see Douglas Van Praet, *Unconscious Branding: How Neuroscience Can Empower (and Inspire) Marketing* (New York, NY: St. Martin's Press: 2014).

7. Ibid.

8. Daniel Kahneman, *Thinking Fast and Slow* (N.p.: Princeton University Press, 2011).

9. Dan Ariely, "The End of Rational Economics," *Harvard Business Review* (July-August 2009).

10. For a more detailed expression of how consumer decisions are affected in this regard, see G. R. Fox et al., "The Behavioral Economics of Consumer Brand Choice," *Journal of Economic Psychology* 24 (2003): 675–695.

11. Michael Schrage, "Daniel Kahneman: The Thought Leader Interview," *Strategy+Business*, 2003, http://www.strategy-business.com/article/03409?gko=7a903.

12. Ibid.

13. Ibid.

14. Ibid.

15. Samuel M. McClure, "Neural Correlates of Behavioral Preference for Culturally Familiar Drinks," *Neuron* 44, no. 2 (October 2004): 379–87.

16. Mary Carmichael, "Neuromarketing: Is It Coming to a Lab Near You?," *PBS*, November 9, 2004, http://www.pbs.org/wgbh/pages/frontline/shows/persuaders/etc/neuro.html.

17. Ibid.

18. Jean-Noel Kapferer, *The New Strategic Brand Management: Advanced Insights and Strategic Thinking* (N.p.: Kogan Page, 2012).

19. John Kearon, "Let's Get Emotional about Advertising," *Contagious*, http://media.brainjuicer.com/media /files/Lets_Get_Emotional_About_Advertising_-_Contagious.pdf.

20. "Nothing More Than Feelings," *Economist*, December 7, 2013, http://www.economist.com/news /business/21591165-admen-have-made-marketing-guru-daniel-kahneman-prizewinning -psychologist-nothing-more.

21. M. Schaefer, "Neuroeconomics: In Search of the Neural Representation of Brands," *NCBI*, 2009, http://www.ncbi.nlm.nih.gov/pubmed/19874974.

22. David A. Aaker, *Brand Relevance: Making Competitors Irrelevant* (San Francisco, CA: Jossey-Bass, 2011).

23. Ibid.

24. "TED Talk," video file, March 1, 2010, http://www.ted.com/speakers/danielkahneman.

25. Ibid.

26. Sonia Gensler, "Managing Brands in the Social Media Environment," *Journal of Interactive Marketing* 27 (2013): 242–56.

27. Ibid.

28. Ibid.

29. Ibid.

30. Ibid.

31. Margaret Mark and Carol S. Pearson, *The Hero and the Outlaw: Building Extraordinary Brands Through the Power of Archetypes* (New York, NY: McGraw-Hill, 2011).

32. Ibid.

33. Jack Neff, "How Well-Defined Is Your Brand's Ideal?," *Advertising Age*, January 16, 2012, http://adage.com/article/news/defined-brand-s-ideal/232097/.

34. Ibid.

35. Jenny Schrade, "A Behind-the-Scenes Look at Tapping into Consumers' Collective Unconscious," *JRS Consulting*, 2011, http://www.jrsconsulting.net/freearticles_43.html.

36. Ibid.

37. Walvis, "Three Laws of Branding."

38. Jorge Alagon and Josh Samuel, "The Meaningfully Different Framework," *Millward Brown*, 2012, http://www.millwardbrown.com/docs/default-source/insight-documents/articles-and-reports /MillwardBrown_MeaningfullyDifferentFramework_April2013.pdf.

39. Ibid.

40. Ibid.

41. Ibid.

42. A. G. Woodside and S. A. Brasel, "Unconscious Thinking, Feelings, and Behavior Toward Products and Brands," *Journal of Brand Management* 18 (2011): 451–56.

43. For Rapaille's latest work, see Clotaire Rapaille, *The Culture Code: How a New Culture of Universal Values Is Reshaping Business and Marketing* (New York, NY: Palgrave Macmillan, 2015).

44. Leon Kaye, "The Seven Obsessions behind Method," *Triple Pundit*, October 10, 2011, http://www.triplepundit.com/2011/10/seven-obsessions-behind-method/.

45. Ibid.

glossary

acquiescence. The failure to defend or protect an IP asset because of delayed or failure or improper registration of a mark.

active engagement. Online consumer behavior such as writing blogs and postings, sharing such postings or blogs, and participating on YouTube productions which point to high degrees of brand loyalty.

adaptation. A go-to-market strategy where some or all of the Ps undergo some degree of adjustment or transformation to accommodate the foreign market and their internal local markets.

advocacy. The extent to which the customer refers others to your brand and of course consistent purchases over time.

affect heuristic. A postulation and mental process that if we think of something, it must be important.

affective commitment. A customer's emotional attachment to a particular brand, based on his or her identification with that brand.

affective/behavioral surveys. Ask questions regarding the experience in an attempt to mine feelings of engagement.

affinity brand. A brand that consumers have intimately embraced and are passionately loyal to because they believe the brand shares their most important values.

aided awareness. Research approach where consumers are shown the brand and asked for the appropriate associated product.

analysis/paralysis. The tendency of consumers to defer a decision when they have too much information.

anchoring. Unrecognized numerical influences affecting the quantitative value of a decision occupying the same time and space as the object or situation being assessed.

antes. Products or service features that are important to consumers but that all competitors offer at a similar level.

archetypes. Universally held generalizations about types of social roles which are anchored in our mental biology which frame our expectations of human behavior and can be the basis of a brand's lasting identity.

artificial inflated pricing. Inordinately high markups are given to products which are then "discounted" to a more reasonable price and promoted as "on sale."

associative halo effect. A strategy that seeks to tie a brand's image to the celebrity's positive persona or stature as a role model for a cohort you wish to reach.

associative projective technique. An idea generation method whereby symbols or representative images are used as stimuli to unleash fresh perspectives and ideas.

associative transference. A variation of the halo effect where the values of a celebrity are associated with the brand.

atelier. An artisan's shop where innovation in product development is the norm.

authenticity. The genuineness of the creative process and the timeless consistency of craftsmanship.

availability. A strategy used by luxury brands to limit inventory and points of distribution to engender desire for the brand.

343

awareness. The brand's presence and message and what consumers should know of the brand and its identity in the market.

b corporation. For-profit companies that pledge to achieve social goals as well as business ones.

bartering. The exchange of goods and services in lieu of money or the availability of currency.

behavioral survey. Questionnaires seek to determine future actions or intent based upon current experiences, such as propensity to purchase or repurchase or to recommend to friends and family.

behavioral economics. Studies the impact of economic stimuli on human behavior.

behavioral segmentation. Organize consumers and data around behavior such as the frequency of store visits, patterns of in-store shopping, departments/brands shopped, or credit cards, cash, or checks.

benchmark brands. Those by which we should measure our processes and our progress.

benchmarking. Setting standards of performance as a means of assessing the progress of your brand relative to competitors in the space where you compete.

best practices. Brands that are recognized as setting the bar of strategic excellence at the highest level of brand loyalty.

beta benchmarking. A valuation method where the objective is to estimate the level of risk and how that might impact the brand strength.

biological determinism. The error of explaining all human behavior as being driven solely or overwhelmingly by our biology.

book value. Assets minus liabilities found on a company's balance sheet.

book-to-market. A metric that has been used to derive brand valuation by subtracting the book value on the company as found on the balance sheet from stock market prices and then multiplied by the number of shares outstanding.

bounce back. A notification to the brand confirming the purchase.

brainstorming. A process of group idea generation where concepts and strategies are subjected to critical assessment until a consensus is reached.

brand advocates. Influencers who talk about, recommend, and spread the word about your brand through engaging their followers.

brand affect. The degree to which brand communication cues resonate with consumers.

brand affinity. The emotional closeness that consumers feel for a brand.

brand alignment. How the ad content aligns with the brand's values.

brand ambassadors. Consumers that pronounce their loyalty for a brand and their unsolicited promotion of the brand to friends, family, and colleagues.

brand associations. The feelings that the brand conjures in the mind of the consumer based on proprietary brand assets such as trademarks and logos and its personality and identity.

brand awareness. The ability to recall and recognize aspects of the brand's position in the market such as the products with which it is associated.

brand book. A book that outlines the marketing, entry strategy, targeted consumers, and prototypical products from the brand.

brand building. The steps such as awareness to create brand strength.

brand communities. Consumers who interface and meet, bonded together by their emotional tie to the brand and its values.

brand concept continuum. A graphic representation of the degrees of difference between mass and luxury brands.

brand development. The process of transforming a name or label into a brand through first creating brand elements.

brand effect. An integrated brand marketing platform that uses the same metrics to online brand assessment that have characterized traditional media measurement.

brand elements. A brand's various intellectual property assets such as brand names, logos, and associated identities.

brand engagement. Fostering emotional relationships with targeted segments.

brand equity. The influence of consumer market perceptions on the value of the brand.

brand equity review (BER). An assessment of the intangible value of the brand from the point of view of consumers.

brand essence. A brand's unique identity by which it differentiates itself from the competition and makes itself relevant to its key consumer cohort.

brand experience. The idea that the experience a luxury brand provides is a product unto itself.

brand extensions. A method of launching a new product or sub-brands by using an existing brand name in a different product category, priced, designed, and imaged to align with and appeal to different consumer segments.

brand fatigue. The extent to which the brand has lost its relevancy and differentiation.

brand ideal. A business strategy that focuses on the customer's hopes and aspirations and commits brand managers to meeting them.

brand identity. (1) What a brand does best. (2) The personality and values of a brand.

brand image. (1) What the market reflects back to the brand managers as to its perception of the brand. (2) The consumer's perception of the personality and values associated with the brand.

brand loyalty. The most dependable consumer purchasers of the brand and its products.

brand loyalty engagement index. Measures how a brand of choice stacks up against the ideal that the consumer has for the brand in the category compared to the averages of a basket of competitive brands.

brand management. A business approach to differentiate, build, protect, and measure the value of a brand.

brand mantra. A promise to consistently deliver to a consumer a set of relevant, functional, and/or emotional experiences. Also known as the brand promise.

brand marketing play. Retail stores that are opened as a strategy to promote the brand image by widening its presence in high-profile retail streets and cities rather than to increase its product sales.

brand persona. A generalized, somewhat fictitious description of what is seen by the brand manager as the typical core consumer of the brand.

brand portfolio yields. Evaluation of the portfolio and how each brand contributes to the overall financial health of the corporation.

brand promise. (1) What a brand conveys in its messaging to consumers regarding its identity. (2) The promise, from a company to the consumer, to consistently deliver a set of relevant, functional, and/or emotional experiences.

brand recall. The ability to recollect certain messages or images in marketing materials associated with the brand.

brand stature. The degree to which the brand is held in high esteem by consumers and the degree of knowledge they have about the brand's identity.

brand strategy. How the brand elements can support business objectives.

brand strength. Brand dimension that is based upon how fully realized relevance and differentiation are in the brand loyalty matrix.

brand touch points. Consumer points of contact with the brand that have a cumulative effect on the ultimate objective of brand management which is to establish brand loyalty.

brand valuation. The influence of financial markets' perception of the value of the brand.

brand value. How much or how little the brand contributes to financial outcomes and business objectives.

brand value chain. The connection and the interdependency between the value of a brand as a marketing asset (brand equity) and the value of a brand as a financial asset (shareholder valuations).

branding. The process of creating communication elements by which to convey the meaning and relevance of a brand.

brand's opinion leader. Bloggers and loyalists who are part of the brand community.

bricks and clicks. The seamless alignment of physical and virtual retail platforms.

bridge lines. Categories in retail departments, where products are priced between better and designer merchandise and the styling trends more contemporary.

business metrics. Information such as brand consideration, market share growth, increased revenues, or heightened profits that show how a company is performing.

buzz marketing. A marketing campaign where the objective is to generate viral conversation about a brand.

cachet. A perception from a fashion market that a brand is viewed by the market as having a distinctive and authentic look.

cannibalize. Brands competing for the same company internal resources and external markets.

capitalization. The value of the company as a function of the number of outstanding shares multiplied by the stock price.

category. The general nature of the product.

category management. A strategy where the major vendor is responsible for helping the distributor manage its departments.

cease and desist letter. A formal letter from an attorney notifying the recipient of his or her breach or impending breach of the client's rights, calling for an immediate cessation of those activities, and threatening further legal action for refusal to do so.

chameleon brands. A brand that changes with every change in the social media space, thereby losing its identity and with it its integrity and customer relevancy.

channels of distribution. Retail points of sale.

character. Invariable identity over time.

chic, cheap fashion. Fashion that follows the trends and is affordable to the vast majority of consumers.

choice analysis. Layer of the consumer journey where the consumer has to come to a decision to purchase.

choice cues. Those visual signs, symbols, images, and auditory and olfactory stimuli that represent the brand promise to the consumer and which drive action.

churn. The rate of turnover relative to the rate of retention in a customer base.

class of trade. The clustering and posting of related types of products or services for determining if a trademark is already owned by a business in a competitive or related area and therefore no longer available.

classification. A subdivision of the category.

click and collect. Concluding the monetary transaction at the point of sale.

clienteling. The development and management of a client base through very personal contact.'

cluster. Individual consumers with common behavior organized into groups for research and marketing purposes.

co-branding. Two brands usually with different but complementary products joining together in a marketing effort capitalizing on the equity in each brand to the unique benefit of both.

co-creation. (1) The creation of brand image and identity through consumer input on products, ads, and services coupled with the mutual contribution of brand managers and brand communities. (2) The role of consumers in creating brand value.

cognitive or rational surveys. Surveys set up to mine utilities or practical outcomes that the consumer expected from the product attributes or benefits.

coherence. The need for brands to be both specific in the brand message (the choice cues) and more frequent, but spaced over time, and across as many touch points as possible.

cohorts. Another word for segments in segmentation discussions; often used as well to designate a subset of a segment.

collateral. Any measurable asset such as stock market capitalization that can be used as security for a loan.

collectibles. When products are valued more for their brand attributes and associations than for their practical use.

collective unconscious. A psychological referent used to describe the cross-cultural existence of archetypes as an expression of our common humanity.

commodities. Grouping of products within a classification that are differentiated by their specific qualities.

competitive differentiation. A clear awareness of who your competitors are and not who you wish them to be, and how you intend to be different.

competitive set. All of the competitors in a product, price channel, or consumer sector.

complementary positioning. The creation of diffusion brands which do not cannibalize the market positions of existing brands within the company's portfolio.

confidence levels. How often we can be confident that the margins of error will fall within a given percentage range (usually 90 to 95 percent) which is a measure of how much variance in the outcome we are willing to tolerate.

conglomerate. A company which owns and markets multiple brands.

connective online community. Those who participate in and identify with social media groups.

connectivity. Characterizes how younger consumers interact with brands and each other in a digital world.

consideration. The act of consumers thinking of your brand and comparing your brand to others in the same competitive category.

consideration index. A consumer's willingness to consider a purchase of a product.

consideration set. When the brand is among other similar brands in the product category under purchase consideration or review.

consideration set model. The processes by which we respond to marketing stimuli in decision making and brand choice.

consistency rule. The visual, verbal, auditory, and tactile brand identity should not be altered across geographies.

conspicuous consumption. The accumulation of wealth often to display it to others as a sign of accomplishments rather than to consume the acquisitions as a function of practical needs.

constant exceeding of expectations. The expectation to surprise and delight.

consumer confusion. The benchmark by which courts ask if everyday consumers in the process of shopping are likely to confuse two similar logos.

consumer-centric. A business model that focuses on creating products and/or services based upon what the consumer wants and is willing to buy.

consumer-oriented economies. Those economies focused on the needs of the end user for building business strategies.

consumption metrics. Metrics that deal with how many people viewed, downloaded, or listened to this piece of content.

contagion. A psychological phenomenon wherein people believe that products become imbued with the values associated with a famous owner, maker, or location which helps explain the power of country of origin as a brand preference driver.

content driven. Being intensely immersed in social messaging that is important to consumers because it touches their emotions and personal values.

content marketing. A focus on relevant communications for and alignment with core consumers.

core competency. The fundamental capabilities that characterize a company or what it does best.

core consumer. Loyal and dependable cohort upon whom the brand managers could project annual business outcomes.

corporate earnings calls. Question-and-answer conference calls to CEOs and brand managers by stock market analysts.

cortical representation. Those brands that because they are most salient win the battle to be called out of memory and are most influential in affecting consumer choices.

cost per customer. To have the right merchandise in stock for best sales.

cost to replace/historical method. Approach to establishing brand valuation by confirming what it costs to re-create a brand.

Costco. A warehouse club retail concept that emphasizes low prices and high volume as its business model.

cottage industries. A business or manufacturing activity carried on within a person's home often with his or her own tools and equipment.

counterfeiting. The illegal copying of logos, designs, and/or products and presenting them for sale as authentic.

country of origin. Where the product is made and the impact of that location on the perception of the brand.

craftsman. The role of the artisan, in both product designs and brand narrative.

Craftsman archetype. The timeless role of the artisan and hand-made in product designs, reflecting the spirit of creativity and its fulfillment.

Creator archetype. An archetype that is innovative in finding solutions

credibility. The result of ensuring authenticity to the core brand identity when adding products and services to a brand's portfolio.

cross-shop. The willingness of consumers to shop at both co-brand retailers.

cult culture. An intense ritualized identification with a brand community that generates and displays extremely high degrees of brand loyalty by its members.

cultural anthropology. Studies how cultural values or codes differ within and among nations and their influence on human behavior.

cultural brand ambassadors. Well-known celebrity who is seen by the consumers in the country as synonymous with the brand.

cultural codes. The unique value systems of national cultures anchored by archetypes that deeply influence human perception and behavior.

culture. Shared patterns of behavior or values by which one group or society identifies itself and differentiates itself from another.

culture clubs. Another name for brand communities whose members have voluntarily joined, bonded together by their emotional tie to a brand identity and its values.

culture of brand engagement. A culture that clarifies the company's brand values and encourages its employees to embrace the vision of the brand.

customer engagement ratio. Ratios which quantify engagement profile results and compare them with lower engaged customers who go to competitors.

customer relationship management (CRM). The managing of customer loyalty and long-term customer engagement through impersonal and personal marketing activities.

customer retention. The savings from having long-term customers and not having to invest in finding new ones.

customer value. The lifetime monetary return on investment from each customer to a brand.

customer-based brand equity. The differential effect of brand knowledge on consumer response to the marketing of the brand.

customer's purchase journey. The steps culminating in a purchase.

customization. The expectation of consumers that products and services should be personalized to their needs and desires.

degree of equity. The strength of the brand helps determine the degree to which the brand can withstand competitive forces, disruptive innovations, and shifting trends and continue to be a market leader.

degree of persuasion. A measure of how the ad content and image were persuasive as to their purpose.

democratization of design. A collaboration between a department store and a well-respected designer bringing a designer's aesthetic to a mass market; the idea that beautiful designs in home goods and fashion, for example, should be and can be made affordable to all.

demographics. Organizing customer profiles by age, gender, education, race, occupation, or income.

desire. An overwhelming passion that drives human consumption and remains even after needs and wants are met.

destination brand. A brand that customers, when planning their shopping for the day, have as top-of-mind to visit, shop, and purchase.

destination decision. Layer in the consumer journey where the product must be at the retailer as promised.

DG. A logo that Dollar General created to represent its brand.

diagnosticians. Those whose job it is to discern the patient's symptoms and from the pattern infer the causes of any brand health issues.

differentiation. The perception of comparative uniqueness that the consumer has of the brand and its products compared with its competitors.

diffusion brands. Brands in a portfolio of related brands that are higher- or lower-priced extensions from the flagship brand. Sometimes referred to as "brand extensions."

dilution. The lessening of IP value due to improper reference or use of the mark.

diminishment. A standard in trademark law prohibiting the blurring of a distinctive quality by a competitor by which the brand is known.

discounted cash flow. The method of brand valuation that subtracts the beta result from the company's cash flow.

distributors. Retailers who are resellers.

DNA. The invariable essence of a brand.

Dollar General. A variety store in competition with Walmart.

dormant brands. A brand that has not been in the market for several years.

drivers. Those values and aspirations that are highly relevant to the consumers, highly differentiated from the competition, and likely to engage customers and build loyalty.

economies of scale. Increasing production to where the greatest cost savings are realized relative to the highest output of units.

EDLP. The "everyday low pricing" position which is meant to convey the idea that the initial pricing on merchandise in the store is the lowest and best value possible day in and day out.

elements. Identifiable symbols and IP assets by which the brand is readily identifiable.

emotional branding. Connecting with consumers through emotional messages relevant to their wants and needs.

emotional surveys. Surveys with questions that speak to feelings and are often driven by whether post-experience needs which motivated the purchase or visit were met.

endorsement contract. A contract with a celebrity to speak and appear on behalf of the brand.

engage. To meaningfully connect and ultimately form a relationship.

exclusive brand. A sought-after opportunity whereby retailers are offered by the brand owner a brand and its products with a promise to exclude them from the retailer's competitors.

exclusivity. A luxury brand objective which seeks to maintain brand value by a commitment to product innovation and a unique brand identity.

existential. Those emotional takeaways that result from the general interaction with brand touch points.

experiencing self. What we personally experience but often do not recall.

experiential brand management. A refocus from the product, the price, and the availability as the center of the business strategy (Waves I and II) to the feelings that consumers experience when they interact with the brand.

experiential marketing. The offers to interface with brand touch points beyond the product itself resulting in an emotional connection for the consumer with the brand.

Explorer archetype. The archetypal values and behavior of risk taking and innovation that accompany it.

fair and square. Pricing model that is based on the actual pricing pattern which eventually is the price at which most products are sold.

familiarity. A layer in the consumer journey where the consumer experiences an increased exposure and comfort level.

fashion brands. Brands that seek to capture fashion trends and translate them into their products.

fashionista. Consumer who follows fashion and wants to be the first to wear the latest trends.

fast fashion. A speed-to-market operational system where the trends from the runways quickly become the retailer's products and get to the retail floor.

fast thinking. Consumer decision making based more on emotional beliefs and values than on reasoned calculations.

features and benefits approach. A product-centric approach to marketing that stresses product functionalities and practical benefits.

feudalism. A system for structuring society around relationships derived from the holding of land in exchange for service or labor.

first usage. In common law (before statutes were enacted), the right of ownership of an IP asset goes to the first user and not necessarily to the first registrant who is not the first user.

fit. In product extensions, the consumer's perception that the brand's associative features fit naturally into the new product category.

flash sales. Brief online opportunities to benefit from designer/luxury product offers at incredible prices.

FMCG. "Fast Moving Consumer Goods," or basic commodities, which describes how frequently they are purchased by consumers.

fool's gold. Touch points that are highly differentiated from those of competing brands but are also of very low relevance to a consumer making a purchase decision among competing brands.

fourth wave. Wave of retail characterized by an intense focus on differential brand experiences as the driving force at retail.

framing. Affecting the outcome of a decision by how information is presented.

free trade agreement. Significantly lowered or removed trade barriers such as tariffs and prohibitive duties on the exchange of goods between nations.

Geek Squad. A highly trained cadre of young technicians available 24/7 for installations, repairs, and understanding the workings and the capabilities of the technology purchased.

General Mills. A corporation that purchased the rights to the Lacoste polos in 1969 but had no apparel or fashion experience.

generification. The loss of a brand's distinctiveness when its name becomes synonymous with its product category and it risks being perceived as and becoming a low-priced commodity.

geo-demographics. Organizing data by region, city, or metro size.

glocal brand management strategy. Adjusting the taste of products to align with local tastes while adhering to their universally understood archetype of innocence and fun in their marketing messages.

Good Housekeeping Seal of Approval. An independent testing lab to evaluate products for the home and for the homemaker.

goodwill. The catchall bucket wherein brand value can be found.

gradualism. Adhering to a reasonable pace in introducing product extensions.

granularity. Whether data about consumers are sufficiently detailed to be useful to the advertiser in making business decisions.

gross profit. The profit before expenses.

halo effect. A benefit derived from being associated with the positive perception of its surrounding elements or other well-established brands.

hang-time. Time consumers spend on the retail floor, often a precondition for a purchase.

hedonic value. A value, or calculus, whereby the luxury brand carries a high prestige value giving it more emotional pull with the consumer's assessment of product extension fit.

heritage narratives. Brands that have deep roots and continuity with the past and build their brand narratives around this.

heuristic. A problem-solving technique whereby one uses mental shortcuts to make decisions.

High Street. High-visibility retail locations that have high traffic of upscale consumers.

high-touch. Extraordinary service, subtle indulgences, and understated aesthetics in the store's environment.

household basket. A grouping of the household items most widely purchased for the week and their prices.

Hunter brands. An archetype that engages consumers and drives the emotional part of shopping.

in commerce. The tendency of courts to recognize commercial usage of IP assets as compelling evidence of rightful ownership of those assets.

in voice. A brand's identity over time.

in-depth interviews. A research method whereby a few interviewees participate in a guided, deep-dive discussion of their attitudes.

Industrial Revolution. The transition to new factory manufacturing processes beginning in the 1760s.

influencers. Those that have a large following who follow their social media sites.

infringement. The unauthorized use or copying by a business of any part of a brand's trademark assets owned by another. See trademark infringement.

intellectual property (IP). Intangible assets such as logos and icons whose value is subject to the protection of the law.

Jokester archetype. A counterpart to the Magician who uses fun and games to create illusions which bring joy to the participants.

jury of executive opinion. In market research, the gathering of experienced managers and soliciting their insights.

key message confirmation. An assessment as to whether the primary message of the ad registered with the ad readers.

key performance indicators. Critical benchmarks by which business objectives and their success are measured.

knock off. The copying of a competitor's product's unique features and attributes to deny it a competitive advantage.

laddering. A process of identifying product attributes, functions, and emotional attachments to discern a brand's essence and the why for a consumer purchase.

lead-gen metrics. Metrics that ask how often does content consumption result in a lead.

less is more. A strategy which evaluates whether inventory levels and assortments are excessive relative to consumers' purchase patterns whereby smaller inventories can still serve most consumers' needs.

licensing. The "renting" of a brand and its IP assets for use by another company to manufacture and market a product not made by the licensor brand.

life stage segmentation. An approach to segmenting markets which recognizes important life events as delineators for marketing strategies; also called socio-graphic segmentation.

lifestyle brand. Brand positioning that focuses on appealing to specific lifestyle choices.

lifestyle fashion brands. Brands that promote themselves as a source of how they can complement and add satisfaction with their products to various aspects of your daily life.

lifestyle segmentation. Organizes consumers and data in terms of how they live and use products or services in their everyday lives. See socio-graphic segmentation.

like2buy. A program that Nordstrom implements where customers can like a photo on Instagram, click, and be taken to the site to buy the product.

Likert scale. A scale that attempts to measure responses by constructing equal gradations of differing values in the choices offered.

limited edition. A product launch that is based on maintaining rarity and exclusivity by limiting inventory and availability.

location, location, location. Referred to as the first rule for a successful store: where it is located.

longitudinal reliability. The ongoing confirmation over time of the research findings.

look book. A compilation of images and pictures of that season's collection.

loyalists. People who shop often, are committed to buying the brand's latest fashions, and are not concerned with purchasing on sale.

loyalty journey. The path taken by a customer from reengaging the brand to the highest level of brand engagement, which is acting as an ambassador for the brand.

luxury. Products and services characterized by innovation and limited accessibility due to limited availability and higher price.

luxury brand management. A business tool to help differentiate and protect the value of the brand, the importance of its heritage, and how these drive business performance.

luxury brand narratives. The story of the brand in terms of its pedigree and vision referencing its genealogy and woven into the tapestry of its marketing communications.

macro-determinants of human behavior. Used to designate segmentation models that seek to understand the big picture drivers of consumer behavior.

Magician archetype. The capacity of a brand such as Disney to evoke the joy of magic and transformation through brand values and associations.

margin of error. A statistical variability concept, not to be confused with a mistake, planned for in the research design to determine how close the sample is to capturing the characteristics of the population studied.

margins. The selling price needed to cover the retailer's cost and expenses with enough left for a profit. See markup.

market dynamics. The competitive factors and the social, political, and economic environments in which a brand must operate.

market impact. How consumer behavior and the behavior of consumer-oriented players, such as retailers, impact brand value.

market orientation. A philosophy of business management based upon a company-wide acceptance of the need for a customer orientation.

market share. A percentage of a company's sales reported in units or dollars in the category and market in which the brand competes.

market valuation. The assessment of the worth of brands from financial institutions such as stock markets.

marketing myopia. A problem that occurs in businesses when managers suffer from "near-sightedness" whereby the big picture becomes out of focus because the focus is on selling products and not being responsive to consumers.

markup. The selling price needed to cover the retailer's cost and expenses with enough left for a profit. See margins.

marquee brands. A brand that the store must have because of consumer demand.

mass brands. (1) Those brands packaged and distributed to reach the greatest number of consumers at the lowest cost to the manufacturer. (2) Brands that define quality as functionality at a low price.

mass customization. The creating of products which reflect the brand's identity but also give the consumer the opportunity to infuse a product with her or his own individuality.

mass marketing. A marketing strategy that targets large segments of the population to sell.

masstige brands. Categories in retail departments where products are priced between better and designer merchandise and the styling trends are more contemporary.

median age. The midpoint delineating two equal clusters of a consumer segment.

men's polo. Knit tops originally worn by Argentinian polo players (hence the name).

metro-sexual. Young, professional male urbanites who stay in shape.

micro-determinants of human behavior. Used to designate segmentation models that seek to discover granular, detailed drivers of consumer behavior.

Millennials. The cohort of 18- to 29-year-old consumers.

mission. A brand's marketplace purpose.

mission statement. A company's communication of a brand's mission and promise; ultimate source of a brand promise and consumer-centric tagline.

monetized benefits. When consumers with high brand loyalty contribute to higher margins, greater revenue, larger share of more markets, and bigger stock valuations.

MRI imaging. Photographic images of areas of the human brain that, when under external stimuli such as marketing messages, control different facets of human behavior.

narratives. Our stories that are part of our wiring for they afford us a sense of control by linking events and painting pictures of cause and effect that seldom mirror the realities.

need states. The intersection between what consumers want and how they want it.

needs. Must-have consumer commodities, products, and services necessary for daily living.

negativity heuristic. A tendency to be instinctively more negative than positive, which reduces the positive to less of an affirmation of quality or value and more to a residue of what remains after the negative calculus is derived.

net present value. The value over a designated period of time less the cost of capital.

net utility. The remainder when the pain utility is subtracted from the pleasure utility.

neural chemistry. The brand's chemical configuration of its identity and DNA.

neuropsychology. Studies the dynamics of biology on human behavior.

neutrals. Products or service features that are important to consumers but that all competitors offer at a similar level.

obsolescence. This season's merchandise designed to offer temporary satisfaction which leads to desire for next season's merchandise successor.

omni-channel brand retail. All of the distribution modes together.

omni-channel communications. A seamless integration of brick-and-mortar stores, direct-mail catalogs, websites, and a mobile apps strategy.

on-brand. Adhering to the brand values as a set of guidelines for merchandise, marketing, and brand management.

one version of the truth. One viewpoint that does away with conflicting or competing data and arrives at a single management strategy.

one-child policy. Former Chinese policy that limited families to one child as a population control device and imposed heavy fines for failing to adhere.

one-off. A transaction that occurs once and is never repeated again.

on-trend. When a brand is capturing what the fashion direction of the season is.

opinion. A layer in the consumer journey where the brand is ranked and rated by the consumer.

opinion leaders. Trend makers and influentials from within their cohorts.

optimize merchandise assortments. To have the right merchandise in stock for best sales.

organic extension. The product additions fit together with the core offerings creating a cohesive and integrated story.

Outlaw archetype. A typology used to personify brands that reflect the rebel in American culture.

outsourcing. Contracting or manufacturing a product or service outside of the country with which the brand is traditionally identified.

parameters. A market's size, growth patterns, geography, and consumers, and its fluctuations in its dimensions and including its players who enter and exit, rise and fall.

parody defense. The claimed right to ridicule or caricature a brand as protected by freedom of speech.

participatory entertainment. The co-creation of the brand experience by how the consumer interacts with the brand and its participatory business model.

passive engagement. Online participants in brand content who read the various content and offered likes and click-throughs but take no active part in creating content suggesting lower degrees of loyalty.

perception map. A rendering of the competition derived from how consumers perceive the brands in a particular competitive landscape.

permission marketing. Obligates retailers to request and receive from phone owners access to their smartphones and apps before messaging is permitted.

personality. A brand's identity over time.

pinyin. Mandarin in romanized letters.

plus business. More than the usual daily pattern of sales.

points-of-difference. A contrast between your brand and that of the nearest competitor's brand.

points-of-similarity. Comparing the similarities between your brand and those of the nearest competitor's brand.

pop-up ads. Ads that seek to create brand awareness by surprise appearances.

pop-up stores. Stores located in high-traffic neighborhoods and are meant to generate awareness by serendipitous discovery and a sense of urgency from consumers to visit.

positioned. How brands are presented as providing solutions that differ from those of their competitors.

positioning. The decision to place and differentiate a brand against those that are seen as the competition.

post-purchase assessment. The moment of truth when the consumer evaluates whether the purchase truly met their needs and whether the brand followed through on its promise.

prelaunch. Preparations prior to being introduced into the market.

premium brands. Those brands that touch on luxury in some aspects of their business strategy such as opening stores in expensive shopping areas.

premium price/gross profit differential. A brand valuation method that is based on the net present value or the price differential in the market that the brand will command over time in comparison with an unbranded or generic product against which it competes in the product category.

price earnings multiple. The relationship between what a stock price is and what it generates in earnings per share.

price elasticity of demand. The degree to which a change in the price of a product or service impacts the level of demand or vice versa.

price point referent. A comparison of similar products that help consumers judge the price, value, and styling.

primary research. A source of research data, such as focus groups or sample surveys customized to ensure relevancy of outcomes for realizing business objectives.

private brand. Brand developed by and exclusive to the retailer.

private label. A brand with names, products, and symbols that are exclusively owned by the retailer and would only be available at that retailer.

PRIZM. A Zip code–driven segmentation method which has organized the U.S. consumer market into sixty-six typologies for in-depth socio-graphic analysis.

producer power. When the demand for goods is much larger than the supply, resulting in the producer having more power over the product, price, and distribution.

product concierge. A presence in the showroom who does not sell the product but helps customers understand the product and how it works.

product integrity. How the brand tells its story.

product-centric. A business model focused on what product can be produced and sold.

product-message-offers. Mass marketing communications customized to each customer segment's wants or needs.

provenance. The place in which a product was originally manufactured. Also another term for country of origin.

psychographic segmentation. Determines the "why" of consumer behavior, or attitudes that motivate the behavior.

public benefit corporation. A corporation's commitment to balance profits with both environmental and social responsibilities.

public brands. A brand with products that are widely distributed and often nationally advertised.

public domain. No ownership of IP rights that others can claim that would restrict usage.

purchase funnel assessment. A diagnostic tool that helps the brand manager assess at what consumer reference point the problem emerged and how best to remedy it.

purchase journey. The path taken by a consumer from awareness to buying.

rarity. A key strategy of luxury brands; controlled scarcity to increase the perceived value and the desire to own a luxury product.

reach. The number of targeted consumers who have seen an ad.

Rebel archetype. An archetype that disrupts the status quo and breaks the rules of the game.

re-branding. When a brand seeks a new name, new consumers, often new products, and new channels of distribution.

relevancy. The extent to which a brand is important to a consumer segment because it fits their lifestyle.

relevant differentiation. The successful integration and optimization of the two variables which frame the brand loyalty matrix.

reliability. Capturing research data that are consistent and transmitting them in research findings whose methodology and result can be replicated.

relief from royalty. The method of ascertaining brand valuation by assessing the amount of royalty that the brand owner would incur as an expense if it had to license the brand it owns.

remembering self. What we retain and around which we choose to fashion a story.

reposition. To retool and redirect brands so they are relevant to another market and/or consumer.

reptilian. (1) The depository of instincts in the human neurological system. (2) The subconscious where we find our deepest survival instincts.

retail availability and accessibility. Readily accessible retail locations where the brand can be bought and sufficient inventory and brand displays are available and properly presented.

retail link. Walmart's proprietary category management software.

retail value chain. All the steps which create value from how products are made.

return on investment (ROI). The measure of the return, monetary and otherwise, from the investment of company resources in pursuit of its business objectives.

revitalization. A change in the messaging strategy.

RFID chip. A radio frequency chip coded with specific instructions to activate a video or audio receptor attached to a garment which generates a series of images on a nearby screen.

richness. Refers to how active the neural connectors are in generating impulses in the synapses in the brain.

rites of passage. Patterns of behavior structured by predefined social events in one's life.

royalty. A percentage of the selling price of each item sold and shipped that the licensor receives from a licensee of the licensor brand.

rule of five. It takes five times the investment to win a new customer than it does to retain an existing one.

Ruler archetype. A typology used to personify brands that command the allegiance of the consumer through their unchallenged authority.

Ruler/Creator archetype. One who has the power to create an experience of lasting consequence.

run-of-press (ROP). Color flyers inserted into newspapers.

sales metrics. Metrics that ask, did we actually make any money from this content?

sample size. The number of respondents required to be representative of the population being surveyed.

satisfaction. A short-term measure of a customer response to a survey question seeking to measure fulfillment.

seamless brand experience. Regardless of where the brand is accessed by the consumer, the same experience unfolds.

secondary meaning. The use of expert opinion, market research, or market prominence to establish a claim of "distinctiveness" in a product attribute as the basis for trademark protection.

securitization. The financial benefits of strong brands whereby the brand can be used as collateral to secure a loan against future earnings, income, and/or cash flow.

segmentation modeling. A technique used to structure and create a deeper and more granular understanding, or the most detailed explanation possible regarding your customer's behavior.

semiotics. The study of signs and symbols and how they convey meaning.

shareholder value. The increase in price of a stock, its dividends, and other monetary benefits derived from stock ownership.

sharing metrics. Metrics that deal with how resonant this content is and how often it is shared with others.

shopping experience. The full effect of all of the store's brand touch points impacting the customer.

signature pieces. Those styles with which the brand is uniquely associated and timelessly identified and which are part of the product line assortment each season.

signature products. Products that represent the unique soul of the brand and its timeless image.

single version of the truth. One set of metrics to measure the return on investment.

size specs. Those calculations that must align with the prototypical figure of the core consumer.

SKUs. Stock counting units which are inventory control records of each item's color, size, and price.

slogans. Brand messages communicated to various consumer advertising mediums.

social ads. Where brands are willing to pay to get their fans to be viral advocates for the brand among their friends.

social media funnels. Funnels which enable managers to manage different types of visits by directing visitors to solutions which align with the purpose for which they engaged the brand.

social media types. Passive versus active engagers.

social shopping. How individuals interact online with each other as interfacing regarding brands.

social stratification. A ranking system of tiered degrees of privileges and power that differentiates members of the same social system from each other.

social value. A measurable increase in realizing the objectives of the charity without exploiting the opportunity to turn the giving into a public relations coup by trumpeting the donations.

socio-graphic segmentation. Looks to social patterns of how people live their lives and as a way of seeing their priorities. See lifestyle segmentation.

standardization. The strategy which characterizes the go-to-market brand identity in terms of the classic four Ps of marketing (product, price, place, promotion) that remain largely unchanged.

statistical tendency. Acceptable variations in statistical ratios that do not negate the soundness of the statistical measure.

staying on-brand. Managing the business from the perspective of the brand values and the brand promise.

STP process. The business planning and execution sequence comprising segmentation, targeting, and positioning of a brand and its offering to the market.

strategic. (1) The idea of what one would want to accomplish based on long-term objectives. (2) Seeing the brand as central to the entire business enterprise, critical for long-term planning and designed and managed with a global business perspective in mind.

sub-brands. A brand that is created under a larger company or brand that is aligned with specific customer segments, prices, and distribution channels.

super rich. Wealthy individuals constituting just 1 percent of the U.S. population. See ultra-high net worth.

switching patterns. Where previously loyal cohorts of customers begin to increasingly switch from your brand to your immediate competitors.

symbiotic. Two parties serving and being mutually dependent upon each other for certain benefits and rewards.

symbolic consumption. When consumers focus on meanings to motivate their purchases beyond the tangible characteristics of material objects.

synaptic connections. Those active depositories of the brain's chemical signals.

System I thinking. Can be discerned when we behave seemingly without needing to reflect before taking action.

System II thinking. Filled with effort, deliberate, and analytical thinking.

tactical. How one communicates and implements a strategy.

taglines. Those emotional takeaways that result from the general interaction with brand touch points.

target. Best customers or opportunities selected from segments whom companies wish to sell to.

targeted marketing. Marketing efforts that reach consumers with specific offers for specific products and services that are of interest to them.

tarnishment. A legal standard prohibiting the promulgation of unfounded associations or accusations regarding IP assets of a company.

The Geneva Seal. An industry certification confirming the highest skills of watch making.

The Great Gatsby. A novel written in the 1920s by F. Scott Fitzgerald fictionalizing the adverse sociological effects of conspicuous consumption.

the post-artisan stage. An integrated strategy for brand extensions, production, distribution, and the transformation of the artisan into designer.

top-of-mind brands. Brands that customers can readily recall when considering a purchasing decision.

touch point. The experience that the customer has and takes away from the brand's operations and personnel during and after every transaction.

trademark infringement. The violation of a myriad of legal standards designed to protect IP rights, unauthorized use, or copying of any part of a brand's trademarked assets. See infringement.

traffic. The number of visitors offline in the stores and online in the social media platform.

transactional. Refers to purchases and the interaction with the brand's salespeople and selling platforms.

transactional brand experience. The tendency of consumers to defer a decision when they have too much information.

travel retail. Retail outlets within travel environments such as airports.

traveler retail. Using any retail outlet to harness growth by appealing to international travelers.

trend-right. When companies have identified the latest trends and created merchandise that their customers are likely to buy.

true distinctiveness. The expectation that the company should be an innovator, successfully rewriting the rules in its category.

turn. The pace at which merchandise sold each week within a predefined seasonal window is sold relative to inventory levels.

types of purchasers. Consumers such as frequent shoppers, ultra-loyalists, bargain hunters, or new shoppers delineated by their shopping behavior patterns.

typologies. A generalization about types of personalities and how they are likely to respond differentially when subjected to marketing messages.

ultra-high net worth (UHNW). Those wealthy individuals constituting just 1 percent of the U.S. population. See super rich.

unaided awareness. Research approach where consumers are asked to recall and/or associate attributes which are in ads and which characterize the brand.

unfair competition. A conscious decision by one company to undermine the integrity of a brand, IP asset, or another company by false advertising and the like.

unfair trade. A legal standard which obligates competitors to cease from, for example, false statements about competitors or price reductions, the purpose of which is to harm another company.

unique value propositions. How a brand identifies itself by what it does best.

utilitarianism. This doctrine held that human beings are motivated to pursue pleasure and to avoid pain.

utilities. The rational value of a product or service derived from its features and benefits.

validity. Actually measuring what research claims to be measuring rather than a spurious or unclear relationship between independent and dependent variables.

VALS. An acronym for "Values, Attitudes and Lifestyles" and a methodology for segmenting and organizing consumer types by lifestyle and psychographic categories.

valuations. Metric to describe the value of financial instruments.

value chain. The entire process and strategy of product creation, marketing, and distribution and how each link contributes value to the final outcome.

value-driven brand engagement. An experience that can be characterized as an emotional exchange between a customer and a brand.

value of a like (VOAL). A formula that was created to put a numerical value on the interaction and worth of a company's social media efforts.

value proposition. What is unique about a brand that makes it relevant to its core consumer.

vision. A brand's future aspirations.

voice-overs. In advertising, a verbal message played while a visual message is displayed.

vulgarity. Overstated or excessive attempts at displays of style.

wants. Consumer preferences for products or services that weren't necessary for everyday living, but were perhaps aspirational choices.

wholesale prices. The price the brand owner/manufacturer would charge a distributor.

wicking. Keeping perspiration from affecting a product's performance and a consumer's comfort.

Zip code clusters. Identifying and organizing postal zip codes whose sociographic consumer types are very similar for purposes of segmentation modeling.

credits

Chapter 1
1.1: Roberto Machado Noa/Getty Images; 1.2: Kim Rogerson/Getty Images; 1.3: Gisele Tellier/Getty Images; 1.4: Neilson Barnard/Wireimage/Getty Images; 1.5: Science and Society Picture Library/Getty Images; 1.6: Courtesy Apple; 1.7: Blank Archives/Getty Images; 1.8: Jeff Schear/Getty Images for Under Armour; 1.9 : Matt McClain/For The Washington Post via Getty Images.

Chapter 2
2.1: Chris Ratcliffe/Bloomberg via Getty Images; 2.2: James Coldrey/Getty Images; 2.3: Visions of America/UIG via Getty Images; 2.4: SimmiSimons/iStock.

Chapter 3
3.1: Evening Standard/Hulton Archive/Getty Images; 3.2: Victor J. Blue/Bloomberg via Getty Images; 3.3: Ritu Manoj Jethani/Shutterstock; 3.4: Fairchild Books; 3.5: Fairchild Books; 3.6: Sean Gallup/Getty Images.

Chapter 4
4.1: Fairchild Books; 4.2: Cyrop/Getty Images; 4.3: Fairchild Books; 4.4: Fairchild Books; 4.5: QBS; 4.6: © Senohrabek/iStock; 4.7: Fairchild Books; 4.8: Hill Street Studios/Getty Images; 4.9: Jim Spellman/WireImage/Getty Images; 4.10: Tasos Katopodis/Getty Images for Tommy Bahama.

Chapter 5
5.1: Ashley Pon/Getty Images; 5.2: © kunertus/iStock; 5.3: TORU YAMANAKA/AFP/Getty Images; 5.4: Fairchild Books; 5.5: Fairchild Books; 5.6: Mark Ashman/Disney Parks via Getty Images; 5.7: Leonard Zhukovsky/Shutterstock.

Chapter 6
6.1: Mariah Wild/Disney Parks via Getty Images; 6.2: Justin Sullivan/Getty Images; 6.3: Doug Kanter/Bloomberg via Getty Images; 6.4: Jin Lee/Bloomberg via Getty Images; 6.5: Fairchild Books; 6.6: Fairchild Books; 6.7: Harold Cunningham/Getty Images.

Chapter 7
7.1: Picture Post/Hulton Archive/Getty Images; 7.2: Al Freni/The LIFE Images Collection/Getty Images; 7.3: Fairchild Books; 7.4: Fairchild Books; 7.5: Fairchild Books; 7.6: William Mancebo/Getty Images.

Chapter 8
8.1: Fairchild Books; 8.2: Fairchild Books; 8.3: Richard Levine/Alamy Stock Photo; 8.4: Ken Wolter/Shutterstock.com; 8.5: Steve Jennings/Getty Images for Men's Health; 8.6: Clicksnap/BuzzFoto/FilmMagic/Getty Images; 8.7: Robert Alexander/Archive Photos/Getty Images; 8.8: Marc Piasecki/Getty Images; 8.9: Mark Ralston/AFP/Getty Images; 8.10: ERIC PIERMONT/AFP/Getty Images.

Chapter 9

9.1: John Lamparski/Getty Images; 9.2: Andrew Harrer/Bloomberg via Getty Images; 9.3: Fairchild Books; 9.4: Tim Boyle/Getty Images; 9.5: Fairchild Books; 9.6: Fairchild Books; 9.7: David Paul Morris/Bloomberg via Getty Images; 9.8: Scott Olson/Getty Images: ; 9.9: Justin Sullivan/Getty Images.

Chapter 10

10.1: Fairchild Books; 10.2: Steve Grayson/Getty Images Sport; 10.3: Fairchild Books; 10.4: Fairchild Books; 10.5: PAOLO COCCO/AFP/Getty Images; 10.6: ullstein bild/ullstein bild via Getty Images; 10.7: JEAN AYISSI/AFP/Getty Images; 10.8: Dario Pignatelli/Bloomberg via Getty Images.

Chapter 11

11.1: Fairchild Books; 11.2: Fairchild Books; 11.3: Fairchild Books; 11.4: Business Wire via Getty Images; 11.5: Charley Gallay/Getty Images for CinemaCon; 11.6: Elenarts/Shutterstock; 11.7: Fairchild Books; 11.8: Dominique Charriau WireImage/Getty Images; 11.9: NoDerog/iStock.

Chapter 12

12.1: McCarthy's PhotoWorks/Shutterstock.com; 12.2: Fairchild Books; 12.3: Eziutka/Shutterstock. com; 12.4: GoBOb/Shutterstock.com; 12.5: Fairchild Books; 12.6: Bloomberg/Getty Images.

Chapter 13

13.1: Bloomberg/Getty images; 13.2: Clemens Bilan/Getty images; 13.3: winhorse/iStock; 13.4: Robert Alexander/Getty Images; 13.5: mgrushin/iStock; 13.6: Bill D'Arienzo; 13.7: Bill D'Arienzo.

Chapter 14

14.1: jorisvo/Shutterstock.com; 14.2: Hulton Archive/Getty Images; 14.3: Traverso/L'Oreal/Getty Images; 14.4: Ron Antonelli/NY Daily News Archive/Getty Images; 14.5: Anthony Kwan/Getty Images.

Chapter 15

15.1: Fairchild Books; 15.2: Fairchild Books; 15.3: Fairchild Books; 15.4: Luke Sharrett/Bloomberg/Getty Images; 15.5: Oli Scarff/Getty Images; 15.6: Fairchild Books; 15.7: Courtesy Method Brand.

index

Note: Page numbers with *f* indicate figures; those with *t* indicate tables.